W9-CZW-513

# ANNUAL EDITIONS

# Computers in Society 09/10
*Fifteenth Edition*

**EDITOR**
**Paul De Palma**
*Gonzaga University*

Paul De Palma is Professor of Computer Science at Gonzaga University. When he discovered computers, he was working on a doctorate in English (at Berkeley). He retrained and spent a decade in the computer industry. After further training (at Temple), he joined the computer science faculty at Gonzaga. He is currently studying computational linguistics (at the University of New Mexico). His interests include artificial intelligence and the social impact of computing.

 **Higher Education**

Boston   Burr Ridge, IL   Dubuque, IA   New York   San Francisco   St. Louis
Bangkok   Bogotá   Caracas   Kuala Lumpur   Lisbon   London   Madrid   Mexico City
Milan   Montreal   New Delhi   Santiago   Seoul   Singapore   Sydney   Taipei   Toronto

**Higher Education**

ANNUAL EDITIONS: COMPUTERS IN SOCIETY, FIFTEENTH EDITION

Published by McGraw-Hill, a business unit of The McGraw-Hill Companies, Inc., 1221 Avenue of the Americas, New York, NY 10020.
Copyright © 2010 by The McGraw-Hill Companies, Inc. All rights reserved. Previous edition(s) 2005, 2007, 2008. No part of this publication may be reproduced or distributed in any form or by any means, or stored in a database or retrieval system, without the prior written consent of The McGraw-Hill Companies, Inc., including, but not limited to, in any network or other electronic storage or transmission, or broadcast for distance learning.

Some ancillaries, including electronic and print components, may not be available to customers outside the United States.

Annual Editions® is a registered trademark of The McGraw-Hill Companies, Inc.
Annual Editions is published by the **Contemporary Learning Series** group within the McGraw-Hill Higher Education division.

1 2 3 4 5 6 7 8 9 0 QPD/QPD 0 9

ISBN 978–0–07–352854–0
MHID 0–07–352854–4
ISSN 1094–2629

Managing Editor: *Larry Loeppke*
Senior Managing Editor: *Faye Schilling*
Developmental Editor: *Dave Welsh*
Editorial Coordinator: *Mary Foust*
Editorial Assistant: *Nancy Meissner*
Production Service Assistant: *Rita Hingtgen*
Permissions Coordinator: *DeAnna Dausener*
Senior Marketing Manager: *Julie Keck*
Marketing Communications Specialist: *Mary Klein*
Marketing Coordinator: *Alice Link*
Project Manager: *Sandy Wille*
Design Specialist: *Tara McDermott*
Senior Production Supervisor: *Laura Fuller*
Cover Graphics: *Kristine Jubeck*

Compositor: Laserwords Private Limited
Cover Image: © Getty Images/RF

**Library in Congress Cataloging-in-Publication Data**
Main entry under title: Annual Editions: Computers in Society. 2009/2010.
 1. Computers in Society—Periodicals. De Palma, Paul, *comp*. II. Title: Computers in Society.
658'.05

www.mhhe.com

# Editors/Advisory Board

Members of the Advisory Board are instrumental in the final selection of articles for each edition of ANNUAL EDITIONS. Their review of articles for content, level, currentness, and appropriateness provides critical direction to the editor and staff. We think that you will find their careful consideration well reflected in this volume.

# Preface

In publishing ANNUAL EDITIONS we recognize the enormous role played by the magazines, newspapers, and journals of the public press in providing current, first-rate educational information in a broad spectrum of interest areas. Many of these articles are appropriate for students, researchers, and professionals seeking accurate, current material to help bridge the gap between principles and theories and the real world. These articles, however, become more useful for study when those of lasting value are carefully collected, organized, indexed, and reproduced in a low-cost format, which provides easy and permanent access when the material is needed. That is the role played by ANNUAL EDITIONS.

In a well-remembered scene from the 1968 movie, *The Graduate,* the hapless Ben is pulled aside at his graduation party by his father's business partner. He asks Ben about his plans, now that the young man has graduated. As Ben fumbles, the older man whispers the single word, "plastics," in his ear. Today, Ben is eligible for the senior discount at movie theatres. What advice would he offer to a new graduate? Surely not plastics, even though petrochemicals have transformed the way we live over the past four decades. Odds are that computers have replaced plastics in the imaginations of today's graduates, this despite the tech bubble that burst in 2000. To test this hypothesis, I did a Google search on the words "plastics," and "plastic." This produced about 240,000,000 hits, an indication that Ben was given good advice. I followed this with a search on "computers," and "computer," to which Google replied with an astonishing 1,340,000,000 hits. The point is that computers are a phenomenon to be reckoned with.

In netting articles for the 15th edition of *Computers in Society* from the sea of contenders, I have tried to continue in the tradition of the previous editors. The writers are journalists, computer scientists, lawyers, economists, and academics, the kinds of professions you would expect to find represented in a collection on the social implications of computing. They write for newspapers, business and general circulation magazines, academic journals, and professional publications. Their writing is free from both the unintelligible jargon and the breathless enthusiasm that prevents people from forming clear ideas about computing. This is by design, of course. I have long contended that it is possible to write clearly about any subject, even one as technically complex and clouded by marketing as information technology. I hope that after reading the selections, you will agree.

*Annual Editions: Computers in Society* is organized around important dimensions of society rather than of computing. The introduction begins the conversation with an article by the late Neil Postman who says "that every technology has a philosophy which is given expression in how the technology makes people use their minds." Sherry Turkle, one of the earliest and most eloquent commentators on the psychological changes wrought by computing, begins the final unit with a similar thought: "computational objects do not simply do things *for* us, they do things *to* us as people, to our ways of being [in] the world, to our ways of seeing ourselves and others." In between, with the help of many other writers, a crucial question recurs like a leitmotif in a complex piece of music: to what extent is technology of any kind without a bias of its own and to what extent does it embody the world view, intentionally or not, of its creators? If the answer were simply that the good and the ill of computing depend upon how computers are used, those of us interested in the interaction of computers and society would be hard-pressed to claim your attention. We could simply exhort you to do no evil, as Google tells its employees. Good advice, certainly. But information technology demands a more nuanced stance. Sometimes, computing systems have consequences not intended by their developers. The vulnerability of government documents is one example (Unit 6). A growing inability to concentrate is another (Unit 4). And at all times, "embedded in every technology there is a powerful idea" (Unit 1, "Five Things You Need to Know about Technological Change"). An essential task for students of technology is to learn to tease out these ideas, so that the consequences might be understood *before* the technology is adopted.

The book's major themes are the economy, community, politics considered broadly, and the balance of risk and reward. In a field as fluid as computing, the intersection of computers with each of these dimensions changes from year to year. Many articles in the 10th edition examined the growing importance of e-commerce. By the time of the 13th edition, e-commerce had nearly disappeared. This is not because e-commerce had become unimportant. Rather, in just a few years, it had moved into the mainstream. The 14th edition replaced over half of the articles from the 13th. The 15th edition eliminates a third of those, replacing them with many new articles. Computing is a rapidly moving target. We race to keep up.

More than any other technology, computers force us to think about limits. What does it mean to be human? Are there kinds of knowledge that should not be pursued? As Sherry Turkle asks, apropos of any complex technology, "Are you really you if you have a baboon's heart inside, had your face resculpted by Brazil's finest plastic surgeons, and are taking Zoloft to give you a competitive edge at work?" (Turkle, 2003:6). Are we developing "increasingly intimate relationship with machines?" as Turkle claims (Unit 8, "A Nascent Robotics Culture"), or, more prosaically, how do we keep e-commerce flowing when public-key cryptography becomes obsolete. These and other unresolved issues are explored in Unit 8, The Frontier of Computing.

A word of caution. Each article has been selected because it is topical and interesting. To say that an article is interesting, however, does not mean that it is right. This is as true of the facts presented in each article as it is of the point of view. When reading startling claims, whether in this volume or in the newspaper, it is wise to remember that writers gather facts from other sources who gathered them from still other sources, who may, ultimately, rely upon a selective method of fact-gathering. There may be no good solution to the problem of unsupported assertions, beyond rigorous peer review. But, then, most of us don't curl up each night with scientific journals, and even these can be flawed. The real antidote to poorly supported arguments is to become critical readers, no less of experts than of the daily newspaper. Having said that, I hope you will approach these articles as you might approach a good discussion among friends. You may not agree with all opinions, but you will come away nudged in one direction or another by reasoned arguments, holding a richer, more informed, view of important issues.

This book includes several features that I hope will be helpful to students and professionals. Each article listed in the table of contents is preceded by a short abstract with key concepts in bold italic type. The social implications of computing, of course, are not limited to the eight broad areas represented by the unit titles. A topic guide lists each article by name and number along still other dimensions of computers in society.

We want *Annual Editions: Computers in Society* to help you participate more fully in some of the most important discussions of the time, those about the promises and risks of computing. Your suggestions and comments are very important to us. If you complete and return the postage-paid article rating form in the back of the book, we can try to incorporate them into the next edition.

## Reference

Turkle, S. (2003). Technology and Human Vulnerability. *Harvard Business Review,* 81(9): 43–50.

Paul De Palma
*Editor*

# Contents

Preface                                                                              iv
Topic Guide                                                                          xii
Internet References                                                                  xiii

## UNIT 1
## Introduction

Unit Overview                                                                        xvi

1. **Five Things We Need to Know about Technological Change,**
   Neil Postman, Address to New Tech '98 Conference, March 27, 1998
   Neil Postman, a well-known cultural critic, suggests that **computer technology**
   is too important to be left entirely to the technologists. "Embedded in every
   technology," he says, "is a powerful idea. . . ."                                3

2. **On the Nature of Computing,** Jon Crowcroft, *Communications
   of the ACM,* February 2005
   The author states, "**Occupying a third place in human intellectual culture,
   computing** is not bound by the need to describe what does exist (as in natural
   science) or what can be built in the real world (as in engineering)."           7

3. **A Place for Hype,** Edward Tenner, *London Review of Books,*
   May 10, 2007
   "A new golden age of **technological hype** seems to be dawning," Tenner
   writes. Despite all predictions, computers still can't tell "whether an object is a
   hat, a chair, or a shoe."                                                        9

## UNIT 2
## The Economy

Unit Overview                                                                        12

4. **Click Fraud: The Dark Side of Online Advertising,** Brian Grow
   and Ben Elgin, *BusinessWeek,* October 2, 2006
   Internet advertisers think they pay only when an interested **customer clicks
   on their ads.** Martin Fleischman, an Atlanta businessman, "noticed a growing
   number of puzzling clicks coming from such places as Botswana, Mongolia,
   and Syria."                                                                      14

5. **Online Salvation?,** Paul Farhi, *American Journalism Review,*
   December 2007/January 2008
   In 2003, **newspapers** earned $1.2 billion through **online services.** By 2006,
   the figure had grown to $2.7 billion. Will the Internet save the beleaguered
   newspaper business?                                                             20

The concepts in bold italics are developed in the article. For further expansion, please refer to the Topic Guide.

6. **The Big Band Era,** Christopher Swope, *Governing,* January 2005
   Even as cities like Philadelphiaare working to transform the, ***entire city into a wireless hot spot***—with government as the Internet service provider of last resort—communications companies are fighting to keep local governments out of the ***broadband business.***      **24**

7. **The Beauty of Simplicity,** Linda Tischler, *Fast Company,* November 2005
   A simple tale about ***simplicity.*** One company hired an editor from *People Magazine* to translate accounting lingo into everyday language, "pared back 125 setup screens to three," and "sold 100,000 units in its first year on the market."      **28**

8. **The Software Wars: Why You Can't Understand Your Computer,** Paul De Palma, *American Scholar,* Winter 2005
   The article argues that ***software development is like military procurement,*** and suffers many of the same woes, including ***excessive complexity*** and cost overruns.      **32**

# UNIT 3
## Work and the Workplace

**Unit Overview**      **38**

9. **National ID: Biometrics Pinned to Social Security Cards,** Ryan Singel, *Wired,* May 15, 2007
   Immigration is in the news again. One proposal before Congress is to issue American workers ***tamper-proof biometric Social Security cards.*** These "would replace the text-only design that's been issued to Americans almost without change for more than 70 years."      **41**

10. **Dilberts of the World, Unite!,** David Sirota, *The Nation,* June 23, 2008
    Faced with industry giants who ***outsource*** work to India on one hand and import ***lower cost engineers*** on the other, software developers have begun to organize.      **43**

11. **Computer Software Engineers,** *Occupational Outlook Handbook,* 2006/07 Edition
    Here is one official source that acknowledges the effect of shipping ***high tech jobs abroad,*** but still predicts that "***software engineers*** are projected to be one of the ***fastest-growing occupations*** from 2004 to 2014."      **46**

12. **How Deep Can You Probe?,** Rita Zeidner, *HR Magazine,* October 2007
    Tales of ***employers searching MySpace pages*** notwithstanding, "Many states limit the extent to which employers can consider off duty conduct in making a hiring decision. . . ."      **50**

13. **Privacy, Legislation, and Surveillance Software,** G. Daryl Nord, Tipton F. McCubbins, and Jeretta Horn Nord, *Communications of the ACM,* August 2006
    The authors tell us that the assumption of ***employee privacy*** in the workplace "may be naïve." Constitutional protections against unreasonable search and seizure "usually apply only to state actions."      **53**

The concepts in bold italics are developed in the article. For further expansion, please refer to the Topic Guide.

14. **The Computer Evolution,** Rob Valletta and Geoffrey MacDonald, *FRBSF Economic Letter,* July 23, 2004

This article uses data from several surveys "to examine two key aspects of the computer evolution: the spread of PCs at work and the ***evolving wage differentials*** between individuals who use them and those who do not."     57

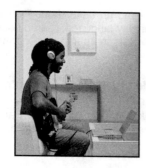

# UNIT 4
## Computers, People, and Social Participation

**Unit Overview**     60

15. **Back-to-School Blogging,** Brock Read, *The Chronicle of Higher Education,* September 3, 2004

It should surprise no one that entering freshmen, who grew up using the Internet, should turn to ***university-sponsored blogs*** to ease the transition to college life.     63

16. **Romance in the Information Age,** Christine Rosen, *The New Atlantis,* Winter 2004

According to Rosen, "our ***technologies enable and often promote*** two ***detrimental forces in modern relationships:*** the demand for total transparency and a bias toward the over sharing of personal information."     66

17. **E-Mail Is for Old People,** Dan Carnevale, *The Chronicle of Higher Education,* October 6, 2006

Reaching students through e-mail has become more difficult as students turn to ***text messaging*** and ***social networking sites.***     73

18. **Girl Power,** Chuck Salter, *Fast Company,* September 2007

How does a seventeen year old run a million dollar ***web site?***     76

19. **Bloggers against Torture,** Negar Azimi, *The Nation,* February 19, 2007

***Authoritarian regimes*** can't always operate in secret, now that bloggers are ***writing.***     81

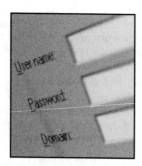

# UNIT 5
## Societal Institutions: Law, Politics, Education, and the Military

**Unit Overview**     84

20. **Piracy, Computer Crime, and IS Misuse at the University,** Timothy Paul Cronan, C. Bryan Foltz, and Thomas W. Jones, *Communications of the ACM,* June 2006

Who are the ***students*** who "openly admit to ***illegally installing software*** on home computers or otherwise misusing computer information systems?" This article provides some clues.     87

The concepts in bold italics are developed in the article. For further expansion, please refer to the Topic Guide.

21. **Can Blogs Revolutionize Progressive Politics?,**
Lakshmi Chaudhry, *In These Times,* February 2006
Liberals have been envious ever since Richard Viguerie's computer-generated mailing lists contributed to Ronald Reagan's victory in 1980. At a time when even Senate Majority Leader Harry Reid has a **blog,** some **Democrats hope** that the computer is finally on their side. **93**

22. **Center Stage,** Carl Sessions Stepp, *American Journalism Review,* April/May 2006
How does a **newspaper's web version** differ from the **print version?** Unlike the print version of a newspaper, the Web version receives little editing. **98**

23. **The Coming Robot Army,** Steve Featherstone, *Harper's Magazine,* February 2007
"Within our lifetime," says Featherstone, "**robots** will give us the ability to **wage war** without committing ourselves to the human cost of actually fighting a war." Sgt. Jason Mero concurs: "These things are amazing. . . . They don't complain. . . . They don't cry. They're not scared. This robot here has no fear." **104**

24. **A Technology Surges,** David Talbot, *Technology Review,* March/April 2008
Real live soldiers still fighting real live wars. A new on-ground reporting system, "*Google Maps* for the *Iraq counterinsurgency*" might help keep these soldiers safe. **111**

25. **Wikipedia in the Newsroom,** Donna Shaw, *American Journalism Review,* February/March 2008
Whether professionals can cite a source that is **collective and anonymous** remains problematic. **114**

26. **E-Mail in Academia: Expectations, Use, and Instructional Impact,** Meredith Weiss and Dana Hanson-Baldauf, *EDUCAUSE Quarterly,* January–March 2008
Studies have shown that there is a relationship between a **student's success** and "the quality of **one-on-one communication** between teacher and student." What happens when you add **e-mail** to the mix? **117**

# UNIT 6
## Risk and Avoiding Risk

**Unit Overview** **124**

27. **Why Spyware Poses Multiple Threats to Security,**
Roger Thompson, *Communications of the ACM,* August 2005
Harm caused by **spyware** ranges from gobbling up computer speed on your PC to enlisting your machine in attacks that can disrupt major businesses or the government. **127**

28. **The Virus Underground,** Clive Thompson, *The New York Times Magazine,* February 8, 2004
Clive Thompson states, "when Mario is bored . . . he likes to sit at his laptop and create computer **viruses** and **worms.**" **129**

The concepts in bold italics are developed in the article. For further expansion, please refer to the Topic Guide.

29. **False Reporting on the Internet and the Spread of Rumors: Three Case Studies,** Paul Hitlin, *gnovis,* April 26, 2004
*Internet news sources* can sometimes be unreliable. Paul Hitlin examines Internet coverage of the *Vince Foster suicide* along with other stories to understand why this is so. **136**

30. **The New Right-Wing Smear Machine,** Christopher Hayes, *The Nation,* November 12, 2007
Some *e-mails* that have gone *viral* in recent political campaigns. **144**

31. **A Growing Watch List,** Karen DeYoung, *The Washington Post National Weekly Edition,* April 2–8, 2007
The *Terrorist Identities Datamart Environment* database contains information on over 450,000 persons, many of them U.S. citizens. What happens if there is an error? **148**

# UNIT 7
## International Perspectives and Issues

Unit Overview **150**

32. **China's Tech Generation Finds a New Chairman to Venerate,** Kevin Holden, *Wired,* May 24, 2007
The *new China* is not a place that would have made Chairman Mao comfortable. One indication is the *popularity of Bill Gates.* **153**

33. **Restoring the Popularity of Computer Science,** David A. Patterson, *Communications of the ACM,* September 2005
While India turns out more and more programmers who are willing to work for a fraction of their American counterparts, *enrollment in computer science classes across the United States is dropping.* The author believes that "inaccurate impressions of opportunities" are behind the decline. **155**

34. **China's Computer Wasteland,** Benjamin Joffe-Walt, *The Progressive,* January 30, 2005
What to do with the *detritus of the digital age* is a growing problem. Shipping it to China seems to be one solution. **157**

35. **In Search of a PC for the People,** Bruce Einhorn, *BusinessWeek,* June 12, 2006
"What features get included in a $200.00 *PC marketed to developing nations?*" and Nicholas Negroponte's remark, "I think of digital access for kids as a human right," are two issues explored in this article. **160**

36. **In Korea, a Boot Camp Cure for Web Obsession,** Martin Fackler, *The New York Times,* November 18, 2007
In a country where online *gaming is a professional sport,* "up to 30% of South Koreans under 18 . . . are at risk of *Internet addiction.*" **162**

37. **New Tech, Old Habits,** Moon Ihlwan and Kenji Hall, *BusinessWeek,* March 26, 2007
*Japan and South Korea* are behind the United States when it comes to the *productivity* of information technology workers. Why? The answer may be as simple as *telecommuting.* **164**

The concepts in bold italics are developed in the article. For further expansion, please refer to the Topic Guide.

# UNIT 8
## The Frontier of Computing

**Unit Overview**      **166**

38. **A Nascent Robotics Culture: New Complicities for Companionship,** Sherry Turkle, *AAAI Technical Report,* July 2006

    "What is a **robot** kind of love?" and "What will we be like, what kind of people are we becoming as we develop increasingly **intimate relationships** with machines?" MIT's pioneering sociologist tries to answer both questions.      **168**

39. **Toward Nature-Inspired Computing,** Jiming Liu and K. C. Tsui, *Communications of the ACM,* October 2006

    Computer scientists are turning to **biology** as a source of inspiration for **models of complex systems.** These biological models change the rules governing systems behavior.      **179**

40. **Google and the Wisdom of Clouds,** Stephen Baker, *BusinessWeek,* December 24, 2007

    Google is teaching researchers around the world how to **extract patterns** using **clusters of computers** that it calls, "**the cloud.**"      **185**

*Test-Your-Knowledge Form*      **190**
*Article Rating Form*      **191**

The concepts in bold italics are developed in the article. For further expansion, please refer to the Topic Guide.

# Topic Guide

This topic guide suggests how the selections in this book relate to the subjects covered in your course. You may want to use the topics listed on these pages to search the Web more easily.

On the following pages a number of Web sites have been gathered specifically for this book. They are arranged to reflect the units of this Annual Editions reader. You can link to these sites by going to *http://www.mhcls.com.*

**All the articles that relate to each topic are listed below the bold-faced term.**

## Artificial intelligence
38. A Nascent Robotics Culture: New Complicities for Companionship
39. Toward Nature-Inspired Computing

## Blogs
15. Back-to-School Blogging
19. Bloggers against Torture
21. Can Blogs Revolutionize Progressive Politics?

## Business
37. New Tech, Old Habits

## Communication
17. E-Mail Is for Old People
26. E-Mail in Academia: Expectations, Use, and Instructional Impact
29. False Reporting on the Internet and the Spread of Rumors: Three Case Studies
30. The New Right-Wing Smear Machine

## Crime
4. Click Fraud: The Dark Side of Online Advertising
20. Piracy, Computer Crime, and IS Misuse at the University

## Education
20. Piracy, Computer Crime, and IS Misuse at the University
26. E-Mail in Academia: Expectations, Use, and Instructional Impact

## E-mail
26. E-Mail in Academia: Expectations, Use, and Instructional Impact
30. The New Right-Wing Smear Machine

## Emerging applications
23. The Coming Robot Army
24. A Technology Surges
35. In Search of a PC for the People
38. A Nascent Robotics Culture: New Complicities for Companionship
39. Toward Nature-Inspired Computing
40. Google and the Wisdom of Clouds

## Employment
9. National ID: Biometrics Pinned to Social Security Cards
10. Dilberts of the World, Unite!
11. Computer Software Engineers
12. How Deep Can You Probe?
13. Privacy, Legislation, and Surveillance Software
14. The Computer Evolution

## Hardware and software design
7. The Beauty of Simplicity
8. The Software Wars: Why You Can't Understand Your Computer
35. In Search of a PC for the People

## Legal and regulatory issues
12. How Deep Can You Probe?
13. Privacy, Legislation, and Surveillance Software
20. Piracy, Computer Crime, and IS Misuse at the University

## Media
5. Online Salvation?
22. Center Stage
25. Wikipedia in the Newsroom

## Military
23. The Coming Robot Army
24. A Technology Surges

## Philosophical/Historical issues
1. Five Things We Need to Know about Technological Change
2. On the Nature of Computing
3. A Place for Hype
38. A Nascent Robotics Culture: New Complicities for Companionship

## Politics
19. Bloggers against Torture
21. Can Blogs Revolutionize Progressive Politics?
29. False Reporting on the Internet and the Spread of Rumors: Three Case Studies
30. The New Right-Wing Smear Machine

## Profiles and personalities
18. Girl Power
32. China's Tech Generation Finds a New Chairman to Venerate

## Privacy
13. Privacy, Legislation, and Surveillance Software
27. Why Spyware Poses Multiple Threats to Security
31. A Growing Watch List

## Youth
18. Girl Power
36. In Korea, a Boot Camp Cure for Web Obsession

# Internet References

The following Internet sites have been selected to support the articles found in this reader. These sites were available at the time of publication. However, because Web sites often change their structure and content, the information listed may no longer be available. We invite you to visit *http://www.mhcls.com* for easy access to these sites.

# Annual Editions: Computers in Society 09/10

## General Sources

### Livelink Intranet Guided Tour
*http://www.opentext.com/*

Livelink Intranet helps companies to manage and control documents, business processes, and projects more effectively. Take this tour to see how.

## UNIT 1: Introduction

### Beyond the Information Revolution
*http://www.theatlantic.com/issues/99oct/9910drucker.htm*

Peter Drucker has written a three-part article, available at this site, that uses history to gauge the significance of e-commerce—"a totally unexpected development"—to throw light on the future of, in his words, "the knowledge worker."

### Short History of the Internet
*http://w3.ag.uiuc.edu/AIM/scale/nethistory.html*

Bruce Sterling begins with the development of the idea for the Internet by the cold war think tank, the Rand Corporation, and goes on to explain how computer networking works. There are links to other sites and to further reading.

## UNIT 2: The Economy

### CAUCE: Coalition Against Unsolicited Commercial Email
*http://www.cauce.org*

This all-volunteer organization was created to advocate for a legislative solution to the problem of UCE, better known as spam. Read about the fight and how you can help at this Web page.

### E-Commerce Times
*http://www.ecommercetimes.com/*

E-Commerce Times is a gateway to a wealth of current information and resources concerning e-commerce.

### The End of Cash (James Gleick)
*http://www.around.com/money.html*

This article, previously published in the *New York Times*, on June 16, 1996, discusses the obsolescence of cash.

### Fight Spam on the Internet
*http://spam.abuse.net*

This is an anti-spam sight that has been in operation since 1996. Its purpose is to promote responsible net commerce, in part, by fighting spam. Up-to-date news about spam can be found on the home page.

### The Linux Home Page
*http://www.linux.org*

This Web site explains that Linux is a free Unix-type operating system, originally created by Linus Torvalds, that is causing a revolution in the world of computers. The site features the latest news about Linux, and everything else you would need to know to switch to the service.

### The Rise of the Informediary
*http://www.ait.unl.edu/crane/misgrad/sglee/informediary.htm*

The author of this site explains what an informediary is and what an informediary does. He also shows why the informediary is so important in today's business environment.

### Smart Cards: A Primer
*http://www.javaworld.com/javaworld/jw-12-1997/jw-12-javadev.html*

This article by Rinaldo Di Giorgio brings the smart card to life with a real-world smart-card example. Five pages explain what a smart card is, how it is used, its limitations, and its strengths.

### Smart Card Group
*http://www.smartcard.co.uk*

This Web site bills itself as "the definitive Web site for Smart Card Technology." At this site you can download Dr. David B. Everett's definitive "Introduction to Smart Cards."

## UNIT 3: Work and the Workplace

### American Telecommuting Association
*http://www.knowledgetree.com/ata-adv.html*

What is good about telecommuting is examined at this site that also offers information regarding concepts, experiences, and the future of telecommuting.

### Computers in the Workplace
*http://www.msci.memphis.edu/~ryburnp/cl/cis/workpl.html*

In this lecture, some of the advantages of computers in the workplace are examined as well as some of the negative aspects, including issues of training, ethics, and privacy.

### InfoWeb: Techno-rage
*http://www.cciw.com/content/technorage.html*

Techno-rage is becoming more and more common. This site provides information and resources regarding techno-rage and techno-stress.

### STEP ON IT! Pedals: Repetitive Strain Injury
*http://www.bilbo.com/rsi2.html*

Data on carpal tunnel syndrome are presented here with links to alternative approaches to the computer keyboard, and links to related information.

# Internet References

## What About Computers in the Workplace
*http://law.freeadvice.com/intellectual_property/computer_law/computers_workplace.htm*

This site, which is the leading legal site for consumers and small businesses, provides general legal information to help people understand their legal rights in 100 legal topics—including the answer to the question, "Can my boss watch what I'm doing?"

## UNIT 4: Computers, People, and Social Participation

### Adoption Agencies
*http://www.amrex.org/*

Here is an example of the much-talked-about new trend of online adoption agencies.

### Alliance for Childhood: Computers and Children
*http://www.allianceforchildhood.net/projects/computers/index.htm*

How are computers affecting the intellectual growth of children? Here is one opinion provided by the Alliance for Childhood.

### The Core Rules of Netiquette
*http://www.albion.com/netiquette/corerules.html*

Excerpted from Virginia Shea's book *Netiquette,* this is a classic work in the field of online communication.

### How the Information Revolution Is Shaping Our Communities
*http://www.plannersweb.com/articles/bla118.html*

This article by Pamela Blais is from the *Planning Commissioners Journal*, Fall 1996 issue, and deals with our changing society. It points out and explains some of the far-reaching impacts of the information revolution, including the relocation of work from office to home.

### SocioSite: Networks, Groups, and Social Interaction
*http://www2.fmg.uva.nl/sociosite/topics/interaction.html*

This site provides sociological and psychological resources and research regarding the effect of computers on social interaction.

## UNIT 5: Societal Institutions: Law, Politics, Education, and the Military

### ACLU: American Civil Liberties Union
*http://www.aclu.org*

Click on the Supreme Court's Internet decision, plus details of the case Reno v. ACLU, and the ACLU's campaign to restore information privacy; "Take Back Your Data"; and cyber-liberties and free speech for opinions on First Amendment rights as they apply to cyberspace.

### Information Warfare and U.S. Critical Infrastructure
*http://www.twurled-world.com/Infowar/Update3/cover.htm*

The "twURLed World" contains a pie chart of URLs involved in IW (information warfare) as well as report main pages that list Internet domains, keywords in contexts and by individual terms, and listing of all URLs and links to details.

### Living in the Electronic Village
*http://www.rileyis.com/publications/phase1/usa.htm*

This site addresses the impact of information in technology on government. Shown is the executive summary, but seven other sections are equally pertinent.

## Patrolling the Empire
*http://www.csrp.org/patrol.htm*

Reprinted from *CovertAction Quarterly*, this article by Randy K. Schwartz details the plans of NIMA (National Imagery and Mapping Agency) for future wars by helping to fuse high-tech surveillance and weaponry.

## United States Patent and Trademark Office
*http://www.uspto.gov/*

This is the official homepage of the U.S. Patent and Trademark Office. Use this site to search patents and trademarks, apply for patents, and more.

## World Intellectual Property Organization
*http://www.wipo.org/*

Visit the World Intellectual Property Organization Web site to find information and issues pertaining to virtual and intellectual property.

## UNIT 6: Risk and Avoiding Risk

### AntiOnline: Hacking and Hackers
*http://www.antionline.com/index.php*

This site is designed to help the average person learn how to protect against hackers.

### Copyright & Trademark Information for the IEEE Computer Society
*http://computer.org/copyright.htm*

Here is an example of how a publication on the Web is legally protected. The section on Intellectual Property Rights Information contains further information about reuse permission and copyright policies.

### Electronic Privacy Information Center (EPIC)
*http://epic.org*

EPIC is a private research organization that was established to focus public attention on emerging civil liberties issues and to protect privacy, the First Amendment, and constitutional values. This site contains news, resources, policy archives, and a search mechanism.

### Internet Privacy Coalition
*http://www.epic.org/crypto/*

The mission of the Internet Privacy Coalition is to promote privacy and security on the Internet through widespread public availability of strong encryption and the relaxation of export controls on cryptography.

### Center for Democracy and Technology
*http://www.cdt.org/crypto/*

These pages are maintained for discussion and information about data privacy and security, encryption, and the need for policy reform. The site discusses pending legislation, Department of Commerce Export Regulations, and other initiatives.

### Survive Spyware
*http://www.cnet.com/internet/0-3761-8-3217791-1.html*

Internet spying is a huge problem. Advertisers, Web designers, and even the government are using the Net to spy on you. CNET.com provides information about spyware and detecting spying eyes that will help you eliminate the threat.

# Internet References

### An Electronic Pearl Harbor? Not Likely
*http://www.nap.edu/issues/15.1/smith.htm*

Is the threat of information warfare real? Yes. Do we need to be completely concerned? Probably not. This site tries to dispel some of the myths and hoaxes concerning information warfare.

## UNIT 7: International Perspectives and Issues

### Information Revolution and World Politics Project
*http://www.ceip.org/files/projects/irwp/irwp_descrip.ASP*

This project, launched by the Carnegie Foundation in 1999, has as its purpose to analyze the political, economic, and social dimensions of the world-wide information revolution and their implications for U.S. policy and global governance.

## UNIT 8: The Frontier of Computing

### Introduction to Artificial Intelligence (AI)
*http://www-formal.stanford.edu/jmc/aiintro/aiintro.html*

This statement describes A.I. Click on John McCarthy's home page for a list of additional papers.

### Kasparov vs. Deep Blue: The Rematch
*http://www.chess.ibm.com/home/html/b.html*

Video clips and a discussion of the historic chess rematch between Garry Kasparov and Deep Blue are available on this site.

### PHP-Nuke Powered Site: International Society for Artificial Life
*http://alife.org/*

Start here to find links to many alife (artificial life) Web sites, including demonstrations, research centers and groups, and other resources.

# UNIT 1
# Introduction

## Unit Selections

1. **Five Things We Need to Know about Technological Change,** Neil Postman
2. **On the Nature of Computing,** Jon Crowcroft
3. **A Place for Hype,** Edward Tenner

## Key Points to Consider

- All American school children learn that the first message Samuel F.B. Morse transmitted over his newly invented telegraph were the words, "What hath God wrought." What they probably do not learn is that Morse was quoting from the poem of Balaam in the Book of Numbers, chapter 23. Read the text of this poem. The overview to this unit presents two ways to understand technical and scientific discoveries. In which camp is Morse?

- Early on in *Walden,* Thoreau famously remarks that "Our inventions are wont to be pretty toys, which distract our attention from serious things. They are but an improved means to an unimproved end, an end that it was already but too easy to arrive at. . . . We are in great haste to construct a magnetic telegraph from Maine to Texas; but Maine and Texas, it may be, have nothing important to communicate." Substitute "Internet" for "magnetic telegraph." Do you agree or disagree with Thoreau? How do you think Jon Crowcroft ("On the Nature of Computing") might respond?

- Richard Lewontin, a Harvard geneticist, says ("The Politics of Science," *The New York Review of Books,* May 9, 2002) that "The state of American science and its relation to the American state are the product of war." What does he mean? Is Lewontin overstating his case? Use the Internet to find out more about Richard Lewontin.

## Student Web Site
www.mhcls.com

## Internet References

**Beyond the Information Revolution**
*http://www.theatlantic.com/issues/99oct/9910drucker.htm*
**Short History of the Internet**
*http://w3.ag.uiuc.edu/AIM/scale/nethistory.html*

This book, *Computers in Society,* is part of a larger series of books published by Dushkin/McGraw-Hill. The series contains over seventy titles, among them *American History, Sociology, and World Politics.* It is instructive to note that not one of them carries the final prepositional phrase "in Society." Why is that? Here is a first approximation. History, sociology, world politics, indeed, most of the other titles in the *Annual Editions* series are not in society, they are society. Suppose we produced an edited volume entitled "History in Society." If such a volume contained reflections on the social implications of the academic study of history, it would have a tiny and specialized readership. But you know that when we speak of "computers in society," we are not talking about the social implications of the academic study of computing. Here is one difference between this volume and the others in the series: it is possible to study computers without studying their social dimension.

But is it? Until not long ago, most people interested in the philosophy and sociology of science considered it value-neutral. That is, a given technology carried no values of its own. The ethics of this or that technology depended on what was done with it. A vestige of this thinking is still with us. When people say, "Guns don't kill people. People kill people," they are asserting that technology somehow stands outside of society, waiting to be put to use for good or ill. The concern about intoxicated drivers is similar. All of us would live happier, safer lives if campaigns to remove drunken drivers from their cars were successful. But this still would not get to the heart of highway carnage that has to do with federal encouragement for far-flung suburbs, local patterns of land use, and a neglect of public transportation. Drunk-driving would not be the issue it is, if driving were not so vital to American life, and driving would not be so vital to American life if a cascade of social and political decisions had not come together in the middle of the twentieth century to favor the automobile.

The first article, "Five Things We Need to Know About Technological Change," makes this point eloquently: "Embedded in every technology there is a powerful idea. . . ." The observation is an important one and is shared by most of the more reflective contemporary commentators on technology. The idea that technology can be studied apart from its social consequences owes some of its strength to the way many people imagine that scientific discoveries are made—since technology is just science applied. It is commonly imagined that scientists are disinterested observers of the natural world. In this view, science unfolds, and technology unfolds shortly after, according to the laws of nature and the passion of scientists. But, of course, scientists study those things that are socially valued. The particular expression of social value in the United States is the National Science Foundation and National Institute of Health funding. We should not be surprised that the medical

© Imagesource/Jupiterimages

and computing sciences are funded generously, or, indeed, that our research physicians and computer scientists are paid better than English professors.

Perhaps a more accurate view of the relationship between technology and computing to society is that social values affect technical discovery which, in turn, affect social values. It is this intricate dance between computers and society—now one leading, now the other—that the writers in this volume struggle to understand, though most of them do it implicitly. But, before we try to understand the dance, it seems reasonable to understand what is meant by the word "computer." You will find in this volume a decided bias toward networked computers. A networked computer is one that can communicate with many millions of others through the global Internet. This is a new definition. As recently as 1996, less than 1 in 5 Americans had used the Internet (Blendon et al., 2001). Just as we mean networked computers when we use the word "computer" today, in the late eighties someone using the word would have meant a stand-alone PC, running, maybe a word processor, a spreadsheet, and some primitive games. A decade before that, the word would have referred to a large, probably IBM, machine kept in an air-conditioned room and tended by an army of technicians. Prior to 1950, the word would have meant someone particularly adept in arithmetic calculations. The point here is that as the meaning of a single word has shifted, our understanding of the dance has to shift with it.

That this shift in meaning has occurred in just a few decades helps us understand why so many commentators use the word "revolution" to describe what computing has wrought. Just as technologies come with hidden meanings, so do words, themselves. The word "revolution" when it is applied to political upheaval is used to describe something thought bad, or at least chaotic—the single counter example is the American

1

Revolution. Not so when the word is applied to computing. Computing is thought to change quickly, but more, it is thought to bring many benefits. A recent survey conducted by the Brookings Institution (Blendon et al, 2001) indicated that 90 percent of Americans believe that science and technology will make their lives easier and more comfortable. The real question to ask is more basic: not whether Americans believe it, but, is it true? First, does the spread of computing constitute a revolution, or just, in Thoreau's words, "an improved means to an unimproved end." Second, revolutionary or not, have we grown smarter, healthier, happier with the coming of the computer? This is still an open question—but, as the Internet morphs from a novelty to an appliance, to a shrinking number of commentators.

Jon Crowcroft's piece, "On the Nature of Computing," is a hymn to its limitless possibilities. As the subtitle asserts, "Computing is its own virtual world, bound only by its practitioners' imaginations and creativity." Read the article and see if you are persuaded.

We end this piece with a book review by Edward Tenner, one of the most refreshing voices among commentators on technology of the past decade. His 1997 book, *Why Things Bite Back* (Vintage) is a cautionary tale for all of us. From improved football helmets that reduced head injuries while turning that very same head into an offensive weapon, to the well-known consequences of DDT, all technologies have a social impact, some less rosy than intended. Here he reviews a book by David Edgerton, another historian of technology who argues that technological change is not "a sequence of revolutionary discoveries, but . . . a complex and often paradoxical interaction between old and new: 'technology in use' as opposed to an 'innovation-centered' history."

## Reference

Blendon, R., Benson, J., Brodie, M., Altgman, D., Rosenbaum, M., Flournoy, R., Kim, M. (2001). Whom to Protect and How? *Brookings Review,* 9(1): 44–48.

# Five Things We Need to Know about Technological Change

Neil Postman

G ood morning your Eminences and Excellencies, ladies, and gentlemen.

The theme of this conference, "The New Technologies and the Human Person: Communicating the Faith in the New Millennium," suggests, of course, that you are concerned about what might happen to faith in the new millennium, as well you should be. In addition to our computers, which are close to having a nervous breakdown in anticipation of the year 2000, there is a great deal of frantic talk about the 21st century and how it will pose for us unique problems of which we know very little but for which, nonetheless, we are supposed to carefully prepare. Everyone seems to worry about this—business people, politicians, educators, as well as theologians.

**The human dilemma is as it has always been, and it is a delusion to believe that the technological changes of our era have rendered irrelevant the wisdom of the ages and the sages.**

At the risk of sounding patronizing, may I try to put everyone's mind at ease? I doubt that the 21st century will pose for us problems that are more stunning, disorienting or complex than those we faced in this century, or the 19th, 18th, 17th, or for that matter, many of the centuries before that. But for those who are excessively nervous about the new millennium, I can provide, right at the start, some good advice about how to confront it. The advice comes from people whom we can trust, and whose thoughtfulness, it's safe to say, exceeds that of President Clinton, Newt Gingrich, or even Bill Gates. Here is what Henry David Thoreau told us: "All our inventions are but improved means to an unimproved end." Here is what Goethe told us: "One should, each day, try to hear a little song, read a good poem, see a fine picture, and, if possible, speak a few reasonable words." Socrates told us: "The unexamined life is not worth living." Rabbi Hillel told us: "What is hateful to thee, do not do to another." And here is the prophet Micah: "What does the Lord require of thee but to do justly, to love mercy and to walk hum-

bly with thy God." And I could say, if we had the time, (although you know it well enough) what Jesus, Isaiah, Mohammad, Spinoza, and Shakespeare told us. It is all the same: There is no escaping from ourselves. The human dilemma is as it has always been, and it is a delusion to believe that the technological changes of our era have rendered irrelevant the wisdom of the ages and the sages.

**. . . all technological change is a trade-off. . . . a Faustian bargain.**

Nonetheless, having said this, I know perfectly well that because we do live in a technological age, we have some special problems that Jesus, Hillel, Socrates, and Micah did not and could not speak of. I do not have the wisdom to say what we ought to do about such problems, and so my contribution must confine itself to some things we need to know in order to address the problems. I call my talk *Five Things We Need to Know About Technological Change*. I base these ideas on my thirty years of studying the history of technological change but I do not think these are academic or esoteric ideas. They are the sort of things everyone who is concerned with cultural stability and balance should know and I offer them to you in the hope that you will find them useful in thinking about the effects of technology on religious faith.

## First Idea

The first idea is that all technological change is a trade-off. I like to call it a Faustian bargain. Technology giveth and technology taketh away. This means that for every advantage a new technology offers, there is always a corresponding disadvantage. The disadvantage may exceed in importance the advantage, or the advantage may well be worth the cost. Now, this may seem to be a rather obvious idea, but you would be surprised at how many people believe that new technologies are unmixed blessings. You need only think of the enthusiasms with which most people approach their understanding of computers. Ask anyone who knows something about computers to talk about them, and you will find that they will, unabashedly and relentlessly, extol the wonders of computers. You will also find that in most cases they will completely neglect to mention any of the liabilities of computers. This is a dangerous imbalance, since the greater the wonders of a technology, the greater will be its negative consequences.

Think of the automobile, which for all of its obvious advantages, has poisoned our air, choked our cities, and degraded the beauty of our natural landscape. Or you might reflect on the paradox of medical technology which brings wondrous cures but is, at the same time, a demonstrable cause of certain diseases and disabilities, and has played a significant role in reducing the diagnostic skills of physicians. It is also well to recall that for all of the intellectual and social benefits provided by the printing press, its costs were equally monumental. The printing press gave the Western world prose, but it made poetry into an exotic and elitist form of communication. It gave us inductive science, but it reduced religious sensibility to a form of fanciful superstition. Printing gave us the modern conception of nation-wide, but in so doing turned patriotism into a sordid if not lethal emotion. We might even say that the printing of the Bible in vernacular languages introduced the impression that God was an Englishman or a German or a Frenchman—that is to say, printing reduced God to the dimensions of a local potentate.

Perhaps the best way I can express this idea is to say that the question, "What will a new technology do?" is no more important than the question, "What will a new technology undo?" Indeed, the latter question is more important, precisely because it is asked so infrequently. One might say, then, that a sophisticated perspective on technological change includes one's being skeptical of Utopian and Messianic visions drawn by those who have no sense of history or of the precarious balances on which culture depends. In fact, if it were up to me, I would forbid anyone from talking about the new information technologies unless the person can demonstrate that he or she knows something about the social and psychic effects of the alphabet, the mechanical clock, the printing press, and telegraphy. In other words, knows something about the costs of great technologies.

Idea Number One, then, is that culture always pays a price for technology.

# Second Idea

This leads to the second idea, which is that the advantages and disadvantages of new technologies are never distributed evenly among the population. This means that every new technology benefits some and harms others. There are even some who are not affected at all. Consider again the case of the printing press in the 16th century, of which Martin Luther said it was "God's highest and extremest act of grace, whereby the business of the gospel is driven forward." By placing the word of God on every Christian's kitchen table, the mass-produced book undermined the authority of the church hierarchy, and hastened the breakup of the Holy Roman See. The Protestants of that time cheered this development. The Catholics were enraged and distraught. Since I am a Jew, had I lived at that time, I probably wouldn't have given a damn one way or another, since it would make no

difference whether a pogrom was inspired by Martin Luther or Pope Leo X. Some gain, some lose, a few remain as they were.

Let us take as another example, television, although here I should add at once that in the case of television there are very few indeed who are not affected in one way or another. In America, where television has taken hold more deeply than anywhere else, there are many people who find it a blessing, not least those who have achieved high-paying, gratifying careers in television as executives, technicians, directors, newscasters and entertainers. On the other hand, and in the long run, television may bring an end to the careers of school teachers since school was an invention of the printing press and must stand or fall on the issue of how much importance the printed word will have in the future. There is no chance, of course, that television will go away but school teachers who are enthusiastic about its presence always call to my mind an image of some turn-of-the-century blacksmith who not only is singing the praises of the automobile but who also believes that his business will be enhanced by it. We know now that his business was not enhanced by it; it was rendered obsolete by it, as perhaps an intelligent blacksmith would have known.

The questions, then, that are never far from the mind of a person who is knowledgeable about technological change are these: Who specifically benefits from the development of a new technology? Which groups, what type of person, what kind of industry will be favored? And, of course, which groups of people will thereby be harmed?

## . . . there are always winners and losers in technological change.

These questions should certainly be on our minds when we think about computer technology. There is no doubt that the computer has been and will continue to be advantageous to large-scale organizations like the military or airline companies or banks or tax collecting institutions. And it is equally clear that the computer is now indispensable to high-level researchers in physics and other natural sciences. But to what extent has computer technology been an advantage to the masses of people? To steel workers, vegetable store owners, automobile mechanics, musicians, bakers, bricklayers, dentists, yes, theologians, and most of the rest into whose lives the computer now intrudes? These people have had their private matters made more accessible to powerful institutions. They are more easily tracked and controlled; they are subjected to more examinations, and are increasingly mystified by the decisions made about them. They are more than ever reduced to mere numerical objects. They are being buried by junk mail. They are easy targets for advertising agencies and political institutions.

In a word, these people are losers in the great computer revolution. The winners, which include among others computer companies, multi-national corporations and the nation state, will, of course, encourage the losers to be enthusiastic about computer technology. That is the way of winners, and so in the beginning they told the losers that with personal computers the average person can balance a checkbook more neatly, keep better track of recipes, and make more logical shopping lists. Then they told them that computers will make it possible to vote at home, shop at home, get all the entertainment they wish at home, and thus make community life unnecessary. And now, of course, the winners speak constantly of the Age of Information, always implying that the more information we have, the better we will be in solving significant problems—not only personal ones but large-scale social problems, as well. But how true is this? If there are children starving in the world—and there are—it is not because of insufficient information. We have known for a long time how to produce enough food to feed every child on the planet. How is it that we let so many of them starve? If there is violence on our streets, it is not because we have insufficient information. If women are abused, if divorce and pornography and mental illness are increasing, none of it has anything to do with insufficient information. I dare say it is because something else is missing, and I don't think I have to tell this audience what it is. Who knows? This age of information may turn out to be a curse if we are blinded by it so that we cannot see truly where our problems lie. That is why it is always necessary for us to ask of those who speak enthusiastically of computer technology, why do you do this? What interests do you represent? To whom are you hoping to give power? From whom will you be withholding power?

I do not mean to attribute unsavory, let alone sinister motives to anyone. I say only that since technology favors some people and harms others, these are questions that must always be asked. And so, that there are always winners and losers in technological change is the second idea.

# Third Idea

Here is the third. Embedded in every technology there is a powerful idea, sometimes two or three powerful ideas. These ideas are often hidden from our view because they are of a somewhat abstract nature. But this should not be taken to mean that they do not have practical consequences.

**The third idea is the sum and substance of what Marshall McLuhan meant when he coined the famous sentence, "The medium is the message."**

Perhaps you are familiar with the old adage that says: To a man with a hammer, everything looks like a nail. We may extend that truism: To a person with a pencil, everything looks like a sentence. To a person with a TV camera, everything looks like an image. To a person with a computer, everything looks like data. I do not think we need to take these aphorisms literally. But what they call to our attention is that every technology has a prejudice. Like language itself, it predisposes us to favor and value certain perspectives and accomplishments. In a culture without writing, human memory is of the greatest importance, as are the proverbs, sayings and songs which

contain the accumulated oral wisdom of centuries. That is why Solomon was thought to be the wisest of men. In Kings I we are told he knew 3,000 proverbs. But in a culture with writing, such feats of memory are considered a waste of time, and proverbs are merely irrelevant fancies. The writing person favors logical organization and systematic analysis, not proverbs. The telegraphic person values speed, not introspection. The television person values immediacy, not history. And computer people, what shall we say of them? Perhaps we can say that the computer person values information, not knowledge, certainly not wisdom. Indeed, in the computer age, the concept of wisdom may vanish altogether.

**The consequences of technological change are always vast, often unpredictable and largely irreversible.**

The third idea, then, is that every technology has a philosophy which is given expression in how the technology makes people use their minds, in what it makes us do with our bodies, in how it codifies the world, in which of our senses it amplifies, in which of our emotional and intellectual tendencies it disregards. This idea is the sum and substance of what the great Catholic prophet, Marshall McLuhan meant when he coined the famous sentence, "The medium is the message."

# Fourth Idea

Here is the fourth idea: Technological change is not additive; it is ecological. I can explain this best by an analogy. What happens if we place a drop of red dye into a beaker of clear water? Do we have clear water plus a spot of red dye? Obviously not. We have a new coloration to every molecule of water. That is what I mean by ecological change. A new medium does not add something; it changes everything. In the year 1500, after the printing press was invented, you did not have old Europe plus the printing press. You had a different Europe. After television, America was not America plus television. Television gave a new coloration to every political campaign, to every home, to every school, to every church, to every industry, and so on.

That is why we must be cautious about technological innovation. The consequences of technological change are always vast, often unpredictable and largely irreversible. That is also why we must be suspicious of capitalists. Capitalists are by definition not only personal risk takers but, more to the point, cultural risk takers. The most creative and daring of them hope to exploit new technologies to the fullest, and do not much care what traditions are overthrown in the process or whether or not a culture is prepared to function without such traditions. Capitalists are, in a word, radicals. In America, our most significant radicals have always been capitalists—men like Bell, Edison, Ford, Carnegie, Sarnoff, Goldwyn. These men obliterated the 19th century, and created the 20th, which is why it is a mystery to me that capitalists are thought to be conservative. Perhaps it is because they are inclined to wear dark suits and grey ties.

I trust you understand that in saying all this, I am making no argument for socialism. I say only that capitalists need to be carefully watched and disciplined. To be sure, they talk of family, marriage, piety, and honor but if allowed to exploit new technology to its fullest economic potential, they may undo the institutions that make such ideas possible. And here I might just give two examples of this point, taken from the American encounter with technology. The first concerns education. Who, we may ask, has had the greatest impact on American education in this century? If you are thinking of John Dewey or any other education philosopher, I must say you are quite wrong. The greatest impact has been made by quiet men in grey suits in a suburb of New York City called Princeton, New Jersey. There, they developed and promoted the technology known as the standardized test, such as IQ tests, the SATs and the GREs. Their tests redefined what we mean by learning, and have resulted in our reorganizing the curriculum to accommodate the tests.

A second example concerns our politics. It is clear by now that the people who have had the most radical effect on American politics in our time are not political ideologues or student protesters with long hair and copies of Karl Marx under their arms. The radicals who have changed the nature of politics in America are entrepreneurs in dark suits and grey ties who manage the large television industry in America. They did not mean to turn political discourse into a form of entertainment. They did not mean to make it impossible for an overweight person to run for high political office. They did not mean to reduce political campaigning to a 30-second TV commercial. All they were trying to do is to make television into a vast and unsleeping money machine. That they destroyed substantive political discourse in the process does not concern them.

## Fifth Idea

I come now to the fifth and final idea, which is that media tend to become mythic. I use this word in the sense in which it was used by the French literary critic, Roland Barthes. He used the word "myth" to refer to a common tendency to think of our technological creations as if they were God-given, as if they were a part of the natural order of things. I have on occasion asked my students if they know when the alphabet was invented. The question astonishes them. It is as if I asked them when clouds and trees were invented. The alphabet, they believe, was not something that was invented. It just is. It is this way with many products of human culture but with none more consistently than technology. Cars, planes, TV, movies, newspapers—they have achieved mythic status because they are perceived as gifts of nature, not as artifacts produced in a specific political and historical context.

When a technology become mythic, it is always dangerous because it is then accepted as it is, and is therefore not easily susceptible to modification or control. If you should propose to the average American that television broadcasting should not begin until 5 P.M. and should cease at 11 P.M., or propose that there should be no television commercials, he will think the idea ridiculous. But not because he disagrees with your cultural agenda. He will think it ridiculous because he assumes you are proposing that something in nature be changed; as if you are suggesting that the sun should rise at 10 A.M. instead of at 6.

## The best way to view technology is as a strange intruder.

Whenever I think about the capacity of technology to become mythic, I call to mind the remark made by Pope John Paul II. He said, "Science can purify religion from error and superstition. Religion can purify science from idolatry and false absolutes."

What I am saying is that our enthusiasm for technology can turn into a form of idolatry and our belief in its beneficence can be a false absolute. The best way to view technology is as a strange intruder, to remember that technology is not part of God's plan but a product of human creativity and hubris, and that its capacity for good or evil rests entirely on human awareness of what it does for us and to us.

## Conclusion

And so, these are my five ideas about technological change. First, that we always pay a price for technology; the greater the technology, the greater the price. Second, that there are always winners and losers, and that the winners always try to persuade the losers that they are really winners. Third, that there is embedded in every great technology an epistemological, political or social prejudice. Sometimes that bias is greatly to our advantage. Sometimes it is not. The printing press annihilated the oral tradition; telegraphy annihilated space; television has humiliated the word; the computer, perhaps, will degrade community life. And so on. Fourth, technological change is not additive; it is ecological, which means, it changes everything and is, therefore too important to be left entirely in the hands of Bill Gates. And fifth, technology tends to become mythic; that is, perceived as part of the natural order of things, and therefore tends to control more of our lives than is good for us.

If we had more time, I could supply some additional important things about technological change but I will stand by these for the moment, and will close with this thought. In the past, we experienced technological change in the manner of sleepwalkers. Our unspoken slogan has been "technology über alles," and we have been willing to shape our lives to fit the requirements of technology, not the requirements of culture. This is a form of stupidity, especially in an age of vast technological change. We need to proceed with our eyes wide open so that we may use technology rather than be used by it.

# On the Nature of Computing

**Computing is its own virtual world, bound only by its practitioners' imaginations and creativity.**

Jon Crowcroft

I would like to propose that computing's innate agenda is the virtual, rather than the natural or the artificial.

Each of us in the computing community experiences periodic bouts of navel gazing about the nature of our business. The related public debate typically polarizes us along a spectrum between engineering and science. At the engineering end are usually the engineers who design and manage systems, networks, and operating systems; at the science end are the ideas describing computability, complexity, and information theory. An extreme view of each end places practitioners within university electrical engineering departments, and theoreticians within university mathematics departments.

I studied the natural sciences at Cambridge University as an undergraduate. I was taught the value of studying the natural world, along with the use (and advance) of mathematics to describe and understand (and predict) its behavior. I have also spent more than a decade teaching courses in an electrical engineering department, where artificial systems are built according to models (often mathematical) with reliable and predictable behavior. Computing has never established a simple connection between the natural and the mathematical. Nowhere is this lack of a clear-cut connection clearer than when Ph.D. students select a problem for their thesis work; their dilemma is the key to understanding why computing represents a third place in the world of discourse—distinct from the natural and from the artificial of science and engineering.

Computing involves (virtual) systems that may never exist, either in nature or through human creation. Ph.D. students find it difficult to settle on a topic because the possibilities are endless and the topic may have no intersection with the real world, either in understanding a phenomenon or in creating an artifact. In trying to define the nature of computing I completely disagree with the late Nobel Prize physicist Richard Feynman.[1] Computing often results in a model of something. Although an object or process that interacts with or describes the real world may be the outcome, it does not have to be.[2]

Computing's disconnection from physical reality has an important consequence when explaining to the public what it is computer scientists do, whether to schoolchildren, noncomputing users in general, or funding agencies and decision makers. Unlike the artificial (the engineering end of the spectrum), some of what we do may not be obviously useful and therefore attractive to commerce and governments for optimizing social welfare or profit. Unlike the natural world (the scientific end of the spectrum), some of what we do may not necessarily be "for the advancement of pure knowledge" and therefore a priori worthwhile. In some sense, though, what we do underpins both of these engineering and scientific activities.

I am comfortable endorsing the claim that computing is less worldly than, say, cosmology. On the other hand, due to the possible use of computing as part of the foundation of practically any kind of system—whether physical or abstract—anyone is likely to build today, computer scientists can also claim that computing is inherently more useful than engineering.

## Examples of the Virtual

To illustrate my argument, consider the following examples of the virtual I've selected from the history of computer science:

**Virtualization.** Within the discipline of computer science itself, the concept of virtualization represents a first-class tool. When confronted with intransigent engineering limitations of memory, processors, I/O, and networks, we've commonly taken the abstract approach. For example, we create virtual memory systems to replace one piece of hardware with another as needed to overcome capacity/performance problems and to choose when it's appropriate to do so; we replace inconvenient low-level processor interfaces (the instruction set) with virtual machines (such as VM, vmware, Xen, and Denali), to provide a more convenient (and stable) interface for systems programmers. We might provide a single API to all I/O devices, so programs need not worry whether, say, an MP3 file is being loaded from a tape, a magnetic disk, an optical disc, flash RAM, or even networked media. We also might replace a network with a virtual private network, allowing users to behave as if they were in an Internet of their own.

**Virtual communities.** In the emerging world of grid computing (notably in the U.K.'s e-Science program), we are creating virtual communities of scientists with virtual laboratories and computing resources dedicated to supporting "in silico" experiments, replacing the expensive, error-prone "in vivo" or "in vitro" experiments of the past. Here, we have virtualized natural systems, whether they involve fluids (such as the atmosphere, oceans, and plasma) or complex biological systems (such as genomes, proteins, and even whole ecologies).

**Entertainment.** The convergence of computer games and the movie industry represents the clearest evidence to support my view that computing is a wholly new discipline. The world of entertainment imposes no natural or artificial constraints on what a system may do. The only limit is the imagination of its creators, combined with knowledge and skills from the computing discipline. Constraints may be imposed from the discipline itself (such as computability, complexity, and plain affability) but may often be orthogonal to the goals (if any) of the computation.

Historically, simple examples of virtual worlds have been used in both games and online environments, as well as for playing with alternate realities (such as in artificial life), so this view is not something that has suddenly become true. It has always been one of the exciting but difficult aspects of working in computing that the bounds are not set from outside the field but by our own choice of what research projects we most want to work on and see developed.

# Conclusion

Occupying a third place in human intellectual culture, computing is not bound by the need to describe what does exist (as in natural science) or what can be built in the real world (as in engineering). This place is the virtual. Although we computer scientists do not need to be complete, consistent, or correct, we have the tools to choose to be part of these categories whenever we wish our systems to be complete, consistent, or correct.

## Notes

1. "Computer science also differs from physics in that it is not actually a science. It does not study natural objects. Neither is it, as you might think, mathematics; although it does use mathematical reasoning pretty extensively. Rather, computer science is like engineering; it is all about getting something to do something, rather than just dealing with abstractions, as in the pre-Smith geology." Richard Feynman, from the book *Feynman Lectures on Computation* (1970).

2. I am tempted to lay claim to the term "magic" [1]. A lot of what computer scientists do is now seen by the lay public as magical. Programmers (especially systems engineers) are often referred to as gurus, sorcerers, and wizards. Given the lofty goals of white magic, understanding the power of names and the value of pure thought, the power of labels is indeed attractive. However, many historically compelling reasons argue against this connotation, including the sad history of Isaac Newton's alchemical pursuit of the philosopher's stone and eternal life, and the religiously driven 17th century witch trials in Salem, MA, and other seemingly rational explanations for irrational behaviors.

## Reference

Penrose, R. *The Road to Reality: A Complete Guide to the Laws of the Universe.* Jonathan Cape, London, U.K., 2004.

**JON CROWCROFT** (Jon.Crowcroft@cl.cam.ac.uk) is the Marconi Professor of Communications Systems in the Computer Laboratory at the University of Cambridge, Cambridge, U.K.

From *Communications of the ACM,* Vol. 48, No. 2, February 2005, pp. 19–20. Copyright © 2005 by Association for Computing Machinery, Inc. Reprinted by permission.

# A Place for Hype

**The Shock of the Old: Technology and Global History since 1900 by David Edgerton. Profile, 270 pp., £18.99, January, 978 1 86197 296 5.**

Edward Tenner

A new golden age of technological hype seems to be dawning. This January, at the Consumer Electronics Show in Las Vegas, a small unfurnished booth cost $24,500. Some 2700 companies proved willing to pay the fee, and 140,000 people visited the show. To coincide with it, Steve Jobs, the Apple CEO, launched the iPhone in San Francisco: a mobile phone with a touch-screen and other familiar functions: web browser, camera, MP3 player. Apple shares went up more than 8 per cent that day, though the phones won't be released until June, will sell for between $499 and $599, and hadn't been independently tested. In January's issue of *Scientific American,* Bill Gates predicted 'a future in which robotic devices will become a nearly ubiquitous part of our day to day lives'. According to Gates, the South Korean government plans to get a domestic robot into all its households by 2013, while the Japanese Robot Association expects there to be a $50 billion a year worldwide personal robot market by 2025.

Ambitious predictions are all very well, but there have also been chastening reminders of previous rounds of misplaced hype. In *New Scientist* last November, the AI researcher Rodney Brooks forecast that at some point in the next fifty years a solution would be found to the 'recognition problem': a computer's inability to tell, as a two-year-old child could, whether an object is a hat, a chair or a shoe on the basis of its general properties. Confident as Brooks was, he acknowledged that his own attempt to solve it in his 1981 PhD dissertation had been unsuccessful.

Academic scientists, medical researchers and technological entrepreneurs are taught to avoid extravagant claims and to rely instead on sober peer review. Yet they are also aware that hype can help win research grants and capital funding and can affect share prices. An adequately supported project may fail, but an overlooked one will not succeed. According to the Thomas Theorem popularised by Robert Merton: 'If men define situations as real, they are real in their consequences.'

David Edgerton's *The Shock of the Old,* with its ironic echoes of bestsellers by Robert Hughes and Alvin Toffler, is not an attack on innovation as such. Rather, it is a call for a new way of thinking about technological change, not as a sequence of revolutionary discoveries, but as a complex and often paradoxical interaction between old and new: 'technology in use' as opposed to an 'innovation-centred' history.

We are said to be living in an age of unprecedented change; indeed, we have been told this in the popular media for the past century at least. Yet much of the technology that now surrounds us would have been clearly recognisable to previous generations. Edgerton doesn't fully explain this paradox, but he does provide many examples, four of which will serve to illustrate the complexities of technology in use: the horse, the Kalashnikov rifle, the B-52 bomber and the flat-pack bookcase.

The horse may be the most surprising case. Edgerton emphasises its continuing role in urban transportation and in warfare in the early to mid-20th century. Hitler's army marched on Moscow with many more horses than Napoleon's, and in 1945 the German army had 1.2 million of them, possibly an even higher ratio of horses to men than in previous centuries of warfare. Horses and other draught animals are still widely used in poor countries: in India, as recently as 1981, animals produced more megawatts of power than all mechanised sources combined, and there were twice as many bullock carts as there had been at independence in 1947. Even in the United States, Amish farmers continue to work with horses, and there seem to be tens of thousands of non-Amish farmers with draught animals, including 3500 oxen teams in New England. Amish artisans continue to develop more efficient agricultural equipment, and have a worldwide market.

It's surprising how many supposedly pre-industrial tools survive in the allegedly post-industrial world. Advocates of development and technology may be embarrassed that horses are still used as draught animals, but they also ignore the proliferation of simple tools and labour-intensive maintenance. In the vast workshop districts of Ghana, known as 'magazines', motor vehicles from the industrialised world have for decades been adapted and refitted for rugged African conditions. They can be maintained indefinitely in this new state, using only simple parts, a sophisticated improvisation that Edgerton calls 'creolisation'. 'At dusk,' he writes, 'bright intermittent light from welding illuminates streets all over the world, issuing from maintenance workshops which might also make simple equipment.'

Edgerton cites the Kalashnikov assault rifle, the AK47, and its descendants to illustrate how effective simplicity can be. Ever since the rifle's introduction in the Soviet Union in 1947 it has been a favourite of both guerrillas and their enemies. Of between

90 and 122 million assault rifles estimated to have been produced since the Second World War, between 70 and 100 million were Kalashnikovs. Together, these small arms have been responsible for more civilian deaths than attacks from the air or the gas chambers. Nuclear weapons, it was once thought, would transform warfare, but they were economically dubious from the start. If the $2 billion spent building the Hiroshima and Nagasaki bombs had been used for conventional weaponry, Edgerton argues, the war might have ended sooner. Likewise, Germany could have built 24,000 fighters for the cost of the V-2 project; each V-2 cost two lives to make and killed on average only one civilian.

The B-52 bomber illustrates a third argument: that the thinking of the military and industrial establishments of the richest countries has changed far less than we imagine. The B-52 was introduced in 1952 and no more were built after 1962, yet in the first Gulf War it dropped 31 per cent of all US bombs. In 2004, the same B-52 used to launch X-15 planes to the edge of space in the 1960s was the platform for testing NASA's latest space aircraft, the X-43A, which was heralded as a dramatic breakthrough even though the X-15 had flown nearly as fast. The B-52 is expected to remain in service until 2040.

Fourth, and perhaps most significant, the globalisation of the trade in wooden furniture is evidence of the conservatism, not the technological transformation, of the industrial order, and also of the continued dominance of rich countries. IKEA has sold 28 million Billy bookcases since 1978, manufactured from wood using conventional mass-production methods. Final transportation and assembly of Billy and other flat-pack IKEA products are left to unpaid consumers. (IKEA and its suppliers employ an estimated one million people worldwide; the founder of this family business is said by some to be worth more than Bill Gates.) The example is even better than Edgerton suggests: the global manufacture and shipping of inexpensive unassembled wooden furniture dates from the middle of the 19th century, when the Thonet brothers of Vienna established factories in the beech forests of Moravia to make virtually indestructible bentwood café chairs.

Edgerton uses stories like these to challenge many of the clichés of technology and business journalism and 'innovation-centric' political rhetoric. He is a formidable polemicist with an encyclopedic grasp of business and economic history and policy, as well as the history of technology, qualities which were manifest in his recent study of British military and industrial history, *Warfare State*. There are many revelations in *The Shock of the Old*, some of them grim: for example, whaling was revived in the 20th century mainly in order to produce margarine. By the 1990s, half of all antibiotics produced in the US were fed to animals, mostly to accelerate growth.

The book's most puzzling theme, though, is one that Edgerton explores only obliquely. Why are older technologies still so prevalent? Or to put it another way: why have so many promising ideas produced less than we expected, at least so far? One 'miracle' after another has turned into a mirage. The future is running behind schedule. Just as the use of horses persisted well into the 20th century, so piston-driven internal combustion engines, developed in the 1870s and 1880s by Otto and Benz, continue to dominate passenger transport. The limited range of all-electric cars has (so far) doomed them commercially. Indeed, poor battery life continues to bedevil devices from cars to digital music players. The miles per gallon achievable by hybrid cars have been even more exaggerated than is

the case with conventional cars. The trains that carry commuters in Europe and the US run on rails similar to those of the 1890s, while diesel trains use an air brake system patented in 1872. Magnetic levitation trains were in service as early as 1984 in Birmingham, yet are still largely at the demonstration stage; a disaster in which 23 people were killed disabled a German experimental project in September 2006.

What of medicine? Cancer survival rates continue to improve, but back in 1971 some of the senators who supported the US National Cancer Act talked of achieving a cure by the Bicentennial of 1976. In rich countries, Aids is now considered a chronic disease rather than a plague; hopes for a vaccine have not been realised. In the mid-1980s one was predicted by the mid-1990s; in 1995, the date was shifted back to 2000. Treatments improve, but no cure is in sight. Bacteria remain just as alarming. In 1969, William Stewart, the US surgeon general, believed we could soon 'close the book on infectious diseases'. But overuse of antibacterial agents helped to promote resistance to antibiotics, leading to today's multi-resistant bacteria, the superbugs of newspaper headlines. Today's antibiotic innovation is a heroic attempt to hold ground thought secured fifty years ago.

Improved medication for progressive diseases such as Parkinson's has made for impressive gains in the control of symptoms. But, as the writer Phyllis Richman recently recalled in a piece for the *Washington Post,* in the 1960s she heard a cure was expected within a decade (the claim seemed credible because of progress made against tuberculosis, polio and malaria), and similar predictions are made today. She repeats a familiar criticism of medical research: 'There's a surer profit in developing another variation of a successful drug than in creating a new kind of drug, for which the clinical trials are not only apt to be more expensive, but the chance of failure runs higher and the approval process is likely to take longer.'

The most significant recent breakthrough in the technology of power transmission, the discovery of high-temperature superconductivity in 1986, seemed to herald virtually resistance-free electric cables, but is still far from being a large-scale application. Consider, too, the crisis over climate change. Optimism about the introduction of nuclear power during the decades before Three Mile Island and Chernobyl may have diverted attention from the dangers of fossil fuel emissions. John von Neumann, the US's most brilliant scientific-political adviser of the postwar decades, wrote in *Fortune* magazine in 1955 that once nuclear power generation had overcome the design limits of older hydrocarbon plants, 'energy may be free—just like the unmetered air—with coal and oil used mainly as raw materials for organic chemical synthesis.' Von Neumann was already aware of the likelihood of global warming from burning hydrocarbons, but saw it not as a cause for worry so much as a possible means for humans to control the climate: we would soon be able to warm or cool the world, or parts of it, mitigate storms and control rainfall. He didn't seem to doubt this would happen; his concerns were over conflicts between winners and losers after the global thermostat had been adjusted.

Von Neumann, who may have known more about computing than any of his contemporaries, believed that increased computer processing power would help make these and other advances—including transmutation of the elements—possible. What he apparently did not foresee was that computational power might have a conservative effect, by prolonging the lives of older technologies.

Consider the Rolamite, a type of bearing patented in 1967 and celebrated in the media as a rare example of a basic new mechanical device. It is basically a band wrapped in an S-shape around two rollers moving in a kind of track. The band can be modified to delay movement until a predetermined force is applied; Rolamites have been used as accelerometers in airbags. But the most ingenious and complex applications predicted were never achieved. The major reason may have been that the Rolamite appeared on the eve of microprocessor control, and it became easier and cheaper to produce programmed chips than to etch patterns into mechanical Rolamite bands.

That so many of the claims made for revolutionary technology between the 1950s and the 1980s have been frustrated leaves us looking for explanations for the surprising technological stability of the present age. There are two possibilities, one structural and one cyclical. The first starts from the premise that the three decades from 1885 to 1915 were unique in the history of technology. (The idea that there was a second industrial revolution, usually dated from 1871 to 1914, originated in 1915 with the Scottish biologist and planner Patrick Geddes, was popularised by David Landes in *The Unbound Prometheus* in 1965, and was affirmed most recently, though with a different starting date, by Vaclav Smil.) Highly developed craft skills, rapid growth in scientific and medical knowledge, and mass promotional techniques came together in the expanding cities of Europe and North America. The basic form of many of today's machines was laid down during these decades and they were mass-marketed surprisingly rapidly, from the Daimler-Maybach engine of 1885 to the Model T Ford of 1908, from the Wright Brothers' flyer of 1905 to the monoplane with joystick control—the basis of most subsequent aircraft design—developed by Louis Blériot and Robert Esnault-Pelterie a few years later. The Rover Safety Bicycle of 1885, designed by an Essex market gardener's son called John Kemp Starley, was the first widely successful design of the type that has dominated ever since. The Scottish vet John Boyd Dunlop introduced the first successful pneumatic tyre in 1888, and most car and bicycle tyres use essentially the same valve patented by George Schrader in 1893.

The same period also saw the extension of continuous processing for mass consumption, with systems that continue to be used today. The crimped bottle cap as we know it was invented in Baltimore in 1891 by William Painter and developed by his company, Crown Cork and Seal, while one of Painter's salesmen, the unsuccessful novelist King C. Gillette, collaborated with the engineer William Nickerson to create the first commercially successful disposable safety razor blade in 1903. Henry Ford's was not the only assembly line: the automatic lasting machine developed in the mid-1880s by Jan Matzeliger increased the number of finished shoes a worker could produce from 50 to 700 a day, laying the foundation of the United Shoe Machinery Co, the international cartel of the 1890s that marketed—with a ruthlessness resulting in decades of antitrust litigation—factory equipment that remains the basis of today's leather shoe industry.

The period from 1945 to 1975 saw radical developments—commercial jet aircraft, antibiotics and vaccines—but in retrospect the great leap forward during these years was in the miniaturisation of electronics. In just three decades we went from publication of von Neumann's proposal for the stored-program computer in universal use today to the unveiling of the Altair 8800 as a 'hobbyist' kit. Bill Gates dropped out of Harvard to develop software for the Altair and its successors. But the paradox remains that the functions of the iPhone, and of today's operating systems and computers, have long been routine.

The structural interpretation of this recent history of innovation is that we have now picked the low-hanging fruit of technology and that the future will be one of continued refinement. This seems to be Edgerton's point of view: he is a partisan of adaptation and improvisation. But a cyclical interpretation is also possible. We may be on the brink of a new era of change, following a thirty-year cycle of incremental improvements, such as the doubling of the Boeing 747's fuel efficiency since its introduction in 1970.

Edgerton does not discuss this alternative. The great strength of his book is its global perspective, which sees poor countries coexisting with rich ones by adopting and adapting. He gives the example of shipbreakers in India, Pakistan and Bangladesh, who dismantle the obsolete vessels of the world's navies and shipping lines, and reroll and rework the steel in them. In this scheme of things, the plans of scientists and engineers in industrial countries are marginal indeed. But Edgerton's viewpoint has its limits. Many poor people in India and Africa can now make inexpensive calls using village cell-phones. Edgerton's linear account sidesteps the intriguing question that can be answered only in real time: will hopes of radical technological progress remain unfulfilled, or will nanotechnology, gene-based medicine, quantum computing and other long-touted innovations eventually find widespread application?

The rhetoric of technological revolution can be hazardous; it can even help hold back innovation. In the 1950s, Lord Cherwell, one of Churchill's senior advisers, successfully recommended against modernising the railways on the grounds that rail was 'obsolete', and that 'helicopters or other formats of transport' would make it less important. Indeed, the railways provide stunning support for Edgerton's argument; computerised analysis has enabled significant improvements in the wheel-rail interface, resulting in greater fuel economy and lower operating costs.

Some commentators are impatient with incremental change; Edgerton sees it as a sensible alternative to the cult of revolutionary transformation as expressed in the hype of the popular press. And so it is, up to a point. But cumulative improvement has left many diseases still incurable, though more humanely managed, and travel times for some air and road journeys have been increasing. (An airline flight from Philadelphia to Los Angeles now takes nearly an hour longer than it did forty years ago.) There may be a legitimate role for hype because of, not despite, the recent absence of anything as 'novel or . . . significant as penicillin or the Model T'. Hype may be an adaptive strategy for building morale and encouraging investment in the face of discouraging experience: the great majority of patents go unrenewed . . .

# UNIT 2
# The Economy

## Unit Selections

4. **Click Fraud S.T,** Brian Grow and Ben Elgin
5. **Online Salvation?,** Paul Farhi
6. **The Big Band Era,** Christopher Swope
7. **The Beauty of Simplicity,** Linda Tischler
8. **The Software Wars,** Paul De Palma

## Key Points to Consider

- The story of automatic underwriting of software is not the first time that software has been blamed for problems in the financial services industry. Use the Internet to find another instance. How are the two stories related? Is the problem with the software or with those that use it? How much responsibility should be shared by those who developed the software?

- Two articles in the unit are about overly complex hardware and software. Is the software that you use overly complex? Do you think the two articles capture what is going on, or can you think of other reasons for why software and hardware are sometimes difficult to use.

- Are you surprised to learn, as the author of "The Software Wars" asserts, that software development can be unsystematic? Do you think this differs from the production of conventional engineering projects, a bridge, for example?

- Intellectual property laws are a contested area. Some—those who engage in music sharing, for instance—would like to eliminate them. Others think they are necessary to encourage creativity. Use the Internet to find out about the Free Software Movement. What would motivate someone to create software and then give it away?

- Joshua Brockman's article on wireless infrastructure raises questions about surveillance. Do you think the increased security offered by remote cameras offset risks to privacy? Use Google Earth to get a satellite view of your house or apartment. Are you concerned that your comings and goings can be monitored?

## Student Web Site
www.mhcls.com

## Internet References

**CAUCE: Coalition Against Unsolicited Commercial Email**
   *http://www.cauce.org*
**E-Commerce Times**
   *http://www.ecommercetimes.com/*
**The End of Cash (James Gleick)**
   *http://www.around.com/money.html*
**Fight Spam on the Internet**
   *http://spam.abuse.net*
**The Linux Home Page**
   *http://www.linux.org*
**The Rise of the Informediary**
   *http://www.ait.unl.edu/crane/misgrad/sglee/informediary.htm*
**Smart Cards: A Primer**
   *http://www.javaworld.com/javaworld/jw-12-1997/jw-12-javadev.html*
**Smart Card Group**
   *http://www.smartcard.co.uk*

Living in the United States in the beginning of the 21st century, it is hard to imagine that the accumulation of wealth once bordered on the disreputable. Listen to William Wordsworth, writing two hundred years ago:

> The world is too much with us; late and soon,
> Getting and spending, we lay waste our powers:
> Little we see in nature that is ours;
> We have given our hearts away, a sordid boon!

These are words that would quicken the pulse of any young protester of globalization. And no wonder. Wordsworth was writing a generation after James Watt perfected the steam engine. England was in the grips of the Industrial Revolution. Just as the developed world now appears to be heading away from an industrial economy and towards a service economy, so Wordsworth's world was moving from an agrarian to an industrial economy. And just as the steam engine has become the emblem of that transformation, the computer has become the symbol of this one.

People, of course, did not stop farming after the Industrial Revolution, nor have they stopped producing steel and automobiles after the Information Revolution, though many commentators write as if this is exactly what has happened. It is true that we in the United States have largely stopped working in factories. In the last three decades, the number of Americans employed has increased by over 50 million. During this same period, the number of manufacturing jobs declined by several hundred thousand. A large handful of these new workers are software and computer engineers, web-site developers, manipulators of digital images—the glamour jobs of the information age. A much larger portion provide janitorial, health, food, and child care services, leading to the charge that the American economy works because we take in one another's laundry.

A service that Americans provide in abundance is advertising. One model in use on the Web is for businesses to pay their Internet hosts only when a potential buyer actually clicks on their site. Sounds good? Read about Martin Fleichmann ("Click Fraud"), who calculates that that invalid clicks have cost his company $100,000. Still, some traditional companies are betting on the wild world Internet advertising to save them. Read Paul Farhi's piece, "Online Salvation," for a look at just how complex the newspaper business has become.

Now what of the decline in manufacturing? It is a rare week when the papers do not include coverage of a plant closure, the weakness of trade unions, or the drop in living wage manufacturing jobs. Large part of this is due to plant relocations to

© Ingram Publishing/AGE Fotostock

countries with lower labor costs. To be convinced, take a look at where almost anything you purchase is made. It is impossible to imagine how a global manufacturing network could be coordinated without computers. Products manufactured abroad—with or without the productivity benefits of computers—pass through a bewildering array of shippers and distributors until they arrive on the shelves of a big box retailer in a Phoenix suburb, or just-in-time to be bolted to the frame of an automobile being assembled outside St. Louis. Or, imagine how Federal Express could track its parcels as they make their way from an office in a San Jose suburb to one in Manhattan. Not surprisingly, cities around the country are scrambling to provide uniform broadband access. "The Big Band Era" reports on a problem many have encountered.

Two articles in the unit describe an important and understudied topic: the complexity of computer hardware and software. Compare Google's home page with just about that of any large company. We have Marissa Mayers to thank for defending it against the natural urge to clutter it up with ads and features. On the other hand, many of us are also burdened by a universal remote: "So many buttons, so little time—and more complicated than the flight deck of the starship Enterprise" ("The Beauty of Simplicity"). "The Software Wars" tells a personal tale of software development and its inefficiencies, while taking its own swipe at the almost willful complexity of the universal remote.

# Click Fraud
## *The Dark Side of Online Advertising*

BRIAN GROW AND BEN ELGIN

Martin Fleischmann put his faith in online advertising. He used it to build his Atlanta company, MostChoice .com, which offers consumers rate quotes and other information on insurance and mortgages. Last year he paid Yahoo! Inc. and Google Inc. a total of $2 million in advertising fees. The 40-year-old entrepreneur believed the celebrated promise of Internet marketing: You pay only when prospective customers click on your ads.

Now, Fleischmann's faith has been shaken. Over the past three years, he has noticed a growing number of puzzling clicks coming from such places as Botswana, Mongolia, and Syria. This seemed strange, since MostChoice steers customers to insurance and mortgage brokers only in the U.S. Fleischmann, who has an economics degree from Yale University and an MBA from Wharton, has used specially designed software to discover that the MostChoice ads being clicked from distant shores had appeared not on pages of Google or Yahoo but on curious Web sites with names like insurance1472.com and insurance060. com. He smelled a swindle, and he calculates it has cost his business more than $100,000 since 2003.

Fleischmann is a victim of click fraud: a dizzying collection of scams and deceptions that inflate advertising bills for thousands of companies of all sizes. The spreading scourge poses the single biggest threat to the Internet's advertising gold mine and is the most nettlesome question facing Google and Yahoo, whose digital empires depend on all that gold.

The growing ranks of businesspeople worried about click fraud typically have no complaint about versions of their ads that appear on actual Google or Yahoo Web pages, often next to search results. The trouble arises when the Internet giants boost their profits by recycling ads to millions of other sites, ranging from the familiar, such as cnn.com, to dummy Web addresses like insurance1472.com, which display lists of ads and little if anything else. When somebody clicks on these recycled ads, marketers such as MostChoice get billed, sometimes even if the clicks appear to come from Mongolia. Google or Yahoo then share the revenue with a daisy chain of Web site hosts and operators. A penny or so even trickles down to the lowly clickers. That means Google and Yahoo at times passively profit from click fraud and, in theory, have an incentive to tolerate it. So do

## Rogues Glossary

The murky world of Web advertising has its own jargon

### Click Fraud
Clicking on Internet advertising solely to generate illegitimate revenue for the Web site carrying the ads; those doing the clicking typically also get paid.

### Parked Web Site
A site typically with little or no content except for lists of Internet ads, often supplied by Google or Yahoo; many of them are the source of false clicks.

### Paid-to-Read
A PTR site pays members to look at other Web sites and offers from marketers; often used to generate fake clicks on parked Web sites.

### Clickbot
Software that can be used to produce automatic clicks on ads; some versions employed in click fraud can mask the origin and timing of clicks.

### Botnet
A collection of computers infected with software that allows them to be operated remotely; networks of thousands of machines can be used in click fraud.

smaller search engines and marketing networks that similarly recycle ads.

## Slipping Confidence

Google and Yahoo say they filter out most questionable clicks and either don't charge for them or reimburse advertisers that have been wrongly billed. Determined to prevent a backlash, the Internet ad titans say the extent of click chicanery has been exaggerated, and they stress that they combat the problem vigorously. "We think click fraud is a serious but manageable issue," says John Slade, Yahoo's senior director for global product management. "Google strives to detect every invalid click that passes through its system," says Shuman Ghosemajumder, the search engine's manager for trust and safety. "It's absolutely in our best interest for advertisers to have confidence in this industry."

That confidence may be slipping. A *BusinessWeek* investigation has revealed a thriving click-fraud underground populated by swarms of small-time players, making detection difficult. "Paid to read" rings with hundreds or thousands of members each, all of them pressing PC mice over and over in living rooms and dens around the world. In some cases, "clickbot" software generates page hits automatically and anonymously. Participants from Kentucky to China speak of making from $25 to several thousand dollars a month apiece, cash they wouldn't receive if Google and Yahoo were as successful at blocking fraud as they claim.

"It's not that much different from someone coming up and taking money out of your wallet," says David Struck. He and his wife, Renee, both 35, say they dabbled in click fraud last year, making more than $5,000 in four months. Employing a common scheme, the McGregor (Minn.) couple set up dummy Web sites filled with nothing but recycled Google and Yahoo advertisements. Then they paid others small amounts to visit the sites, where it was understood they would click away on the ads, says David Struck. It was "way too easy," he adds. Gradually, he says, he and his wife began to realize they were cheating unwitting advertisers, so they stopped. "Whatever Google and Yahoo are doing [to stop fraud], it's not having much of an effect," he says.

Spending on Internet ads is growing faster than any other sector of the advertising industry and is expected to surge from $12.5 billion last year to $29 billion in 2010 in the U.S. alone, according to researcher eMarketer Inc. About half of these dollars are going into deals requiring advertisers to pay by the click. Most other Internet ads are priced according to "impressions," or how many people view them. Yahoo executives warned on Sept. 19 that weak ad spending by auto and financial-services companies would hurt its third-quarter revenue. Share prices of Yahoo and Google tumbled on the news.

Google and Yahoo are grabbing billions of dollars once collected by traditional print and broadcast outlets, based partly on the assumption that clicks are a reliable, quantifiable measure of consumer interest that the older media simply can't match. But the huge influx of cash for online ads has attracted armies of con artists whose activities are eroding that crucial assumption and could eat into the optimistic expectations for online advertising. (Advertisers generally don't grumble about fraudulent clicks coming from the Web sites of traditional media outlets. But there are growing concerns about these media sites exaggerating how many visitors they have—the online version of inflating circulation.)

---

**The success of Google and Yahoo is based partly on the idea that clicks are reliable.**

---

Most academics and consultants who study online advertising estimate that 10% to 15% of ad clicks are fake, representing roughly $1 billion in annual billings. Usually the search engines divide these proceeds with several players: First, there are intermediaries known as "domain parking" companies, to which the search engines redistribute their ads. Domain parkers host "parked" Web sites, many of which are those dummy sites containing only ads. Cheats who own parked sites obtain search-engine ads from the domain parkers and arrange for the ads to be clicked on, triggering bills to advertisers. In all, $300 million to $500 million a year could be flowing to the click-fraud industry.

Law enforcement has only lately started focusing on the threat. A cybercrime unit led by the FBI and U.S. Postal Inspection Service just last month assigned two analysts to examine whether federal laws are being violated. The FBI acted after noticing suspected cybercriminals discussing click fraud in chat rooms. The staff of the Senate Judiciary Committee has launched its own informal probe.

Many advertisers, meanwhile, are starting to get antsy. Google and Yahoo have each settled a class action filed by marketers. In late September a coalition of such major brands as InterActive Corp.'s Expedia.com travel site and mortgage broker Lending-Tree is planning to go public with its mounting unease over click fraud, *BusinessWeek* has learned. The companies intend to form a group to share information and pressure Google and Yahoo to be more forthcoming. "You can't blame the advertisers for being suspicious," says Robert Pettee, search marketing manager for LendingTree, based in Charlotte, N.C. "If it's your money that's going out the door, you need to be asking questions." He says that up to 15% of the clicks on his company's ads are bogus.

In June, researcher Outsell Inc. released a blind survey of 407 advertisers, 37% of which said they had reduced or were planning to reduce their pay-per-click budgets because of fraud concerns. "The click fraud and bad sites are driving people away," says Fleischmann. He's trimming his online ad budget by 15% this year.

Google and Yahoo insist there's no reason to fret. They say they use sophisticated algorithms and intelligence from advertisers to identify the vast majority of fake clicks. But the big search engines won't disclose the specifics of their methods, saying illicit clickers would exploit the information.

Some people who have worked in the industry say that as long as Google and Yahoo distribute ads to nearly anyone with a rudimentary Web site, fraud will continue. "Advertisers should be concerned," says a former Yahoo manager who requested anonymity. "A well-executed click-fraud attack is nearly impossible, if not impossible, to detect."

Although 5 feet 6 and 135 pounds, Marty Fleischmann is no one to push around. He barked orders at much bigger oarsmen while serving as coxswain on the varsity crew team at Yale in the mid-1980s. His shyness deficit surfaced again when he later played the role of Jerry Seinfeld in the student follies at Wharton. Married and the father of three children, he tends to pepper his conversation with jargon about incentives and efficiencies.

# Follow the Money

Click fraud schemes vary and often involve a complicated chain of relationships. Here's one way the process can work:

1. XYZ Widgets signs up with Google or Yahoo to advertise on the Internet, agreeing to pay the search engine every time somebody clicks on an XYZ ad.
2. Google or Yahoo displays the ad on its own site but also recycles it to millions of affiliates, including "domain parking" companies.
3. Domain-parking outfits feed the Google or Yahoo ad to thousands of "parked" Web sites, some of which are nothing more than lists of ads.
4. A fraud artist who owns a parked site circulates it to "paid to read" (PTR) groups, whose members receive small payments to visit sites and click on ads.
5. When a PTR member clicks on the XYZ ad, the company is billed. Yahoo or Google shares the proceeds with the domain parker, the fraudster, and the clickers.

Before he and partner Michael Levy co-founded their financial-information company in 1999, Fleischmann worked in Atlanta at the management consulting firm A.T. Kearney Inc., advising major corporations in the shipping and pharmaceutical industries. One lesson he says he learned is that big companies are loath to cut off any steady source of revenue. Google and Yahoo are no different, he argues.

That cynicism several years ago contributed to MostChoice's assigning an in-house programmer to design a system for analyzing every click on a company ad: the Web page where the ad appeared, the clicker's country, the length of the clicker's visit to MostChoice's site, and whether the visitor became a customer. Few companies go to such lengths, let alone companies with only 30 employees and revenue last year of just $6.4 million.

To Fleischmann, the validity of his clicks, for which he pays up to $8 apiece, has become an obsession. Every day he pores over fresh spreadsheets of click analysis. "I told Yahoo years ago," he says, " 'If this was costing you money instead of making you money, you would have stopped this.' "

Google, he says, does a better job than Yahoo of screening for fraud. But neither adequately protects marketers, he argues. Until March, 2005, Google, based in Mountain View, Calif., charged advertisers twice for "double clicks," meaning those occasions when a user unnecessarily clicks twice in quick succession on an ad. Confirming this, Google's Ghosemajumder says that before the company made the change, it felt it had to focus "on issues of malicious behavior," though now it identifies double clicks and bills for only one.

# Korean Clones

Fleischmann's daily immersion in click statistics fuels his indignation. How, he wants to know, did he receive traffic this summer from PCs in South Korea which are clicking on insurance1472.com and insurance060.com? The only content on these identical sites—and five other clones with similar names—are lists of Yahoo ads, which occasionally have included MostChoice promotions. Fleischmann's spreadsheets revealed, not surprisingly, that all of the suspected Korean clickers left his site in a matter of seconds, and none became customers. The two individuals registered as owning the mysterious insurance sites are based in South Korea. They didn't respond to requests for comment, and most of the sites disappeared in late summer, after MostChoice challenged Yahoo about them.

## "If this was costing [Yahoo] money instead of making it," they would have stopped it.

Fleischmann, like most other advertisers, has agreed to let Google and Yahoo recycle his ads on affiliated sites. The search engines describe these affiliates in glowing terms. A Google "help" page entitled "Where will my ads appear?" mentions such brand names as AOL.com and the Web site of *The New York Times*. Left unmentioned are the parked Web sites filled exclusively with ads and sometimes associated with click-fraud rings.

Google and Yahoo defend their practice of recycling advertising to domain-parking firms and then on to parked sites, saying that the lists of ads on the sites help point Internet surfers toward relevant information. Google notes that it allows advertisers to identify sites on which they don't want their ads to run.

But this Google feature doesn't apply to many parked sites, and Yahoo doesn't offer the option at all. In any event, excluding individual sites is difficult for marketers that don't do the sort of time-consuming research MostChoice does. Whether they know it or not, many other companies are afflicted in similar ways. At *BusinessWeek's* request, Click Forensics Inc., an online auditing firm in San Antonio, analyzed the records of its 170 financial-services clients and found that from March through July of this year, 13 companies had received clicks from Web sites identified as dubious by MostChoice.

Yahoo declined to comment on insurance1472, -060, and other suspect sites in its ad network. The Sunnyvale (Calif.) search giant stressed that in many cases it doesn't deal directly with parked sites; instead, it distributes its ads by means of domain-parking firms.

*BusinessWeek's* independent analysis of the MostChoice records turned up additional indications of click fraud. Over the past six months, the company received 139 visitors through an advertisement on the parked site healthinsurancebids.com, which offers only ads supplied by Yahoo. Most of these visitors were located in Bulgaria, the Czech Republic, Egypt, and

# Taking the Search Engines to Court

Under pressure from advertisers, Google Inc. and Yahoo! Inc. are adjusting the way they deal with click fraud. Several lawsuits filed on behalf of hundreds of advertisers have helped fuel the modest changes.

In June, Yahoo agreed to settle a class action filed in federal court in Los Angeles on behalf of advertisers alleging they had been billed for fake clicks. Without admitting wrongdoing, yahoo said it would grant refunds for bad clicks since January, 2004, that advertisers bring to its attention. The potential cost to Yahoo isn't clear. The company also agreed to appoint an in-house advocate to represent advertisers. The search engine said it would periodically invite marketers to inspect its now-secret fraud-detection systems. Separate from the settlement, Yahoo says that next year it will give marketers more control over where their ads appear.

Google reached its own settlement with unhappy advertisers in July in state court in Texarkana, Ark., where a judge approved a pact valued at $90 million. The agreement provides $30 million in cash for lawyers but only advertising credits for class members. Dissatisfied, a group of advertisers is seeking to challenge the settlement in appellate court. "The rot is so pervasive," says Clarence E. Briggs, III, a leader of the breakaway group. Briggs, a former Army ranger, says his company, Advanced Internet Technologies in Fayetteville, N.C., has detected $90,000 of bad clicks on its Google ads.

Google, which denied any liability, has since announced it will pull back its cloak of secrecy and show individual advertisers the proportion of their clicks it has deemed invalid and for which they weren't billed.

—Ben Elgin and Brian Grow

## Evolution of a Scam

The purpose of click fraud has changed in recent years

### Version 1.0

Companies clicked on a rival's Internet advertisements, running up its ad bills and squeezing the competition. The ads in question typically appeared on Google, Yahoo and other search engine sites.

### Version 2.0

Today click fraud is much more likely to occur on small Web sites that carry ads recycled from Yahoo and Google. Fraudsters arrange for fake clicks on the ads and split the resulting revenue with the search engines.

---

Ukraine. Their average stay on MostChoice.com was only six seconds, and none of them became a customer.

Healthinsurancebids.com offers a revealing entry point into the click-fraud realm. It is one of several parked sites registered to Roland Kiss of Budapest. Kiss also owns BestPTRsite .com. "PTR" refers to "paid to read." In theory, paid-to-read sites recruit members who agree to read marketing e-mails and Web sites tailored to their interests. PTR site operators pay members for each e-mail and Web site they read, usually a penny or less.

In reality, many PTR sites are click-fraud rings, some with hundreds or thousands of participants paid to click on ads. BestPTRsite says it has 977 members. On Aug. 23 its administrator sent an e-mail to members containing a list of parked sites filled with ads. One of these sites, mortgagebg.com, which is also registered to Kiss, has been a source of apparently bogus clicks on MostChoice. The e-mail instructed members to click on different links every day, a common means to avoid detection. Members were also told to cut and paste text from the Web pages they click as proof of their activity. "If you send us back always the same link you will get banned and not paid! So take care and visit everyday a new link," the e-mail said.

Reached by telephone, Kiss says that his registration name is false and declines to reveal the real one. He says he's the 23-year-old son of computer technicians and has studied finance. He owns about 20 paid-to-read sites, he says, as well as 200 parked sites stuffed with Google and Yahoo advertisements. But he says he will take down healthinsurancebids.com to avoid discovery. He claims to take in $70,000 in ad revenue a month, but says that only 10% of that comes from PTRs. The rest, he says, reflects legitimate clicks by real Web surfers. He refrains from more PTR activity, he claims, because "it's no good for advertisers, no good for Google, no good for Yahoo." It's not unusual for people who are involved in PTR activity to profess that they restrict their behavior in some way for the good of advertisers and the big search engines.

After joining several PTR groups, *BusinessWeek* reporters received a torrent of e-mail showcasing hundreds of parked sites filled with Google and Yahoo ads. The groups urged participants to click aggressively on ads. "People don't click because they're interested in the subject," says Pam Parrish, a medical editor in Indianapolis who has participated in PTR sites. "They're clicking on ads to get paid."

Parrish, 52, says that when she started three years ago, PTR sites drew clickers like herself: potential customers looking to pick up a few spare dollars. At one point, she says she belonged to as many as 50 such sites but earned only about $200 all told. More recently, she says, most PTR sites have dropped the pretense of caring whether members are interested in the sites they visit. Parrish and others active on PTR sites say click fraud became more blatant as Google and Yahoo made their ads more widely available to parked sites.

Google and Yahoo say they filter out most PTR activity. "We manage that very well," says Google's Ghosemajumder. "It hasn't been an issue across our network, but it's something we take very seriously." Yahoo adds that PTR sites carrying its ads are in "very serious violation" of its standard distribution

# Advertisers in China Are Getting Burned, Too

China has a reputation in the U.S. as a haven for click-fraud artists. Now, Chinese advertisers say they, too, have fallen victim to the proliferating racket.

In August, Chinese advertisers carrying placards even staged a small demonstration in front of the Beijing office of Baidu.com. China's top search engine. Leading the protest was Dr. Liu Wenhua, director of the Beijing Zhongbei Cancer Medical Research Center. Liu claims that his center, which advertises its services online, has suffered from fraudulent clicks on its ads on a Baidu-affiliated music and entertainment site. Baidu has offered a refund, Liu says, but he turned it down, preferring to take Baidu to court. "I'm not satisfied," the doctor says.

Zhang Xinwei, a partner with the Beijing Hetong Law Office, represents Liu and four other advertisers that also have sued Baidu, alleging fraud. "The problem is very serious," says Zhang. Another plaintiff, Land of Maples Tourism & Culture Exchange, a Beijing travel agency specializing in trips to Canada, has hired a different lawyer. Steven Donne, who runs the agency, says he became suspicious of a batch of 600 clicks this summer because they all came from one source. But Donne feared he wouldn't be able to prove click fraud, so his suit focuses on a claim that Baidu manipulates search results to punish certain advertisers. The legal cases are all in a preliminary stage.

Baidu officials declined to comment but provided a statement denying any impropriety. "Baidu places the highest priority on preventing fraudulent clicks," it said. "We have set up numerous measures both through automated technology and manual efforts to prevent fraudulent clicks and the effectiveness of which [has] been verified by [an] independent third party. . . . We are, however, continuing to invest aggressively in safeguarding measures which will help ensure that our customers and users continue to have the best possible experience."

Despite such assurances, advertisers say concern is spreading. Executives at Analysys International, an info tech researcher in Beijing, noted earlier this year that clicks on its ads on Baidu soared without any uptick in business. In April alone, Analysys burned through one-third of its modest yearly online marketing budget of $3,800. "It was like crazy," says CEO Edward Yu.

This spring, Analysys conducted a survey of 2,000 online advertiser in China and found that one-third believe they have been click-fraud victims. Yu continues to patronize. Google's Chinese affiliate, but he has stopped buying advertising from Baidu and Yahoo China, which is owned by Alibaba.com. Porter Erisman, a spokesman for Alibaba, said in an e-mail that "click fraud is a serious but manageable issue," adding that less than 0.01% of his company's customers have complained.

—Bruce Einhom

---

agreement. Yahoo says it scans its network for PTR activity, but declines to describe its methods.

PTR impresarios often don't fit the profile of an illicit kingpin. Michele Ballard runs a 2,200-member network called theOwl-Post.com from her home in the small town of Hartford, Ky. On disability since a 1996 car accident, Ballard, 36, lives with her ailing mother and her cat, Sassy. She says she works day and night running Owl-Post, a five-year-old group named after the postal system in the Harry Potter novels. Sometimes, Ballard says she takes a break at lunchtime to tend her vegetable garden or help her elderly neighbors with theirs.

She sends her members a daily e-mail containing links to parked Web pages, many of them filled with Google ads. Her e-mails, decorated with smiley faces, suggest to members: "If you could just give a click on something on each page." She owns some of the parked pages, so she gets a share of the revenue when ads on them are clicked. She claims her take amounts to only about $60 a month, noting that if she made more than $85, the government would reduce her $601 monthly disability check.

In August, Google cut off a domain parking firm that hosted some of Ballard's sites. Showing her resilience, she moved the sites to other domain parkers, although none of those currently distributes Google ads. "Google would prefer you not to send out ads on paid e-mails, because they get too much crappy traffic," she says in a phone interview. She realizes that advertisers would get angry "if they knew we were just sitting here, clicking and not interested" in their wares. But, she adds, "They haven't figured that out yet."

Despite these views, Ballard says she doesn't think she's doing anything improper, let alone illegal. While investigations of some Internet criminals have revealed evidence of click fraud, the activity itself hasn't been the subject of prosecution. Ballard says Owl-Post is "like a huge family" whose members sometimes help out colleagues in financial distress. She says the network includes people who have low incomes and are desperate to earn cash to pay their bills. "A lot of people would be hurt if [the PTR business] crashed," she says.

Google's Ghosemajumder says any operation inviting people to click on ads is encouraging fraud, but he expresses skepticism about the overall scale of PTR activity: "People have a great tendency to exaggerate when they say they can attack Google's service."

Networks of human clickers aren't the only source of fake Web traffic. Scores of automated clicking programs, known as clickbots, are available to be downloaded from the Internet and claim to provide protection against detection. "The primary use is to cheat advertising companies," says Anatoly Smelkov, creator of Clicking Agent, a clickbot he says he has sold to some 5,000 customers worldwide.

The brazen 32-year-old Russian software developer lives in the city of Novosibirsk in western Siberia and says he received a physics degree from the state university there. A fan of the British physicist and author Stephen W. Hawking, Smelkov says Clicking Agent is a sideline that generates about $10,000 a year for him; he also writes software for video sharing and other purposes.

> **"A lot of people would be hurt [if the paid-to-read business] crashed," says one organizer.**

Clickbots are popular among online cheats because they disguise a PC's unique numerical identification, or IP address, and can space clicks minutes apart to make them less conspicuous. Smelkov shrugs off his role in facilitating deception. He points out that the first four letters of the name of his company, Lote-Soft Co., stand for "living on the edge." Teasing, he asks: "You aren't going to send the FBI to me, are you?"

## Past Media Scandals

Allegations that some publishers and TV companies deceive advertisers go back many decades. Now the problem has moved online:

### Newspapers and Magazines

Outrage over circulation fraud, employed to boost ad rates, led to the 1914 creation of the Audit Bureau of Circulations. But that didn't stop some publishers from faking the numbers. In 2004 a scandal tainted Tribune's *Newsday* and its Spanish-language *Hoy*, Belo's *Dallas Morning News*, and Sun-Times Media's *Chicago Sun-Times*.

### Television

Broadcasters set ad rates using surveys of how many people are tuned in during four "sweeps" periods a year. Advertisers complain that some networks and local stations use contests and other stunts to attract extra attention during sweeps. The American Association of Advertising Agencies says this practice "has been going on for decades."

### Internet

Click fraud, generating bogus mouse clicks on an online ad, isn't the only way advertisers can get ripped off on the Internet. Some ads are priced according to "impressions," the number of Web surfers who see it, regardless of whether they click. Now there is concern that some media companies commit impression fraud by overstating the number of visitors to their sites.

Google and Yahoo say they can identify automated click fraud and discount advertisers' bills accordingly. Jianhui Shi, a Smelkov customer who goes by the name Johnny, says that for this very reason he steers away from Google and Yahoo ads. An unemployed resident of the booming southern Chinese city of Shenzhen, Jianhui says he has used Clicking Agent to click all sorts of ads on sites he controls, making about $20,000 a year from this activity. While he doesn't click on Google and Yahoo ads, he says that more skilled Chinese programmers modify Clicking Agent to outwit the American search engines. "Many in China use this tool to make money," he wrote in an e-mail to *BusinessWeek*.

Back at the bare-bones MostChoice offices in north Atlanta, Marty Fleischmann continues to demand recompense. He says he has received refunds from Google and Yahoo totaling only about $35,000 out of the $100,000 he feels he is owed. In one exchange, MostChoice e-mailed Google to point out 316 clicks it received in June from ZapMeta.com, a little-known search site. MostChoice paid an average of $4.56 a click, or roughly $1,500 for the batch. Only one converted into a customer. Google initially responded that "after a thorough manual review" some bad clicks were filtered out before MostChoice was charged. Refund request: denied.

But as clicks from ZapMeta kept arriving, Fleischmann demanded in an Aug. 7 e-mail to Google: "You should be trusting us and doing something about [ZapMeta] as a partner, instead of finding more ways to refute our data or requests." (*BusinessWeek*'s e-mail to ZapMeta's site and its registered owner, Kevin H. Nguyen, elicited no response.)

Finally, on Aug. 8, Google admitted that clicks from ZapMeta "seem to be coming through sophisticated means." A Google employee who identified himself only as "Jason" added in an e-mail: "We are working with our engineers to prevent these clicks from continuing." MostChoice received a $2,527.93 refund that included reimbursement for suspect clicks from an additional site as well.

Google says it has refunded MostChoice for all invalid clicks and won't charge for any additional ZapMeta clicks until the situation is resolved. But Google also says it doesn't believe ZapMeta has done anything improper. As of late September, ZapMeta continued to carry ads that had been recycled from Google, although not MostChoice ads.

Randall S. Hansen, a professor of marketing at Stetson University in Deland, Fla., sees a larger lesson in tales of this sort. "We are just beginning to see more and more mainstream advertisers make the Internet a bigger part of their ad budget, and move dollars from print and TV," says Hansen, who has held marketing jobs at *The New Yorker* and *People* magazines. "But if we can't fix this click-fraud problem, then it is going to scare away the further development of the Internet as an advertising medium. If there is an undercurrent of fraud, then why should a large advertiser be losing $1 million, or maybe not know how much it is losing?"

With Moira Herbst.

# Online Salvation?

**The embattled newspaper business is betting heavily on Web advertising revenue to secure its survival. But that wager is hardly a sure thing.**

Paul Farhi

Even the most committed newspaper industry pessimist might begin to see a little sunshine after talking to Randy Bennett. Yes, the print business is "stagnant," acknowledges the Newspaper Association of America's new-media guru. And yes, he says, newsrooms are under pressure. But—and here comes the sun—newspapers have staked out a solid position on the Internet, he says. Internet revenue is growing smartly: In 2003, Bennett points out, newspapers collected a mere $1.2 billion from their online operations; last year the figure was nearly $2.7 billion. "We're growing at a double-digit rate," he says.

This is the kind of news that soothes beleaguered publishers and journalists. As print circulation and advertising swoon, the newspaper industry, and news providers generally, have looked for a lifeboat online. Newspapers were the first of the mainstream media to extend their traditional news franchises into the world of pixels, giving them an important "first mover" advantage. Web sites run by local newspapers typically remain the most popular sources of news and the largest sources of online advertising in their local communities.

Predictions about where the Internet is headed are, of course, hazardous. A dozen or so years after it began to become a fixture in American life, the Internet is still in a formative stage, subject to periodic earthquakes and lightning strikes. Google didn't exist a decade ago. Five years ago, no one had heard of MySpace. Facebook is just four years old, and YouTube is not quite three. Washington Post Executive Editor Leonard Downie Jr. compares the current state of the Internet to television in the age of "Howdy Doody."

Even so, a few dark clouds are starting to form in the sunny vista. Consider a few distant rumbles of thunder:

- After years of robust increases, the online newspaper audience seems to have all but stopped growing. The number of unique visitors to newspaper Web sites was almost flat—up just 2.3 percent—between August 2006 and August 2007, according to Nielsen/NetRatings. The total number of pages viewed by this audience has plateaued, growing just 1.8 percent last year.
- Newspaper Web sites are attracting lots of visitors, but aren't keeping them around for long. The typical visitor

to nytimes.com, which attracts more than 10 percent of the entire newspaper industry's traffic online, spent an average of just 34 minutes and 53 seconds browsing its richly detailed offerings in October. That's 34 minutes and 53 seconds per month, or about 68 seconds per day online. Slim as that is, it's actually about three times longer than the average of the next nine largest newspaper sites. And it's less than half as long as visitors spent on the Web's leading sites, such as those run by Google, Yahoo! and Microsoft.

Many news visitors—call them the "hard-core"—linger longer online, but they're a minority. Greg Harmon, director of Belden Interactive, a San Francisco-based newspaper research firm, estimates that as many as 60 percent of online newspaper visitors are "fly-bys," people who use the site briefly and irregularly. "Everyone has the same problem," says Jim Brady, editor of washingtonpost.com. The news industry's continuing challenge, Brady says, is to turn "visitors into residents."

- As competition for visitors grows, news sites are rapidly segmenting into winners and losers. In a yearlong study of 160 news-based Web sites (everything from usatoday.com to technorati.com), Thomas E. Patterson of Harvard University found a kind of two-tier news system developing: Traffic is still increasing at sites of well-known national brands (the New York Times, CNN, the Washington Post, etc.), but it is falling, sometimes sharply, at mid-size and smaller newspaper sites.

"The internet is redistributing the news audience in ways that [are] threatening some traditional news organizations," concluded Patterson in his study, produced for the Joan Shorenstein Center on the Press, Politics and Public Policy. "Local newspapers have been the outlets that are most at risk, and they are likely to remain so."

Patterson suggests that some of the declines at newspaper sites may be due to increased competition from local broadcast stations, particularly TV. Although they got a late start on the Internet, local TV stations are beginning to catch up, thanks to copious video news clips and strong promotional capabilities.

"A lot of papers are close to maxing out their local audiences," Patterson said in an interview. "It's hard to know where more readers will come from. . . . They have to figure out how to deal with a pretty difficult future."

In other words, for many, that first-mover advantage has vanished.

Most ominous of all is that online ad growth is beginning to slow. Remember those confidence-building double-digit increases in online advertising revenue? They're fading, fast. In the first quarter of this year, the newspaper industry saw a 22 percent gain in online revenue. Not exactly shabby, but still the smallest uptick (in percentage terms) since the NAA started keeping records in 2003. In the second quarter, the industry rate slipped again, to 19 percent. The third quarter promises even less, considering what various companies have been reporting lately. E.W. Scripps Co. saw a 19 percent increase. The Washington Post Co. said its online revenue was up 11 percent in the period, the same as Gannett's. Tribune Co. saw a gain of 9 percent. McClatchy was almost in negative territory, with a weak 1.4 percent increase for the quarter and the year to date.

All of which begins to hint at one of the deeper economic challenges facing online news providers. Even as advertisers move from traditional media to new media, a big question lingers: Can online ad revenue grow fast enough to replace the dollars that are now being lost by the "old" media? And what happens if they don't?

At the moment, the Internet has a long way to go. Newspapers collected $46.6 billion from print advertisers last year; they took in another $11 billion in circulation revenue in 2004, the last time the NAA compiled the total. Even with the double-digit increases online, that's more than 20 times what they're generating from the Internet. Among the industry's most cutting-edge publishers, the Internet still accounts for only a fraction of the overall pie. The leading online newspaper company, the New York Times Co., derives only about 11 percent of its revenue from the Web. This fall, MediaNews Group, which publishes 57 daily newspapers, including the Denver Post and the San Jose Mercury News, touted plans to increase its share of Internet revenue to 20 percent—by 2012.

Philip Meyer, author of "The Vanishing Newspaper" and a former journalist and University of North Carolina journalism professor, believes that it's "in the interest of both newspapers and advertisers to shift content to the Internet." Advertisers get narrower target audiences for their products, he notes, and greater accountability, since they can monitor consumers' behavior. "Newspapers can at last grow their businesses without being held back by the variable costs of newsprint, ink and transportation," he said in an e-mail interview. "In the recent past, newspaper owners have preferred to cut fixed costs, like editorial staff, which gives a quick boost to the bottom line but weakens their hold on the audience. Using technology to cut the variable costs is a better strategy even though the payoff takes longer."

Shedding the big overhead costs of the old media is certainly an attraction of the new one. The problem is, an Internet visitor isn't yet as valuable as a print or broadcast consumer. The cost of reaching a thousand online readers—a metric known in advertising as CPM, or cost per thousand—remains a fraction of the print CPM. The price differential can be as much as 10-to-1, even though many newspaper Web sites now have online audiences that rival or exceed the number of print readers.

Some of this disparity is a result of the witheringly competitive nature of the Web. Unlike the print business, in which newspaper publishers generally enjoy near-monopoly status, the online news world is littered with entrants—from giants like MSNBC.com and AOL.com, to news aggregators like drudgereport.com, to blogs by the millions. This makes it tough for any online ad seller to do what newspaper publishers have done for years—keep raising their ad rates. "Ultimately, it comes down to supply and demand," observes Leon Levitt, vice president of digital media for Cox Newspapers. "And there's an awful lot of supply out there."

Harvard's Patterson offers a more intriguing, and perhaps more unsettling, theory about why it's hard to squeeze more money out of online advertisers: Web ads may not be as effective as the traditional kind. "I'm not sure [advertisers] are convinced yet about how terrific a sales tool [a Web display ad] is," he says. "The evidence isn't strong yet that it can drive people into a store the way a full-page newspaper ad can. They're less confident about what they're getting online." Moreover, unlike their here-and-gone counterparts on the Internet, print subscribers still stay around long enough to see an ad. Some 80 percent of print readers say they spent 16 or more minutes per day with their newspaper, according to Scarborough Research.

These dynamics could change, perhaps as stronger news sources emerge on the Web and weaker ones disappear. But even if the newspaper industry continued to lose about 8 percent of its print ad revenue a year and online revenue continued to grow at 20 percent a year—the pace of the first half of 2007—it would take more than a decade for online revenue to catch up to print.

Journalists, or indeed anyone with an interest in journalism, had better pray that doesn't happen. Because online revenue is still relatively small and will remain so even at its current pace, this scenario implies years of financial decline for the newspaper industry. Even a 5 percent decline in print revenue year after year might look something like Armageddon. Newspapers were already cutting their staffs before this year's advertising downturns. A sustained frost of similar intensity would likely lead to even more devastating slashing. The cuts could take on their own vicious momentum, with each one prompting a few more readers to drop their subscriptions, which would prompt still more cuts. Some daily papers would undoubtedly fold.

Some remain confident that these dire scenarios won't come to pass. "I don't foresee [print dying] in my lifetime," says Denise F. Warren, chief advertising officer for the New York Times Co. and its Web sites. "I'm still bullish on print. It's still an effective way to engage with the audience." On the other hand, she adds, "The business model will keep evolving."

Yes, says Phil Meyer, but it may evolve in ways that render many daily newspapers unrecognizable to today's subscribers: "You want a prediction?" he says. "There will be enough ads for ink on paper to survive, but mainly in niche products for specialized situations."

## Adding It Up

Here is how much print and online ad revenue newspapers have attracted in recent years:

| Year | Print Total $Mill | Print Total %change | Online Total $Mill | Online Total %change | Print and Online Total $Mill | Print and Online Total %change |
|---|---|---|---|---|---|---|
| 2000 | $48,670 | 5.10% | | | | |
| 2001 | $44,305 | −9.00% | | | | |
| 2002 | $44,102 | −0.50% | | | | |
| 2003 | $44,939 | 1.90% | $1,216 | | $46,156 | |
| 2004 | $46,703 | 3.90% | $1,541 | 26.70% | $48,244 | 4.50% |
| 2005 | $47,408 | 1.51% | $2,027 | 31.48% | $49,435 | 2.47% |
| 2006 | $46,611 | −1.68% | $2,664 | 31.46% | $49,275 | −0.32% |
| 2007 | | | | | | |
| **Quarter** | | | | | | |
| First | $9,840.16 | −6.40% | $750.04 | 22.30% | $10,590.20 | −4.80% |
| Second | $10,515.23 | −10.20% | $795.68 | 19.30% | $11,310.90 | −8.60% |

Source: Newspaper Association of America.

Question: Do you see a smart online business model for traditional media that will permit newspapers and other publications to continue to do deep reporting and attract talented journalists?

Craig Newmark: Not yet. While there are people working on it . . . no one's figured it out yet.

—From an online Q&A with Craigslist founder Newmark, posted on nytimes.com on October 10.

To restore the industry's momentum online, executives like Denise Warren suggest the key may simply be more. More new editorial features that will attract new visitors and keep the old ones engaged on the site for longer.

The Times, for instance, expanded three "vertical" news and feature sections last year (real estate, entertainment and travel) and this year is fleshing out similar sections on business, health and technology. In early December, the paper will launch a Web version of its fashion and luxury goods magazine, called T. The paper has also stopped charging for its op-ed columns, after having determined that it could attract more readers—and hence more advertising dollars—by removing the "pay wall" that blocked unlimited access. (The Wall Street Journal is also considering doing away with online subscriptions and moving to a free, ad-supported model, the Journal's new owner, Rupert Murdoch, said in mid-November.)

Washingtonpost.com has added more blogs, more video and special features, like a religion and ethics discussion called On Faith. In June, it started a hyper-local site-within-the-site called LoudounExtra.com that focuses on exurban Loudoun County in Virginia. Coming next summer: a complete redesign of the site. With so much movement, Brady isn't concerned about traffic slowing down. "I'm not worried that people's interest in the Internet has peaked," he says. "There's a whole generation coming up that uses the Internet a lot more."

Cox Newspapers is focusing on its papers' local markets with freestanding niche offerings that target specific demographic groups underserved by the main newspaper, such as young mothers and pet owners and local sports fans, says Leon Levitt. The idea is to assemble a larger, geographically concentrated online readership bit by bit, with as many as seven to nine specialized publications, he says.

Harvard's Patterson has a simpler idea: Just play the news better online. His study of news sites found "substantial variation" in how local sites display news, with some pushing blogs, ads and "activity lists" over breaking news. "If local news is downplayed, local papers are conceding a comparative advantage in their competition with other community sites for residents' loyalties," the study concluded. "If national and international news is downplayed, local papers may increase the likelihood that local residents will gravitate to national brand-name outlets."

The news may be the primary product, but the way the news is served online needs to be updated, too, says Mark Potts, a Web-news entrepreneur and consultant. He says newspaper-run sites are falling behind the rest of the industry in their use of technology. "For the most part, once you get past the bigger papers, newspapers are not up to date" online, he says. "They've got some video, a podcast, some blogs, yes, but mostly . . . they're just pasting the newspaper up on the screen. That was barely OK five years ago." Potts ticks off the tools that news sites usually lack: social networking applications, database-search functions, mapping, simplified mobile-device delivery technology, services that let readers interact with one another, etc. His one-word description for the state of newspapers online: "Stodgy."

On the ad side, traditional news organizations are starting to join, rather than trying to fight, some of the Internet's giants. In recent months, major newspaper companies have struck alliances with Yahoo! and Google in an attempt to pair newspapers' strength in selling local advertising with the search engines' superior technology and national reach. (See The Online Frontier, page 42.)

In the first phase of a multipart alliance, some 19 newspaper companies that own 264 daily papers have linked their online help-wanted advertising to Yahoo!'s HotJobs recruitment site. When an advertiser seeking to hire, say, a nurse, in St. Louis buys an ad through the St. Louis Post-Dispatch, the newspaper places the ad on its site, which is co-branded with HotJobs and automatically linked to HotJobs' national listings. As a result, the advertiser gets his message in front of both local job candidates and others across the country. HotJobs, in turn, gets a local sales agent—the Post-Dispatch—to sell more listings. Although the partners have revealed few financial details about the arrangement, revenue from such ads is split between the newspaper and Yahoo!, with the newspapers taking a majority of each dollar generated.

In a second phase of the alliance that is now being tested, publishers such as McClatchy, Lee Enterprises, Media General, Cox and others will attempt to do something similar with display ads. Using Yahoo!'s search capabilities and technology, the companies hope to marry national and local display ads to their visitors' interests. People interested in, say, pickup trucks (as identified by tracking software and registration questionnaires), would likely see national ads for Ford, and perhaps for local Ford dealers, when they logged on to a newspaper's site. Such highly targeted advertising would command much higher CPMs than plain old banner ads, says Cox's Levitt.

While it's still too early to declare victory, the general scheme of the partnership has drawn praise from Wall Street. Deutsche Bank analyst Paul Ginocchio has estimated that some members of the consortium could see online ad growth rates of 40 percent for the next two years, thanks in large part to revenue generated by the Yahoo! tie-in.

However, other publishers have declined to join the Yahoo! consortium, in part out of concern that newspapers may be giving away too much to Yahoo! and leaving readers little reason to visit the newspapers' own sites. For example, Gannett and Tribune Co. are developing a display advertising network of their own.

Another group of publishers, including Hearst, E.W. Scripps and the New York Times Co., have turned to Google. Under an experimental program that was expanded this summer, Google is running auctions that enable thousands of smaller advertisers to bid on ad space—size, section and date of their choosing—on some 225 newspaper Web sites. The newspapers are free to accept the offer, reject it or make a counteroffer (Google says more than half the bids have been accepted). The process is streamlined by Google's technology, which automates billing and payments.

A little less cooperation might help, too. Some argue that news providers made a huge strategic mistake when they decided to make their content available to others online. "Free riders" like Yahoo.com, MSN.com, Google and AOL.com have built massive franchises—far larger than any traditional mainstream news site—in part by posting news stories created and paid for by others. These days, of course, anyone can assemble a series of links and headlines to become a "news" site. The Shorenstein Center put it bluntly in its recent study of news on the Internet: "The largest threat posed by the Internet to traditional news organizations . . . is the ease with which imaginative or well positioned players from outside the news system can use news to attract an audience."

"It's a terribly unfair deal," says Randy Siegel, the publisher of Parade, the weekly newspaper magazine. "Newspapers need to negotiate a more equitable share with search engines that are making billions of dollars by selling ads around newspaper content without the costs of creating that content. . . . The book industry and the movie industry don't give their content away."

Arkansas Publisher Walter Hussman Jr. knows he sounds like a man from another century when he says it, but he thinks newspapers shouldn't be free, online or off. He rues the day that the Associated Press, which is owned by the newspaper industry, agreed to sell stories to the Yahoo!s and AOLs of the world. Free or bargain-priced news, Hussman says, cheapens everyone's news. Free, he says, "is a bad business model."

Hussman has an idea that's so old and abandoned it seems almost new: Make people pay for the news they want, even in the Internet age. Hussman obviously is swimming upstream with this notion. Not long after the New York Times stopped charging for its op-ed columns under the now-jettisoned Times-Select initiative, the Sacramento Bee dropped subscription fees for Capitol Alert, the paper's Web site for political news.

The newspaper Hussman publishes, the Arkansas Democrat-Gazette in Little Rock, is one of the few that charge a fee ($4.95 a month) for full access to its site. The site has a modest base of 3,000 subscribers, but Hussman says walling it off protects a more lucrative franchise: the newspaper. He believes it's no coincidence that the Democrat-Gazette's print circulation is growing—about 2,000 daily in the latest six-month period that ended in September—at a time when so many others are sliding.

But what about the ad revenue that the newspaper is giving up with such a restricted Web site? Hussman says ad rates are so low online that they often don't cover the cost of producing original journalism. Example: An online gallery of photos from a local high school football game might generate 4,000 page views. If an advertiser paid $25 for each thousand views—a premium figure, by the way—the photo feature might generate $100, barely enough to pay the photographer for his work.

"I know what I'm saying is going to sound too simplistic to some people, but it seems to be working," he says. "The reason I advocate this is not some ideological or esoteric reason or because of pride of authorship. I'm basing this on experience."

Hussman sees an industry that generates nearly $60 billion a year in print ad sales and subscription fees, and that supports the expenditure of roughly $7 billion a year on newsgathering operations, and worries about it all slipping away in an era in which news is so abundant—and so free. "It would be wonderful if someone could figure out a way" to do all that online, he says before concluding, "but I just don't see it now."

PAUL FARHI (farhip@washpost.com) is a Washington Post reporter who writes frequently about the media for the *Post* and *AJR*. He has written about the *San Francisco area's news blues*, *hyperlocal news Web sites* and the *business magazine Portfolio* in recent issues of *AJR*.

# The Big Band Era

**The quest for rapid and robust Internet access has cities grappling with how to bring the best of broadband to their businesses and residents.**

Christopher Swope

Talk to Chris O'Brien about broadband access, and the city of Chicago's technology chief will tell you that more Internet traffic flows through Chicago than anywhere else in the world. That's a difficult point to prove, a bit like saying that Chicago-style pizza is better than New York's. No matter. O'Brien knows that broadband means business, and that most companies can't survive today without superfast access to the Internet. So the Windy City has taken to selling itself as Broadband City—as much a national hub for Internet infrastructure as it's always been for railroads, highways and airports.

That claim is an easy one to believe from the vantage point of O'Brien's 27th-floor downtown office. Underneath the traffic-clogged streets below, private companies have buried miles of fiber-optic cable—an Internet backbone that is indeed as quick as any in the world. Here, big finance and technology firms that require huge amounts of bandwidth for the fastest Internet speeds don't have too much trouble getting it.

But you don't have to wander far from downtown to see how quickly Chicago's broadband prowess breaks down. In South Side neighborhoods and industrial corridors slated for economic development, fiber is much harder to find. Business customers have fewer broadband options here, and what they do have can be prohibitively expensive. For the modest bandwidth of a T-1 line, they can pay as much as $1,000 a month—more than the rent for some of them. Or they can look into two other broadband options: DSL and cable modem. Those are more limited still and aren't yet available in some pockets of the city.

The broadband landscape looks even more speckled over the city line. In the suburbs, researchers at federal laboratories and universities enjoy top-speed broadband at work but some can't get the modest speeds of DSL at home. The suburbs, however, are better off than the prairie towns that lie farther out. There, most computer users are making do with pokey dial-up Internet service that moves data along at a glacial pace.

Broadband access is an essential item for business, and it is quickly becoming one at home too, as everything digital, from e-mail to phone calls to "The Sopranos," tries to squeeze through the same Internet pipe. Yet as the Chicago region shows, the state of American broadband in 2005 ranges from Tiffany to the country store. This new digital divide—the broadband divide—leaves state and local officials facing a lot of tough questions. What's the best way to smooth out these disparities? And what's the proper role of the public sector? Should government build and own some of the infrastructure itself, as it does with highways? Or should broadband look more like the railroads, built and run by profit-seeking companies?

## A Broad Reach

The current situation is cause for either hope or despair, depending on how one looks at it. As of last July, 63 million Americans were connecting to the Internet via broadband at home, according to Nielsen//NetRatings. Millions more use broadband at the office—DSL, T-1 or better—making workers more efficient and innovative. Entrepreneurs can now dream up new services to sell over broadband—founding new companies that create new jobs.

The bad news is that as quickly as broadband is catching on, the U.S. is a laggard compared with other nations. South Korea, Denmark, Japan and Canada have higher rates of residential broadband penetration. In fact, the U.S. is 11th in the world, according to the International Telecommunications Union in Geneva. Part of the problem is that Americans are more spread out than, say, the South Koreans, half of whom live in apartment buildings. But public policy also plays a big role. Japan and South Korea have national broadband strategies. The U.S. doesn't. Broadband deployment is largely up to the giant telephone and cable companies that currently compete with each other in the courtroom just as much as they slug it out in the marketplace. An upside of the American laissez-faire approach is innovation: Carriers have developed lots of technologies for delivering broadband, some using old existing wires, some requiring new lines and others using wireless. The downside is that they only deploy these products in markets where they believe they can turn a profit quickly.

There may be no national policy, but that doesn't mean cities, suburbs and rural communities are sitting on the sidelines.

In fact, localities are at the forefront of the broadband debate, stirring up controversy. For example, Philadelphia, like dozens of other cities, is looking at offering cheap broadband service by turning the whole city into a wireless "hot spot." Opponents of the idea, led by Verizon Communications, think that cities should stay out of broadband. They persuaded the Pennsylvania legislature in November to pass a law that makes it harder for cities to offer municipal broadband. (Verizon is letting Philadelphia proceed with its plans, however.)

Politics may be the least of local officials' worries. As they attack the broadband divide, they're finding that it's a terrifically complex problem, one that is only growing more complicated as technology advances and bandwidth needs grow. Realistically, they can't hope to "solve" the divide so much as manage it over time. Moreover, there's not just one broadband divide. There are at least four of them:

- **Access.** Millions of Americans still can't get basic DSL or cable modem service, or the local provider has a monopoly on the market.
- **Service.** There's lots of high-speed fiber in the ground in the U.S., but outside of dense business districts, the "last mile" problem of tapping into it is expensive to solve.
- **Cost.** Even where basic broadband is available, the monthly cost remains higher than many consumers are willing or able to pay.
- **Don't Need It.** More than one-third of U.S. households still don't have computers—let alone high-speed Internet. And many Internet users don't mind using slow dial-up service.

## The Gatekeepers

You see a range of thinking about these issues across the Chicago region. The most controversial idea came from three cities on the western edge of the Chicago suburbs. Batavia, Geneva and St. Charles, also known as the Tri-Cities, are among the 2,000 U.S. cities that are in the electricity business. Public power has been pretty good for the Tri-Cities. Their electric rates are about 30 percent lower than neighboring towns. So it wasn't a stretch when they proposed getting into the broadband business as well.

The idea first came up two years ago. Comcast, the dominant cable company in the Chicago region, hadn't yet rolled out its cable modem service. The local phone company, SBC Communications, had started offering DSL—but large swaths of the Tri-Cities still couldn't get it.

The city governments held a trump card, however. Each owned a fiber-optic network—a valuable byproduct of running an electric utility. Officials began thinking that if they could build that fiber out directly to homes and businesses, it would be a huge draw for economic development. Municipal broadband—offering superfast Internet, cable TV and telephone—would compete directly with Comcast and SBC.

The towns put the question to a referendum in April 2003. Scared by the $62 million price tag, voters turned it down decisively. The plan went before voters again this past November with a new financing scheme. It got steam rolled again. Comcast and SBC waged an overwhelming campaign against the measure. They bused in employees to knock on doors, and Comcast even sent Hallmark greeting cards to voters' homes.

There was another factor at play. Not all residents saw the issue as a compelling one. As Jeffery Schielke, the mayor of Batavia, puts it, "When we put in sanitary sewers 100 years ago, a number of people said they'd prefer to go to the outhouse."

Proponents of municipal broadband are still bitter about the outcome. They argue that Comcast and SBC, by fighting the referendum, are holding back technology. "They think it's okay to give us limited bandwidth and charge us an arm and a leg for it," says Annie Collins, whose citizens' group was behind the second referendum. As Collins sees it, cities should view broadband as they do roads, sewers or any other essential infrastructure they provide. "Putting the infrastructure in place is just like pavement," she says. "It's basic infrastructure, and the cities should own it."

Comcast and SBC share a different view: Municipal broadband is a bad idea. "It's wrong of the government to get involved in areas where private corporations are offering choices," says Carrie Hightman, president of SBC Illinois. What about the argument that cities should provide broadband as basic infrastructure? "These aren't vital services," says Bob Ryan, a Comcast lobbyist. "They're nice services. But you're not going to die if you don't get video, data and telephony from the government."

All is not lost in the Tri-Cities. By the time of the second vote, Comcast and SBC had rolled out their networks almost ubiquitously there. Just two weeks before the election, SBC held a "digital ribbon-cutting" ceremony in Batavia. Both companies deny wooing voters by bumping the Tri-Cities up their to-do lists. But many observers in Illinois think that the squeaky wheel got the grease. "All of a sudden the Tri-Cities are getting better service," says Edward Feser, a University of Illinois professor who studies broadband. "Maybe the vote is looked at as a failure, but for the end-market consumer the whole effort has been a bonus."

## At Your Service

Farther west, in the prairie town of Princeton, the broadband battle is playing out somewhat differently. A couple of years ago, manufacturers in town began complaining that the T-1 lines they used for broadband weren't fast or robust enough. Rural towns across Illinois have been hit hard lately by manufacturers going overseas. Princeton has fared pretty well so far. But officials there figured that if they could offer manufacturers more bandwidth, it might be all the more reason for companies to stay put.

**Big cities have to show corporations that their broadband will stay on even if terrorists strike, says Chris O'Brien, Chicago's technology chief.**

Princeton officials met with the local phone company—Verizon in this part of Illinois—to see if there was something it could do to upgrade service. But as Princeton's Jason Bird puts it, "at the end of the day, it came down to the fact that we needed to take on this endeavor ourselves." Princeton owns its electric utility, just as the Tri-Cities do. Unlike the Tri-Cities, however, Princeton is not proposing to go into the broadband business on a retail level. Instead, Princeton will build out the broadband infrastructure and let a local company called Connecting Point sell the service to customers.

Princeton's plan is to build fiber out to any customers who say they need it—most likely the big industrial users. Smaller customers and residential users will be handled differently. They'll be among the first in the nation to receive broadband over the same power lines that pump electricity into peoples' homes. This new technology is a convenient solution to the notorious "last mile" problem. Customers simply plug a box into a power outlet and plug their computers into the box. Bird thinks Princeton's approach to broadband represents a lighter touch to government intervention. "We have a partnership here," he says. "We didn't want to get into the business of being the provider. We didn't feel comfortable with that."

> **"Wireless really gives you the opportunity, on a relatively low-cost basis, to put technology into neighborhoods that could never afford it before."**
>
> —Bob Lieberman
> Center for Neighborhood Technology

But that distinction doesn't mean much to the big telephone and cable companies. They argue that any form of municipal broadband enjoys unfair advantages, such as tax-free bond financing. Comcast, SBC and other broadband providers are expected to lobby the legislature for a law similar to Pennsylvania's, either banning municipal broadband or severely restricting it. Similar laws have passed in 15 other states, and the U.S. Supreme Court recently found such bans constitutional. "This is an area where the powerful incumbents want to snuff out consumer option and choice," says Illinois Lieutenant Governor Pat Quinn. "They're snarling in Illinois. It looks like they'll try to wipe out the municipal option for our state this year. We'll see."

## Broadband Browser

| Technology | Speed | Consumer Cost | Upsides | Downsides |
|---|---|---|---|---|
| **WIRED** | | | | |
| **DSL** | Moderate to fast | $25–$60/mo. for residential; $40–$300 for business | Uses existing copper telephone wires | Available only within 3 miles of the telephone company's switch |
| **Cable modem** | Moderate | $40–$70/mo. | Uses existing coaxial cable networks | Customers share bandwith, not as prevalent in commercial areas |
| **Broadband over power lines (BPL)** | Moderate | $25–$50/mo. | Uses existing power lines; just plug into a wall socket | Not widely available yet |
| **T-1 line** | Fast | $200–$1,000/mo. depending on location | Widely used by small businesses | Expensive to install; monthly charge can be more than the rent. |
| **Fiber-optic lines** | Fast to lightning fast | $35–$80/mo. for residential; varies widely for business | Fastest and most reliable for voice, data, video; huge capacity makes it "future proof" | Laying new fiber to the home or to business is expensive |
| **WIRELESS** | | | | |
| **Wi-Fi** | Moderate | Free in public "hot spots"; $8–$10/day in private hot spots | Cheap and easy to deploy in libraries, parks, hotels and airports | Limited range; security remains a concern |
| **Cellular broadband** | Very slow to moderate | $30–$80/mo. | Rides off cell phone networks; better range than Wi-Fi | Available only in select cities |
| **Satellite** | Slow to moderate | $400–$800 for dish; $60–$150/mo. for service | The only option in many rural areas | Pricey start-up costs; slow uploads |
| **WiMax** | Very fast | Expected to be moderate | Future option in both cities and rural areas | Won't beat fiber, especially for online video |

Chicago is more hesitant to use a heavy hand when it comes to broadband. Of course, the city also enjoys two luxuries: a dense downtown and a wealthy mix of corporations that broadband providers are hungry to serve. During the dot-com boom, lots of telecom companies trenched fiber-optic lines under downtown streets. It was a gold rush fueled by the exuberant Internet dreams of the age. Many of those companies later went bankrupt. But their fiber is still there, waiting to be used.

In the Loop, Chicago's busy downtown business section, the biggest broadband problem is figuring out where all the fiber is—and who owns it. That's an economic development issue: Businesses looking to tap into that fiber don't know whom to call. But it's increasingly a homeland security issue, too. After 9/11, many big corporations are queasy about locating critical operations such as data banks in big cities, fearing a terror attack. They want some assurance that their Internet traffic has redundant routes should disaster strike. "Corporate boards are asking whether it's dangerous to locate in a big city," Chris O'Brien says. "We have to prove to them that it's not."

Chicago's neighborhoods are a different story. Back in 2000, Chicago announced a big idea to wire the whole city for broadband. The plan was called CivicNet, and the idea was to aggregate all the public schools, firehouses and city offices into one massive telecom contract. In exchange for a 10-year deal, Chicago expected the winning bidder to lay broadband infrastructure to some 1,600 city facilities. It wouldn't wire the whole city, but since there's a police station, library or some city building in nearly every neighborhood, it would come pretty close.

CivicNet never happened. The telecom bust killed the industry's interest. And Chicago's budget bust killed the city's interest. The silver lining, as O'Brien sees it, is that Comcast and SBC have since pumped millions of dollars of their own into rolling out cable modem and DSL service across nearly all of Chicago. "The residential issue is not solved," O'Brien says. "But we're a lot closer to eliminating access as a problem because of cable modem and DSL." Of all the broadband divides, the one that now concerns O'Brien the most is level of access for small businesses that require more bandwidth than Comcast and SBC are offering. To target this problem, Chicago is considering a CivicNet Lite: a stripped-down version of the original broadband plan, targeted solely at six or seven underserved industrial corridors.

## Wire Works

Others are more concerned about another of the broadband divides: cost. Comcast charges between $43 and $58 a month for cable Internet in Chicago. SBC charges between $27 and $37 a month for the most basic residential DSL. Bob Lieberman thinks that wireless broadband might be a cheaper alternative.

Lieberman heads the Center for Neighborhood Technology in Chicago, and is experimenting with wireless projects in three neighborhoods in the region. One is Lawndale, a predominantly African-American neighborhood west of the Loop. "The median household income in Lawndale is $22,000, so $600 a year for broadband is a big chunk," Lieberman says. "That's a lot of money for what is arguably entertainment."

The tallest building in Lawndale is an historic brick tower that rises 260 feet above an old Sears distribution center. "It's the first Sears Tower," Lieberman says. Just as the namesake skyscraper downtown is crowned with radio antennae, Lieberman has placed a small, barely visible antenna in the Lawndale tower. The antenna is wired to the Internet and beams a signal out to "nodes" scattered atop row houses in the neighborhood, which relay the signal back and forth to computers in peoples' homes. An unusual feature of this so-called "mesh" network is that the system actually becomes stronger and more reliable as more people use it.

The Lawndale project is up to 100 users, who for the time being are getting the service for free (the Center hooks people up with used computers, too). Lieberman thinks it could serve as a prototype for small cities or neighborhoods. He estimates the municipal cost of providing such a service would ring in at about $8 to $10 per month, per household. "Wireless really gives you the opportunity, on a relatively low-cost basis, to put technology into neighborhoods that could never afford it before," Lieberman says.

A lot of other cities are having exactly the same thought. The technology is cheap enough that Philadelphia thinks it could fill the air with a cloud of Internet signals for just about $10 million. And wireless technology is advancing quickly. A new generation of wireless broadband, called WiMax, is due out in the next year or so. WiMax will offer greater bandwidth than the current Wi-Fi does and work to a range of 30 miles. In other words, a single antenna could blanket entire cities, or large swaths of countryside, with broadband coverage.

A lot of people in city government around the country are very excited about wireless. Chicago has created Wi-Fi hot spots at all its city libraries, and in places where business travelers congregate, such as the airport and convention center. Yet Chris O'Brien is skeptical of taking on a broader, city-wide wireless project. Simply put, Chicago doesn't want to step on the private sector's turf. "Government needs to tread a very fine line," O'Brien says. "We could create a wireless network for the entire city if we wanted to. We own enough fiber that we could get into the telecom business, too. Figuring out where our leverage ends and where we leave it to the private sector is the tough issue."

CHRISTOPHER SWOPE can be reached at cswope@governing.com.

From *Governing*, January 2005, pp. 20–22, 24–25. Copyright © 2005 by Congressional Quarterly, Inc. Reprinted by permission.

# The Beauty of Simplicity

**I'm snuggled under the covers with Jon Stewart and the remote. The "Evolution/Schmevolution" skit is funny, but it's been a long day, and I'm fading fast. The promise of technology is that I'm one click away from slumberland. I hit the power button. The picture disappears, but the TV is still glowing a creepy blue that will haunt my dreams if I don't make it go away. I try the TV button. Nothing. The cable button. Nothing. What the %$\*&?? I kick off the blankets and trudge over to turn off the miserable box at the source. I can't help but wonder, as I lie there, now wide awake, how it is that all the things that were supposed to make our lives so easy instead made them more complex. Why is so much technology still so hard?**

LINDA TISCHLER

It is innovation's biggest paradox: We demand more and more from the stuff in our lives—more features, more function, more power—and yet we also increasingly demand that it be easy to use. And, in an Escher-like twist, the technology that's simplest to use is also, often, the most difficult to create.

Marissa Mayer lives with that conundrum every day. As Google's director of consumer Web products, she's responsible for the search site's look and feel. Mayer is a tall, blond 30-year-old with two Stanford degrees in computer science and an infectious laugh. She's also Google's high priestess of simplicity, defending the home page against all who would clutter it up. "I'm the gatekeeper," she says cheerfully. "I have to say no to a lot of people."

The technology that powers Google's search engine is, of course, anything but simple. In a fraction of a second, the software solves an equation of more than 500 million variables to rank 8 billion Web pages by importance. But the actual experience of those fancy algorithms is something that would satisfy a Shaker: a clean, white home page, typically featuring no more than 30 lean words; a cheery, six-character, primary-colored logo; and a capacious search box. It couldn't be friendlier or easier to use.

Here is how Mayer thinks about the tension between complexity of function and simplicity of design: "Google has the functionality of a really complicated Swiss Army knife, but the home page is our way of approaching it closed. It's simple, it's elegant, you can slip it in your pocket, but it's got the great doodad when you need it. A lot of our competitors are like a Swiss Army knife open—and that can be intimidating and occasionally harmful."

It would be lovely if Google's corporate mythology included an enchanting tale to account for the birth of this pristine marvel. But the original home-page design was dumb luck. In 1998, founders Sergey Brin and Larry Page were consumed with writing code for their engine. Brin just wanted to hack together something to send queries to the back end, where the cool technology resided. Google didn't have a Web master, and Brin didn't do HTML. So he designed as little as he could get away with.

The accident became an icon, of course, and a key reason the company enjoys a commanding lead. Google's design has been mimicked on the search pages of MSN and Yahoo, whose portals are messy throwbacks to the "everything but the kitchen sink" school of Web design. But they're poor imitations; according to Hitwise, Google controls 59.2% of the search market, up from 45% a year ago; MSN's share is down to 5.5% and Yahoo's is 28.8%.

No surprise that a site easy enough for a technophobe to use has caught the public imagination. Like desperate Gullivers, we're pinned down by too much information and too much stuff. By one estimate, the world produced five exabytes (one quintillion bytes) of content in 2002—the same amount churned out between 25,000 B.C. and A.D. 2000. Little wonder that *Real Simple* has been the most successful magazine launch in a decade, and the blogosphere is abuzz over the season's hottest tech innovation—the Hipster PDA: 15 index cards held together by a binder clip.

With Google's extraordinary trajectory and the stratospheric success of Apple's iPod—itself a marvel of simplicity and, with 20 million units sold, a staggering hit—we seem to be nearing

# The Simple, and the Simply Awful

**A pantheon of technology products that marry great performance with simplicity of design—and those that miss the mark**

## Products we love . . .

**TiVo, by TiVo.** It's not often that owners refer to their pet technology as "life changing," but the ability to watch 24 at 3 A.M. surely counts as one of the decade's greatest humanitarian breakthroughs. The remote, the intuitive menus, the crisp instructions—everything about it can make even your parents feel smart.

**iPod, by Apple.** You don't have to be a hipster to love iPod, which plays Henry Mancini as easily as it blasts Cannibal Corpse.

**Skype's Voice-over-Internet service.** Cheap long distance? Without having to deal with the phone company? What's not to love?

**Google's search engine.** So good it's a verb. The real question is, How did we find anything in the pre-Google era?

**BlackBerry by RIM.** Love 'em or hate 'em, their ubiquity speaks for itself. Sure beats lugging around an eight pound laptop just to get e-mail.

## . . . and love to hate

**Universal remote.** So many buttons, so little time—and more complicated than the flight deck of the starship *Enterprise.* If you're an engineering prof (or a 14-year-old), it's heaven on earth. For the rest of us, it's easier to haul our weary bodies out of the La-Z-Boy than to figure out how to turn of the TV with this thing.

**PeopleSoft software.** The product most likely to induce about of Tourette's syndrome in the office.

**LG VX6100 cell phone.** Why is it so hard to make it shut up? Finding the MUTE button requires digging through the innards of the user's manual.

**HP Officejet 7110 printer.** It does it all—printing, scanning, copying, faxing—and does it all badly.

**Sony Synthesized Radio.** One aggravated owner complained, "It's impossible to program. You can't get the clock to stop blinking . . . and the antenna is useless." But it looks cool.

a seminal moment. Whereas endless Sunday Styles stories may have failed to get its attention, the tech industry's interest is invariably galvanized by cash. If the equation T (technology) + E (ease of use) = $ can be proven, the time may be right for the voice of the technologically challenged who can't operate their remotes to be heard.

In a 2002 poll, the Consumer Electronics Association discovered that 87% of people said ease of use is the most important thing when it comes to new technologies. "Engineers say, 'Do you know how much complexity we've managed to build in here?' But consumers say, 'I don't care. It's just supposed to work!'" says Daryl Plummer, group vice president at Gartner Group.

It's often that tension—between the desire to cram in cool new features and the desire to make a product easy to use—that makes delivering on the simplicity promise so hard, particularly in companies where engineers hold sway. At Google, it's an ongoing battle. As developers come up with ever sexier services—maps! news alerts! scholarly papers!—the pressure to lard on links is fierce. Mayer holds them at bay with a smile and strict standards.

To make it to the home page, a new service needs to be so compelling that it will garner millions of page views per day. Contenders audition on the advanced-search page; if they prove their mettle—as image search did, growing from 700,000 page views daily to 2 million in two weeks—they may earn a permanent link. Few make the cut, and that's fine. Google's research shows that users remember just 7 to 10 services on rival sites. So Google offers a miserly six services on its home page. By contrast, MSN promotes more than 50, and Yahoo, over 60. And both sell advertising off their home pages; Google's is a commercial-free zone.

> I want to figure out how to combine simplicity, which is basic human life, with this thing—technology—that's out of control.

So why don't those sites simply hit the DELETE button and make their home pages more Googlesque? Hewing to the simplicity principle, it turns out, is tougher than connecting with tech support, particularly if you try it retrospectively. "Once you have a home page like our competitors'," Mayer says, "paring it back to look like Google's is impossible. You have too many stakeholders who feel they should be promoted on the home page." (MSN says more than half its customers are happy with its home page—but it's experimenting with a sleeker version called "start.com.")

Google understands that simplicity is both sacred and central to its competitive advantage. Mayer is a specialist in artificial intelligence, not design, but she hits on the secret to her home page's success: "It gives you what you want, when you want it, rather than everything you could ever want, even when you don't."

That, says Joe Duffy, founder of the award–winning Minneapolis design firm Duffy & Partners and author of *Brand Apart,* is a pretty good definition of good design. He quotes a famous line from the eminent designer Milton Glaser: "Less isn't more; just enough is more." Just enough, says Duffy, contains an aesthetic component that differentiates one experience from another.

It's just that holding the line on what constitutes "just enough" is harder than it looks.

It's early September, and the streets of Cambridge, Massachusetts, are teeming with young technorati in flip-flops and shorts. But there is calm at the MIT Media Lab, just upstairs from the List Visual Arts Center, the university's preeminent gallery. It's a fitting juxtaposition, a place where art and technology seek common ground.

John Maeda runs the Media Lab's Simplicity Consortium. His goal is to find ways to break free from the intimidating complexity of today's technology and the frustration of information overload. He is a gentle, soft-spoken man, dressed elegantly in a crisp, white collarless shirt and black pants. And he is an unusual amalgam: having the mathematical wizardry of a computer geek with the soul of an artist. Indeed, in 1990, he left MIT for four years to study art. "My whole life changed," he says. "I thought, this is a great way to live." But rather than throwing over his digital life entirely, he conceived a mission. "I came back to MIT to figure out how you could combine simplicity, which is basic human life, with this thing—technology—that's out of control."

Maeda's ability to toggle back and forth between right brain and left affords him unusual insight into how we got stuck in this technological quagmire. On one level, he says, the problem is simply one of scale. Before computer technology, small things were simple; big things were more likely complex. But the microchip changed that. Now small things can be complex, too. But small objects have less room for instruction—so we get cell phones with tip calculators buried deep in submenus and user manuals the size of the Oxford English Dictionary to help us figure it all out.

Blame the closed feedback loop among engineers and industrial designers, who simply can't conceive of someone so lame that she can't figure out how to download a ringtone; blame a competitive landscape in which piling on new features is the easiest way to differentiate products, even if it makes them harder to use; blame marketers who haven't figured out a way to make "ease of use" sound hip. "It's easier," says Charles Golvin, principal analyst with Forrester Research, "to market technology than ease of use."

Across the river from MIT, in the Boston suburb of West Newton, Aaron Oppenheimer runs the product behavior group of Design Continuum, one of the country's preeminent design firms. He is the sympathetic counselor who gently points out that for each feature clients want to include—"Hey, if we've got a microprocessor in there, let's add an alarm clock!"—they're trading off a degree of ease of use. It's a never-ending battle. "I spend a lot of time talking clients out of adding features," he says with a sigh. "Every new feature makes things more complicated, even if you never use them."

In the past, he says, adding features usually meant adding costs. Put a sound system or power windows into a car, and you've upped the price, so you better make sure consumers really want what you're peddling. But in the digital world, that cost-benefit calculus has gone awry. "The incremental cost to add 10 features instead of one feature is just nothing," says Oppenheimer. "Technology is this huge blessing because we can do anything with it, and this huge curse because we can do anything with it."

But the issue is also our conflicted relationship with technology. We want the veneer of simplicity but with all the bells and whistles modern technology can provide. "The market for simplicity is complex," says Dan Ariely, a business-school professor who is spending a year off from MIT figuring out how to quantify the value of simplicity at Princeton's Institute for Advanced Study. "If I offer you a VCR with only one button, it's not all that exciting, even if when you use it, it's likely to be easier."

We also want our devices to talk to each other—cell phone to the Web, digital camera to printer. That requires a level of interoperability that would be difficult to attain in a perfect world, but is well nigh impossible in one where incompatibility is a competitive strategy. "In business, it's all about war," says Maeda. "I hate to sound like a hippie, but if there were just some sense of peace and love, products would be much better."

In his quiet way, Maeda hopes to right the balance between man and machine. He and his students are working on software, code-named OPENSTUDIO, that would create an "ecosystem of design"—connecting designers with customers on a broad scale. That could lead to bespoke products—a cell phone, for example, with 30 features for Junior, 3 for Gran. "You can't make the world simpler unless you can get in touch with design," he says, "and the only way you can do that is to get in touch with designers."

How do you make your company's products simpler? You can start by simplifying your company.

In the late 1990s, Royal Philips Electronics was a slow-footed behemoth whose products, from medical diagnostic imaging systems to electric shavers, were losing traction in the marketplace. By 2002, a new CEO, Gerard Kleisterlee, determined that the company urgently needed to address the dynamic global marketplace and become more responsive to consumers' changing needs.

Philips deployed researchers in seven countries, asking nearly 2,000 consumers to identify the biggest societal issue that the company should address. The response was loud and urgent. "Almost immediately, we hit on the notion of complexity and its relationship to human beings," says Andrea Ragnetti, Philips's chief marketing officer. Consumers told the researchers that they felt overwhelmed by the complexity of technology. Some 30% of home-networking products were returned because people couldn't get them to work. Nearly 48% of people had put off buying a digital camera because they thought it would be too complicated.

Strategists recognized a huge opportunity: to be the company that delivered on the promise of sophisticated technology without the hassles. Philips, they said, should position itself as a simple company. Ragnetti was dumbstruck. "I said, 'You must be joking. This is an organization built on complexity, sophistication, brainpower.'" But he and Kleisterlee responded with an even more audacious plan. Rather than merely retooling products, Philips would also transform itself into a simpler, more market-driven organization.

## The market for simplicity is complex. If I offer you a VCR with only one button, it's not all that exciting, even if when you use it, it's likely to be easier.

That initiative has been felt from the highest rungs of the organization to the lowest. Instead of 500 different businesses, Philips is now in 70; instead of 30 divisions, there are 5. Even things as prosaic as business meetings have been nudged in the direction of simplicity: The company now forbids more than 10 slides in any PowerPoint presentation. Just enough, they decided, was more.

The campaign, christened "Sense and Simplicity," required that everything Philips did going forward be technologically advanced—but it also had to be designed with the end user in mind and be easy to experience. That ideal has influenced product development from conception—each new product, like the ShoqBox, an MP3 mini-boom box, must be based on a user need that's tested and validated—to packaging. Philips invited 15 customers to its Consumer Experience Research Centre in Bruges, Belgium, to see how they unpacked and set up a Flat TV. After watching people struggle to lift the heavy set from an upright box, designers altered the packaging so the TV could be removed from a carton lying flat on the ground.

While many of the new products have yet to hit the market, early results of the business reorganization, particularly in North America, have been dramatic. Sales growth for the first half of 2005 was up 35%, and the company was named Supplier of the Year by Best Buy and Sam's Club. Philips's Ambilight Flat TV and GoGear Digital Camcorder won European iF awards for integrating advanced technologies into a consumer-friendly design, and the Consumer Electronics Association handed the company 12 Innovation Awards for products ranging from a remote control to a wearable sport audio player.

Maeda, who, as a member of Philips's Simplicity Advisory Board has had a front-row seat for this transformation, is impressed. "The best indication of their sincerity is that they're embracing the concept at a management level," says Maeda. "It isn't just marketing to them. That's quite a radical thing."

Designing products that are easy to use is nothing new for Intuit, the big tax- and business-software company. Indeed, it's been the mantra since founder Scott Cook developed Intuit's first product, Quicken, back in 1983 after listening to his wife complain about writing checks and managing bills.

But even by Intuit's standards, Simple Start, a basic accounting package that debuted in September 2004, was a leap. For one thing, the target market was tiny businesses that used no software at all. "These were people who said, 'I have a simple busi-ness, and I don't want the complexity of having to learn this. I don't want to use the jargon, I don't want the learning curve, and besides, I'm afraid of it,' " says project manager Terry Hicks.

But the potential was huge: some 9 million microbusiness owners that Intuit wasn't reaching with its current line. So Hicks's team first tried a knockoff of Intuit's QuickBooks Basic, with a bunch of features turned off. Then they confidently took the product out for a test-drive with 100 potential customers.

And it bombed. It was still too hard to use, still riddled with accounting jargon, still too expensive. They realized they had to start from scratch. "We had to free ourselves and say, 'Okay, from an engineering point of view, we're going to use this code base, but we need to design it from a customer's point of view.' " says Lisa Holzhauser, who was in charge of the product's user interface.

The designers followed more customers home. They heard more complaints about complexity, but also anxiety that things in their business might be falling through the cracks. So the team distilled two themes that would guide their development: The product had to be simple, and it had to inspire confidence. Terms such as "aging reports" and "invoicing" were edited out, and the designers drew on the experience of the SnapTax division, which had hired an editor from *People* magazine to help translate accountant-speak into real-world language. Accounts receivable became "Money In," accounts payable, "Money Out." They pared back 125 setup screens to three, and 20 major tasks to six essentials. They spent days worrying about the packaging, knowing that to this audience, something labeled "Simple Accounting" was an oxymoron.

Above all, they subjected their work to the demanding standards of Intuit's usability lab, run by Kaaren Hanson. To get a product by her, users must be able, 90% of the time, to accomplish the tasks deemed most critical. It's a draconian standard. But "if our goal was to make it 'as easy as we can,' " Hanson says, "we wouldn't be as successful as if we had set a concrete number."

The Simple Start team thought they had nailed the user-interface problem after their third iteration of the product got rave reviews for its look and feel. But task completion results from the lab were dismal. The launch was delayed for months while the team reengineered the tools until they measured up.

The additional time was worth it. Simple Start—a product with 15 years of sophisticated QuickBooks code lurking behind an interface even a Luddite could love—sold 100,000 units in its first year on the market. Even better, reviews from target customers indicate that Intuit hit the mark. Ken Maples, owner of a tiny flight-instruction school in Cupertino, California, summed it up: "It's easy to use. It's got everything I need and nothing more." Ah . . . just enough. Good. Somewhere, Milton Glaser is smiling.

**LINDA TISCHLER** (ltischler@fastcompany.com) is a *Fast Company* senior writer. TiVo changed her life, but she can't find the MUTE button on her new phone. Jennifer Reingold contributed to this story.

# The Software Wars
## *Why You Can't Understand Your Computer*

PAUL DE PALMA

O n a bright winter morning in Philadelphia, in 1986, my downtown office is bathed in sunlight. I am the lead programmer for a software system that my firm intends to sell to the largest companies in the country, but like so many systems, mine will never make it to market. This will not surprise me. If the chief architect of the office tower on whose twenty-sixth floor I am sitting designed his structure with the seat-of-the-pants cleverness that I am using to design my system, prudence would advise that I pack my business-issue briefcase, put on my business-issue overcoat, say good-bye to all that sunlight, and head for the front door before the building crumbles like a Turkish high-rise in an earthquake.

But I am not prudent; nor am I paid to be. Just the opposite. My body, on automatic pilot, deflects nearly all external stimuli. I can carry on a rudimentary conversation, but my mind is somewhere else altogether. In a book-length profile of Ted Taylor, a nuclear-weapons designer, that John McPhee wrote for *The New Yorker*, Dr. Taylor's wife tells McPhee a wonderful story about her husband. Mrs. Taylor's sister visits for the weekend. Taylor dines with her, passes her in the hall, converses. He asks his wife on Monday morning— her sister having left the day before—when she expects her sister to arrive. Mrs. Taylor calls this state "metaphysical absence." You don't have to build sophisticated weaponry to experience it. When my daughter was younger, she used to mimic an old John Prine song. "Oh my stars," she sang, "Daddy's gone to Mars." As you will see, we workaday programmers have more in common with weapons designers than mere metaphysical absence.

My mind reels back from Mars when a colleague tells me that the *Challenger* has exploded. The *Challenger*, dream child of NASA, complex in the extreme, designed and built by some of the country's most highly trained engineers, is light-years away from my large, and largely uninspired, piece of data-processing software. If engineering were music, the *Challenger* would be a Bach fugue and my system "Home on the Range." Yet despite the differences in technical sophistication, the software I am building will fail for many of the same reasons that caused the *Challenger* to explode seconds after launch nearly twenty years ago.

S oftware's unreliability is the stuff of legend. *Software Engineering Notes,* a journal published by the ACM, the largest professional association of computer scientists, is known mostly for the tongue-in-cheek catalogue of technical catastrophes that appears at the beginning of each issue. In the March 2001 issue—I picked this off my shelf at random—you can read about planes grounded in L.A. because a Mexican air-traffic controller keyed in too many characters

of flight description data, about a New York database built to find uninsured drivers, which snared many of the insured as well, about Florida eighth graders who penetrated their school's computer system, about Norwegian trains that refused to run on January 1, 2001, because of a faulty Year 2000 repair. The list goes on for seven pages and is typical of a column that has been running for many years.

> **People often claim that one of every three large-scale software systems gets canceled midproject. Of those that do make it out the door, three-quarters are never implemented: some do not work as intended; others are just shelved.**

People often claim that one of every three large-scale software systems gets canceled midproject. Of those that do make it out the door, three-quarters are never implemented: some do not work as intended; others are just shelved. Matters grow even more serious with large systems whose functions spread over several computers—the very systems that advances in networking technology have made possible in the past decade. A few years ago, an IBM consulting group determined that of twenty-four companies surveyed, 55 percent built systems that were over budget; 68 percent built systems that were behind schedule; and 88 percent of the completed systems had to be redesigned. Try to imagine the same kind of gloomy numbers for civil engineering: three-quarters of all bridges carrying loads below specification; almost nine of ten sewage treatment plants, once completed, in need of redesign; one-third of highway projects canceled because technical problems have grown beyond the capacity of engineers to solve them. Silly? Yes. Programming has miles to go before it earns the title "software engineering."

In civil engineering, on the other hand, failures are rare enough to make the news. Perhaps the best-known example is the collapse of the Tacoma-Narrows Bridge. Its spectacular failure in 1940, because of wind-induced resonance, was captured on film and has been a staple of physics courses ever since. The collapse of the suspended walkway in the Kansas City Hyatt Regency in 1981 is a more recent example. It failed because structural engineers thought that verifying the design of connections joining the walkway segments was the job of their manufacturer. The manufacturer had a different recollection. The American Society of Civil Engineers quickly adopted a protocol for checking shop designs. These collapses are remarkable for two related reasons. First, bridge and building failures are so rare in the United States that when they do occur we continue to talk about them half a century later. Second, in both cases, engineers correctly determined the errors and took steps not to repeat them. Programmers cannot make a similar claim. Even if the cause of system failure is discovered, programmers can do little more than try not to repeat the error in future systems. Trying not to repeat an error does not compare with building well-known tolerances into a design or establishing communications protocols among well-defined players. One is exhortation. The other is engineering.

None of this is new. Responding to reports of unusable systems, cost overruns, and outright cancellations, the NATO Science Committee convened a meeting of scientists, industry leaders, and programmers in 1968. The term *software engineering* was invented at this conference in the hope that, one day, systematic, quantifiable approaches to software construction would develop. Over the intervening years, researchers have created a rich set of tools and techniques, from design practices to improved programming languages to techniques for proving program correctness. Sadly, anyone who uses computers knows that they continue to fail regularly, inexplicably, and, sometimes, wonderfully—*Software Engineering Notes* continues to publish pages of gloomy tales each quarter. Worse, the ACM has recently decided not to support efforts to license software engineers because, in its words, "there is no form of licensing that can be instituted today assuring public safety." In effect, software-engineering discoveries of the past thirty years may be interesting, but no evidence suggests that understanding them will improve the software-development process.

As the committee that made this decision surely knows, software-engineering techniques are honored mostly in the breach. In other words, business practice, as much as a lack of technical know-how, produces the depressing statistics I have cited. One business practice in particular ought to be understood. The characteristics of software often cited as leading to failure—its complexity, its utter plasticity, its free-floating nature, unhampered by tethers to the physical world—make it oddly, even paradoxically, similar to the practice of military procurement. Here is where the *Challenger* and my system, dead these twenty long years, reenter the story.

I n the mid-eighties I worked for a large management-consulting firm. Though this company had long employed a small group of programmers, mostly to support in-house systems, its software-development effort and support staff grew substantially, perhaps by a factor of ten, over a period of just a few years. A consulting firm, like a law firm, has a cap on its profits. Since it earns money by selling time, the number of hours its consultants can bill limits its revenue. And there is a ceiling to that. They have to eat and sleep, after all. The promise of software is the promise of making something from nothing. After development, only the number of systems that can be sold limits return on investment. In figuring productivity, the denominator remains constant. Forget about unhappy unions, as with cars and steel; messy sweatshops, as with clothing and shoes; environmental regulations, as with oil and petrochemicals. Software is a manufacturer's dream. The one problem, a very sticky problem indeed, is that it does not wear out. The industry responds by adding features, moving commercial software one step closer to military systems. More on this later. For now, just understand that my company, like so many others under the influence of the extraordinary attention that newly introduced personal computers were receiving at the time, followed the lure of software.

My system had one foot on the shrinking terra firma of large computers and the other in the roiling, rising sea of microcomputers. In fact, mine was the kind of system that three or four years earlier would have been written in COBOL, the language of business systems. It perhaps would have used a now obsolete database design, and it would have gone to market within a year. When told to build a similar system for a microcomputer, I did what I knew how to do. I designed a gray flannel system for a changing microcomputer market.

Things went along in a predictable if uninspired way until there was a shift in management. These changes occur so frequently in business that I had learned to ignore them. The routine goes like this. Everyone gets a new organization chart. They gather in conference rooms for mandatory pep talks. Then life goes on pretty much as before. Every so often, though, management decisions percolate down to the geeks, as when your manager arrives with a security officer and gives you five minutes to empty your desk, unpin your *Dilbert* comics, and go home. Or when someone like Mark takes over.

When that happened, I assumed falsely that we would go back to the task of producing dreary software. But this was the eighties. Junk bonds and leveraged buyouts were in the news. The arbitrageur was king. Business had become sexy. Mark, rumor had it, slept three hours a night. He shuttled between offices in New York, Philadelphia, and Montreal. Though he owned a house in Westchester County, now best known as the home of the Clintons, he kept an apartment in Philadelphia, where he managed to spend a couple of days each week. When Mark, the quintessential new manager ("My door is always open"), arrived, we began to live like our betters in law and finance. Great bags of bagels and cream cheese arrived each morning. We lunched in trendy restaurants. I, an erstwhile sixties radical, began to ride around in taxis, use my expense account, fly to distant cities for two-hour meetings. Life was sweet.

During this time, my daughter was an infant. Her 4:00 A.M. feeding was my job. Since I often had trouble getting back to sleep, I sometimes caught an early train to the office. One of these mornings my office phone rang. It was Mark. He sounded relaxed, as if finding me at work before dawn was no more surprising than bumping into a neighbor choosing apples at Safeway. This was a sign. Others followed. Once, Mark organized a dinner for our team in a classy hotel. When the time came for his speech, Mark's voice rose like Caesar's exhorting his troops before the Gallic campaign. He urged us to bid farewell to our wives and children. We would, he assured us, return in six months with our shields or upon them. I noticed then that a few of my colleagues were in evening dress. I felt like Tiresias among the crows. When programmers wear tuxedos, the world is out of joint.

Suddenly, as if by magic, we went from a handful of programmers producing a conventional system to triple that number, and the system was anything but conventional. One thing that changed was the programming language itself. Mark decided that the system would be splashier if it used a database-management system that had recently become commercially available for mainframes and was promised, shortly, for microcomputers. These decisions—hiring more people to meet a now unmeetable deadline; using a set of new and untested tools—represented two of the several business practices that have been at the heart of the software crisis. Frederick Brooks, in his classic book, *The Mythical Man-Month,* argues from his experience building IBM's System 360 operating system that any increased productivity achieved by hiring more people gets nibbled at by the increased complexity of communication among them. A system that one person can develop in thirty days cannot be developed in a single day by thirty people. This simple truth goes down hard in business culture, which takes, as an article of faith, the idea that systems can be decreed into existence.

The other practice, relying on new, untested, and wildly complex tools, is where software reigns supreme. Here, the tool was a relational database-management system. Since the late sixties, researchers have realized that keeping all data in a central repository, a database, with its own set of access techniques and backup mechanisms, was better than storing data with the program that used it. Before the development of database-management systems, it was common for every department in a company to have its own data, and for much of this data to overlap from department to department. So in a university, the registrar's office, which takes care of student records, and the controller's office, which takes care of student accounts, might both have copies of a student's name and address. The problem occurs when the student moves and the change has to be reported to two offices. The argument works less well for small amounts of data accessed by a single user, exactly the kind of application that the primitive microcomputers of the time were able to handle. Still, you could argue that a relational database-management system might be useful for small offices. This is exactly what Microsoft Access does. But Microsoft Access did not exist in 1986, nor did any other relational database-management system for microcomputers. Such systems had only recently become available for mainframes.

> Something unique to software, especially new software: no experts exist in the sense that we might speak of an expert machinist, a master electrician, or an experienced civil engineer. There are only those who are relatively less ignorant.

One company, however, an infant builder of database-management systems, had such software for minicomputers and was promising a PC version. After weeks of meetings, after an endless parade of consultants, after trips to Washington, D.C., to attend seminars, Mark decided to go with the new product. One of these meetings illustrates something unique to software, especially new software: no experts exist in the sense that we might speak of an expert machinist, a master electrician, or an experienced civil engineer. There are only those who are relatively less ignorant. On an early spring evening, we met in a conference room with a long, polished wood table surrounded by fancy swivel chairs covered in gorgeous, deep purple fabric. The room's walls turned crimson from the setting sun. As the evening wore on, we could look across the street to another tower, its offices filled with miniature Bartlebys, bent over desks, staring into monitors, leafing through file cabinets. At the table with representatives from our company were several consultants from the database firm and an independent consultant Mark had hired to make sure we were getting the straight scoop.

Here we were: a management-consulting team with the best, though still less than perfect, grasp of what the proposed system was supposed to do, but almost no grasp of the tools being chosen; consultants who knew the tools quite well, but nothing about the software application itself, who were fully aware that their software was still being developed even as we spoke; and an independent consultant who did not understand either the software or its application. It was a perfect example of interdependent parasitism.

My company's sin went beyond working with complex, poorly understood tools. Neither the tools nor our system existed. The database manufacturer had a delivery date and no product. Their consultants were selling us a nonexistent system. To make their deadline, I am confident they hired more programmers and experimented with unproven software from still other companies with delivery dates but no products. And what of *those* companies? You get the idea.

No one in our group had any experience with this software once we adopted it. Large systems are fabulously complex. It takes years to know their idiosyncrasies. Since the introduction of the microcomputer, however, nobody has had years to develop this expertise. Because software does not wear out, vendors must consistently add new features in order to recoup development costs. That the word processor you use today bears almost no resemblance to the one you used ten years ago has less to do with technological advances than with economic realities. Our company had recently acquired a smaller I company in the South. This company owned a mini computer for which a version of the database software had already been released. Mark decided that until the PC database was ready for release, we could develop our system on this machine, using 1,200-baud modems, a modem about one-fiftieth as fast as the one your cable provider tells you is too slow for the Web, and a whole lot less reliable.

Let me put this all together. We had a new team of programmers who did not understand the application, using ersatz software that they also did not understand, which was running on a kind of machine no one had ever used before, using a remote connection that was slow and unstable.

Weeks before, I had begun arguing that we could never meet the deadline and that none of us had the foggiest idea of how to go about building a system with the tools we had. This was bad form. I had been working in large corporations long enough to know that when the boss asks if something can be done, the only possible response is "I'm your boy." Business is not a Quaker meeting. Mark didn't get to be my boss by achieving consensus. I knew that arguing was a mistake, but somehow the more I argued, the more I became gripped by a self-righteous fervor that, while unattractive in anyone (who likes a do-gooder?), is suicide in a corporate setting. Can-do-ism is the core belief. My job was to figure out how to extend the deadline, simplify the requirements, or both—not second-guess Mark. One afternoon I was asked if I might like to step down as chief architect and take over the documentation group. This was not a promotion.

Sitting in my new cubicle with a Raskolnikovian cloud over my head, I began to look more closely at the database-management system's documentation. Working with yet another consultant, I filled a paper database with hypothetical data. What I discovered caused me to win the argument but lose the war. I learned that given the size of the software itself and the amount of data the average client would store, along with the overhead that comes with a sophisticated database, a running system would fill a microcomputer hard disk, then limited to 30 megabytes, several times over. If, by some stroke of luck, some effort of will, some happy set of coincidences that I had yet to experience personally, we were able to build the system, the client would run up against hardware constraints as soon as he tried to use it. After weeks of argument, my prestige was slipping fast. I had already been reduced to writing manuals for a system I had designed. I was the sinking ship that every clearheaded corporate sailor had already abandoned. My triumphant revelation that we could not build a workable system, even if we had the skill to do so, was greeted with (what else?) complete silence.

Late in 1986 James Fallows wrote an article analyzing the *Challenger* explosion for the *New York Review of Books*. Instead of concentrating on the well-known O-ring problem, he situated the failure of the *Challenger* in the context of military procurement, specifically in the military's inordinate fondness for complex systems. This fondness leads to stunning cost overruns, unanticipated complexity, and regular failures. It leads to Osprey aircraft that fall from the sky, to anti-missile missiles for which decoys are easy to construct, to FA-22 fighters that are fabulously over budget. The litany goes on. What these failures have in common with the *Challenger* is, Fallows argues, "military procurement disease," namely, "over-ambitious schedules, problems born of too-complex design, shortages of spare parts, a 'can-do' attitude that stifles embarrassing truths ('No problem, Mr. President, we can lick those Viet Cong'), and total collapse when one component unexpectedly fails." Explanations for this phenomenon include competition among the services; a monopoly hold by defense contractors who are building, say, aircraft or submarines; lavish defense budgets that isolate military purchases from normal market mechanisms; the nature of capital-intensive, laptop warfare where hypothetical justifications need not—usually cannot—be verified in practice; and a little-boy fascination with things that fly and explode. Much of this describes the software industry too.

Fallows breaks down military procurement into five stages:

*The Vegematic Promise,* wherein we are offered hybrid aircraft, part helicopter, part airplane, or software that has more features than could be learned in a lifetime of diligent study. Think Microsoft Office here.

*The Rosy Prospect,* wherein we are assured that all is going well. I call this the 90 percent syndrome. I don't think I have ever supervised a project, either as a software manager overseeing professionals or as a professor overseeing students, that was not 90 percent complete whenever I asked.

*The Big Technical Leap,* wherein we learn that our system will take us to regions not yet visited, and we will build it using tools not yet developed. So the shuttle's solid-fuel boosters were more powerful than any previously developed boosters, and bringing it all back home, my system was to use a database we had never used before, running on a computer for which a version of that software did not yet exist.

*The Unpleasant Surprise,* wherein we learn something unforeseen and, if we are unlucky, calamitous. Thus, the shuttle's heat-resistant dies, all 31,000 of them, had to be installed at the unexpected rate of 2.8 days per tile, and my system gobbled so much disk space that there was scarcely any room for data.

*The House of Cards,* wherein an unpleasant surprise, or two, or three, causes the entire system to collapse. The Germans flanked the Maginot Line, and in my case, once we learned that our reliance on a promised database package outstripped operating-system limits, the choices were: one, wait for advances in operating systems; two, admit a mistake, beg for forgiveness, and resolve to be more prudent in the future; or, three, push on until management pulls the plug.

In our case, the first choice was out of the question. We were up against a deadline. No one knew when, or if, the 30 MB disk limit would be broken. The second choice was just as bad. The peaceable kingdom will be upon us, the lamb will lie down with the lion, long before you'll find a hard-driving manager admitting an error. These guys get paid for their testosterone, and for men sufficiently endowed, in the famous words of former NASA flight director Gene Kranz, "failure is not an option." We were left with the third alternative, which is what happened. Our project was canceled. Inside the fun house of corporate decision making, Mark was promoted—sent off to manage a growing branch in the South. The programmers left or were reassigned. The consultant who gave me the figures for my calculations was fired for reasons that I never understood. I took advantage of my new job as documentation chief and wrote an application to graduate school in computer science. I spent the next few years, while a student, as a well-paid consultant to our firm.

J ust what is it about software, even the most conventional, the most mind-numbing software, that makes it similar to the classiest technology on the planet? In his book *Trapped in the Net,* the Berkeley physicist turned sociologist, Gene Rochlin, has this to say about computer technology:

> Only in a few specialized markets are new developments in hardware and software responsive primarily to user demand based on mastery and the full use of available technical capacity and capability. In most markets, the rate of change of both hardware and software is dynamically uncoupled from either human or organizational learning logistics and processes, to the point where users not only fail to master their most recent new capabilities, but are likely to not even bother to try, knowing that by the time they are through the steep part of their learning curve, most of what they have learned will be obsolete.

To give a homey example, I spent the last quarter hour fiddling with the margins on the draft copy of this article. Microsoft Word has all manner of arcane symbols—Exacto knives, magnifying glasses, thumbtacks, globes—plus an annoying little paper clip homunculus that pops up, seemingly at random, to offer help that I always decline. I don't know what any of this stuff does. Since one of the best-selling commercial introductions to the Microsoft Office suite now runs to nearly a thousand pages, roughly the size of Shakespeare's collected works, I won't find out either. To the untrained eye, that is to say, to mine, the bulk of what constitutes Microsoft Word appears to be useful primarily to brochure designers and graphic artists. This unused cornucopia is not peculiar to Microsoft, nor even to microcomputer software. Programmers were cranking out obscure and poorly documented features long before computers became a consumer product.

---

**Though the medium on which it is stored might decay, the software itself, because it exists in the same ethereal way as a novel, scored music, or a mathematical theorem, lasts as long as the ability to decode it.**

---

But why? Remember the nature of software, how it does not wear out. Adding features to a new release is similar, but not identical, to changes in fashion or automobile styling. In those industries, a change in look gives natural, and planned, obsolescence a nudge. Even the best-built car or the sturdiest pair of jeans will eventually show signs of wear. Changes in fashion just speed this process along. Not so with software. Though the medium on which it is stored might decay, the software itself, because it exists in the same ethereal way as a novel, scored music, or a mathematical theorem, lasts as long as the ability to decode it. That is why Microsoft Word and the operating systems that support it, such as Microsoft Windows, get more complex with each new release.

But this is only part of the story. While software engineers at Oracle or Microsoft are staying up late concocting features that no one will ever use, hardware engineers at Intel are inventing ever faster, ever cheaper processors to run them. If Microsoft did not take advantage of this additional capacity, someone else would. Hardware and software are locked in an intricate and pathological dance. Hardware takes a step. Software follows. Hardware takes another step. Software follows, and so on. The result is the Vegematic Promise. Do you want to write a letter to your bank? Microsoft Word will work fine. Do you need to save your work in any one of fifteen different digital formats? Microsoft Word will do the job. Do you want to design a Web page, lay out a brochure, import clip art, or include the digitally rendered picture of your dog? The designers at Microsoft have anticipated your needs. They were able to do this because the designers at Intel anticipated theirs. What no one anticipated was the unmanageable complexity of the final product from the user's perspective and the stunning, internal complexity of the product that Microsoft brings to market. In another time, this kind of complexity would have been reserved for enterprises of true consequence, say the Manhattan Project or the *Apollo* missions. Now the complexity that launched a thousand ships, placed men on the moon, controlled nuclear fission and fusion, the complexity that demanded of its designers years of training and still failed routinely, sits on my desk. Only this time, developers with minimal, often informal, training, using tools that change before they master them, labor for my daughter, who uses the fruits of their genius to chat with her friends about hair, makeup, and boys.

As I say, accelerating complexity is not just a software feature. Gordon Moore, one of Intel's founders, famously observed, in 1965, that the number of transistors etched on an integrated circuit board doubled every year or so. In the hyperbolic world of computing, this observation, altered slightly for the age of microprocessors, has come to be called Moore's Law: the computing power of microprocessors tends to double every couple of years. Though engineers expect to reach physical limits sometime in the first quarter of this century, Moore has been on target for the past couple dozen years. As a related, if less glamorous example, consider the remote control that accompanies electronic gadgetry these days. To be at the helm of your VCR, TV, DVD player, stereo (never mind lights, fans, air-conditioning, and fireplace), is to be a kind of Captain Kirk of home and hearth. The tendency, the Vegematic Promise, is to integrate separate remote controls into a single device. A living room equipped with one of these marvels is part domicile, part mission control. I recently read about one fellow who, dazzled by the complexity of integrated remotes, fastened his many devices to a chunk of four-by-four with black electrical tape. I have ceded operation of my relatively low-tech equipment to my teenage daughter, the only person in my house with the time or inclination to decipher its runic symbols.

But software is different in one significant way. Hardware, by and large, works. When hardware fails, as early versions of the Pentium chip did, it is national news. It took a computer scientist in Georgia doing some fairly obscure mathematical calculations to uncover the flaw. If only software errors were so well hidden. Engineers, even electrical engineers, use well-understood, often off-the-shelf, materials with well-defined limits. To offer a simple example, a few years ago I taught a course in digital logic. This course, standard fare for all computer science and computer engineering majors, teaches students how to solve logic problems with chips. A common lab problem is to build a seven-segment display, a digital display of numbers, like what you might find on an alarm clock. Students construct it using a circuit board and chips that we order by the hundreds. These chips are described in a catalogue that lists the number and type of logical operations encoded, along with the corresponding pins for each. If you teach software design, as I do, this trespass into the world of the engineer is instructive. Software almost always gets built from scratch. Though basic sorting and string manipulation routines exist, these must be woven together in novel ways to produce new software. Each programmer becomes a craftsman with a store of tricks up his sleeve. The more experienced the programmer, the more tricks.

To be fair, large software-development operations maintain libraries of standard routines that developers may dip into when the need arises. And for the past ten years or so, new object-oriented design and development techniques have conceived of ways to modularize and standardize components. Unfortunately, companies have not figured out how to make money by selling components, probably for the same reason that the music industry is under siege from Napster's descendants. If your product is only a digital encoding, it can be copied endlessly at almost no cost. Worse, the object-oriented programming paradigm seems often to be more complex than a conventional approach. Though boosters claim that programmers using object-oriented techniques are more productive and that their products are easier to maintain, this has yet to be demonstrated.

Software is peculiar in another way. Though hardware can be complex in the extreme, software obeys no physical limits. It can be as feature-rich as its designers wish. If the computer's memory is too small, relatively obscure features can be stored on disk and called into action only when needed. If the computer's processor is too slow, just wait a couple of years. Designers want your software to be very feature-rich indeed, because they want to sell the next release, because the limits of what can be done with a computer are not yet known, and, most of all, because those who design computer systems, like the rich in the world of F. Scott Fitzgerald, are different from you and me. Designers love the machine with a passion not constrained by normal market mechanisms or even, in some instances, by managerial control.

On the demand side, most purchases are made by institutions, businesses, universities, and the government, where there is an obsessive fear of being left behind, while the benefits, just as in the military, are difficult to measure. The claims and their outcomes are too fuzzy to be reconciled. Since individual managers are rarely held accountable for decisions to buy yet more computing equipment, it should not surprise you that wildly complex technology is being underused. Thus: computer labs that no one knows what to do with, so-called smart classrooms that are obsolete before anyone figures out how to use them, and offices with equipment so complicated that every secretary doubles as a systems administrator. Even if schools and businesses buy first and ask questions later, *you* don't have to put up with this. You could tell Microsoft to keep its next Windows upgrade, your machine is working very nicely right now, thank you. But your impertinence will cost you. Before long, your computer will be an island where the natives speak a language cut off from the great linguistic communities. In a word, you will be isolated. You won't be able to buy new software, edit a report you wrote at work on your home computer, or send pictures of the kids to Grandma over the Internet. Further, a decision to upgrade later will be harder, perhaps impossible, without losing everything your trusted but obsolete computer has stored. This is what Rochlin means when he writes that hardware and software are "dynamically uncoupled from either human or organizational learning." To which I would add "human organizational need."

What if the massively complex new software were as reliable as hardware usually is? We still wouldn't know how to use it, but at least our screens wouldn't lock up and our projects wouldn't be canceled midstream. This reliability isn't going to happen, though, for at least three reasons. First, programmers love complexity, love handcrafted systems, with an ardor that most of us save for our spouses. You have heard about the heroic hours worked by employees of the remaining Internet start-ups. This is true, but true only partly so that young men can be millionaires by thirty. There is something utterly beguiling about programming a computer. You lose track of time, of space even. You begin eating pizzas and forgetting to bathe. A phone call is an unwelcome intrusion. Second, nobody can really oversee a programmer's work, short of reading code line by line. It is simply too complex for anyone but its creator to understand, and even for him it will be lost in the mist after a couple of weeks. The 90 percent syndrome is a natural consequence. Programmers, a plucky lot, always think that they are further along than they are.

It is difficult to foresee an obstacle on a road you have never traveled. Despite all efforts to the contrary, code is handcrafted. Third—and this gets to the heart of the matter—system specifications have the half-life of an adolescent friendship. Someone—the project manager, the team leader, a programmer, or, if the system is built on contract, the client—always has a new idea. It is as if a third of the way through building a bridge, the highway department decided it should have an additional traffic lane and be moved a half mile downstream.

Notice that not one of the reasons I have mentioned for failed software projects is technical. Researchers trying to develop a discipline of software engineering are fond of saying that there is no silver bullet: no single technical fix, no single software-development tool, no single, yet-to-be-imagined programming technique that will result in error-free, maintainable software. The reason for this is really quite simple. The problem with software is not technical. Remember my project. It fell into chaos because of foolish business decisions. Had Mark resisted the temptation to use the latest software-development products, a temptation he succumbed to not because they would produce a better system, but because they would seem flashier to prospective clients, we might have gone to market with only the usual array of problems.

Interestingly, the geek's geek, Bruce Schneier, in his recent book, *Secrets and Lies*, has come to similar conclusions about computer security: the largest problems are not technical. A computer security expert, Schneier has recanted his faith in the impermeability of crypto-graphic algorithms. Sophisticated cryptography is as resistant as ever to massive frontal attacks. The problem is that these algorithms are embedded in computer systems that are administered by real human beings with all their charms and foibles. People use dictionary entries or a child's name as passwords. They attach modems to their office computers, giving hackers easy access to a system that might otherwise be more thoroughly protected. They run versions of Linux with all network routines enabled, or they surreptitiously set up Web servers in their dormitory rooms. Cryptographic algorithms are no more secure than their contexts.

---

**Until computing is organized like engineering, law, and medicine through a combination of self-regulating professional bodies, government-imposed standards, and the threat of litigation, inviting a computer into your house or office is to invite complexity masquerading as convenience.**

Though the long march is far from over, we know a lot more about managing the complexity of software systems than we did twenty years ago. We have better programming languages and techniques, better design principles, clever software to keep track of changes, richly endowed procedures for moving from conception to system design to coding to testing to release. But systems still fail and projects are still canceled with the same regularity as in the bad old days before object-oriented techniques, before software engineering becomes an academic discipline. These techniques are administered by the same humans who undermine computer security. They include marketing staff who decree systems into existence; companies that stuff yet more features into already overstuffed software; designers and clients who change specifications as systems are being built; programmers who are more artist than engineer; and, of course, software itself that can be neither seen, nor touched, nor measured in any significant way.

There is no silver bullet. But just as the *Challenger* disaster might have been prevented with minimal common sense, so also with software failure. Keep it simple. Avoid exotic and new programming techniques. Know that an army of workers is no substitute for clear design and ample time. Don't let the fox, now disguised as a young man with a head full of acronyms, guard the chicken coop. Make only modest promises. Good advice, certainly, but no one is likely to listen anytime soon. Until computing is organized like engineering, law, and medicine through a combination of self-regulating professional bodies, government-imposed standards, and, yes, the threat of litigation, inviting a computer into your house or office is to invite complexity masquerading as convenience. Given the nature of computing, even these remedies may fall short of the mark.

But don't despair. If software engineering practice is out of reach, you still have options. For starters, you could just say no. You could decide that the ease of buying plane tickets online is not worth the hours you while away trying to get your printer to print or your modem to dial. Understand that saying no requires an ascetic nature: abstinence is not terribly attractive to most of us. On the other hand, you could sign up for broadband with the full knowledge that your computer, a jealous lover, will demand many, many Saturday afternoons. Most people are shocked when they learn that their computer requires more care than, say, their refrigerator. Yet I can tell you that its charms are immeasurably richer. First among them is the dream state. It's almost irresistible.

---

**PAUL DE PALMA** is associate professor of mathematics and computer science at Gonzaga University. His essay "http://www.when_is_enough_enough?.com" appeared in the *Winter 1999* issue.

---

From *American Scholar*, Vol. 74, No. 1, Winter 2005, pp. 69–83. Copyright © 2005 by Paul De Palma. Reprinted by permission of American Scholar.

# UNIT 3
# Work and the Workplace

## Unit Selections

9. **National ID,** Ryan Singel
10. **Dilberts of the World, Unite!,** David Sirota
11. **Computer Software Engineers,** *Occupational Outlook Handbook*
12. **How Deep Can You Probe?,** Rita Zeidner
13. **Privacy, Legislation, and Surveillance Software,** G. Daryl Nord, Tipton F. McCubbins, and Jeretta Horn Nord
14. **The Computer Evolution,** Rob Valletta and Geoffrey MacDonald

## Key Points to Consider

- Some European democracies require their citizens to carry government-issued identification. This has been problematic in the United States? Why do you think this is so?

- Were you surprised to learn that there is no constitutional right to privacy at work?

- Find out how work-place privacy issues are handled in other Western democracies.

- How do you feel about prospective employers searching the Internet for information about you?

- David Sirota presents the resistance of tech workers to union organization as misguided. What are two of the reasons for their resistance? Do you think that anti-union sentiment in the tech sector is misguided?

## Student Web Site
www.mhcls.com

## Internet References

**American Telecommuting Association**
*http://www.knowledgetree.com/ata-adv.html*

**Computers in the Workplace**
*http://www.msci.memphis.edu/~ryburnp/cl/cis/workpl.html*

**InfoWeb: Techno-rage**
*http://www.cciw.com/content/technorage.html*

**STEP ON IT! Pedals: Repetitive Strain Injury**
*http://www.bilbo.com/rsi2.html*

**What About Computers in the Workplace**
*http://law.freeadvice.com/intellectual_property/computer_law/computers_workplace.htm*

**W**ork is at the center of our lives. The kind of work we do plays a part in our standard of living, our social status, and our sense of worth. This was not always the case. Read some of the great Victorian novels, and you will find a society where paid employment, at least among the upper classes, does not exist. Even those men from the nineteenth century and before, whose discoveries and writings we study and admire, approached their work as an avocation. It is hard to imagine William Wordsworth, kissing his wife goodbye each morning, and heading off to the English Department where he will direct a seminar in creative writing before he gets to work on a sticky line in Ode Composed at Tintern Abbey. Or, think of Charles Darwin, donning a lab coat, and supervising an army of graduate students before he touches up his latest National Science Foundation proposal. In the nineteenth century, there were a handful of professionals—doctor, lawyer, professor, clergyman, military officer; a larger handful of craftsmen—joiner, miller, cooper, blacksmith, and an army of agricultural workers and an increasing number of displaced peasants toiling in factories, what William Blake called England's "dark Satanic mills."

The U.S. Census records tell us that there were only 323 different occupations in 1850, the butcher, the baker, and the candlestick maker that all children read about. The butcher is still with us, as well as the baker, but both of them work for national supermarket chains, using digitally-controlled tools and manage their 401k's on-line. The candlestick maker has morphed into a refinery worker, watching digital displays in petrochemical plants that light up the Louisiana sky. The Canadian National Occupational Classification lists more than 25,000 occupational titles. It was once feared that first, machines in the early twentieth century, and then computers in the later, would render work obsolete, transforming us into country gentlemen, like Charles Darwin in the utopian view or nomadic mobs of starving proletarians in the distopian.

It appears instead that fabulously productive farms and factories—as well as a third world willing to make our shoes, clothing, and electronics for pennies an hour—have opened up opportunities that did not exist in Darwin's time. We are now sales clerks, health care workers, state license examiners, light truck drivers, equal opportunity compliance officers, and, yes, also software engineers, database analysts, web-site designers, and entrepreneurs.

Many of the lowest-paid jobs in the new economy are held by the foreign-born, some illegally, prompting the current immigration debate. That debate, in turn, has prompted some to propose a mechanism to determine who may and may not work in the United States. One proposal is a tamper-proof Social Security card, complete with biometric data. See Ryan Singel's article, "National ID," for the details.

© Tetra Images/Getty Images

We have grown used to hearing stories in the news about the blush coming off the rose of software development. The computer industry is happy to reduce labor costs by outsourcing skilled work and importing skilled workers. David Sirota's piece, "Dilberts of the World, Unite!" is in that genre, but with a new twist. Instead of just grumbling about declining conditions in the computer industry, some engineers in Washington State have begun to organize.

As a corrective to gloomy talk about the tech sector, take a look at the piece from the Bureau of Labor Statistics, "Computer Software Engineers." There you will find that, news of outsourcing notwithstanding, "software engineers are projected to be one of the faster-growing occupations from 2004 to 2014."

"The Computer Evolution" confirms what every working American has noticed, namely, that computers have spread throughout the workplace. It also confirms what many observers have long suspected: "the ability to use a computer is not a 'sufficient' condition for earning high wages, but it is increasingly a 'necessary' condition."

Another topic, much in the news, is the predictable response to employers who have learned that their applicants maintain MySpace pages. They scan them looking for information—an interest in violent films, pictures from a party that got out of hand—that didn't come up when interviewees are on their best behavior. Rita Zeidner's piece from *HR Magazine,* ought to please job applicants with wild oats still to sow: "Many states limit the extent to which employers can consider off duty conduct in making a hiring decision. . . ."

We end this section with a clear advice for both employees and employers. For employees, don't expect constitutional protections against unreasonable search and seizure to prevent your boss from reading your e-mail. These protections usually apply only to government action. See G. Daryl Nord and his colleagues for a persuasive account ("Privacy, Legislation, and Surveillance Software").

# National ID
## *Biometrics Pinned to Social Security Cards*

RYAN SINGEL

The Social Security card faces its first major upgrade in 70 years under two immigration-reform proposals slated for debate this week that would add biometric information to the card and finally complete its slow metamorphosis into a national ID.

The leading immigration proposal with traction in Congress would force employers to accept only a very limited range of approved documents as proof of work eligibility, including a driver's license that meets new federal Real ID standards, a high-tech temporary work visa or a U.S. passport with an RFID chip. A fourth option is the notional tamper-proof biometric Social Security card, which would replace the text-only design that's been issued to Americans almost without change for more than 70 years.

A second proposal under consideration would add high-tech features to the Social Security card allowing employers to scan it with specially equipped laptop computers. Under that proposal, called the "Bonner Plan," the revamped Social Security card would be the only legal form of identification for employment purposes.

Neither bill specifies what the biometric would be, but it could range from a simple digital photo to a fingerprint or even an iris scan. The proposals would seem to require major changes to how Social Security cards are issued: Currently, new and replacement cards are sent in the mail. And parents typically apply for their children before they're old enough to give a decent fingerprint.

There are also logistical problems to overcome before forcing all of the nation's employers to verify a biometric card—given the nation has millions of employers, many of whom may not have computer equipment at all.

"This is an exact example of why IDs are so ludicrous as a form of security," American Civil Liberties Union legislative counsel Tim Sparapani said. "Do we really think the migrant workers are going to show up at the pickle farm and the farmer is going to demand ID and have a laptop in the field to check their ID?"

That's one of the problems that Rep. Zoe Lofgren (D-California), who heads a key House immigration subcommittee, says she's thinking about.

"There seems to be a fairly strong sentiment that there needs to be an easy way to reliably enforce whatever rules we adopt and the biometric is something being discussed in all the House bills," Lofgren told Wired News. "Obviously every small business isn't going to have a biometric card reader, but perhaps the post office might have a reader since every community in America has a post office."

The proposed biometric feature would apply to newly issued or replaced Social Security cards—you won't be asked to hand in your old one. Nevertheless, the plan doesn't sit well with privacy and civil liberties advocates like Sparapani. And immigrant-rights groups foresee rampant database errors, and an inevitable mission drift, with biometric cards—whether the Social Security card or one of the other cards pushed in the proposals—being used for purposes other than employment.

Currently, U.S. employers can accept a range of documents, including expired U.S. passports, tribal documents, refugee documents, birth certificates, driver's licenses and even school report cards, to establish an employee's eligibility for work.

Michele Waslin, the policy research director at the National Council of La Raza, a Latino civil rights group, supports immigration reform but emphasizes that employment-eligibility verification must be effective and have safeguards.

"This is one provision that would impact every single person that gets a job in the United States," Waslin said. "Given the inaccuracy of government databases, it is likely that some Americans will show documents and the answer will come back as a 'non-confirmation' and (they) could be denied employment based on a government mistake."

Waslin also fears that the existence of a document that proves immigration status will lead to widespread document checks, even from shop clerks.

"You can imagine arriving at a polling place and some people are being asked for a Real ID, while people who look 'American' aren't asked for a Real ID," Waslin said.

The controversy is likely to heat up this week. Senate Majority Leader Harry Reid is set to schedule two weeks of immigration-reform debate Tuesday, setting a deadline for a bipartisan panel of lawmakers to craft legislation that combines tighter border enforcement, avenues for current undocumented workers to earn legal status, and stringent employee-verification requirements for employers.

If they succeed, the bill will probably have roughly the same contours as the leading House bill, known as the *Strive Act*, co-authored by Reps. John Flake (R-Arizona) and Luis Gutierrez (D-Illinois).

The Strive Act would require employers to verify a new employee's credentials—by telephone or the internet—against databases maintained by the Social Security Administration and the Department of Homeland Security. If the answer comes back as a "non-confirmation," the new hire would have the opportunity to update any incorrect records.

The Strive Act's verification system is based on the Basic Pilot Program, a currently voluntary program that lets busi-nesses verify new employees' work eligibility over the web. But that program relies on databases prone to inaccuracy, according to Tyler Moran, the employment policy director at the National Immigration Law Center.

"The Basic Pilot program has given more power to employers to oppress workers," Moran said. "It's the worker's burden to prove they are work-authorized, and employers are taking adverse action when there is a problem, such as demoting or fir-ing workers before they have a chance to correct the database."

A recent report by the Social Security Administration's inspector general backs up Moran's criticism with findings that 17.8 million records in the government's employment databases contained inaccuracies that could initially and erroneously flag individuals as ineligible for employment.

# Dilberts of the World, Unite!

## Can a populist uprising flourish in a sector traditionally hostile to collective action?

DAVID SIROTA

In the 1990s, dot-com celebrations were happening everywhere. From Silicon Valley to Boston, from Austin to Seattle, the geeky Lambda Lambda Lambda frat brothers from *Revenge of the Nerds* were suddenly big men on campus, starting computer companies, swimming in cash—partying, as Prince might say, like it was 1999 (it actually *was* 1999). As the kegger raged upstairs, though, a group of Microsoft employees at its headquarters in Redmond, Washington, called the Washington Alliance of Technology Workers—WashTech for short—was shrieking from the basement about an impending economic massacre. Sadly, very few were listening. Now the party's over—and a white-collar uprising is on.

If you haven't heard much about this, don't blame yourself. We live in a media environment that trumpets the price of the Apple iPhone as big financial news and adultery as major political news. But the fight WashTech is contributing to is hugely important for two reasons—one is obvious, but the other is rarely discussed.

First, the obvious: the white-collar sector is growing fast. Between 1977 and 2004 the number of professional and high-skilled US workers more than doubled. The government predicts that roughly one-third of all employment growth between now and 2012 will be in the white-collar sector. In contemporary America, though, sheer size is no longer the primary determinant of change. The better gauge is demographics, which brings us to the second reason this white-collar uprising is so significant: if politics and culture still react to the mass public at all, they react almost exclusively to the upper middle professional class. That's pretty awful, but it's absolutely true. Business misbehavior, for example, was rarely a Congressional focus when CEOs were cutting blue-collar wages. But when Enron's collapse hit the stock market and undermined the retirement savings of the upper middle class, lawmakers raced to pass corporate accountability legislation. Housing affordability and predatory lending received little attention in Washington when only the working poor couldn't meet their mortgage payments. But now that defaults are convulsing Wall Street, the problem is deemed a crisis. So this white-collar uprising is not just about professional office workers and their fight. It is also about whether an uprising can flourish in the very demographic the Establishment most responds to—a demographic that also happens to be skeptical of collective action.

How did WashTech begin, and what is its role in the larger uprising roiling America? Not too long ago, on a typically gray Seattle winter day, the group's president, Marcus Courtney, sat down with me at a Starbucks in the University District to tell the story. In 1993 Courtney was one of many starry-eyed college grads who migrated to Seattle just as the tech boom was moving to warp speed. He found one of those Great Jobs at Microsoft in technical support—only his job turned out to be not so great. He was one of roughly 6,000 employees known as "permatemps," a classification that allows a company to pay a temp-agency middleman for full-time, indefinite labor. The designation, which covers roughly a quarter of Microsoft workers in the Seattle area, means employers don't have to pay regular benefits.

"Around the middle of 1997," Courtney tells me, "me and my office mate were talking about how we weren't getting real raises or cost-of-living increases, and I was like, this permatemp stuff is kinda bullshit. The contract agencies are ripping us off. I was like, God, I wonder if there's an organization to help us." So he started phoning state agencies and labor councils. "Everyone was totally fucking clueless," he says. "All anyone knew about the new economy was that people make millions. No one had any idea that here in Seattle a huge percentage of the employment is contracted out." So Courtney and two others began building an e-mail list of permatemps and other high-tech workers who were interested in getting more politically active.

In December 1997 their efforts were bolstered when the *Seattle Times* published a front-page story about how Microsoft used its connections in state government to secure a regulatory change exempting high-tech companies from having to pay temps time-and-a-half for overtime. It was a screwing of bipartisan proportions: the rule change was approved by Democratic Governor Gary Locke, and it was designed to bring the state's labor regulations into conformity with federal law, which was changed by the then-Republican Congress. The *Times* also noted that the local labor movement had hung the permatemps out to dry: two unions supported the rule change after it was revised to make sure their own members were protected.

For the uprising, the episode was like a match being dropped into a pool of gasoline. Sold out by both political parties and ignored by organized labor, "we decided to get serious," Courtney tells me. From the flames of outrage, WashTech was born. The organization's mission is straightforward: to get high-tech workers to vote to form unions so they can collectively bargain for improved wages, benefits and job security.

Microsoft countered the organizing drive by claiming that the status of the workers as permatemps meant the company had no statutory obligation to listen to the union, even though roughly two-thirds of all permatemps had been working full-time for more than a year. "Issues of collective bargaining are issues between employees and their employer," said a company spokesman at the time. "In this case, the employers are the staffing companies." The *Times* reported that when the workers and WashTech began the byzantine process of trying to bargain with four separate temp agencies, the agencies claimed that because the workers were temps, they were not "an appropriate bargaining unit under the federal labor laws." Courtney and his colleagues were caught in no man's land—call it Dilbert's Purgatory. "Permatemps were getting the worst of all worlds," Courtney says, taking a sip of coffee.

When it came to wages, they were considered high-level computer professionals, thus not entitled to overtime pay, thanks to the state ruling and change in federal law. When it came to benefits, they were treated as temps unworthy of healthcare coverage and stock options. And when it came to basic union rights, they were treated as "a second class of subordinate workers," as the former chair of the National Labor Relations Board said at the time. They had none of the organizing privileges that other company employees enjoyed.

After two failed organizing attempts, one at Microsoft and one at Amazon.com, Courtney and his allies enlisted the aid of the Communications Workers of America to build WashTech's "at large" membership—workers who are not covered by any union contract but who are sympathetic to the cause and pay $11 a month in dues. Courtney remained visible in the local media as an increasingly effective advocate for tech workers.

W ashTech finally got a break in 2005. That year 900 call-center workers at Cingular in suburban Seattle voted to form a union and affiliate with WashTech. As of mid-2007 WashTech had roughly 1,500 dues-paying members—1,100 at Cingular (now AT&T) and 400 at large. It also had an e-mail list of 17,000 subscribers. Whether WashTech's work can expand the white-collar uprising beyond that, however, is very much an open question.

Certainly the conditions seem ripe. Between 2000 and 2004, 221,000 US tech jobs were eliminated as offshore outsourcing accelerated. In 2005 the Institute of Electrical and Electronics Engineers reported the first drop in median income for tech workers in the thirty-one years it had been producing annual wage and salary analyses. And WashTech's survey of IT workers found that the majority said their healthcare premiums had increased and their wages had either remained flat or dropped. As these trends have intensified, WashTech's membership has grown. Nonetheless, there are reasons that only 2 to 5.5 percent of high-tech workers are unionized—reasons that have little to do with concrete economic factors.

"Many people in these industries say, 'I hate unions' just on principle," Courtney tells me as we walk out of Starbucks. "But these same people will then go to the Mini-Microsoft website and voice their complaints because they know the company is reading the site." This constituency is a key component of today's white-collar uprising. They are swing voters, but they aren't the socially liberal, economically conservative suburbanites pundits always say are the key swing demographic in presidential elections. They are folks whose libertarianism has led them to vote Republican and dislike unions but whose economic self-interest is now pulling them in a populist direction.

A ccording to a national poll commissioned by WashTech in late 2003, 73 percent of IT workers describe themselves as either Independents (32 percent) or Republicans (41 percent)—a demographic that is typically hostile to the ideology of the labor movement and the concept of collective action. However, an overwhelming majority of this same group told pollsters they support strongly progressive legislation to expand unemployment benefits and to prohibit government contracts from going to companies that outsource jobs. And despite decades of antiunion propaganda from industry and its allied consultants, think tanks and politicians, a majority of Americans still tell pollsters that, if given the chance, they would vote to join a union.

This sentiment persists even in the white-collar world. Groups like WashTech, however, haven't been able to expand persistent positive feelings about unions into a more mature movement because they face the Fantastic Four: a quartet of pernicious and dishonest story lines that play to tech workers' unique self-image and that discourage full participation in the uprising.

The first and most powerful of these myths is the Marlboro Man Fable. Doug, a Microsoft employee and WashTech at-large member, who asks me to use a pseudonym to protect him from blacklisting, tells me that while tech workers certainly have complaints about wages and benefits, they do not see unions as being congruent with their deeply held beliefs in "rugged individualism"—the Marlboro Man spirit that says everyone is a lone cowboy who can tough it out on his or her own. "One of the successful things the high-tech industry has done is to have sold people on the idea that if you just struggle all by yourself, you can be Bill Gates, too," he says over lunch at Microsoft's cafeteria in Redmond. "That's kind of what we sell in our whole country as the self-made man. There's no such thing, really, but that's what lots of folks believe."

The gulf between the Marlboro Man Fable and reality is one of the most combustible ingredients in today's uprising. People's economic experiences—stagnant wages, rising healthcare costs, decreasing retirement benefits—indict the fable in a far deeper way than even the best uprising leader could. However, as Doug says, the awakening has been slow in a white-collar world that matured during the go-go 1990s. The Marlboro Man Fable poses the toughest challenge to WashTech because it drills directly into white-collar workers' psychology—specifically, their belief "that interests of employers and employees are the same," as sociologist Seymour Martin Lipset found in his groundbreaking research on the subject.

Antiunionism is being sustained not solely by the Marlboro Man Fable but also by the Legend of Job Security—the second of the Fantastic Four. Shrewd corporate PR and workers' career ambitions predispose white-collar employees to view the boss and the company as inherently benevolent. Many workers believe they don't need a union because they think such benevolence will protect them from the outsourcing buzz saw. WashTech's 2005 poll showed that about half of all tech workers do not believe outsourcing will affect their jobs—even though simultaneous polls of high-tech executives show that most are planning to radically accelerate outsourcing.

Whereas surmounting the Marlboro Man Fable requires changing deep psychologies and self-images, breaking through the Legend of Job Security is a much easier task, thanks to harsh realities. Princeton economist Alan Blinder reports that up to 42 million jobs could be outsourced in the coming years, especially impersonal services like software programming. Many high-tech workers are starting to get a handle on this. "A lot of full-timers who have been at Microsoft a long time are finally believing that sometime in the next few years, five years maximum, some whole division is going to show up one Monday morning and their card keys aren't going to work," one WashTech activist tells me. "Their work will have been sent to India." WashTech has deftly played its role as information conduit to expose outsourcing practices in provocative ways. For example, the group has leaked internal Microsoft documents revealing that company managers are encouraging those under them to hire foreign workers.

The frustrations of another WashTech member, a permatemp named Rennie, illustrate the third great myth of the Fantastic Four. Like most veteran permatemps, Rennie has been trying to switch to full-time work. "I've interviewed for jobs, and they always say they are going to hire me, but before they get an offer on the table, the job gets outsourced or an H-1B gets brought in," he says in disgust. H-1B is a bland, IRS-tax-form kind of term, but it is at the heart of the Great Labor Shortage Lie.

For the better part of two decades, tech companies have complained about a dearth of high-skilled US computer programmers and engineers. This narrative is dutifully echoed by the media. A 2007 *BusinessWeek* headline is typical: Where Are All the Workers? the magazine asked, stating that "companies worldwide are suddenly scrambling to manage a labor crunch."

---

## 'They say they can't find a qualified American, but what they really mean is they can't find a *cheap* American.'

—Microsoft temp worker

---

There's just one snag: there is no labor shortage. In 2007 a comprehensive Duke University study found "no indication of a shortage of engineers in the United States." As *BusinessWeek* admits in that same story about a supposed "global labor crunch," many "so-called shortages could quickly be solved if employers were to offer more money." But that's not happening. In fact, the magazine grudgingly acknowledged, "the strongest evidence that there's no general shortage today is that overall worker pay has barely outpaced inflation." So why is the lie still being spread? To drive down wages. To "fix" the alleged shortage, Congress in 1990 created the H-1B program, which allows employers like Microsoft to bring in temporary foreign workers for high-skill jobs. "They say they need H-1Bs because they can't find a qualified American, but what they really mean is they can't find a *cheap* American," Rennie tells me during a coffee break at his Microsoft office. His assertion is supported by the data. In 2005 the Center for Immigration Studies released a report on government statistics showing that H-1B employees are paid an average of $13,000 a year less than American workers in the same job in the same state.

Today Microsoft ranks third in the country among companies hiring H-1Bs, so Rennie works with H-1B workers all the time. His anger is not the quasinationalism of Lou Dobbs or the xenophobia of the Minutemen. The rage is not directed at H-1B workers but at people he feels are abusing the program—and chief among them, he says, is Bill Gates.

In early 2007, the richest man in America brought his boyish happy talk to the nation's capital, testifying before the Senate in an attempt to persuade lawmakers to eliminate the government's annual cap on the number of H-1B visas. Almost all the WashTech members I met brought up Gates's testimony, making sure I understood what an atrocity they think it was. Here they are, working as permatemps, and the founder of their company spits out the Great Labor Shortage Lie by telling Congress he can't find qualified full-time workers.

The union published a full-page ad in *Roll Call* to pressure Congress to oppose Gates's H-1B request. The ad was not partisan, which is smart for two reasons. First, rank-and-file tech workers have mixed partisan loyalties, and they are more likely to donate to something bipartisan. Second, the Washington problem on these issues is truly bipartisan. Republicans may be the party of Wall Street, but Democrats—thanks to oodles of tech-industry campaign contributions—have become the party of Silicon Valley. "The people in the Senate were all praising Gates, telling him, Oh, you're such a great guy," Rennie says, his hand balled up into a fist, tapping his knee. "I just couldn't believe some of the stuff that was being said."

In particular, Rennie cites the last of the Fantastic Four—the Great Education Myth. Parroted by just about everybody in business, politics and media, this fairy tale tells us that if everyone just gets a college degree, our problems with outsourcing, stagnant wages and pension cuts will magically vanish. In the white-collar world, this myth says all you have to do is go back to school and you'll be fine. But Census figures show that between 2000 and 2004, earnings of college grads dropped by more than 5 percent. The *Financial Times* reports that "earnings of average US workers with an undergraduate degree have not kept up with gains in productivity in recent decades," primarily because "a change in labor market institutions and norms [has] reduced the bargaining power of most US workers" (translation: the loss of unions has meant less worker leverage). Even *Fortune* concedes that "just maybe the jobs most threatened by outsourcing are no longer those of factory workers with a high school education . . . but those of college-educated desk workers [who] look more outsourceable by the day."

The potentially insurmountable obstacle for WashTech, though, is something it cannot fully control. It can gradually break down the Fantastic Four and update the labor movement's image for its union-averse constituency. But without the intangible of inspiration, it will be having a "fight with a windmill," as Saul Alinsky would say. Those who join the uprising do so because they are tired of a political and economic system that ignores them. But for those folks, like white-collar workers, who may be less political by nature, that feeling of disenfranchisement can serve as a suppressant. Their apolitical, nonconfrontational disposition means that they, more than most others, need an inspiration that proves the value of joining the uprising. And without that inspiration, whatever sympathies they may have are easily quashed by a sense of helplessness.

Rennie sums it up in distinctly Microsoft terms. "It's hard to change things when people turn on the television and see someone like Gates with all the Congressmen fawning all over him." They need to see something else. With the rise of populism in the 2008 election campaign, perhaps they soon will.

---

**DAVID SIROTA** is a bestselling author and nationally syndicated newspaper columnist. This article is adopted from his newest book, *The Uprising: An Unauthorized Tour of the Populist Revolt Scaring Wall Street and Washington* (Crown).

# Computer Software Engineers

## Significant Points

- Computer software engineers are projected to be one of the fastest growing occupations over the 2004–14 period.
- Very good opportunities are expected for college graduates with at least a bachelor's degree in computer engineering or computer science and with practical work experience.
- Computer software engineers must continually strive to acquire new skills in conjunction with the rapid changes that are occurring in computer technology.

## Nature of the Work

The explosive impact of computers and information technology on our everyday lives has generated a need to design and develop new computer software systems and to incorporate new technologies into a rapidly growing range of applications. The tasks performed by workers known as computer software engineers evolve quickly, reflecting new areas of specialization or changes in technology, as well as the preferences and practices of employers. Computer software engineers apply the principles and techniques of computer science, engineering, and mathematical analysis to the design, development, testing, and evaluation of the software and systems that enable computers to perform their many applications. (A separate statement on Computer hardware engineers appears elsewhere in the *Handbook.*)

Software engineers working in applications or systems development analyze users' needs and design, construct, test, and maintain computer applications software or systems. Software engineers can be involved in the design and development of many types of software, including software for operating systems and network distribution, and compilers, which convert programs for execution on a computer. In programming, or coding, software engineers instruct a computer, line by line, how to perform a function. They also solve technical problems that arise. Software engineers must possess strong programming skills, but are more concerned with developing algorithms and analyzing and solving programming problems than with actually writing code.

*Computer applications software engineers* analyze users' needs and design, construct, and maintain general computer applications software or specialized utility programs. These workers use different programming languages, depending on the purpose of the program. The programming languages most often used are C, C++, and Java, with Fortran and COBOL used less commonly. Some software engineers develop both packaged systems and systems software or create customized applications.

*Computer systems software engineers* coordinate the construction and maintenance of a company's computer systems and plan their future growth. Working with the company, they coordinate each department's computer needs—ordering, inventory, billing, and payroll recordkeeping, for example—and make suggestions about its technical direction. They also might set up the company's intranets—networks that link computers within the organization and ease communication among the various departments.

Systems software engineers work for companies that configure, implement, and install complete computer systems. These workers may be members of the marketing or sales staff, serving as the primary technical resource for sales workers and customers. They also may be involved in product sales and in providing their customers with continuing technical support. Since the selling of complex computer systems often requires substantial customization for the purchaser's organization, software engineers help to explain the requirements necessary for installing and operating the new system in the purchaser's computing environment. In addition, systems software engineers are responsible for ensuring security across the systems they are configuring.

Computer software engineers often work as part of a team that designs new hardware, software, and systems. A core team may comprise engineering, marketing, manufacturing, and design people, who work together until the product is released.

## Working Conditions

Computer software engineers normally work in well-lighted and comfortable offices or laboratories in which computer equipment is located. Most software engineers work at least 40 hours a week; however, due to the project-oriented nature of the work, they also may have to work evenings or weekends to meet deadlines or solve unexpected technical problems.

Like other workers who sit for hours at a computer, typing on a keyboard, software engineers are susceptible to eyestrain, back discomfort, and hand and wrist problems such as carpal tunnel syndrome.

As they strive to improve software for users, many computer software engineers interact with customers and coworkers. Computer software engineers who are employed by software vendors and consulting firms, for example, spend much of their time away from their offices, frequently traveling overnight to meet with customers. They call on customers in businesses ranging from manufacturing plants to financial institutions.

As networks expand, software engineers may be able to use modems, laptops, e-mail, and the Internet to provide more technical support and other services from their main office, connecting to a customer's computer remotely to identify and correct developing problems.

## Training, Other Qualifications, and Advancement

Most employers prefer to hire persons who have at least a bachelor's degree and broad knowledge of, and experience with, a variety of computer systems and technologies. The usual degree concentration for applications software engineers is computer science or software engineering; for systems software engineers, it is computer science or computer information systems. Graduate degrees are preferred for some of the more complex jobs.

Academic programs in software engineering emphasize software and may be offered as a degree option or in conjunction with computer science degrees. Increasing emphasis on computer security suggests that software engineers with advanced degrees that include mathematics and systems design will be sought after by software developers, government agencies, and consulting firms specializing in information assurance and security. Students seeking software engineering jobs enhance their employment opportunities by participating in internship or co-op programs offered through their schools. These experiences provide the students with broad knowledge and experience, making them more attractive candidates to employers. Inexperienced college graduates may be hired by large computer and consulting firms that train new employees in intensive, company-based programs. In many firms, new hires are mentored, and their mentors have an input into the performance evaluations of these new employees.

For systems software engineering jobs that require workers who have a college degree, a bachelor's degree in computer science or computer information systems is typical. For systems engineering jobs that place less emphasis on workers having a computer-related degree, computer training programs leading to certification are offered by systems software vendors. Nonetheless, most training authorities feel that program certification alone is not sufficient for the majority of software engineering jobs.

Persons interested in jobs as computer software engineers must have strong problem-solving and analytical skills. They also must be able to communicate effectively with team members, other staff, and the customers they meet. Because they often deal with a number of tasks simultaneously, they must be able to concentrate and pay close attention to detail.

As is the case with most occupations, advancement opportunities for computer software engineers increase with experience. Entry-level computer software engineers are likely to test and verify ongoing designs. As they become more experienced, they may become involved in designing and developing software. Eventually, they may advance to become a project manager, manager of information systems, or chief information officer. Some computer software engineers with several years of experience or expertise find lucrative opportunities working as systems designers or independent consultants or starting their own computer consulting firms.

As technological advances in the computer field continue, employers demand new skills. Computer software engineers must continually strive to acquire such skills if they wish to remain in this extremely dynamic field. For example, computer software engineers interested in working for a bank should have some expertise in finance as they integrate new technologies into the computer system of the bank. To help them keep up with the changing technology, continuing education and professional development seminars are offered by employers, software vendors, colleges and universities, private training institutions, and professional computing societies.

## Employment

Computer software engineers held about 800,000 jobs in 2004. Approximately 460,000 were computer applications software engineers, and around 340,000 were computer systems software engineers. Although they are employed in most industries, the largest concentration of computer software engineers—almost 30 percent—are in computer systems design and related services. Many computer software engineers also work for establishments in other industries, such as software publishers, government agencies, manufacturers of computers and related electronic equipment, and management of companies and enterprises.

Employers of computer software engineers range from start-up companies to established industry leaders. The proliferation of Internet, e-mail, and other communications systems is expanding electronics to engineering firms that are traditionally associated with unrelated disciplines. Engineering firms specializing in building bridges and powerplants, for example, hire computer software engineers to design and develop new geographic data systems and automated drafting systems. Communications firms need computer software engineers to tap into growth in the personal communications market. Major communications companies have many job openings for both computer software applications engineers and computer systems engineers.

An increasing number of computer software engineers are employed on a temporary or contract basis, with many being self-employed, working independently as consultants. Some consultants work for firms that specialize in developing and maintaining client companies' Web sites and intranets. About 23,000 computer software engineers were self-employed in 2004.

## Job Outlook

Computer software engineers are projected to be one of the fastest-growing occupations from 2004 to 2014. Rapid employment growth in the computer systems design and related services industry, which employs the greatest number of computer software engineers, should result in very good opportunities for those college graduates with at least a bachelor's degree in computer engineering or computer science and practical experience working with computers. Employers will continue to seek computer professionals with strong programming, systems analysis, interpersonal, and business skills. With the software industry beginning to mature, however, and with routine software engineering work being increasingly outsourced overseas, job growth will not be as rapid as during the previous decade.

Employment of computer software engineers is expected to increase much faster than the average for all occupations, as businesses and other organizations adopt and integrate new technologies and seek to maximize the efficiency of their computer systems. Competition among businesses will continue to create an incentive for increasingly sophisticated technological innovations, and organizations will need more computer software engineers to implement these changes. In addition to jobs created through employment growth, many job openings will result annually from the need to replace workers who move into managerial positions, transfer to other occupations, or leave the labor force.

Demand for computer software engineers will increase as computer networking continues to grow. For example, the expanding integration of Internet technologies and the explosive growth in electronic commerce—doing business on the Internet—have resulted in rising demand for computer software engineers who can develop Internet, intranet, and World Wide Web applications. Likewise, expanding electronic data-processing systems in business, telecommunications, government, and other settings continue to become more sophisticated and complex. Growing numbers of systems software engineers will be needed to implement,

safeguard, and update systems and resolve problems. Consulting opportunities for computer software engineers also should continue to grow as businesses seek help to manage, upgrade, and customize their increasingly complicated computer systems.

New growth areas will continue to arise from rapidly evolving technologies. The increasing uses of the Internet, the proliferation of Web sites, and mobile technology such as the wireless Internet have created a demand for a wide variety of new products. As individuals and businesses rely more on hand-held computers and wireless networks, it will be necessary to integrate current computer systems with this new, more mobile technology. Also, information security concerns have given rise to new software needs. Concerns over "cyber security" should result in businesses and government continuing to invest heavily in software that protects their networks and vital electronic infrastructure from attack. The expansion of this technology in the next 10 years will lead to an increased need for computer engineers to design and develop the software and systems to run these new applications and integrate them into older systems.

As with other information technology jobs, employment growth of computer software engineers may be tempered somewhat as more software development is contracted out abroad. Firms may look to cut costs by shifting operations to lower wage foreign countries with highly educated workers who have strong technical skills. At the same time, jobs in software engineering are less prone to being sent abroad compared with jobs in other computer specialties, because the occupation requires innovation and intense research and development.

## Earnings

Median annual earnings of computer applications software engineers who worked full time in May 2004 were about $74,980. The middle 50 percent earned between $59,130 and $92,130. The lowest 10 percent earned less than $46,520, and the highest 10 percent earned more than $113,830. Median annual earnings in the industries employing the largest numbers of computer applications software engineers in May 2004 were as follows:

Software publishers ............................................. $79,930
Management, scientific,
    and technical consulting services ...................... 78,460
Computer systems design and related services ....... 76,910
Management of companies and enterprises ............ 70,520
Insurance carriers ................................................ 68,440

Median annual earnings of computer systems software engineers who worked full time in May 2004 were about $79,740. The middle 50 percent earned between $63,150 and $98,220. The lowest 10 percent earned less than $50,420, nd the highest 10 percent earned more than $118,350. Median annual earnings in the industries employing the argest numbers of computer systems software engineers in May 2004 are as follows:

Scientific research and development services.......$91,390
Computer and peripheral equipment
     manufacturing......................................................87,800
Software publishers.....................................................83,670
Computer systems design and related services.......79,950
Wired telecommunications carriers.........................74,370

According to the National Association of Colleges and Employers, starting salary offers for graduates with a bachelor's degree in computer engineering averaged $52,464 in 2005; offers for those with a master's degree averaged $60,354. Starting salary offers for graduates with a bachelor's degree in computer science averaged $50,820.

According to Robert Half International, starting salaries for software engineers in software development ranged from $63,250 to $92,750 in 2005. For network engineers, starting salaries in 2005 ranged from $61,250 to $88,250.

## Related Occupations

Other workers who use mathematics and logic extensively include computer systems analysts, computer scientists and database administrators, computer programmers, computer hardware engineers, computer support specialists and systems administrators, engineers, statisticians, mathematicians, and actuaries.

From *Occupational Outlook Handbook,* 2006/07 Edition, pp. ONET codes 15-1031.00, 15-1032.00. Published by Bureau of Labor Statistics, U.S. Department of Labor. http://www.bls.gov/oco/

# How Deep Can You Probe?

**Many employers are going online to check out job candidates. But does the practice carry hidden risks?**

RITA ZEIDNER

When Mary Willoughby was looking to hire a technology director, she went online to check out the leading candidate.

On his page on MySpace, a popular social networking site, the applicant talked at length about his interest in violent films and boasted about his romantic exploits.

Based on what she saw, Willoughby, the human resources director for a New York nonprofit that provides assistance to people with disabilities, decided to keep her search open and ultimately offered the job to someone else.

"It's not that he did anything wrong" Willoughby says of the young man she passed over. "But we're an organization that serves the disabled. We decided that this was not a good fit."

Several high-profile cases of resume fraud, widely reported by the media, underscore the problems that can occur when an applicant is not adequately vetted. Earlier this year, a previously well-regarded Massachusetts Institute of Technology admissions officer was forced to resign after admitting she lied about where she had gone to school. Last year, RadioShack Corp.'s chief executive, David Edmundson, was forced from his job for lying about his credentials.

Eager to keep their own companies' names out of the headlines, many employers are trying to be more vigilant. A recent survey by the Society for Human Resource Management (SHRM) found that nearly half of the HR professionals who responded run a candidate's name through a search engine like Google or Yahoo! before making an offer. About one in five of those HR professionals who conduct such searches said they have disqualified a candidate because of what they uncovered.

## Looking for Trouble

Many employers do online background searches to identify fraudsters before they are brought on board. And even if a search turns up nothing negative about a candidate, it may help an employer show due diligence and fend off a negligent hiring charge if relations with a new hire turn ugly later.

Some 15 percent of the HR professionals who responded to the SHRM survey said they check social networking sites like MySpace and its fast-growing competitor Facebook to see what a job candidate has posted. And their ranks are likely to increase. Some 40 percent of the surveys respondents who don't now go to the sites say they are "somewhat likely" or "very likely" to visit them in the next 12 months. In most cases, checking such a site only takes a few moments.

Recruiter Tom Darrow of Talent Connections in Atlanta says he doesn't check such sites when scoping out candidates, but he can understand why employers do. Darrow offers a hypothetical example of a pharmaceutical company concerned about infiltration by radical animal fights advocates. While information about a candidate's attitude toward animal testing might not come up in an interview, or be revealed in a traditional background check, it might be disclosed on a networking site.

"The only downside of checking out the candidate's MySpace page," Darrow says, "is that it takes time."

## Recognizing Hidden Risks

But some HR practitioners say they are unnerved by the trend and question whether it is ethical, responsible or even legal for employers to be trolling such sites. "I've had some heated

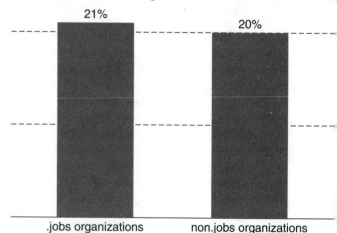

**Making the Cut.** Respondents who said they eliminated a job candidate based on information discovered from a search engine within the past 12 months.

Source: SHRM 2007 Advances in E-Recruiting: Leveraging the .jobs Domain.

discussions on this with my colleagues," says Willoughby of the Center for Disability Rights in Rochester, N.Y., a member of SHRM's Workplace Staffing and Deployment Special Expertise Panel who has earned SPHR certification.

Inadvertent violations of the federal Fair Credit Reporting Act (FCRA) and related state consumer protection laws are a hidden risk of online screening, according to Les Rosen, a former California deputy district attorney and a founding member of the National Association of Professional Background Screeners, a Morrisville, N.C. based trade group representing more than 500 background investigators.

The FCRA requires employers to notify job applicants and obtain their consent before conducting a background check. And while the law is geared toward obtaining official reports such as criminal histories and driving records, it's a good idea for employers doing online checks to follow the same notification and consent rules, says Rosen, author of *The Safe Hiring Manual* (On Demand Press, 2005) and head of a background screening firm. For a company bent on running Google searches on its potential hires, Rosen recommends that such an inquiry be conducted post-offer and only with the applicant's consent. An employer who changes his mind about a worker after finding disparaging information online generally would not be required to provide an explanation, Rosen says.

Employers also increase their exposure to discrimination claims when they gather too much information about a candidate. Companies suspected of rejecting a candidate based on race, religion or marital status can find themselves being hit with a claim of hiring based on unlawful factors.

Robert E. Capwell, chief knowledge officer at Employment Background Investigations Inc. in Pittsburgh, says if an employer does turn up information that a candidate could claim was used to discriminate against him or her, "You can't turn back the clock."

And just because a hiring official is turned off by the raunchy material someone posts on Facebook or MySpace doesn't mean she can use it to disqualify a candidate. Many states limit the extent to which employers can consider off-duty conduct in making a hiring decision, according to Capwell.

"If [the activity] is not related to the job and it doesn't change how the applicant does [his or her] work, then maybe it shouldn't be considered," says Capwell.

When it comes to a job candidate's political activities, the line for employers is often blurry and may depend on specific circumstances. For example, in the hypothetical case of the pharmaceutical company that is considering a candidate who criticizes animal testing on his Facebook page, "I feel, absolutely, that this is job-related," says Darrow, who maintains that an employer has the right not to hire someone who opposes the way the company does business.

Using networking sites for hiring purposes may also violate these sites' terms, some lawyers say. Both Facebook and MySpace post rules prohibiting the use of information on their sites for commercial purposes. That arguably includes vetting employment candidates. The sites also ban the collection of e-mail addresses and the dissemination of unsolicited e-mails and solicitations—common practices for many recruiters.

Some lawyers warn that using social networking sites to vet job candidates may hurt employers by turning off good candidates who don't want the company snooping on them without their consent.

Another reason for employers to exercise caution: There's always the possibility that the information found online about job candidates simply isn't true.

Human resource consultant Becky Strickland of HR Matters in Pueblo, Colo., says she takes any information gleaned from the Internet with a grain of salt. Even an incriminating photo of a job candidate isn't necessarily proof positive that the person has engaged in bad behavior. The photo could have been created by an imposter.

"The Internet is not necessarily a reliable source" Strickland says.

## Screening e Screeners

Online databases can be another potential landmine for do-it-yourself screeners. While some legitimate information is accessible to employers over the Internet for a fee, many databases shortcut background screening industry standards. Unbeknownst to their paying clients, some databases rely on incomplete data sources or on information that is out-of-date. Some databases that provide criminal histories don't distinguish between arrest records and convictions. That could be a problem since using arrest records to disqualify an employee is illegal in some states.

"National databases are a tool, but the information always needs to be verified," advises Capwell.

A thorough criminal background check almost always requires a trip to the county courthouse in each of the jurisdictions where the applicant has lived, Capwell says.

To illustrate the problem with large commercial databases, Rosen cites in his book a 2004 study in which a University of Maryland professor obtained the criminal records of 120 Virginia parolees and submitted their names to a popular online background check company. Sixty names came back showing the person had no criminal record, and other reports were so jumbled it was hard to identify specific offenses.

In some cases, database inaccuracies can prompt an employer to take the wrong action. In June, a coalition of labor, privacy and civil rights groups filed a complaint with the Federal Trade Commission urging the agency to investigate four transportation companies that fired 100 railroad workers after conducting criminal background checks. The complaint alleges that at least

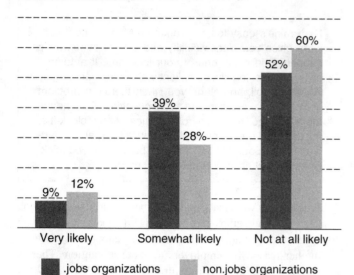

**Using Search Engines.** Respondents who indicated the likelihood that their organization will begin using search engines to review online information posted by job candidates within the next 12 months.

Source: SHRM 2007 Advances in E-Recruiting: Leveraging the .jobs Domain.

some of the firings were related to database errors. In addition, several of the workers had clean records but were victims of identity theft.

"The ability of an ordinary American to get a job, qualify for credit or even find a place to live depends increasingly on the information collected and stored by massive data aggregators," says Ari Schwartz, deputy director of the Center for Democracy and Technology in Washington, D.C., one of the groups filing the complaint. "If you're using data to make a hiring decision, there's an ethical obligation to tell the individual why you made that decision—especially if the information may not be correct."

## Tapping Technology

Notwithstanding the pitfalls of the Interact, technology does provide some relief to those looking for speedy ways to identify falsehoods and root out those hiding a criminal past.

Some system designers are partnering directly with screening companies to ensure that data flows smoothly from an employer's human resource information system to a background screening company.

"If we can get data directly out of an HR system and don't have to read it off a fax or decipher someone's handwriting, we avoid the potential for error and save time," Capwell says. He can then send the information electronically to court researchers anywhere in the country for verification.

Streamlining the process even further, a few large data brokers, including Little Rock, Ark. based Acxiom and Alpharetta, Ga. based ChoicePoint have gotten into the applicant tracking business and are now marketing all-in-one applicant tracking and background checking systems.

Anne Nimke of Pinstripe Talent in Brookfield, Wis., says she depends on SkillSurvey, an online reference collection tool that allows potential employers to send a preselected set of screening questions to candidates' references via e-mail. The tool then scores the responses.

Other resources employers can access online include employment verification tools available on the web sites of the Social Security Administration and the Department of Homeland Security.

Employers and background screeners also are increasingly relying on the Internet to obtain the signature necessary to conduct a background check. Many companies get authorization with a click-through process. More-advanced software allows an applicant to scribble a signature by clicking and dragging the mouse.

RITA ZEIDNER is manager of the SHRM Online HR Technology Focus Area.

*E-Monitoring in the Workplace*

# Privacy, Legislation, and Surveillance Software

## Protecting the corporation while respecting employee privacy— an old puzzle made more complex with new software.

G. DARYL NORD, TIPTON F. MCCUBBINS, AND JERETTA HORN NORD

*"Through advanced computer technology, employers can now continuously monitor employees' actions without the employee even knowing he or she is being 'watched.' The computer's eye is unblinking and ever-present. Sophisticated software allows every minute of the day to be recorded and evaluated [1]."*

Increasingly, personnel in institutions worldwide use email and the Internet on a daily basis at work. This daily reliance and dependency on technology has created new issues with respect to employee privacy in the workplace and has added new stress to the employer-employee relationship. Employee privacy, long considered a basic right, is often taken for granted by employees. However, as a result of technological monitoring, this view may be naïve.

According to the annual survey, *Workplace Monitoring and Surveillance Survey 2001* conducted by the American Management Association, more than three-quarters of all major U.S. firms (nearly double the 1997 survey results) are recording and/or reviewing the email messages, telephone calls, Internet connections, and computer files of their employees. Workplace monitoring has existed for a long time in one form or another and will undoubtedly continue to proliferate and become increasingly sophisticated as technology advances. This article examines the employer/employee workplace privacy relationship, identifies the existing federal and state law governing workplace privacy, and discusses the rapidly developing monitoring software market.

## Workplace Privacy

Most U.S. citizens are accustomed to the expectation of privacy. Privacy, as defined by the Merriam-Webster dictionary is a: the quality or state of being apart from company or observation; b: freedom from unauthorized intrusion <one's right to *privacy*>. But in the workplace, to what degree can workers expect privacy and protection from observation and unauthorized intrusion? Workers may sometimes expect they have the same privacy rights at the office as they have at home. Others may assume that since they have an account number and

password on their software and email system their individual privacy is protected and secure.

Do you know anyone who occasionally takes a moment out of his or her day to check a stock quote, sports score, or movie listing online at work? As of January 2002, approximately 55 million U.S. adults accessed the Internet at work, up from 43 million in March 2000. Fifty-five percent of those with Internet access at work went online on a typical day in 2001, compared to 50% in 2000, and many were going online more frequently throughout the day than they had in 2001 [10]. More than 72% of Internet users do more than just surf the Web. Popular Internet activities include instant messaging, downloading music, and watching video clips [9]. In another Internet work-related study, Yankelovich Partners discovered that 62% of workers go online at work for personal reasons at least once a day, while about 20% do so 10 or more times a day. In a 2002 study by the Computer Security Institute (CSI), 78% of polled enterprises reported employee abuse of Internet access privileges by workers, including downloading pirated software or pornography, shopping on the Internet, and inappropriate use of email systems. These studies readily show the escalating magnitude of non-work related Internet use at work.

Employers want to make sure their employees are using company time productively and not creating a legal liability for their business as a result of harassing or offensive communications. A recent study revealed that 10% of U.S. companies have received subpoenas resulting from employee email [5]. In addition, employers have security concerns relating to the intentional or accidental sending of sensitive data via email attachments as well as the ongoing concern of viruses entering the business from outside communications. Consequently, employers are monitoring employee's computer and Internet access to a greater degree than in the past. As illustrated in Table 1, the American Management Association surveys conducted from 1999 to 2001 and again in 2005, exposed the growing trend of employer monitoring of employees' computer files, email messaging, and Internet connections [2].

## Table 1 Survey Results by AMA on Employee Monitoring

| | 1999 | 2000 | 2001 | 2005 |
|---|---|---|---|---|
| Storage and review of computer files | 21.4% | 30.8% | 36.1% | 50% |
| Storage and review of email messages | 27% | 38.1% | 46.5% | 55% |
| Monitoring Internet connections | NA | 54.1% | 62.8% | 76% |

According to another recent AMA survey, the 2003 E-mail Rules, Policies and Practices Survey, over half (52%) of employers monitor email. Three-fourths of the 1,100 employers surveyed have put written email policies in place. And 22% have terminated an employee for violating email policy [3].

# Federal Privacy Legislation in the Workplace

Most U.S.-based employees assume they have a constitutional right to privacy. However, constitutional rights to privacy are generally inferred through the U.S. Constitution's Fourth Amendment's rights to freedom from unreasonable search and seizure. These freedoms usually apply only to state actions. In an employment context, state actions are fairly narrowly limited to protecting federal, state, and municipal employees. Private-sector employees must look elsewhere for protection. Possible sources for such protection from employer snooping include federal legislation and state common law tort actions such as invasion of privacy [4].

The primary piece of federal legislation suggesting employee privacy interest is the Electronic Communications Privacy Act (ECPA). However, there are three exceptions under the ECPA that effectively eliminate any substantial expectation of privacy an employee might have with respect to his/her employer.

> **Workplace monitoring has existed for a long time in one form or another and will undoubtedly continue to proliferate and become increasingly sophisticated as technology advances.**

The first of the ECPA exceptions is the "provider exception." If an employer actually owns and is providing the telephone, email, or Internet services to the employee being monitored, there is little doubt that the employer is protected from employee privacy claims. However, if the employer is merely providing email services through a third-party Internet provider, it is not as clear that the employer would enjoy the same protection. Nevertheless, given the fact the employer is "providing" the provider, coupled with the generous interpretation that most courts have granted employers, there is good reason to believe that even these providers of providers would enjoy protection from employee privacy suits [7].

The second exception is the "ordinary course of business" exception. It really provides an exception to the definition of an electronic device, and therefore excludes the employer's monitoring from the ECPA and the employee protections provided therein. Under this exception the employer may monitor employee communications to ensure such legitimate business objectives as assuring quality control, preventing sexual harassment, and preventing unauthorized use of equipment, such as excessive telephone or email usage.

However, the "course of business" language also implies a limitation on the extent of monitoring in the event the employer discovers he has accessed a personal conversation. In monitoring telephone conversations it is well established that employers can continue to listen only for so long as it takes to determine the conversation is in fact personal. At that point, the employer must cease the surveillance. The case setting the standard for this limitation is a 1983 case dealing with the use of the telephone. A thorough examination of the standard as it applies to email usage has not yet occurred, but a similar application should probably be expected. However, at least one case has suggested that no monitoring of an employee's personal email may be allowed without prior notification [8].

The third exception is the "consent" exception. If at least one party to the communication is either the party who intercepts the communication or gives consent to the interception then the ECPA has not been violated. The "consent" exception apparently applies even when the sender of the intercepted communication has been assured that all email communications would remain confidential and privileged. In *Smyth v. The Pillsbury Company,* Smyth sent his supervisor emails that contained inappropriate and unprofessional comments from Smyth's home computer. The supervisor received the email over Pillsbury's email system. The email included such statements such as "kill the backstabbing . . . " and referred to the company's holiday party as the "Jim Jones Koolaid affair." At a later date the company intercepted these email messages and terminated Smyth's employment based upon their content.

Although the court did not explain exactly how the interception took place, the email messages were apparently retrieved from storage with the supervisor's consent. As a result of the consent, even the prior promise of confidentiality did not provide the employee with privacy protection.

# State Privacy Case Law

The common law tort of invasion of privacy is recognized by most states. The Restatement (Second) of Torts §652B defines invasion of privacy as: " . . . intentionally intruding, physically or otherwise, upon the solitude or seclusion of another . . . , if the intrusion would be highly offensive to a reasonable person." Employees have tried to use this tort as a protection for privacy in the workplace. Although it shows some potential for privacy protection, it has generally stumbled over two problems. The first is that the employee must have a reasonable expectation of privacy, and the second is that the intrusion would be highly offensive to the reasonable person.

> **Along with the ever-increasing exploitation of technology in the workplace has come the capability for employers to see and measure nearly every aspect of company usage.**

In *McLaren v. Microsoft* (1999), Microsoft made available to McLaren, as part of his employment, use of an email system owned and administered by Microsoft. McLaren had the right and ability to store email he received either in the server-based "inbox" or in a "personal folder" protected by a personal store password. As part of a harassment investigation, Microsoft decrypted McLaren's personal store password and broke into his personal folder even though it had been specifically requested by McLaren not to do so.

McLaren argued that the password-protected personal folder was basically the same as a locked storage locker provided by a company for employees to store personal items in while at work. It has long been accepted that employees have a legitimate expectation of privacy with regard to such lockers. However, the court rejected this argument. It stated that because the email was first received and stored in the "inbox," which was subject to inspection, McLaren could have no expectation of privacy simply by moving it to a protected folder. How this is different from a telephone call that can only be monitored long enough to determine if it is of a business or personal nature the court did not explain. True, in this case, the fact that the email messages were pertinent to a harassment investigation would make them subject to legitimate business scrutiny. However, the court did not seem to rely on this fact in declaring a blanket open season on email monitoring. Second, although it is possible to distinguish between illicit information being carried through public space from the front door of a business to an employee's locked storage locker and an email message sitting in an inbox before being transferred to a protected personal folder, such distinctions are not so obvious as to deny a need for recognition. However the court seemed sufficiently confident in its analysis that it did not address the issue.

In determining that the intrusion was not highly offensive, the court properly recognized the importance of whether the intrusion was justified. The fact that McLaren was under investigation, and that he had notified Microsoft that the email was relevant to that investigation, clearly support the court's finding that Microsoft's actions were justified. Therefore, they were not highly offensive even though the actions had been specifically forbidden by McLaren and led to his dismissal.

# Company Electronic Communications Policy

In a case [11] in which the California Appellant Court ruled in favor of the employer strictly on the basis of a signed electronic communications policy, the court stated that at a minimum the policy should contain a statement that:

1. Electronic communication facilities provided by the company are owned by the company and should be used solely for company business.
2. The company will monitor all employee Internet and email usage. It should state who may review the information, the purposes for which the information may be used, and that the information may be stored on a separate computer [6, 7].
3. The company will keep copies of the Internet and email passwords.
4. The existence of a separate password is not an assurance of the confidentiality of the communication or other "protected" material.

5. The sending of any discriminatory, offensive, or unprofessional message or content is strictly prohibited.
6. The accessing of any Internet site that contains offensive of discriminatory content is prohibited.
7. The posting of personal opinions on the Internet using the company's access is strictly prohibited. This is particularly true of, but not limited to, opinions that are political or discriminatory in nature.
8. Although not included in the court's list, the policy should clearly state potential repercussions to the employee for violating the policy [4].

Legally, these requirements are considered minimum standards that a sound policy should meet. They should be clear and unequivocal, and they should be read and signed by each employee. However, the employer should also remain aware of the employee's normal human desire for reasonable amounts of privacy. Therefore the employer should try to minimize unnecessary intrusion into this privacy expectation in order to reduce the negative impact on employee morale.

# Monitoring Software

Along with the ever-increasing exploitation of technology in the workplace has come the capability for employers to see and measure nearly every aspect of company computer usage. The dilemma that employers must resolve is how to balance the obvious benefits of employee use of technological tools with the risks inherent in providing those tools to employees. As stated earlier, many employers have sought to achieve this balance by electronically monitoring the use that their employees make of email, the Internet, and other computer-related activities.

Monitoring software allows employers to see, measure, and manage employees' computer systems, monitors, disks, software, email, and Web and Internet access. The software can automatically archive all collected information into a corporate network server for review at a later time. The list in Table 2 illustrates the many capabilities of typical monitoring software readily available on the market today by companies such as Spectorsoft and DynaComm.

# Conclusion

E-monitoring and employee workplace privacy are issues that will continue to present questions and problems for some time to come. In addition, it looks as if there will be ongoing efforts to balance employee workplace privacy with the need for employers to manage and protect company resources from non-productive, non-work related activities. Federal and state legislation governing monitoring and workplace privacy will undoubtedly continue to evolve and be tested in the court systems.

There are many legitimate reasons for organizations to want to know what is occurring on their computer systems. Those reasons range from workplace harassment, to loss of productivity, and even to company sabotage. Therefore, it is easy to understand why it would be prudent for companies to have such a strong incentive to find a healthy balance between employee privacy rights and organizational concerns.

## Table 2 Surveillance Capabilities of Monitoring Software on the Market Today

The workplace end user types any keystroke in any window on his/her remote PC, that text appears on the network administrator's screen in real time or archived to a corporate server.

Typed text that is monitored may include email messages, online chat conversations, documents, passwords and all other keystrokes.

The network administrator can view the actual screen of the workplace desktops being monitored.

Internet usage can be monitored in real time and a log file recording of all Internet activity can be made.

A spy module can see and list software running on the remote PC and can view in real time the software applications and run executions.

A record and activity log for all workstations on the local or shared network location can be produced.

Monitoring software provides the ability to take snapshots of a remote PC screen or active window in specified time intervals and save them on the local or shared network location.

The workplace user's system can be turned off, restarted, and actually logged completely off the network.

The network administrator can run programs and execute commands on remote computers, open Web pages or documents, send instant messages for remote users, and terminate remote processes.

Files can be readily copied including logs and screenshots from the desktop computers. The administrator can have the same file access permissions, as a current user has on the workplace computer.

Multiple employee computers can simultaneously be monitored from a single workstation in the LAN.

Workplace surveillance software that runs on monitored computers is hidden and difficult for an employee to locate or even know that the software is present and monitoring their every keystroke. The monitoring software usually cannot be terminated without the network administrator's permission.

# References

1. American Civil Liberties Union (ACLU). Workplace Rights on Electronic Monitoring, ACLU online archives; archive.aclu.org/issues/worker/legkit2.html.
2. American Management Association, AMA Research: Workplace Monitoring and Surveillance, 1999, 2000, 2001 and 2005; www.amanet.org/research/archive_2001_1999.htm.
3. American Management Association, Survey on Workplace E-Mail Reveals Disasters in the Making, May 28, 2003; www.amanet.org/press/amanews/Email_Survey2003.htm.
4. Bloom, E., Schachter, M., and Steelman, E. Justice in a Changing World: Competing Interests in the Post 9-11 Workplace: The New Line Between Privacy and Safety. 29 Wm. Mitchell L. Rev. 897 (2003).
5. Crimmins, J. Even federal judges come under surveillance when online. *Chicago Daily Law Bulletin 147,* 159 (Aug. 14, 2001).
6. *Deal v. Spears,* 980 F.2d 1153, 1155-1157 (8th Cir. 1992).
7. DiLuzio, S. Workplace E-Mail: It's Not as Private as You Might Think. 25 Del. J. Corp. L. 741 (2000).
8. Kopp, K. Electronic Communications in the Workplace: E-Mail Monitoring and the Right of Privacy. 8 Seaton Hall Const. L. J. 861 (1998).
9. Neilson//NetRankings, U.S. Online Population Internet Use. (Dec. 18, 2002); www.nielsen-netratings.com/pr/pr_021218.pdf.
10. Pew Internet & American Life, Getting Serious Online: As Americans Gain Experience, They Use the Web More at Work, Write Emails with More Significant Content, Perform More Online Transactions, and Pursue More Serious Activities, (Mar. 3, 2002); www.pewinternet.org/reports/toc.asp?Report555.
11. *TBG Insurance Services Corporation v. The Superior Court of Los Angeles Co.;* Robert Zieminski, Real Party in Interest, 96 Cal. App. 4th 443; 117 Cal. Rptr. 2d 155 (Cal. App. 2002).

**G. DARYL NORD** (daryl.nord@okstate.edu) is a professor of Management Science & Information Systems in the William S. Spears School of Business, at Oklahoma State University, Stillwater, OK. **TIPTON F. MCCUBBINS** (tipton.mccubbins@okstate.edu) is an associate professor of Legal Studies in Business in the William S. Spears School of Business, at Oklahoma State University, Stillwater, OK. **JERETTA HORN NORD** (jeretta.nord@okstate.edu) is a professor of Management Science & Information Systems and Associate Dean for Undergraduate Programs in the William S. Spears School of Business, at Oklahoma State University, Stillwater, OK.

# The Computer Evolution

Rob Valletta and Geoffrey MacDonald

Since the introduction of the IBM PC in 1981, desktop computers have become a standard fixture in most workplaces. Through their ubiquity and impact on how work is done, personal computers (PCs) arguably have transformed the workplace. At the same time, the use and impact of PCs varies across worker groups with different educational and skill levels. As a result, an extensive body of research suggests that the spread of computers, or perhaps increased workplace emphasis on skills that are closely related to computer use, has altered the distribution of wages as well. This process has been marked not so much by abrupt change as by slow and steady change—it is an "evolution" rather than a "revolution."

In this Economic Letter, we use data from five special surveys, covering the period 1984–2001, to examine two key aspects of the computer evolution: the spread of PCs at work and the evolving wage differentials between individuals who use them and those who do not. Although the spread of computers has been relatively uniform across labor force groups, the wage returns associated with computers tilted sharply in favor of the highly educated at the end of our sample frame. This finding appears consistent with the increase in trend productivity growth that occurred around the same time.

## Computers and Workers

By the middle to late 1980s, the rapid expansion of computer power embodied in PCs, combined with software that enhanced the overall ease of PC use and application to common business tasks, suggested to researchers and casual observers alike that computers were playing an increasingly important role in the determination of worker productivity and wages. In the first systematic analysis of the impact of computer use on wages, Krueger (1993) used data for the years 1984 and 1989 to estimate standard wage regressions that included controls for computer use at work. As such his estimates reflect wage differences between workers who use and do not use computers, adjusted for other observable differences across such workers that are systematically related to wages as well (age, educational attainment, sex, etc.). His results suggested that workers who used computers earned about 10%–20% more than workers who did not. Moreover, Krueger found that differences between highly educated and less educated workers in the incidence of and returns to computer use could account for 40%–50% of the increased return to education during the 1980s.

Krueger's analysis tied in well with earlier work regarding the contribution of technological change to increased dispersion in the U.S. wage distribution. Since then, wage gaps have widened even further, intensifying the research focus on how equipment like computers can alter the wage distribution by altering the demand for workers with the skills to use such equipment effectively. In a notable recent piece, Autor, Levy, and Murnane (2003) argue that increased computer use can explain most of the increase in nonroutine job tasks, hence the advanced skill content of jobs, during the 1970s, 1980s, and 1990s, and as such can explain most of the increased relative demand for college-educated workers. Although Autor et al. do not directly address the question of computer effects on earnings, their results indirectly suggest that rising computer use also explains a substantial portion of the rising wage gaps between highly educated and less educated workers over these three decades.

## PC Diffusion and Wage Effects

Given these existing findings about computer use, skill demand, and wages, an updated assessment of the returns to computer use is in order. To do so, we use the School Enrollment and the Computer and Internet Use Supplements to the federal government's Current Population Survey (CPS). The CPS covers about 60,000 households each month; the resulting sample of individuals serves as a primary source of information on U.S. employment, unemployment, and income patterns. The supplements we use were conducted in 1984, 1989, 1993, 1997, and 2001 (Krueger's work relied on the first two of these). In these surveys, the respondents were asked about computer use at home, work, and school. Although the exact content of the supplements changed over time (for example, Internet use was first addressed in 1997), the question about computer use at work has been essentially unaltered. We rely on samples of about 60,000 employed individuals in each survey to calculate rates of computer use at work; of these, information on wages and related variables is provided for a bit under one-fourth of the sample (about 12,000–14,000 individuals). We restrict the analysis to individuals age 18 to 65.

Figure 1 shows the time series of computer use rates for college graduates, nongraduates, and the combined population. Although the level of computer use is significantly higher for workers with a bachelor's degree (82.3% in 2001) than for those without it (42.7%), the diffusion over time has been relatively

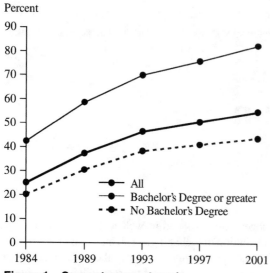

Percent

**Figure 1   Computer use at work.**

Note: Authors' tabulations of CPS computer use supplement data.

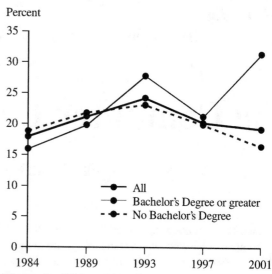

Percent

**Figure 2   Wage returns to computer use.**

Note: Authors' estimates.

uniform across these groups. Additional tabulations show a similar pattern of diffusion when the sample is broken down into narrower educational groups or by additional characteristics such as gender, race, age, geography, and occupation. In percentage terms, we find the sharpest increase in computer use at work for groups with low initial use, including older workers, part-time workers, blue-collar workers, and workers without a high school degree. Moreover, the diffusion of computer use at work slowed after 1993. These patterns are consistent with common models of technology diffusion, in which individuals and firms with the most to gain adopt the new technology first and the rate of diffusion slows as the group that has not yet adopted it shrinks.

To estimate the effect of computer use on wages, we use a regression model similar to Krueger's (1993). The model controls for observable characteristics that are systematically related to wages, including age, education, race, sex, marital status, veteran status, union status, part-time status, and geographic location (region and urban/rural residence), allowing us to isolate the effect of computer use on wages independent of the influence of these other characteristics. Given the potentially important interaction between computer use and education level, we also allow for separate estimates of the return to computer use for individuals who have attained at least a college degree versus those who have not. After applying an appropriate mathematical transformation based on the logarithmic regression function, we obtain the estimated percentage effect of computer use on wages.

Figure 2 plots how the estimated return to computer use at work has changed over time. For the full sample of workers, the return to computer use reached a peak in 1993, with a 24.2% wage advantage over otherwise similar workers. The estimated return to computer use for the full sample declined to 19.2% in 2001. However, the return for individuals with a college or graduate degree increased dramatically during the last period, reaching 31.4% in 2001. This sharp change is surprising, as it

conflicts with the general expectation, based on economic reasoning, that the return to scarce skills (those needed for computer use) should decline as that skill becomes less scarce. As shown in Figure 1, only about one in five college-educated workers did not use computers at work in 2001, which suggests that the skills needed to use computers are far from scarce among the highly educated.

Although the spread of computer skills suggests that the wage returns to computer use should decline, this argument ignores the possibility that production technology is changing rapidly and in ways that support increased rewards for workers with the skills needed for effective use of critical technologies such as computers. Available evidence suggests that rapid expansion of information technology capital (mainly computers and software) in the workplace accounts for a substantial portion of the increased growth in labor productivity during the period 1996–2001 (see for example Oliner and Sichel 2003). While computers make some tasks easier and reduce required skill levels, many advances in computer technology have enabled increasingly sophisticated applications that require complex analytical and evaluative skills. A leading reason to attend college is to acquire such skills. It appears that these skills commanded an increasing premium as workplace computer use intensified between 1997 and 2001, enabling college-educated workers to capture the largest benefits from the spread of computers in the workplace during this period.

## Implications

Our findings confirm that workers who use computers earn more than otherwise similar workers who do not. We also find that this effect has been especially large for highly educated workers in recent years. Some researchers, however, have questioned whether the computer effect on wages is fundamentally meaningful in an economic sense. For example, DiNardo and Pischke (1997) have shown that workers who use simple office ools like pencils earn a wage premium similar to that estimated for computer users. This suggests the possibility that the estimated effect of computer use on wages reflects unobserved aspects of skilled workers and their jobs, such that these workers would earn higher wages even if they did not use computers. In other words, DiNardo and Pischke argue that computer use does not have an independent "causal" impact on wages but instead serves as a mediating or auxiliary factor, reflecting related skills that are more fundamental than the direct ability to use a computer.

Nevertheless, an abundance of evidence regarding close relationships among the use of advanced technology and the demand for and wages of skilled workers suggests an important causal role for computers and the skills needed to use them. In that regard, an emphasis on "causal" impacts may be misplaced. For many jobs, effective performance requires computer use, which suggests a close relationship between computer use and critical job skills. In technical parlance, the ability to use a computer probably is not a "sufficient" condition for earning high wages, but it is increasingly a "necessary" condition.

Overall, we interpret the evidence as suggesting that direct computer skills or skills that closely relate to computer use command a substantial premium in the labor market, especially in conjunction with a college degree. It remains to be seen whether the recent increase in returns to computer use for highly educated individuals will continue. However, the trend over the past few years suggests that U.S. productivity growth remains on (or even above) the accelerated growth path that was established during the late 1990s. Going forward, it is likely that these productivity gains will be largely reflected in wage gains for highly educated individuals who use computers, much as was the increase in the relative return to computer use for these individuals during the period 1997–2001.

# References

Autor, David H., Frank Levy, and Richard J. Murnane. 2003. "The Skill Content of Recent Technological Change: An Empirical Exploration." *Quarterly Journal of Economics* 118(4) (November), pp. 1279–1333.

DiNardo, John, and Jörn-Steffen Pischke. 1997. "The Return to Computer Use Revisited: Have Pencils Changed the Wage Structure Too?" *Quarterly Journal of Economics* 112(1) (February), pp. 291–303.

Krueger, Alan. 1993. "How Computers Have Changed the Wage Structure: Evidence from Microdata, 1984–1989." *Quarterly Journal of Economics* 108(1) (February), pp. 33–60.

Oliner, Stephen D., and Daniel E. Sichel. 2003. "Information Technology and Productivity: Where Are We Now and Where Are We Going?" *Journal of Policy Modeling* 25(5) (July), pp. 477–503.

Reprinted with permission from the *FRBSF Economic Letter,* No. 2004-19, July 23, 2004, pp. 1–3, by Rob Valletta and Geoffrey MacDonald. The opinions expressed in this article do not necessarily reflect the views of the management of the Federal Reserve Bank of San Francisco, or of the Board of Governors of the Federal Reserve System.

# UNIT 4

# Computers, People, and Social Participation

## Unit Selections

15. **Back-to-School Blogging,** Brock Read
16. **Romance in the Information Age,** Christine Rosen
17. **E-Mail Is for Old People,** Dan Carnevale
18. **Girl Power,** Chuck Salter
19. **Bloggers against Torture,** Negar Azimi

## Key Points to Consider

- The overview to this unit mentions de Tocqueville's observation that Americans tend to form civic associations and Putnam's argument that this tendency is declining. Do you think that computing has played any part in the decline? What does Putnam say? What do other scholars say about Putnam's work?

- Ben Franklin's autobiography is considered a classic of American literature. There, he describes several civic associations that he formed in early Philadelphia. What were they?

- Social scientists sometimes say that the likelihood of participating in civic life declines ten per cent for every ten miles one commutes. What is the source for this figure? Is there a similar figure relating civic participation to daily minutes spent on-line?

- Do you agree that "E-Mail Is for Old People?"

- Who uses Internet dating services? Can you generalize about age, income, ethnicity, education, or religion?

- Do you read books for pleasure? What about your family?

## Student Web Site

www.mhcls.com

## Internet References

**Adoption Agencies**
*http://www.amrex.org/*
**Alliance for Childhood: Computers and Children**
*http://www.allianceforchildhood.net/projects/computers/index.htm*
**The Core Rules of Netiquette**
*http://www.albion.com/netiquette/corerules.html*
**How the Information Revolution Is Shaping Our Communities**
*http://www.plannersweb.com/articles/bla118.html*
**SocioSite: Networks, Groups, and Social Interaction**
*http://www2.fmg.uva.nl/sociosite/topics/interaction.html*

The early and astute observer of American culture, Alexis de Tocqueville (1805–1859), had this to say about the proclivity of Americans to form civic associations:

> Americans of all ages, all conditions, and all dispositions constantly form associations. . . . The Americans make associations to give entertainments, to found seminaries, to build inns, to construct churches, to diffuse books, to send missionaries to the Antipodes; in this manner they found hospitals, prisons, and schools. If it is proposed to inculcate some truth or to foster some feeling by the encouragement of a great example, they form a society. Wherever at the head of some new undertaking you see the government in France, or a man of rank in England, in the United States you will be sure to find an association. . . . The first time I heard in the United States that a hundred thousand men had bound themselves publicly to abstain from spiritous liquors, it appeared to me more like a joke than a serious engagement, and I did not at once perceive why these temperate citizens could not content themselves with drinking water by their own firesides. . . . Nothing, in my opinion is more deserving of our attention than the intellectual and moral associations of America. . . . In democratic countries the science of association is the mother of science; the progress of all the rest depends upon the progress it has made (Tocqueville, 1945: v. 2, pp. 114–118)

He laid this tendency squarely at the feet of democracy. If all men—we're talking about the first half of the 19th century here—are equal before the law, then, to do any civic good requires that these equal, but individually powerless, men band together.

A century and a half later, we have the technical means to communicate almost instantly and effortlessly across great distances. But we are banding together less. In 1995, Robert D. Putnam, made the news with an article, later expanded into a book, called *Bowling Alone* (Putnam 2000). He argued that the civil associations de Tocqueville had noticed so long ago were breaking down. Americans were not joining the PTA, the Boy Scouts, the local garden club, or bowling leagues in their former numbers. Putnam discovered that although more people are bowling than ever, participation in leagues was down by 40 percent since 1980. The consequences for a functioning democracy are severe.

Although the articles in this unit do not directly address the idea of civic participation, one question is the glue that holds them together. Do computers assist or detract from civic life? Another French social observer, Emile Durkheim (1858–1917), argued that a vital society must have members who feel a sense of community. Community is easily evident in pre-industrial societies where kinship ties, shared religious belief, and custom reinforce group identity and shared values. Not so in modern societies, particularly in the United States, where a mobile

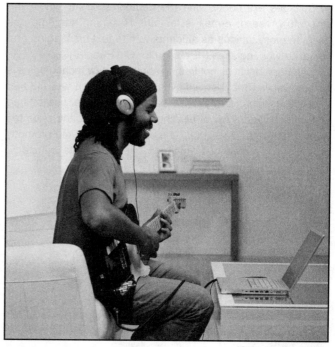

© Royalty-Free/Corbis

population commutes long distances and retreats each evening to the sanctity and seclusion of individual homes. Contemporary visitors to the United States are struck by the cultural cafeteria available to Americans. They find a dizzying array of religions, beliefs, moral and philosophical perspectives, modes of social interaction, entertainment venues and, now, networked computers. One need only observe a teenager frantically instant-messaging her friends from a darkened bedroom to know that while computer technology has surely given us great things, it has taken away something as well. The capacity to maintain friendships without face-to-face contact, the ability to construct a computer profile that edits anything not in line with one's interests, seems to push society a step closer to self-interested individualism.

On the other hand, one can argue that the new communications technologies permit relationships that were never before possible. To cite a large example, the organization, moveon.org, organized many thousands of people, in a matter of weeks, entirely over the Internet, to oppose the invasion of Iraq in the spring of 2003. Or a smaller one. Immigration, always a wrenching experience, is less wrenching now, since immigrants to the United States can be in daily touch with their families across the globe. Or consider how the virtual bazaar, eBay, surely one of the extraordinary aspects of the Internet, puts Americans in touch with Japanese, Latvians, Montenegrans, peoples whom we might never have known. Recall Postman: "Technology giveth and technology taketh away."

What technology seems to have "giveth" in the past few years is the ability to find love online. Christine Rosen's "Romance in the Information Age" provides a critical look at a practice that is not only becoming common but lucrative, as well. Eager to distinguish themselves from the competition, some Internet dating sites have turned to social scientists to hone their matching skills.

Colleges are confronting the demographic for whom the staccato prose of e-mail is tedious. Reaching students has become more difficult as students turn to text messaging and social networking sites ("E-mail Is for Old People").

One person who is not fretting about the new technologies is Ashley Qualls. She founded WhateverLife.com, a website that supplies designs for MySpace pages. When she was offered $1.5 million "and a car of her choice—as long as the price tag wasn't more than $100,000," the seventeen year old promptly dropped out of school to manage her improbable company. Read about it in Chuck Salter's "Girl Power."

It's easy enough for commentators of a certain age to find fault with emerging technologies. Read Negar Azimi's piece, "Bloggers against Torture," to get another perspective. Activists in developing nations are turning to blogs to evade tight media controls. The story of Emad Mohamed Ali Mohamed, a young Egyptian bus driver, whose torture at the hands of police had been videotaped and passed around Egyptian blogs, is evidence enough, to reverse Postman (Article 1): "Though technology taketh away, it also giveth."

## References

Tocqueville, Alexis de. (1945). *Democracy in America.* New York: Vintage Books, 1945.

Putnam, Robert D. (2000). *Bowling Alone: The Collapse and Revival of American Community.* New York: Simon & Schuster.

# Back-to-School Blogging

**Web logs help new students prepare for campus life.**

<small>BROCK READ</small>

L ike almost any student preparing to move into a freshman dormitory, Nora Goldberger spent much of the summer batting around questions about college life: Would she struggle to make friends? Which courses should she take, and which ones should she avoid? How would she get her laundry done?

Such concerns are the stuff that precollege apprehension is made of. But Ms. Goldberger, a Philadelphia native who is beginning her studies at Davidson College, says she feels more at ease than most of her friends. Credit for that, she says, goes to her computer.

Throughout the summer she joined her peers in posting questions on a Web log, or blog, for students at the North Carolina college. Using the informal discussion forum, maintained by students at Davidson, she chatted with her soon-to-be-classmates and hit up wizened upperclassmen for advice on the coming year.

When Ms. Goldberger wondered if she could trust the university's laundry service—which collects students' dirty clothes and washes them at no cost—she asked her fellow bloggers. Within a day, several upperclassmen had given her a consensus opinion: Don't be afraid to use the service, but wash delicate items yourself.

When she wanted to know how much she should expect to pay for a semester's worth of textbooks, she quickly got a number of estimates. And after she mentioned offhandedly that she'd been listening to a song by the band Sister Hazel, she compared notes with two other students who owned all of the cult group's albums.

The popularity of blogs is helping students across the country meet their dorm mates, form study groups, and make friends before they set foot on their new campuses.

Free, Web-based tools like Xanga and LiveJournal, which allow users to easily create their own blogs, have attracted a large following among high-school and college students. At institutions like Davidson, enterprising students have used the popularity of the medium to create thriving communities in which incoming freshmen meet to exchange practical questions, personal information, movie recommendations, and jokes.

Administrators say the sites constitute an important new trend: Students who grow up using the Web as a social tool can now ask their peers, instead of college officials, for counseling on the process of preparing for college. The colleges aren't about to get rid of their orientation sessions, but officials say freshmen who use the Internet for college planning may become more self-reliant students.

Meanwhile, students like Ms. Goldberger relish the chance to get a head start on college socializing. "This has definitely made me feel more excited and better about coming here," she says. "I have friendly faces and people to look out for, and I'm just a little bit better informed."

## Flood of Questions

The success of the Davidson students' Web log (http://www .livejournal.com/community/davidson college) has exceeded the expectations of its creator, Emily McRae, a sophomore.

Ms. McRae started the site—a group journal that allows anyone to post comments—this summer after speaking to an incoming freshman who found her own blog inundated with questions about Davidson from people she'd never met.

The flood of questions, Ms. McRae says, proves that first-year students are eager to touch base with their peers—and that information travels quickly among bloggers. A Web log, she reasoned, would let incoming freshmen share questions about Davidson among a broad pool of college-age bloggers.

The blog is hosted on LiveJournal, a free service. Anyone can see the postings, but only those who have signed up with the service can contribute. On pages that resemble discussion boards, users with pseudonymous screen names like "onenoisygirl" and "atrain14" post questions or comments, and others respond.

At first the site was popular with freshmen who logged on to do little more than introduce themselves and post their course schedules. But soon upperclassmen happened onto the Web log and made their presence known. Students began asking about cafeteria food, required courses, dorm-room accouterments, and other concerns of campus life, and the community took off.

"I think freshmen became really interested when there were upperclassmen giving sage advice on classes, orientation, and living in Davidson," says Peter Benbow, a sophomore who regularly contributes to the site as "crazydcwildcat7."

"We know what it's like to come wide-eyed and mystified onto a college campus," he says.

The site now has almost 80 users, including alumni and prospective students. "The alumni get to reconnect, the freshmen get to ask advice, the upperclassmen get to consult one another, and the prospectives get lots of answers for 'Why did you come to Davidson?'" says Ms. McRae.

The site has a generally earnest tone, with posts that range from informational to motivational. During the week before freshmen headed to campus for orientation activities in August, students sought tips for decorating their rooms and updated classmates on their packing progress. One first-year student tried to set up a knitting party, a sophomore offered an inspirational poem, another student asked her classmates for help in choosing a gym class, and an alumnus reminded frantic packers to bring cold medicine.

The site has caught on with upperclassmen and alumni because they remember how daunting the transition to dormitory life can be, says Rachel Andoga, a sophomore who helps run the LiveJournal blog and posts regularly under the name "rachigurl5." "I imagine that if I'd had something like this when I came to college, I wouldn't have been as insanely nervous about starting out," she says. "Everyone's so friendly on the site."

Ms. Andoga hopes that the blog will survive the start of the academic year and become an informal bulletin board where first-year students can organize study sessions and publicize extracurricular activities. The bonds that students have formed on the site are real, she says. She expects to drop in on several freshman bloggers to see how they are adjusting to college, and she is helping to plan a party for all the Davidson students who joined the LiveJournal community.

## Lurking Administrators

Davidson administrators, too, have been tuning in to the blog—even though they had no part in its creation—in an effort to determine what issues freshmen are most worried about.

"I think I've spent as much time on the site as the students have," jokes Leslie Marsicano, director of residence life at the college. "It's been riveting and addicting for me."

She has recommended the site to students and parents who called her office with niggling questions about bedsheets and laundry arrangements. Some students have speculated that she had recruited upperclassmen to log on and serve as mentors to incoming students.

To the contrary, she says she's strictly a watcher of the blog. "I think if we tried to encourage the site we'd spoil it," she says. "It works so much better because it comes from the grass roots, and there's no administration figures for students to be suspicious of."

But Davidson officials do have a vested interest in the online gathering. For many prospective students, Ms. Marsicano says, the Web log may be a more effective form of advertisement than a glossy brochure or even a college visit. High-school students

---

# Chemistry 115, Midnight Treks, and Knitting: Online Reassurance at Davidson College

Users who post messages on Davidson College's student-run Web log, or blog, discuss a wide range of topics, including course schedules, extracurricular activities, and their views of college life. A sampling of comments:

**sleeprocker (August 13, 1:27 A.M.):** I signed up for Organic Chemistry, but now I think I want to drop back to Chem 115. The course schedule says that all the sections are full right now. How likely is it that I can make the switch?

**nayetter (August 13, 7:17 A.M.):** Go to the 115 class on the first day (or both 115 classes, if you can) and talk to the professor, and explain your situation to him. He won't be able to raise the ceiling beyond how many students can fit in the lab at once, but if you talk to him then he'll do his best to accommodate your needs.

Also, watching the "add/drop" page like a hawk is a good idea.

**squirrelhanded (August 15, 10:18 P.M.):** Here's a piece of advice. . . . If you have the choice between having an incredible talk with a good friend in the hallway or getting 3 extra hours of sleep . . . take the talk. If it's between ANOTHER 5-point math assignment and a midnight magi-cal mystery trek through town. . . . go crazy. Have a good time.

Don't get me wrong, academics are priority. They're the reason we're all here in the first place. . . . but choose your memories. Make them lasting ones.

**rachigurl5 (August 16, 8:28 A.M.):** Exactly. Education isn't limited to the classroom . . . God, if I had a nickel for every Great Thing I've learned from long midnight talks . . . le sigh!

**superluci (August 18, 3:23 A.M.):** I haven't been able to find out anything about this online. I'm a knitter, and I'm looking for yarn stores in the Davidson area. Are there any stores selling yarn and knitting supplies near the college? I'm stocked up reasonably well coming in but I doubt my supply will last long. I love knitting with other people so if anybody wants to knit with me or have stitch & bitch parties that would be awesome! See you all. . . . TODAY!: Belk 243, come by and chat!

**advice_and_ice (August 18, 6:51 A.M.):** There's a knitting store on main street. Would a crocheter be welcome occasionally?

choosing between Davidson and its competitors are adept at tracking down student Web logs and are likely to trust them to provide an unfiltered view of college life, she says.

Davidson is lucky: The blog has been consistently cheery and cordial. But Ms. Marsicano says she'd be unhappy if she felt that students were misrepresenting the institution. "When parents call me to ask how long the beds are, they're really asking if there's some nice person who will look after their baby," she says. "I'd like to be able to keep pointing to this site to say, 'The kids can take care of each other.'"

## Bonding Online

Blogs are not the only online forums that have developed to help incoming students break the ice with classmates. Many students are using e-mail lists and social-networking sites like Friendster and Thefacebook to make bonds before arriving on the campus.

For Anna Dinndorf, a freshman at Washington University in St. Louis, a personal Web log and an online discussion group led to romance. Last spring she mentioned her early-admission acceptance in her online journal, a daily blog she maintains on the popular Web site Diaryland. Another blogger who had been admitted to Washington spotted the entry and invited Ms. Dinndorf to join a growing group of incoming students in a discussion forum that makes use of a free service by Yahoo, the popular search site.

"I had never spoken to her before, and I never spoke to her after that, but she clued me in, and for that I'm very thankful," Ms. Dinndorf says.

In the Yahoo group, users not only post questions about courses and dorm preparations at Washington, but contribute to a database of students' contact information, exchange screen names so they can chat on instant-messaging software, and create informal polls that ask their peers to comment on matters both political and personal. For example, almost none of the incoming freshmen approve of the Bush administration's proposed Constitutional amendment to ban gay marriage. On a lighter note, most students said they order soft drinks by asking for "soda" instead of "pop" or "Coke."

## Chattier Comments

With more than 200 students registered, the discussion at Washington is chattier and less focused than the Davidson blog. It's also a bit franker: Some students grouse about their housing assignments or other matters. But the incoming students, by and large, seem to have few quibbles with Washington, and administrators surfing the site would find little to worry about.

For most students, the site is more about socializing than it is for airing serious concerns. Ms. Dinndorf says she's spent much of her time on the site just meeting people, including a fellow freshman whom she now calls her boyfriend. The pair, it turns out, have met only once in real life, but they've gotten to know each other through posts on the discussion board and on AOL Instant Messenger chats.

"We started out talking online and things developed, and then we met in person when I went to Washington for a weekend in July," says Ms. Dinndorf. "It's so great to be going down to school and already have all these connections."

The connections, she says, are forged by jokes and gossip as much as by serious conversations. Some students took notice when a rumor popped up on the board that the radio "shock jock" Howard Stern's daughter would be part of the Class of 2008 at Washington, but, ultimately, the claim was debunked.

For Ms. Dinndorf, that light touch is a welcome distraction from the often tense process of preparing to move away from home. "Basically, the site has been like a sounding board for all the precollege jitters and worries and questions and everything that everyone goes through at this point," she says. "And I'm really addicted to it."

# Romance in the Information Age

Christine Rosen

When Samuel F. B. Morse sent his first long-distance telegraph message in 1844, he chose words that emphasized both the awe and apprehension he felt about his new device. "What hath God wrought?" read the paper tape message of dots and dashes sent from the U.S. Capitol building to Morse's associates in Baltimore. Morse proved prescient about the potential scope and significance of his technology. In less than a decade, telegraph wires spread throughout all but one state east of the Mississippi River; by 1861, they spanned the continent; and by 1866, a transatlantic telegraph cable connected the United States to Europe.

The telegraph, and later, the telephone, forever changed the way we communicate. But the triumph wrought by these technologies was not merely practical. Subtly and not so subtly, these technologies also altered the range of ways we reveal ourselves. Writing in 1884, James Russell Lowell wondered a bit nervously about the long-term consequences of the "trooping of emotion" that the electric telegraph, with its fragmented messages, encouraged. Lowell and others feared that the sophisticated new media we were devising might alter not just how we communicate, but how we feel.

Rapid improvement in communication technologies and the expansion of their practical uses continue unabated. Today, of course, we are no longer tethered to telegraph or telephone wires for conversation. Cell phones, e-mail, Internet chatrooms, two-way digital cameras—we can talk to anyone, anywhere, including those we do not know and never see. The ethical challenges raised by these new communication technologies are legion, and not new. Within a decade of the invention of the telephone, for example, we had designed a way to wiretap and listen in on the private conversations flourishing there. And with the Internet, we can create new or false identities for ourselves, mixing real life and personal fantasy in unpredictable ways. The "confidence man" of the nineteenth century, with his dandified ruses, is replaced by the well-chosen screen name and false autobiography of the unscrupulous Internet dater. Modern philosophers of technology have studied the ethical quandaries posed by communication technologies—questioning whether our view of new technologies as simply means to generally positive ends is naïve, and encouraging us to consider whether our many devices have effected subtle transformations on our natures.

But too little consideration has been given to the question of how our use of these technologies influences our emotions. Do certain methods of communication flatten emotional appeals, promote immediacy rather than thoughtful reflection, and encourage accessibility and transparency at the expense of necessary boundaries? Do our technologies change the way we feel, act, and think?

## Love and E-Mail

There is perhaps no realm in which this question has more salience than that of romantic love. How do our ubiquitous technologies—cell phones, e-mail, the Internet—impact our ability to find and experience love? Our technical devices are of such extraordinary practical use that we forget they are also increasingly the primary medium for our emotional expression. The technologies we use on a daily basis do not merely change the ways, logistically, we pursue love; they are in some cases transforming the way we think and feel about what, exactly, it is we should be pursuing. They change not simply how we find our beloved, but the kind of beloved we hope to find. In a world where men and women still claim to want to find that one special person—a "soul mate"—to spend their life with, what role can and should we afford technology and, more broadly, science, in their efforts?

### *Love after Courtship*

The pursuit of love in its modern, technological guise has its roots in the decline of courtship and is indelibly marked by that loss. Courtship as it once existed—a practice that assumed adherence to certain social conventions, and recognition of the differences, physical and emotional, between men and women—has had its share of pleased obituarists. The most vigorous have been feminists, the more radical of whom appear to take special delight in quelling notions of romantic love. Recall Andrea Dworkin's infamous equation of marriage and rape, or Germaine Greer's terrifying rant in *The Female Eunuch:* "Love, love, love—all the wretched cant of it, masking egotism, lust, masochism, fantasy under a mythology of sentimental postures, a welter of self-induced miseries and joys, blinding and masking the essential personalities in the frozen gestures of courtship, in the kissing and the dating and the desire, the compliments and the quarrels which vivify its barrenness." Much of this work is merely an unpersuasive attempt to swaddle basic human bitterness in the language of female empowerment. But such sentiments have had their effect on our culture's understanding of courtship.

More thoughtful chroniclers of the institution's demise have noted the cultural and technological forces that challenged courtship in the late nineteenth and early twentieth century, eroding the power of human chaperones, once its most effective guardians. As Leon Kass persuasively argued in an essay in *The Public Interest,* the obstacles to courtship "spring from the very heart of liberal democratic society and of modernity altogether." The automobile did more for unsupervised sexual exploration than many technologies in use today, for example, and by twentieth century's end, the ease and availability of effective contraceptive devices, especially the birth control pill, had freed men and women to pursue sexual experience without the risk of pregnancy. With technical advances came a shift in social mores. As historian Jacques Barzun has noted, strict manners gave way to informality, "for etiquette is a barrier, the casual style an invitation."

Whether one laments or praises courtship's decline, it is clear that we have yet to locate a successful replacement for it—evidently it is not as simple as hustling the aging coquette out the door to make way for the vigorous debutante. On the contrary, our current courting practices—if they can be called that—yield an increasing number of those aging coquettes, as well as scores of unsettled bachelors. On college campuses, young men and women have long since ceased formally dating and instead participate in a "hooking up" culture that favors the sexually promiscuous and emotionally disinterested while punishing those intent on commitment. Adults hardly fare better: as the author of a report released in January by the Chicago Health and Social Life Survey told CNN, "on average, half your life is going to be in this single and dating state, and this is a big change from the 1950s." Many men and women now spend the decades of their twenties and thirties sampling each other's sexual wares and engaging in fits of serial out-of-wedlock domesticity, never finding a marriageable partner.

In the 1990s, books such as *The Rules,* which outlined a rigorous and often self-abnegating plan for modern dating, and observers such as Wendy Shalit, who called for greater modesty and the withholding of sexual favors by women, represented a well-intentioned, if doomed, attempt to revive the old courting boundaries. Cultural observers today, however, claim we are in the midst of a new social revolution that requires looking to the future for solutions, not the past. "We're in a period of dramatic change in our mating practices," Barbara Dafoe Whitehead told a reporter for *U.S. News & World Report* recently. Whitehead, co-director of the National Marriage Project at Rutgers University, is the author of *Why There are No Good Men Left,* one in a booming mini-genre of books that offer road maps for the revolution. Whitehead views technology as one of our best solutions—Isolde can now find her Tristan on the Internet (though presumably with a less tragic finale). "The traditional mating system where people met someone in their neighborhood or college is pretty much dead," Whitehead told

CBS recently. "What we have is a huge population of working singles who have limited opportunities to go through some elaborate courtship."

Although Whitehead is correct in her diagnosis of the problem, neither she nor the mavens of modesty offer a satisfactory answer to this new challenge. A return to the old rules and rituals of courtship—however appealing in theory—is neither practical nor desirable for the majority of men and women. But the uncritical embrace of technological solutions to our romantic malaise—such as Internet dating—is not a long-term solution either. What we need to do is create new boundaries, devise better guideposts, and enforce new mores for our technological age. First, however, we must understand the peculiar challenges to romantic success posed by our technologies.

## Full Disclosure

Although not the root cause of our romantic malaise, our communication technologies are at least partly culpable, for they encourage the erosion of the boundaries that are necessary for the growth of successful relationships. Our technologies enable and often promote two detrimental forces in modern relationships: the demand for total transparency and a bias toward the over-sharing of personal information.

# To Google or Not to Google

With the breakdown of the old hierarchies and boundaries that characterized courtship, there are far fewer opportunities to glean information about the vast world of strangers we encounter daily. We can little rely on town gossips or networks of extended kin for background knowledge; there are far fewer geographic boundaries marking people from "the good part of town"; no longer can we read sartorial signals, such as a well-cut suit or an expensive shoe, to place people as in earlier ages. This is all, for the most part, a good thing. But how, then, do people find out about each other? Few self-possessed people with an Internet connection could resist answering that question with one word: Google. "To google"—now an acceptable if ill-begotten verb—is the practice of typing a person's name into an Internet search engine to find out what the world knows and says about him or her. As one writer confessed in the *New York Observer,* after meeting an attractive man at a midtown bar: "Like many of my twenty-something peers in New York's dating jungle, I have begun to use Google.com, as well as other online search engines, to perform secret background checks on potential mates. It's not perfect, but it's a discreet way of obtaining important, useless and sometimes bizarre information about people in Manhattan—and it's proven to be as reliable as the scurrilous gossip you get from friends."

That is—not reliable at all. What Google and other Internet search engines provide is a quick glimpse—a best and worst list—of a person, not a fully drawn portrait. In fact, the transparency promised by technologies such as Internet search engines is a convenient substitute for something we used to assume would develop over time, but which fewer people today seem willing to cultivate patiently: trust. As the single Manhattanite writing in the *Observer* noted, "You never know. He seemed nice that night, but he could be anyone from a rapist or murderer to a brilliant author or championship swimmer."

In sum, transparency does not guarantee trust. It can, in fact, prove effective at eroding it—especially when the expectation of transparency and the available technological tools nudge the suspicious to engage in more invasive forms of investigation or surveillance. One woman I interviewed, who asked that her name not be revealed, was suspicious that her live-in boyfriend of two years was unfaithful when her own frequent business trips took her away from home. Unwilling to confront him directly with her doubts, she turned to a technological solution. Unbeknownst to him, she installed a popular brand of "spyware" on his computer, which recorded every keystroke he made and took snapshots of his screen every three minutes—information that the program then e-mailed to her for inspection. "My suspicions were founded," she said, although the revelation was hardly good news. "He was spending hours online looking at porn, and going to 'hook-up' chatrooms seeking sex with strangers. I even tracked his ATM withdrawals to locations near his scheduled meetings with other women."

She ended the relationship, but remains unrepentant about deploying surveillance technology against her mate. Considering the amount of information she could find out about her partner by merely surfing the Internet, she rationalized her use of spyware as just one more tool—if a slightly more invasive one—at the disposal of those seeking information about another person. As our technologies give us ever-greater power to uncover more about each other, demand for transparency rises, and our expectations of privacy decline.

The other destructive tendency our technologies encourage is over-sharing—that is, revealing too much, too quickly, in the hope of connecting to another person. The opportunities for instant communication are so ubiquitous—e-mail, instant messaging, chatrooms, cell phones, Palm Pilots, Black-Berrys, and the like—that the notion of making ourselves unavailable to anyone is unheard of, and constant access a near-requirement. As a result, the multitude of outlets for expressing ourselves has allowed the level of idle chatter to reach a depressing din. The inevitable result is a repeal of the reticence necessary for fostering successful relationships in the long term. Information about another person is best revealed a bit at a time, in a give-and-take exchange, not in a rush of overexposed feeling.

## The Bachelor

Perhaps the best example of this tendency is reality TV and its spawn. Programs like *The Bachelor* and *The Bachelorette,* as well as pseudo-documentary shows such as *A Dating Story* (and *A Wedding Story* and *A Baby Story*) on The Learning Channel, transform the longings of the human heart into top Nielsen ratings by encouraging the lovelorn to discuss in depth and at length every feeling they have, every moment they have it, as the cameras roll. Romances begin, blossom, and occasionally end in the space of half an hour, and audiences—privy to even the most excruciatingly staged expressions of love and devotion—nevertheless gain the illusion of having seen "real" examples of dating, wedding, or marriage.

On the Internet, dating blogs offer a similar sophomoric voyeurism. One dating blogger, who calls himself Quigley, keeps a dreary tally of his many unsuccessful attempts to meet women, peppering his diary with adolescent observations about women he sees on television. Another dating blogger, who describes herself as an "attractive 35-year old," writes "A Day in the Life of Jane," a dating diary about her online dating travails. Reflecting on one of her early experiences, she writes: "But what did I learn from Owen? That online dating isn't so different from regular dating. It has its pros and cons: Pros—you learn a lot more about a person much more quickly, that a person isn't always what they seem or what you believe them to be, that you have to be really honest with yourself and the person you are communicating with; Cons—uh, same as the pros!"

## BadXPartners.com

Successful relationships are not immune to the over-sharing impulse, either; a plethora of wedding websites such as SharetheMoments.com and TheKnot.com offer up the intimate details of couples' wedding planning and ceremonies—right down to the brand of tie worn by the groom and the "intimate" vows exchanged by the couple. And, if things go awry, there are an increasing number of revenge websites such as BadXPartners.com, which offers people who've been dumped an opportunity for petty revenge. "Create a comical case file of your BadX-Partners for the whole world to see!" the website urges. Like the impulse to Google, the site plays on people's fears of being misled, encouraging people to search the database for stories of bad exes: "Just met someone new? Think they are just the one for you? Well remember, they are probably someone else's X. . . . Find out about Bill from Birmingham's strange habits or Tracy from Texas' suspect hygiene. Better safe than sorry!"

Like the steady work of the wrecking ball, our culture's nearly-compulsive demand for personal revelation, emotional exposure, and sharing of feelings threatens the fragile edifice of newly-forming relationships. Transparency and complete access are exactly what you want to avoid in the early stages of romance. Successful courtship—even successful flirtation—require the gradual peeling away of layers, some deliberately constructed, others part of a person's character and personality, that make us mysteries to each other.

Among Pascal's minor works is an essay, "Discourse on the Passion of Love," in which he argues for the keen "pleasure of loving without daring to tell it." "In love," Pascal writes, "silence is of more avail than speech . . . there is an eloquence in silence that penetrates more deeply than language can." Pascal imagined his lovers in each other's physical presence, watchful of unspoken physical gestures, but not speaking. Only gradually would they reveal themselves. Today such a tableau seems as arcane as Kabuki theater; modern couples exchange the most intimate details of their lives on a first date and then return home to blog about it.

"It's difficult," said one woman I talked to who has tried—and ultimately soured on—Internet dating. "You're expected to be both informal and funny in your e-mails, and reveal your likes and dislikes, but you don't want to reveal so much that you appear desperate, or so little so that you seem distant." We can, of course, use these technologies appropriately and effectively in the service of advancing a relationship, but to do so both people must understand the potential dangers. One man I interviewed described a relationship that began promisingly but quickly took a technological turn for the worse. After a few successful dates, he encouraged the woman he was seeing, who lived in another city, to keep in touch. Impervious to notions of technological etiquette, however, she took this to mean the floodgates were officially open. She began telephoning him at all hours, sending overly-wrought e-mails and inundating him with lengthy, faxed letters—all of which had the effect not of bringing them closer together, which was clearly her hope, but of sending him scurrying away as fast as he could. Later, however, he became involved in a relationship in which e-mail in particular helped facilitate the courtship, and where technology—bounded by a respect on the part of both people for its excesses—helped rather than harmed the process of learning about another person. Technology itself is not to blame; it is our ignorance of its potential dangers and our unwillingness to exercise self-restraint in its use that makes mischief.

## The Modern-Day Matchmaker

Internet dating offers an interesting case study of these technological risks, for it encourages both transparency and oversharing, as well as another danger: it insists that we reduce and market ourselves as the disembodied sum of our parts. The woman or man you might have met on the subway platform or in a coffee shop—within a richer context that includes immediate impressions based on the other person's physical gestures, attire, tone of voice, and overall demeanor—is instead electronically embalmed for your efficient perusal online.

And it is a booming business. Approximately forty percent of American adults are single, and half of that population claims to have visited an online dating site. Revenue for online dating services exceeded $302 million in 2002. There is, not surprisingly, something for the profusion of tastes: behemoth sites such as Match.com, Flirt.com, Hypermatch.com, and Matchmaker.com traffic in thousands of profiles. Niche sites such as Dateable.org for people with disabilities, as well as sites devoted to finding true love for foot fetishists, animal lovers, and the obese, cater to smaller markets. Single people with religious preferences can visit Jdate.com (for Jewish dates), CatholicSingles.com, and even HappyBuddhist.com to find similarly-minded spiritual singles. As with any product, new features are added constantly to maintain consumer interest; even the more jaded seekers of love might quail at Match.com's recent addition to its menu of online options: a form of "speed dating" that offers a certain brutal efficiency as a lure for the time-challenged modern singleton.

## A Case Study

One woman I interviewed, an attractive, successful consultant, tried online dating because her hectic work schedule left her little time to meet new people. She went to Match.com, entered her zip code, and began perusing profiles. She quickly decided to post her own. "When you first put your profile on Match.com," she said, "it's like walking into a kennel with a pork chop around your neck. You're bombarded with e-mails from men." She received well over one hundred solicitations. She responded to a few with a "wink," an electronic gesture that allows another person to know you've seen their profile and are interested—but not interested enough to commit to sending an e-mail message. More alluring profiles garnered an e-mail introduction.

After meeting several different men for coffee, she settled on one in particular and they dated for several months. The vagaries of online dating, however, quickly present new challenges to relationship etiquette. In her case, after several months of successful dating, she and her boyfriend agreed to take their Match.com profiles down from the site. Since they were no longer "single and looking," but single and dating, this seemed to make sense—at least to her. Checking Match.com a week later, however, she found her boyfriend's profile still up and actively advertising himself as available. They are still together, although she confesses to a new wariness about his willingness to commit.

The rapid growth of Internet dating has led to the erosion of the stigma that used to be attached to having "met someone on the Internet" (although none of the people I interviewed for this article would allow their names to be used). And Internet dating itself is becoming increasingly professionalized—with consultants, how-to books, and "expert" analysis crowding out the earlier generation of websites. This February, a "commonsense guide to successful Internet dating" entitled *I Can't Believe I'm Buying This Book* hit bookstores. *Publishers Weekly* describes the author, an "Internet dating consultant," as "a self-proclaimed online serial dater" who "admits he's never sustained a relationship for more than seven months," yet nevertheless "entertainingly reviews how to present one's self on the Web."

Designing the "dating software" that facilitates online romance is a science all its own. *U.S. News & World Report* recently described the efforts of Michael Georgeff, who once designed software to aid the space shuttle program, to devise similar algorithms to assess and predict people's preferences for each other. "Say you score a 3 on the introvert scale, and a 6 on touchy-feely," he told a reporter. "Will you tend to like somebody who's practical?" His weAttract.com software purports to provide the answer. On the company's website, amid close-ups of the faces of a strangely androgynous, snuggling couple, weAttract—whose software is used by Match.com—encourages visitors to "Find someone who considers your quirks adorable." Fair enough. But the motto of weAttract—"Discover your instinctual preferences"—is itself a contradiction. If preferences are instinctual, why do you need the aid of experts like weAttract to discover them?

We need them because we have come to mistrust our own sensibilities. What is emerging on the Internet is a glorification of scientific and technological solutions to the challenge of finding love. The expectation of romantic happiness is so great that extraordinary, scientific means for achieving it are required—or so these companies would have you believe. For example, Emode, whose pop-up ads are now so common that they are the Internet equivalent of a swarm of pesky gnats, promotes "Tickle Matchmaking," a service promising "accurate, Ph.D. certified compatibility scores with every member!"

# EHarmony.com

The apotheosis of this way of thinking is a site called eHarmony.com, whose motto, "Fall in love for the right reasons," soothes prospective swains with the comforting rhetoric of professional science. "Who knew science and love were so compatible?" asks the site, which is rife with the language of the laboratory: "scientifically-proven set of compatibility principles," "based on 35 years of empirical and clinical research," "patent-pending matching technology," "exhaustively researched" methods, and "the most powerful system available." As the founder of eHarmony told *U.S. News & World Report* recently, we are all too eager—desperate, even—to hustle down the aisle. "In this culture," he said, "if we like the person's looks, if they have an ability to chatter at a cocktail party, and a little bit of status, we're halfway to marriage. We're such suckers." EHarmony's answer to such unscientific mating practices is a trademarked "Compatibility Matching System" that promises to "connect you with singles who are compatible with you in 29 of the most important areas of life." As the literature constantly reminds the dreamy romantics among us, "Surprisingly, a good match is more science than art."

EHarmony's insistence that the search for true love is no realm for amateurs is, of course, absurdly self-justifying. "You should realize," their website admonishes, after outlining the "29 dimensions" of personality their compatibility software examines, "that it is still next to impossible to correctly evaluate them on your own with each person you think may be right for you." Instead you must pay eHarmony to do it for you. As you read the "scientific" proof, the reassuring sales pitch washes over you: "Let eHarmony make sure that the next time you fall in love, it's with the right person."

In other words, don't trust your instincts, trust science. With a tasteful touch of contempt, eHarmony notes that its purpose is not merely dating, as it is for megasites such as Match.com. "Our goal is to help you find your soul mate." Four pages of testimonials on the website encourage the surrender to eHarmony's expertise, with promises of imminent collision with "your" soul mate: "From the minute we began e-mailing and talking on the phone, we knew we had found our soul mate," say Lisa and Darryl from Dover, Pennsylvania. "It took some time," confessed Annie of Kansas City, Missouri, "but once I met John, I knew that they had made good on their promise to help me find my soul mate."

Some observers see in these new "scientific" mating rituals a return to an earlier time of courtship and chaperoned dating. *Newsweek* eagerly described eHarmony as a form of "arranged marriage for the digital age, without the all-powerful parents," and Barbara Dafoe Whitehead argues that the activities of the Internet love seeker "reflect a desire for more structured dating." Promoters of these services see them as an improvement on the mere cruising of glossy photos encouraged by most dating sites, or the unrealistic expectations of "finding true love" promoted by popular culture. Rather, they say, they are like the chaperones of courtship past—vetting appropriate candidates and matching them to your specifications.

# Not Real Matchmakers

As appealing as this might sound, it is unrealistic. Since these sites rely on technological solutions and mathematical algorithms, they are a far cry from the broader and richer knowledge of the old-fashioned matchmaker. A personality quiz cannot possibly reveal the full range of a person's quirks or liabilities. More importantly, the role of the old-fashioned matchmaker was a social one (and still is in certain communities). The matchmaker was embedded within a community that observed certain rituals and whose members shared certain assumptions. But technological matchmaking allows courtship to be conducted entirely in private, devoid of the social norms (and often the physical signals) of romantic success and failure.

Finally, most Internet dating enthusiasts do not contend with a far more alarming challenge: the impact such services have on our idea of what, exactly, it is we should be seeking in another person. Younger men and women, weaned on the Internet and e-mail, are beginning to express a preference for potential dates to break down their vital stats for pre-date perusal, like an Internet dating advertisement. One 25-year old man, a regular on Match.com, confessed to *U.S. News & World Report* that he wished he could have a digital dossier for all of his potential dates: "It's, 'OK, here's where I'm from, here's what I do, here's what I'm looking for. How about you?' " One woman I spoke to, who has been Internet dating for several years, matter-of-factly noted that even a perfunctory glance at a potential date's résumé saves valuable time and energy. "Why trust a glance exchanged across a crowded bar when you can read a person's biography in miniature before deciding to strike up a conversation?" she said. This intolerance for gradual revelation increases the pace of modern courtship and erodes our patience for many things (not the least of which is commencement of sexual relations). The challenge remains the same—to find another person to share your life with—but we have allowed the technologies at our disposal to alter dramatically, even unrecognizably, the way we go about achieving it.

## *The Science of Feeling*

This impulse is part of a much broader phenomenon—the encroachment of science and technology into areas once thought the province of the uniquely intuitive and even the ineffable. Today we program computers to trounce human chess champions, produce poetry, or analyze works of art, watching eagerly as they break things down to a tedious catalog of techniques: the bishop advances, the meter scans, the paintbrush strokes across the canvas. But by enlisting machines to do what once was the creative province of human beings alone, we deliberately narrow our conceptions of genius, creativity, and art. The *New York Times* recently featured the work of Franco Moretti, a comparative literature professor at Stanford, who promotes "a more rational literary history" that jettisons the old-fashioned reading of texts in favor of statistical models of literary output. His dream, he told reporter Emily Eakin, "is of a literary class that would look more like a lab than a Platonic academy."

Yet this "scientific" approach to artistic work yields chillingly antiseptic results: "Tennyson's mind is to be treated like his intestines after a barium meal," historian Jacques Barzun noted with some exasperation of the trend's earlier incarnations. Critic Lionel Trilling parodied the tendency in 1950 in his book, *The Liberal Imagination.* By this way of thinking, Trilling said, the story of Romeo and Juliet is no longer the tragic tale of a young man and woman falling in love, but becomes instead a chronicle of how, "their libidinal impulses being reciprocal, they activated their individual erotic drives and integrated them within the same frame of reference."

What Barzun and Trilling were expressing was a distaste for viewing art as merely an abstraction of measurable, improvable impulses. The same is true for love. We can study the physiological functions of the human heart with echocardiograms, stress tests, blood pressure readings, and the like. We can examine, analyze, and investigate ad nauseum the physical act of sex. But we cannot so easily measure the desires of the heart. How do you prove that love exists? How do we know that love is "real"? What makes the love of two lovers last?

There is a danger in relying wholly or even largely on science and technology to answer these questions, for it risks eroding our appreciation of the ineffable things—intuition and physical attraction, passion and sensibility—by reducing these feelings to scientifically explained physiological facts. Today we catalog the influence of hormones, pheromones, dopamine, and serotonin in human attraction, and map our own brains to discover which synapses trigger laughter, lying, or orgasm. Evolutionary psychology explains our desire for symmetrical faces and fertile-looking forms, even as it has little to tell us about the extremes to which we are taking its directives with plastic surgery. Scientific study of our communication patterns and techniques explains why it is we talk the way we do. Even the activities of the bedroom are thoroughly analyzed and professionalized, as women today take instruction from a class of professionals whose arts used to be less esteemed. Prostitutes now run sex seminars, for example, and a recent episode of Oprah featured exotic pole dancers who teach suburban housewives how to titillate their husbands by turning the basement rec room into a simulacrum of a Vegas show girl venue.

Science continues to turn sex (and, by association, love and romance) into something quantifiable and open to manipulation and solution. Science and technology offer us pharmaceuticals to enhance libido and erectile function, and popular culture responds by rigorously ranking and discussing all matters sexual—from the disturbingly frank talk of female characters on Sex and the City to the proliferation of "blind date" shows which subject hapless love-seekers to the withering gaze of a sarcastic host and his viewing audience. "What a loser!" cackled the host of the reality television program Blind Date, after one ignominious bachelor botched his chance for a good night kiss. "The march of science," Barzun wrote, "produces the feeling that nobody in the past has ever done things right. Whether it's teaching or copulation, it has 'problems' that 'research' should solve by telling us just how, the best way."

## *Test-Driving Your Soul Mate*

Why is the steady march of science and technology in these areas a problem? Shouldn't we be proud of our expanding knowledge and the tools that knowledge gives us? Not necessarily. Writing recently in the journal Techné, Hector Jose Huyke noted the broader dangers posed by the proliferation of our technologies, particularly the tendency to "devalue the near." "When a technology is introduced it, presumably, simply adds options to already existing options," he writes. But this is not how technology's influence plays out in practice. In fact, as Huyke argues, "as what is difficult to obtain becomes repeatedly and easily accessible, other practices and experiences are left out—they do not remain unchanged." The man who sends an e-mail to his brother is not merely choosing to write an e-mail and thus adding to his range of communication options; he is choosing not to make a phone call or write a letter. A woman who e-mails a stranger on the Internet is choosing not to go to a local art exhibit and perhaps meet someone in person. "Communications technologies indeed multiply options," says Huyke. "An increase in options, however, does not imply or even serve an advance in communications." Technologies, in other words, often make possible "what would otherwise be difficult to obtain." But they do so by eliminating other paths.

## Personal Ads

Love and genuine commitment have always been difficult to attain, and they are perhaps more so today since it is the individual bonds of affection—not family alliance, property transfer, social class, or religious orthodoxy—that form the cornerstone of most modern marriages. Yet there remains a certain grim efficiency to the vast realm of love technologies at our disposal. After a while, perusing Internet personal ads is like being besieged by an aggressive real estate agent hoping to unload that tired brick colonial. Each person points out his or her supposedly unique features with the same banal descriptions ("adventurous," "sexy," "trustworthy") never conveying a genuine sense of the whole. Machine metaphors, tellingly, crop up often, with women and men willingly categorizing themselves as "high maintenance" or "low maintenance," much as one might describe a car or small kitchen appliance. As an executive of one online dating service told a reporter recently, "If you want to buy a car, you get a lot of information before you even test-drive. There hasn't been a way to do that with relationships."

But we have been "test driving" something: a new, technological method of courtship. And although it is too soon to deliver a final verdict, it is clear that it is a method prone to serious problems. The efficiency of our new techniques and their tendency to focus on people as products leaves us at risk of understanding ourselves this way, too—like products with certain malfunctioning parts and particular assets. But products must be constantly improved upon and marketed. In the pursuit of love, and in a world where multiple partners are sampled before one is selected, this fuels a hectic culture of self-improvement—honing the witty summary of one's most desirable traits for placement in personal advertisements is only the beginning. Today, men and women convene focus groups of former lovers to gain critical insights into their behavior so as to avoid future failure; and the perfection of appearance through surgical and non-surgical means occupies an increasing amount of people's time and energy.

Our new technological methods of courtship also elevate efficient communication over personal communication. Ironically, the Internet, which offers many opportunities to meet and communicate with new people, robs us of the ability to deploy one of our greatest charms—nonverbal communication. The emoticon is a weak substitute for a coy gesture or a lusty wink. More fundamentally, our technologies encourage a misunderstanding of what courtship should be. Real courtship is about persuasion, not marketing, and the techniques of the laboratory cannot help us translate the motivations of the heart.

The response is not to retreat into Luddism, of course. In a world where technology allows us to meet, date, marry, and even divorce online, there is no returning to the innocence of an earlier time. What we need is a better understanding of the risks of these new technologies and a willingness to exercise restraint in using them. For better or worse, we are now a society of sexually liberated individuals seeking "soul mates"—yet the privacy, gradualism, and boundaries that are necessary for separating the romantic wheat from the chaff still elude us.

# Alchemy

Perhaps, in our technologically saturated age, we would do better to rediscover an earlier science: alchemy. Not alchemy in its original meaning—a branch of speculative philosophy whose devotees attempted to create gold from base metals and hence cure disease and prolong life—but alchemy in its secondary definition: "a power or process of transforming something common into something precious." From our daily, common interactions with other people might spring something precious—but only if we have the patience to let it flourish. Technology and science often conspire against such patience. Goethe wrote, "We should do our utmost to encourage the Beautiful, for the Useful encourages itself." There is an eminent usefulness to many of our technologies—e-mail and cell phones allow us to span great distances to communicate with family, friends, and lovers, and the Internet connects us to worlds unknown. But they are less successful at encouraging the flourishing of the lasting and beautiful. Like the Beautiful, love occurs in unexpected places, often not where it is being sought. It can flourish only if we accept that our technologies and our science can never fully explain it.

---

**CHRISTINE ROSEN** is a senior editor of *The New Atlantis* and resident fellow at the Ethics and Public Policy Center. Her book *Preaching Eugenics: Religious Leaders and the American Eugenics Movement* was just published by Oxford University Press.

---

# E-Mail Is for Old People

**As students ignore their campus accounts, colleges try new ways of communicating.**

Dan Carnevale

Maurice Johnson, a freshman studying interior design at Harcum College, spends hours each day online, both for work and play. One thing he rarely does, though, is open his campus e-mail account. "I check it about every other month," he says.

Moe, as his friends call him, has his own fashion label and regularly corresponds with other designers through his MySpace page. He chats with friends through instant messaging. He also has a few commercial e-mail accounts that he checks daily.

But his Harcum account lies dormant. Not only does he prefer other means of communication, but the college e-mail addresses—created by a combination of a student's first and last names plus part of the student's identification number—are too complicated to give out to friends or to check online. "I don't like the Harcum e-mail," he says. "It's too confusing."

Mr. Johnson is not alone in his disdain for campus e-mail. College officials around the country find that a growing number of students are missing important messages about deadlines, class cancellations, and events sent to them by e-mail because, well, the messages are sent to them by e-mail.

In response, some institutions require that students check their college e-mail accounts so they do not miss announcements, holding students responsible for official information that comes through that medium. Other institutions are attempting to figure out what technology students are using to try to reach them there.

A 2005 report from the Pew Internet and American Life Project called "Teens and Technology" found that teenagers preferred new technology, like instant messaging or text messaging, for talking to friends and use e-mail to communicate with "old people." Along the same lines, students interviewed for this article say they still depend on e-mail to communicate with their professors. But many of the students say they would rather send text messages to friends, to reach them wherever they are, than send e-mail messages that might not be seen until hours later.

Students have not given up on e-mail altogether. In fact, a survey of more than 1,300 students at the University of Illinois at Chicago earlier this year found that 86 percent of them still use campus e-mail regularly. Eszter Hargittai, an assistant professor of communication studies and sociology at Northwestern University who conducted the survey, says students often ignore messages coming from their colleges, considering them a form of spam.

Brian Niles, chief executive officer of TargetX, a company that helps colleges use technology to recruit new students, says colleges need to branch out and find new ways to connect with students.

"It's not that they don't read e-mail," Mr. Niles says. "It's that they have their own world, and you need to know how to reach them in that world."

## 'Big Family'

Harcum, a two-year college outside Philadelphia, enrolls about 900 students. It is the type of institution where the college president's wife can be found tending to the plants in front of campus buildings. "Harcum's a very big family," says Lisa A. Mixon, assistant director of public relations and marketing.

Ms. Mixon created the college's MySpace page (http://myspace.com/harcumcollege) after she realized that many students were missing important messages. They were paying no attention to the college e-mail newsletter. They were not even showing up for ice-cream socials—and everyone likes ice cream.

It seemed clear that students were not ignoring their MySpace pages, though. Some students here have more than one such page. Some have MySpace pages for their pet snakes.

A key feature of MySpace and other social-networking sites is the ability to link with another user by designating him or her a "friend." Friends are able to send each other messages and announcements, and view pictures and items that are blocked from other users.

After the college put up its site in August, Ms. Mixon searched online for Harcum students with MySpace pages and found more than 200 of them. She contacted the students individually, over the course of a few weeks, and asked each of them to become a friend of the college. So far, more than 160 have said yes.

Joseph J. Diorio, Harcum's director of public relations and marketing, who admits that he relies on Ms. Mixon to keep him "hip," says he finds the online service to be a good way for the college and its students to get to know each other better.

Using MySpace is like "being able to walk into a residence hall and everybody's door is open," says Mr. Diorio. "We knew that's where students were going."

Harcum keeps its MySpace page lively, with photos of students on the campus. Officials have also posted a picture of a cartoon rabbit with the caption: "College prepares you for the real world, which also sucks."

"We thought, What the heck, it's not the official Harcum Web page," Mr. Diorio says.

A student also writes a weekly blog for the college MySpace page. Current blog posts include some complaints about cafeteria food interjected in discussions about forthcoming events. Ms. Mixon plans to invite additional students to write for the blog, letting them vent honestly about anything on their minds.

---

## Reaching Students

As some students reduce their use of e-mail in favor of other means of communication, colleges are trying new technologies to reach them. Among the new techniques:

### Cellphone Text Messages

Students live and die by their cellphones. A few colleges now provide information, including snow closures and sports scores, to students instantly, wherever they are.

### Instant Messages

Some professors now make themselves available to students via instant-messaging software, especially during office hours. And some admissions counselors use it to answer questions from prospective students faster, and through a medium in which many students are most comfortable.

### MySpace and Facebook

Some colleges have begun using the popular social-networking services to provide information to their students, including calendars of events, deadlines, and other announcements. College officials also use the services to present a lighter side of an institution—something different from the stuffy main Web page.

---

"They like Harcum," she says, "but they'd be honest about things they didn't like."

## 'Not as Formal'

In addition, the Harcum MySpace page includes dates of important events, such as volleyball games and alumni weekends. It also allows students to pose general questions to college officials, if they are not sure whom they need to talk to. "If they have a question and they can't get to the right person," Ms. Mixon says, "they have someplace to go."

Ashley M. Elliott, a veterinary-technology student in her second year at Harcum, says the Harcum MySpace page shows the college is making an effort to reach students. "It's down to the student's level," she says. "It's not as formal as the Web site."

Becoming MySpace friends with a college may seem lame to some students. But Steven J. Arnone, another veterinary-technology student in his second year at Harcum, wants to convince his classmates that all the cool kids are doing it.

"I'm spreading the word that it's not stupid," Mr. Arnone says. "To be honest, I'm proud. It's like slapping a college sticker on the back of your car."

The MySpace service asks users to rank their friends, which could put Harcum in the awkward position of seeming to play favorites. Ms. Mixon says she picks the college's top friends randomly. "I just keep rotating them," she says.

She says that the college may have a contest to determine who deserves to be listed as Harcum's favorite friend, possibly judging how much school spirit a student displays on his or her MySpace page.

While Harcum has convinced a good portion of its student population to be its friends, some friends are closer than others.

"I'm a friend, but I've never actually been to the site," says Shay Curry, who is in her first year studying early-childhood education at Harcum.

Ms. Curry says she felt obligated to befriend Harcum when the request came in—even though the invitation did not indicate that it was mandatory to do so.

Matthew J. Roane, a Harcum psychology major who has four e-mail accounts, says he never uses his Harcum account or the college MySpace page. He finds out about announcements and events the old-fashion way—from printed fliers.

## Trying Too Hard?

Just because students use new means of communication does not mean that colleges should, however.

Some students at the University of Maryland at College Park, for instance, say they would rather keep talking to professors and campus officials through e-mail.

"I like to separate my personal life from my school life," says Amanda J. Heilman, a freshman studying animal sciences at the university.

Emily Diehl, another freshman majoring in animal sciences, agrees. "It would be weird if all your professors had Facebook," she says.

But even the students who use their campus e-mail accounts will sometimes not open messages that appear to be from the college.

"These students are walking spam filters," says Paul Lehmann, the director of student activities at Utica College. "They are masters of multiple forms of communication and have perfected the skill of cutting through the multiple forms of communication that they are bombarded with to find what they are interested in and want to reply to."

The result, he says, is that no matter how important the message from the college, students will often choose to ignore it.

"Students receive multiple 'official' messages a day, with information that runs the gamut of importance," says Stephanie Dupaul, director of undergraduate business admissions at Southern Methodist University's business school. "A reminder that there is a free movie in the student center on Friday night hits their in boxes with the same level of urgency as an announcement of registration deadlines or changes in official university policies."

Pennsylvania State University has been trying different ways to use technology to reach students, including podcasts, RSS feeds, and Web video clips.

The university's latest attempt is to use cellphone text messaging, by setting up a service that can blast announcements to students using the technology.

Subscribers to the service can let the university know what types of messages they want to receive. Many choose to get updates on emergency announcements, such as school closures, and some also want to be notified about upcoming concerts or sports scores, which are available seconds after a Nittany Lions game has ended.

Bill Mahon, assistant vice president for university relations at Penn State, says many students use text messaging more than e-mail. So administrators expected the plan to be popular with the students.

"We thought maybe in a year we'd get 2,000 people," Mr. Mahon says of the program, which started in August. "As it turns out, in the first three weeks or so we have 1,000 subscribers."

Mr. Mahon says the service will really come in handy in the winter, when snow can create havoc on campus. And the service has already proved useful, he says. Not long ago, a road near the campus was closed because of an oil spill. Penn State officials were able to let subscribers know immediately, so they could plan an alternate route.

"In the old days, we couldn't do that," Mr. Mahon says. "We just let thousands of people drive on that road to find policemen sending them in a different direction."

Not all students want the cell-phone service, he says. It is best to give them many options. "The key is, you can't do just one thing," he says.

## Web Portals

Harrisburg University of Science and Technology, a new institution that began enrolling students last year, has already run into difficulties communicating with students.

Because many students do not check their e-mail, officials are creating a Web portal for students. James B. Young, associate vice president for information services at the university, says the portal will be a place that lets students register for courses and find out about upcoming events, and that provides other services.

But, he says, it will be much more informal than the main university Web page. He hopes to put a "youthful edge to it."

"We're brand new and we're pushing habits early," Mr. Young says. "Hopefully MyHU will become an indispensable space."

The University of South Carolina Upstate, on the other hand, is sticking with campus e-mail accounts. Officials have informed students that e-mail is the official means of communication and that they must check it.

In the past, any student could send a message via campus e-mail to the entire student population. Students used the capability to find roommates and for other informal matters, but it also led to many unwanted messages for students.

"So they stopped checking it," says Laura Puckett-Boler, assistant vice chancellor for student and diversity affairs. "They were missing announcements."

So the university set up an electronic newsletter, called E-blast, that is sent out once a week with students' informal announcements and requests. Now only certain administrators can send bulk e-mail.

Despite the requirement, not everybody on the campus uses their university e-mail accounts, she says. But students manage to get by, either by forwarding the information to another account, or just learning what they need to know through friends.

"They're still responsible for the information," Ms. Puckett-Boler says. "Students figure out what to do."

# Girl Power

**No rich relatives? no professional mentors? no problem. Ashley Qualls, 17, has built a million-dollar Web site. She's lol all the way to the bank.**

CHUCK SALTER

L ate last year, Ian Moray stumbled across a cotton-candy-pink Web site called Whateverlife.com. As manager of media development at the online marketing company ValueClick Media, he was searching for under-the-radar destinations for notoriously fickle teenagers. Beyond MySpace and Facebook, countless sites come and go in the teen universe, like soon forgotten pop songs. But Whateverlife stood out. It was more authentic somehow. It featured a steady supply of designs for MySpace pages and attracted a few hundred-thousand girls a day. "Clever design, a growing base—that's a no-brainer for us," Moray says.

He approached Ashley Qualls, Whateverlife's founder, about incorporating ads from ValueClick's 450 or so clients and sharing the revenue. At first, she declined. Then a few weeks later she changed her mind. He was in Los Angeles and she was in Detroit, so they arranged everything by phone and email. They still have yet to meet in person.

When did Moray, who's 40, learn that his new business partner was 17 years old?

Pause.

"When our director of marketing told me why FAST COMPANY was calling," says Moray, now ValueClick's director of media development. "I assumed she was a seasoned Internet professional. She knows so much about what her site does, more than people three times her age."

It's like that famous *New Yorker* cartoon. A dog typing away at a computer tells his canine buddy, "On the Internet, nobody knows you're a dog."

At 17 going on 37 (at least), Ashley is very much an Internet professional. In the less than two years since Whateverlife took off, she has dropped out of high school, bought a house, helped launch artists such as Lily Allen, and rejected offers to buy her young company. Although Ashley was flattered to be offered $1.5 million and a car of her choice—as long as the price tag wasn't more than $100,000—she responded, in effect, Whatever.:) "I don't even have my license yet," she says.

Ashley is evidence of the meritocracy on the Internet that allows even companies run by neophyte entrepreneurs to compete, regardless of funding, location, size, or experience—and she's a reminder that ingenuity is ageless. She has taken in more than $1 million, thanks to a now-familiar Web-friendly business model. Her MySpace page layouts are available for the bargain price of . . . nothing. They're free for the taking. Her only significant source of revenue so far is advertising.

According to Google Analytics, Whateverlife attracts more than 7 million individuals and 60 million page views a month. That's a larger audience than the circulations of *Seventeen, Teen Vogue,* and *CosmoGirl!* magazines combined. Although Web-site rankings vary with the methodology, Quantcast, a popular source among advertisers, ranked Whateverlife.com a staggering No. 349 in mid-July out of more than 20 million sites. Among the sites in its rearview mirror: Britannica.com, AmericanIdol .com, FDA.gov, and CBS.com.

And one more, which Ashley can't quite believe herself: "I'm ahead of Oprah!" (Oprah.com: No. 469.) Sure, Ashley is a long way from having Oprah's clout, but she is establishing a platform of her own. "I have this audience of so many people, I can say anything I want to," she says. "I can say, 'Check out this movie or this artist.' It's, like, a rush. I never thought I'd be an influencer." (Attention pollsters: 1,500 girls have added the Join Team Hillary '08 desktop button to their MySpace pages since Ashley offered it in March.)

She has come along with the right idea at the right time. Eager to customize their MySpace profiles, girls cut and paste the HTML code for Whateverlife layouts featuring hearts, flowers, celebrities, and so on onto their personal page and—presto—a new look. Think of it as MySpace clothes; some kids change their layouts nearly as frequently. "It's all about giving girls what they want," Ashley says.

These days, she and her young company are experiencing growing pains. She's learning how to be the boss—of her mother, her friends, developers-for-hire in India. And Whateverlife, one of the first sites offering MySpace layouts specifically for girls, needs to mature as well. "MySpace layouts" was among the top 30 search terms on Google in June. Ashley knows that she needs new content—not just more layouts, but more features, to distinguish Whateverlife from the thousands of sites in the expanding MySpace ecosystem. Earlier this year, she created an online magazine. Cell-phone wallpaper, a new source of revenue at 99 cents to $1.99 a download, is in the works.

Running a growing company without an MBA, not to mention a high-school diploma, is hard enough, but Ashley confronts another extraordinary complication. Business associates may forget that she is 17, but Detroit's Wayne County Probate Court has not. She's a minor with considerable assets—"business affairs that may be jeopardized," the law reads—that need protection in light of the rift her sudden success has caused in an already fractious family. In January, a probate judge ruled that neither Ashley nor her parents could adequately manage her finances. Until she turns 18, next June, a court-appointed conservator is controlling Whateverlife's assets; Ashley must request funds for any expense outside the agreed-upon monthly budget.

The arrangement, she says, affects her ability to react in a volatile industry. "It's not like I'm selling lemonade," she says. Besides, it's her company. If she wants to contract developers or employ her mother, Ashley says, why shouldn't she be able to do it without the conservator's approval?

So the teenager has hired a lawyer. She wants to emancipate herself and be declared an adult. Now. At 17. Why not just sit tight until June? The girl trying to grow up fast can't wait that long.

> I'm doing what everyone says they want to do, "live like there's no tomorrow."
>
> —Ashley in her blog, "The Daily Life of a Simple Kind of Gal," July 1, 2006; 2:43 A.M.

Ashley is different from the recent crop of high-profile teen entrepreneurs. True, her eighth-grade class did vote her "most likely to succeed," but it's safe to say they were predicting 20 or 30 years out, not three years removed from middle school. She created her company almost by accident and without the resources that typically give young novices a leg up. Catherine Cook, 17, started myYearbook.com by teaming up with her older brother, a Harvard grad and Internet entrepreneur. Ben Casnocha, the 19-year-old founder of software company Comcate and author of the new memoir *My Start-Up Life,* is the son of a San Francisco lawyer and has tapped Silicon Valley brains and bank accounts.

But Ashley had no connections. No business professionals in the family. No rich aunt or uncle. In the working-class community of downriver Detroit, south of downtown and the sprawling Ford plant in Dearborn, Michigan, she bounced back and forth between her divorced parents, neither of whom attended college. Her father is a machinist, her mother, until recently, a retail data collector for ACNielsen. "My mom still doesn't understand how I do it," Ashley says. To be fair, she did go to her mother for the initial investment: $8 to register the domain name. Ashley still hasn't spent a dime on advertising.

It all started as a hobby. She began dabbling in Web-site design eight years ago, when she was 9, hogging the family's Gateway computer in the kitchen all day. When she wasn't playing games, she was teaching herself the basics of Web design.

To which her mother, Linda LaBrecque, responded, "Get off that computer. *Now!*" For Ashley's 12th birthday, her mother splurged on an above-ground swimming pool—"just so she'd go outside," LaBrecque says.

Whateverlife just sort of happened, another accidental Web business. Originally, Ashley created the site in late 2004 when she was 14 as a way to show off her design work. "I was the dorky girl who was into HTML," she says. It attracted zero interest beyond her circle of friends until she figured out how to customize MySpace pages. So many classmates asked her to design theirs that she began posting layouts on her site daily, several at first, then dozens.

By 2005, her traffic had exploded; she needed her own dedicated server. Ashley, who had bartered site designs for free Web hosting, couldn't afford the monthly rental, not on her babysitting income. Her Web host suggested Google AdSense, a service that supplies ads to a site and shares the revenue. The greater the traffic, the more money she'd earn.

"She would look up how much she had made," says Jen Carey, 17, one of her closest friends. "It was $50. She thought that was the coolest."

The first check, her first paycheck of any kind, was even cooler: $2,790.

"It was more than I made in a month," her mother says.

"It made me want to do even more designs," Ashley says. But first, she went on a shopping spree at a nearby mall with Bre Newby, her best friend since third grade. Ashley walked out with eight pairs of jeans from J.C. Penney and an armful of other clothes. Without a credit card or a bank account, the 15-year-old paid $600 in cash—the most she'd ever spent.

"Before, I would ask my mom, 'Can I have $10?' and she'd say, 'No, you have to wait a few weeks,' " Ashley recalls.

She hasn't asked since.

In January 2006, a few months after that first payday and six months before her 16th birthday, she withdrew from school. Instead of taking AP English, French, and algebra II, instead of being a straight-A sophomore at Lincoln Park High School, Ashley stayed home to nurture her budding business and take classes through an online high school. "Everybody was shocked," she says. "They asked, 'Are you sure you know what you're doing?' But I had this crazy opportunity to do something different."

That "something different" was Whateverlife. The name came to Ashley in a moment of frustration. After losing a video game to Bre, she dropped the controller and blurted out, "Whatever, life." She liked it instantly. She thought it would be a great name for a Web site, for "whatever life you lead."

Now her life is centered around working in the basement of the two-story, four-bedroom house that she bought last September for $250,000. It's located in a fenced-off subdivision in the community of Southgate, a couple of blocks removed from Dix Highway, a thoroughfare dotted with body shops and convenience stores. She lives with her mother; her 8-year-old sister, Shelby; three cats; two turtles; a Rottweiler; a hamster; and a fish.

Ashley's home office is the physical embodiment of her Web site. The business brings in as much as $70,000 a month, but there's not a whiff of corporate convention. It's fun, whimsical, and unabashedly pink. Pink walls. Pink rug. Pink chairs, pillows, and lamp. Even the blue, green, and silver stick-on robots dancing on the wall have tiny pink hearts. It's a teenager's version of the workplace, which earned raves when she posted pictures on MySpace:

"SOO FLIPPING CUTE!"

"OMG I want that office."

"Geez. That's just incredible. I'm what . . . almost ten years your senior and I am inspired by you."

The space reflects Ashley's personality, like everything else about her business. Therein lies one of the main reasons for Whateverlife's success, says Robb Lippitt, whom Ashley considers the only good thing to come out of her legal issues. When her lawyer realized she was running her company alone, he arranged a meeting with Lippitt, the former COO of ePrize, an online promotions outfit that is one of Detroit's fastest-growing companies. Having helped build ePrize to $30 million in annual revenue and 325 employees, he now helps other local entrepreneurs scale the mountain. In April, he became her $200-an-hour consultant and first business mentor.

Since Ashley, his youngest client ever, had never taken a class in accounting or read a business book, she needed a crash course on the basics, such as maintaining two accounts, business and personal. "She was running her business like a piggy bank," says Lippitt, 38.

But he found her to be a quick study and, in many ways, a natural entrepreneur. "She lacks experience, but I was blown away by her instincts," he says. How she makes her layouts compatible with social-networking sites other than MySpace, so her company isn't tied to one site. How she decided to offer her designs as cell-phone wallpaper, creating a new service and revenue stream based on existing inventory. Ashley, he realized, has a vision for Whateverlife that goes beyond a MySpace tools site. It could be a multifaceted community for girls.

Convinced that her fans need help building Web sites, she hired developers in India to create an easy-to-use application and wrote one-teen-to-another tutorials. After the site builder launched in May, though, she told Lippitt she was disappointed by delays and early bugs. Hiccups were common, he assured her; he expected modest results, maybe a few hundred users. But 28,000 signed up in the first week. "There are CEOs across the country who would be dancing in their offices if they got that reaction," he says.

Ashley is the demographic she's serving, which gives her a powerful advantage over far more experienced adults trying to channel their inner teen or glean clues from focus groups. Her site looks and sounds like something made by a teenager, not something manufactured to look that way.

The risk, of course, is that she could lose touch with her audience as she outgrows it. But Lippitt says she already grasps the importance of understanding her customers, not simply assuming they share her taste. She conducts polls about their favorite stores, celebrities, and *American Idol* contestants. She solicits feedback on new features. And she's thinking of the next step: "I may have to hire people younger than me."

Some days I miss school. I miss the laughter, the lunch lines, the jackass of the class, the evil ass teacher, sometimes I even miss the drama.

August 4, 2006; 1:30 A.M.

On a Wednesday in early June, the gang's all here after school. Well, everyone except Bre. Shayna Bone, 17, and Jen—outfitted in matching Whateverlife T-shirts, featuring row after row of multicolored hearts—sit at a table reviewing their W-4 forms. It's official: The staff is doubling for the summer.

Mike Troutt, 16, who's stretched across a white L-shaped couch, won't be joining them. A past contributor to the Whateverlife magazine, he's working as an apprentice at a local tattoo shop for the summer. He's contemplating where he'll get his first tattoo, he announces. Tomorrow's the big day.

As usual, Ashley is working away at her computer, a new desktop with a touch-screen monitor, one of three computers in her basement. Often, she's up at 7 or working into the wee hours on a "designfest" with Bre, fueled with music and Monster energy drinks.

In just 15 minutes, she creates a layout. Blue and pink streaks on a black background with blocks of pink rap lyrics. Her fingers race across the keyboard as she tries different fonts, sizes, compositions, switching out HTML coding as she talks. "Don't worry," she tells a wary Shayna, "I'll teach you."

Ashley the CEO, who has no fewer than 14 hearts on her business card, is both utterly familiar and a complete mystery to her friends. In some ways, she's the same old "Ash"—or "AshBo," a nickname they coined because she didn't have her own room at one point (Ashley + hobo = AshBo). She still plays *The Sims*, still giggles when Jen laughs like Eddie Murphy, and is still up for silliness, like standing by the road holding a sign that says, HONK IF YOU BELIEVE IN THE LOCH NESS MONSTER, or taking breaks on the swing set down the street.

AshBo looks even younger than 17. She has straight brown hair with light streaks down to the middle of her back. She has a French pedicure, like Jen and her mother. Her clothes are nothing fancy. "I don't need $2,000 shirts," Ashley says. "I'm fine with Target." Or a University of Michigan sweatshirt over a summer dress.

In other ways, she's an alien among normal teens. She can go on about hiring freelance developers, studying site-traffic trends, calculating ad rates, maintaining low overhead (her main operating expense is seven servers). "Sometimes when I talk about the site, my friends just stare at me," she says. She carries a BlackBerry and a Coach bag (a recent birthday present to herself). Her friends tease her about her last ring tone, which consisted of The Donald, someone they couldn't care less about, barking, "This is Donald Trump telling you to have an ego!"

Whateverlife has definitely brought out a bolder side. "One minute, she's joking around with us, and then, 'Oh, guys, hold on, I gotta take this call,' " says Mike. "She turns it on like a light switch." She's no longer the shy 15-year-old who would ask her mother or father to make a difficult phone call. Who didn't know how to respond to advertisers' cold calls. Who didn't know how to negotiate. Now, it's "Is that the best you can do for me?"

"Something clicked," says her mother, who can be direct herself. "She's not letting people walk over her."

At one point, Ashley takes a call upstairs in the kitchen, where a fax machine sits on the countertop. The company that's building the application for her cell-phone wallpaper is on the line. The developer walks her through the latest mock-up, answering Ashley's questions. She's one of those teens who has mastered the art of talking to adults as a peer, of making eye contact rather than looking down or away at a moment's blush.

Her mother, whom Ashley hired recently to keep the books, listens in, hand on hip, a cigarette cocked. Afterward, she asks, "What was he talking about?"

Ashley translates. She'll ask her mother for advice, but she doesn't necessarily take it. "I'm stubborn, like her," she says. Ashley has more leverage than the typical teen. She's the breadwinner. And yet for all her newfound independence, she still needs to be driven everywhere. She hasn't taken driver's ed because she wants to take the class with a friend, not alone.

Occasionally, she feels the tug of her old life, traditions like Lincoln Park's Spirit Week, when she'd paint her cheeks orange and blue, the school colors. More than once, she has returned, just for the day, hanging out in her French teacher's classroom. Ashley wonders if she'll be allowed to participate in graduation. By then, she may have already earned an associate's degree in design, at Henry Ford Community College.

She's determined to bring her friends along for this strange and wonderful ride. They rode in the limo to her over-the-top sweet-16 party at the local Masonic Temple, where guests wore pink Whateverlife rubber bracelets and the door prize was an Xbox. She took Bre on a family vacation to Hawaii, Ashley's first flight. And when the friends go out—tonight it's to Chili's—she picks up the tab.

This summer, she's the boss. One of Ashley's friends had pitched in making layouts last year, but things got a tad awkward when Ashley thought her friend's productivity was dipping. Now she insists they've made up—BFF. But after the misunderstanding, she wrote up employee guidelines. She wanted to spell out her expectations. Lippitt is impressed. She's learning from her mistakes, a challenge for any new entrepreneur.

"I told them I need a minimum of 25 layouts a week to get paid," Ashley says. "It's just business."

> Do I keep my site?
> Do I sell and be set for life?
> God, it's all so overwhelming.
>
> August 4, 2006; 1:30 A.M.

L ast year, Steve Greenberg, the former president of Columbia Records and now the head of indie label S-Curve Records, witnessed the power of Whateverlife. Greenberg discovered Joss Stone, produced the Hanson brothers, and helped make Baha Men's "Who Let the Dogs Out" an unofficial sports anthem. Last year, he decided to promote Jonas Brothers, an unknown pop trio, online instead of on radio. He

turned to Nabbr, a company that had developed a viral widget, a small desktop application that plays videos and can be easily shared with other sites. It's like "a music poster on a bedroom wall," says Mike More, Nabbr's CEO.

The widget made its Internet debut on Whateverlife. While surfing MySpace for leads, More had noticed how many Jonas Brothers fans used Whateverlife layouts. In less than two months, 60,000 fans transferred the Jonas Brothers' three-part video from Whateverlife to their MySpace pages, in effect becoming 60,000 new distribution points. "This teenage girl in the Midwest got more views for our video than YouTube," says Greenberg, 46. "It wasn't even close." The viral campaign encouraged fans to vote for the band on MTV's *Total Request Live,* and the group's song "Mandy" hit No. 4, unheard of without radio play.

Since then, Whateverlife has become one of the primary vehicles for Nabbr's viral campaigns for artists and movies, breaking acts such as the Red Jumpsuit Apparatus and 30 Seconds to Mars, as well as Lily Allen. More's staff sends Ashley signed CDs and photos to pass on to Whateverlife fans, and artists record personal shout-outs to her and Whateverlife that play on her site. She's light years ahead of traditional media such as *Teen Vogue,* More says. "If I were Condé Nast, I'd figure out a way to buy her," he says. "I would."

As previous suitors can attest, that wouldn't be easy. In March 2006, an associate of MySpace cofounder Brad Greenspan approached Ashley with a bid valued at more than $1.5 million. She passed. Three months later, Greenspan's people came back with a second offer: $700,000, a car, and her own Internet show with a marketing budget of $2 million.

Sorry, fellas. "I created this from nothing, and I want to see how far I can take it," Ashley says. "If I wanted to do an Internet show, I could do it on my own. I have the audience."

Until now, she has maintained a remarkably low profile in the offline world. Her scheduled appearance on the "Totally Wired Teen Superstars" panel at Mashup, a teen-marketing conference in July, was to be her first public-speaking appearance—and her first business trip. An even bigger gig is possible: her own reality-TV show. Rick Sadlowski, a TV production executive in Detroit who worked with Eminem when he was still Marshall Mathers, is eager to pitch the idea to MTV. Ashley is mulling it over.

Move over, Paris Hilton. It's Whateverlife: The Not-So-Simple Life.

> Got evaluated by my therapist for emancipation—
> need to get a few teachers' written letters; should
> be cool.
>
> April 7, 2007; 9:53 P.M.

I n February 2006, following a falling-out with her mother, Ashley moved in with her father and older brother. With her business booming, she says, she began supporting them—groceries, bills, rent, renovations. At first, she didn't mind. One of the benefits of Whateverlife was the ability to take care of her family in a way she'd never imagined, certainly not when she was a child overhearing arguments about unpaid bills. Ashley says she bought her brother a used car and paid her grandmother's taxes. The insurance through Whateverlife covered her mother's back surgery. But in August, Ashley moved back in with her mother. She hasn't spoken to her father since. Or to her brother, who later filed (then withdrew) a petition to become her conservator. "I used to trust easily," Ashley says. "I've learned to be careful."

When her brother took his name off a joint bank account with her, Lincoln Park Community Credit Union petitioned the probate court to assign a conservator. After several months, the judge tapped attorney Alan May. He has 40 years' worth of experience with conservatorships, but Ashley's situation makes the case unique in his career. Although May's role is protecting Ashley's interests, it hasn't always felt that way to her, not when she hasn't had complete control over the money she made. But she says, "I don't want this to come across like a war."

Until recently, though, the tension was undeniable. Ashley was unhappy having to get May's approval for expenses such as her mother's nearly $500-a-week pay. May declined to discuss the case, but in papers filed last spring with the court, he characterized LaBrecque as uncooperative and evasive.

"They're making me out to be the bad guy," Ashley's mother says. LaBrecque, 42, had little growing up herself. Her father worked on the assembly line at General Motors until he died of a heart attack at 42, leaving his wife to raise six kids on Social Security. "It was rough but we survived," she says. "I feel so lucky my daughter doesn't have to live the life I lived."

In mid-July, seven months after being assigned a conservator, Ashley finally sat down with everybody for the first time: her mother, her lawyer, her consultant, her guardian ad litem, and her conservator. She says that she feels much better about the situation.

But that doesn't change the fact that she wants to be on her own. The typical conservatorship case involves a minor with an inheritance or an elderly person who has lost his faculties. "It's unusual to be emancipated to run your own business," says Darren Findling, Ashley's lawyer. "But she's the perfect candidate—an Internet superstar who happens to be a minor."

For now, she's trying to block all this out and concentrate on her business.

On Thursday, while her friends are slaving through exams, Ashley meets with Lippitt for two hours. They couldn't appear more different. He's a low-key, analytical sort with a law degree. Lives on the other side of town, in the Tony Bloomfield Hills suburb. Drives a black Lexus, a rarity on her block. As an entrepreneur, though, she relates to him better than anyone else right now.

"I know, I'm always jumping on 10,000 things," Ashley says and then pitches her latest brainstorm, her own social-networking application for girls.

"Hmm," he says. "How do you think the reaction of MySpace would be?"

A teenage CEO, Lippitt is learning, is even more easily distracted and more fearless than an adult entrepreneur. "Failure is an abstract concept to her, and I want it to stay that way," he says. When he was a teenager, his father lost his body shop and had to start over, attending law school in his forties.

Lippitt urges Ashley to prioritize and think about profits as well as design. As clever as her site-building tool is, it doesn't allow a way to run ads on the pages it creates. "You're leaving revenue on the table," he tells her.

At times, Lippitt has to remind himself that she's only 17. "Even if she could go a lot faster, I don't know if that's the best thing for her," he says. "She's already in the adult world doing adult things. I'm reluctant to drive her away from living an important and fun time in her life."

But he's not shy about pushing her when she needs it. Today, he tells her it's time to consider approaching companies to advertise. So far, she has relied largely on Google AdSense, which supplies ads in exchange for what she says is a 40% cut. The direct model is not only potentially more lucrative but also allows her to target brands more suited to teens than, say, Microsoft Office 2007. "I'm not sure that's a good fit," he says of the software ad placed by ValueClick.

Ashley is excited about the idea. And a little nervous. She'll need a sales presentation, a company logo, and ad rates. Eventually, she may want to hire a sales rep, a job she'd never heard of until Lippitt described it. More important, she'll need to sell herself to name-brand companies. "If she can combine 'I'm 17' with a little more about her business, I think she's unstoppable," Lippitt says.

This could be the next growth spurt for Ashley and Whateverlife. It's scary, sure, but she's getting used to the demands and challenges of "this crazy opportunity." She's learning, stretching, getting that much-needed seasoning.

She and Lippitt brainstorm about which brands would resonate with girls like her. This is the fun part. No petitions. No regrets. No family feud. Just a 17-year-old and her big dreams in a pink, pink, pink world full of promise. And if they don't come true? Well, there's always college.

# Bloggers against Torture

NEGAR AZIMI

The video that circulated on Egyptian blogs this winter showed Emad Mohamed Ali Mohamed, a 21-year-old bus driver, lying on the floor stripped naked from the waist down—his hands bound behind his back and his legs held in the air. He screams and begs as he is sodomized with a stick while those around him, whose faces are not visible to us, taunt him.

Hours earlier, Ali Mohamed (known among friends as Emad al-Kabir) had been picked up by two plain-clothes police officers in Bulaq alDaqrur, a roughish slum in Giza, across the river from downtown Cairo's crumbling Europeanate area. The young man's offense was venturing to break up a scuffle between police officers and his cousin. Despite the inhospitable treatment he endured, al-Kabir was released thirty-six hours later with no charges to speak of. After all, torture of this variety is commonplace. Protesting its manifestations, or questioning the logic behind it, is usually met with a shrug, even contemptuous indifference.

And so, when it was announced in late December that the two police officers who had supervised the abuse, Capt. Islam Nabih and Cpl. Reda Fathi, had been detained and their case transferred to a criminal court for investigation, it seemed that something had changed. With the simple act of uploading the video to a blog, a web impresario known as Demagh MAK had unleashed a storm of attention both at home and abroad around the case of the diminutive, soft-spoken bus driver. (A still image from the video is reproduced on this page and on this magazine's cover.) A link to the video, passed around among activists and journalists and posted on YouTube (until it was removed for graphic content), was finally picked up by the more intrepid Egyptian independent papers as well as Arab satellite channels such as Al Jazeera and Dream TV. Even a handful of jihadi websites chimed in, fuming about the excesses of the infidel Egyptian regime. Within days, the video had taken on a life of its own.

Watching the revelations unfold, one couldn't help but think there was more to come. Sure enough, before long another leak— also spread via blogs—revealed a man (later identified as Ah med Gad) receiving sharp slaps to the face from a belligerent officer. And then came the jarring image of a young woman, ostensibly a murder suspect, pleading for mercy while suspended from a stick held across two chairs, in what seemed a throwback to a medieval interrogation method. Whoever was behind the camera, presumably a police officer, seemed to relish the ability to capture the scene: As the woman screams "Please, *ya basha!*" (a sign of prostration) over and over, the camera moves in and out, making use of the zoom function with abandon.

Indeed, this may be just the beginning. Wael Abbas, a Cairo-based blogger who was among the first to post the torture videos, has received nearly a dozen additional videos since the beginning of December. Most have been forwarded anonymously, and most, like al-Kabir's, were captured with simple cellphone cameras.

I met Abbas in late December in Cairo, just as the stir created by the al-Kabir video was reaching its peak. "We know people get raped, beaten all the time. And who's going to stick up for a bus driver? But now it's public, and everyone is talking. The government has to do something. They've lost face," he explained.

## While the capacity of the web to jump-start democracy has been exaggerated, blogs have enormous potential as an advocacy tool.

Bloggers in the developing world have long been the subject of romantic odes in the Western press (give a young man a blog and he will start a revolution). While the capacity of digital technologies to jump-start democracy has often been exaggerated, recent events in Egypt demonstrate blogs' enormous potential as an advocacy tool and, more broadly, as an alternative source of news. Here, a number of bloggers seem to have cracked into a hitherto tightly sealed state monopoly on information dissemination, breaking stories in many cases before the mainstream press.

In this neighborhood, the official press dominates circulation numbers—with a single state-controlled paper producing up to 1 million copies a day, while the whole of the independent press puts out 10,000–40,000, according to Arab Press Freedom Watch. Though a handful of independent papers, such as *Al-Dustour* (whose editor, Ibrahim Issa, faces charges of "insulting the president") and *Al Masry Al Youm* (whose writers have faced similar charges), have managed to push the bounds of what is allowable in the public sphere, until recently it would have been unheard of to take on such subjects as torture carried out by officials without being summarily shut down.

But things are changing. In many cases blogs, working hand in hand with the modest independent press as well as satellite television channels ("We are the children of Al Jazeera," one blogger recently told me), have broken a number of big stories—from sectarian strife in Alexandria to state-sponsored violence during the last parliamentary elections, and even the type of routine crackdowns that occur during demonstrations. Together these forces have not only created an alternative source of information but have increasingly managed to shame the government into punishing those responsible for abuses. Since the leak of the notorious "slaps" video, the officer charged with the abuse of Gad, for example, has been suspended while his case is under investigation. The Interior Ministry, meanwhile, has publicly called for the identification of the pleading woman hanging from the stick, as well as the officers who carried out that abuse.

Still, whatever happens to the perpetrators of the recent spate of leaked abuses, torture will likely remain routine in Egypt for the time being. The sort of roughing up that takes place in dark alleys, security checkpoints and dingy police stations daily—normally targeting ordinary citizens—continues to pass unquestioned. Not only are torture and abuse tolerated; in the security services violence is broadly valued as a sign of authority, strength, bravado. It is not uncommon for lower-level officers to get promotions for such theatrics. In fact, the original video of al-Kabir appears to have circulated for months (the abuse was carried out in January 2006) among police officers and taxi drivers, Abu Ghraib–style, before it was leaked to the public. The images were likely shared for bragging purposes—and to serve as a sort of warning to those who would dare to tread on police turf, as al-Kabir had. It's hardly surprising that, following the video's wide circulation and al-Kabir's statements on a satellite television channel about his experience, he received a torrent of phone calls demanding his silence and threatening both him and his family.

This is not the first time that bloggers in this country have roused the ire of the authorities. Last spring at least six bloggers were arrested in connection with demonstrations in solidarity with senior judges demanding independence of the judiciary from the executive branch. Although the bloggers were not explicitly picked up for their writings, their arrests revealed the deep links between electronic activism and the street at large. In Egypt in particular, blogging as a phenomenon was not born in a vacuum but rather has emerged as an extension of existing popular movements—whether it is the country's modest street opposition movement, Kifaya, or even the banned Muslim Brotherhood, which has equally embraced the web and the blogosphere (just look at ikhwanweb.net). Together with e-mail and text messaging, blogging has undeniably changed the way activism is carried out.

Alaa Abd El Fattah, a 24-year-old who blogs with his wife at manalaa.net and also runs omraneya.net, an aggregator for more than 1,500 Egyptian blogs (with 2,000 in queue), was among the detained last spring—held for forty-six days on various charges ranging from insulting the president to obstructing traffic to inciting citizens to topple the regime. As he was leaving state security upon his release one official took him aside, making it clear that he was an avid reader of blogs.

"The people they targeted at the time of the judges' demonstrations used the Internet to mobilize. We've gotten as far as we have as a movement because we're linked to the street. We spread word of demonstrations through blogs, we organize and gain supporters through them, we publicize abuses at protests. Kifaya even started as a petition on the Internet," El Fattah tells me. He counts himself among the self-proclaimed "geeks" who helped make building a community of bloggers a possibility in Egypt and ultimately made the Egyptian blogosphere a success story in the region.

Another young blogger, Mohamed al-Sharkawi, was arrested twice during the judges' demonstrations. On his blog, he had not only supported the striking judges but also posted strident editorials critical of President Hosni Mubarak. In detention, he was blindfolded, beaten and molested with a rolled-up cardboard tube. When I met him in January at his rooftop apartment, he recalled the experience. "All I remember is three voices hanging above me. 'Why are you attending demonstrations? Why did you write on your blog that we treated you badly in prison? Do you think you'll become a star?'" When I asked al-Sharkawi what he would do if the authorities eventually shut down his blog, which he continues to update daily, he replied, "I'll set up another one. They have nearly killed me already—what more can they do?"

But how threatening, we may wonder, can a handful of bloggers be—and how much of a threat could they be to the twenty-five-year-and-running rule of a leader like Mubarak? After all, many of them are simply tech-savvy twenty somethings recently out of university. And besides, how big a role can bloggers play in a country in which they number just over 3,000—a mere fraction of whom write political content?

Hossam el-Hamalawy runs arabawy.org, a blog that has been central to documenting what he has dubbed Egypt's very own Videogate. "We're exploding," he tells me. "The government didn't see it coming, and it's creating a domino effect. You read bloggers in Tunisia, Yemen, Libya, and they take pride in the Egyptian gains. Once you get this far, there's no going back. You can't take the plug out." As recently as January 2005, there were only about thirty blogs in the country. "My dream is that one day there will be a blogger with a digital camera in every street in Egypt."

Exploding or not, this sort of electronic activism defies facile definitions. No longer simply an upper- or middle-class phenomenon, blogging has become an outlet for expression among a broad spectrum of people. Some bloggers post exclusively from Internet cafes (those without PCs), some are without a university education, many are women. Today there is a blogger in every urban center in Egypt—from the stark Sinai Peninsula to Mansoura in the Nile Delta. Most write in Arabic. Recently one blogger went so far as to set up a site devoted to bringing attention to police brutalities taking place in the Sinai following bouts of terrorism (hundreds, even thousands of Bedouins have been disappeared by state security, often locked away and abused with impunity). Other blogs broach the sensitive subject of how the country's religious minorities are treated—particularly the Copts, who make up Egypt's Christian community. Blogs have also been a crucial space for engaging such uncomfortable topics as sexuality, race and beyond. Suddenly, the (improvised) Arabic word *mudawena,* signifying a blogger, has found its way into the lexicon.

The turning point in Egypt in particular, if one were to identify one, may go back to May 2005. Under pressure from his Western patrons to engage in what is casually referred to as "reform," President Mubarak had called for a referendum vote on a constitutional amendment that would provide for the country's first multiparty elections. The proposed amendment, however, was dismissed by many within the country as little more than window dressing to appease the United States, an empty gesture at best. Protests calling for boycotts of the vote on referendum day devolved into a melee marked by hundreds of men—many of them hired government thugs—harassing and sexually abusing women who had gathered on downtown streets. While the government vehemently denied allegations of sexual abuse (dismissing the "fantasies" and "fabrications" of a few "creative minds"), images shot by both participants and observers on small digital cameras and phones wound up on blogs like Wael Abbas's in the following days—making it virtually impossible to explain away the accusations. Since that time, blogs have become a repository for everything from stories about striking ambulance workers threatening to commit suicide to debates about corruption in the health sector to accounts of camel butch-ers shouting obscenities at parliamentary speaker Fathi Sorour. In other words, these are stories that would never see the light of day given the conventions and dictates of the state press.

For good reason, the government is growing jittery about blog-ging. At the moment, at least one blogger, Abdul Kareem Nabeil Suleiman (who goes by the Internet name Kareem Amer), remains in solitary confinement, awaiting trial for his criticisms of Islam in general and conservative Al-Azhar University, where he was once a student, in particular. The charges against him include "defaming the president of Egypt." One Coptic blogger, Hala Helmy Botros (she goes by the Internet name Hala El Masry), who has written at length about persecution of the Coptic minority, clearly went too far recently; the computers at an Internet cafe she once frequented have been confiscated. (Proprietors of Internet cafes are often given lists of people who may not use their services, checking ID is de rigueur and prominent signs announce "No entry to political or sexual sites by order of the State Security.") And on January 8 a reporter from Al Jazeera named Howeida Taha was detained as she was leaving the country. Taha had tapes in hand for work on a forthcoming docu-mentary on torture; she had recorded testimonies of victims and had amassed various videos of police brutality. Al Jazeera, for its part, announced on its Arabic-language website that Egyptian pros-ecutors had accused the journalist of "filming footage that harms the national interest of the country, possessing and giving pictures contradicting the truth, and giving a wrong description of the situ-ation in the country."

There are additional signs that the government campaign against electronic activism may be escalating. The Interior Ministry has been pursuing this campaign through a special unit called the Department for Confronting Computer and Internet Crime. Thanks to a 2006 court ruling, websites can be shut down if they are deemed a threat to national security. Some of the country's more active political bloggers, such as Abbas and al-Sharkawi, are regularly trailed, harassed and intimidated by state security. And the official press has been launching rhetorical attacks against blog-gers at large, accusing them of "spreading malicious rumors about Egypt," "working for the Americans," "engaging in satanic sexual fantasy" and so on.

## Middle Eastern bloggers are engaging in a sort of citizen journalism that stands, in its own modest way, to alter the political terrain.

Across the Middle East bloggers are engaging in a sort of citizen journalism that stands, in its own modest way, to alter the political terrain. In Bahrain they have clamored for freedom of expression on the web, also having played a large role in pushing for female participation in that country's parliamentary elections. Earlier this year Bahraini bloggers used Google Earth satellite maps to juxtapose the vast wealth of the ruling family against increasingly destitute areas, exposing the rampant inequities in the Gulf kingdom at large

(imagine palace meets slum). The Google Earth site was shut down for three days until international attention seemed to shame the Bahraini government into lifting the ban. In Lebanon blogs provided a home for reactions to last summer's war, along with documenta-tion of its ravages. In Qaddafi's Libya blogs persist, though a number of political bloggers have been imprisoned, and in one especially sordid case a writer covering government corruption had his fingers chopped off before he was murdered—presumably a sign to others who would consider following his lead. And this is to say nothing of Iran, where Internet activity is so significant that despite restrictions, Farsi has cracked the top ten represented languages in the global blogosphere.

But where, you may ask, are the Western governments that have lent such impassioned rhetorical support to the demo-cratic aspirations of citizens of the Middle East since 9/11? In Egypt, the US government in particular has undeniably played some role in creating openings for activists, bloggers among them. But today that commitment seems to have ebbed, the enthusiasm for democracy promotion dampened by the prospect of Islamist groups like the Muslim Brotherhood, Hamas and Hezbollah gain-ing power via elections throughout the region.

And so when Secretary of State Condoleezza Rice passed through Cairo on one leg of a Middle East tour in January, she made it crystal clear that her Administration had opted to favor stability over rocking the boat. She uttered hardly a whisper about the events of recent weeks (torture revelations, jailed bloggers) or the country's dismal human rights record in general. At a news conference in the historic city of Luxor, Rice intoned, "Obviously the relationship with Egypt is an important strategic relationship—one that we value greatly." On previous trips to the country, Rice had been more confrontational, raising issues such as the importance of free and fair elections, the need for an independent judiciary and even the country's subpar treatment of its political prisoners. This time around, however, there was not a peep about anything that could compromise the postcard image of Egypt as a reliably mod-erate, pro-Western Arab regime. As the US government's grandiose plan to democratize the region stumbles—and Iraq in particular (which was to be the jewel in the crown of this new Middle East) slips further into pandemonium—even the requisite lip service to reform has all but disappeared. The noose on local democracy activists, in the meantime, tightens.

Just days before the Secretary of State's visit, in what seemed an uncanny twist of fate, al-Kabir, the young bus driver, was sentenced to three months in prison. The charge: "resisting authorities." While the police officers responsible for his abuse will face a trial in March, his lawyer and human rights groups expressed concern that al-Kabir would face further torture in prison. His bizarre sentence seemed to signal that little may have changed, despite the glimmer of hope offered by the media frenzy of the past weeks. Indeed, as the ruling was announced, it seemed that for the Egyptian regime as well as the US government that readily accommodates it, it was back to business as usual.

NEGAR AZIMI is senior editor of *Bidoun,* an arts and culture magazine based in New York.

# UNIT 5

# Societal Institutions: Law, Politics, Education, and the Military

## Unit Selections

20. **Piracy, Computer Crime, and IS Misuse at the University,** Timothy Paul Cronan, C. Bryan Foltz, and Thomas W. Jones
21. **Can Blogs Revolutionize Progressive Politics?,** Lakshmi Chaudhry
22. **Center Stage,** Carl Sessions Stepp
23. **The Coming Robot Army,** Steve Featherstone
24. **A Technology Surges,** David Talbot
25. **Wikipedia in the Newsroom,** Donna Shaw
26. **E-Mail in Academia: Expectations, Use, and Instructional Impact,** Meredith Weiss and Dana Hanson-Baldauf

## Key Points to Consider

• The overview to this unit mentions that civil institutions were overlooked in the excitement after the collapse of the former Soviet Union. Find on the Internet and read Francis Fukuyama's essay, "The End of History." Do you agree with his arguments? Does computing have any role to play in the development of civil institutions?

• Find out how profitable some big-city U.S. papers are. Are you surprised at the results?

• Use the Internet to find out if commentators have anything to say about the difficulty of managing complex weaponry in outposts around the globe.

• How has high-tech weaponry fared in the Iraq war?

• Do you read political blogs? Why would someone read a political blog rather than *The New Statesman* (on the right) or *The Nation* (on the left)?

• Do you e-mail your professors? Under what circumstances?

• Do your professor's allow you to cite *Wikipedia* in your papers?

## Student Web Site
www.mhcls.com

## Internet References

**ACLU: American Civil Liberties Union**
  *http://www.aclu.org*
**Information Warfare and U.S. Critical Infrastructure**
  *http://www.twurled-world.com/Infowar/Update3/cover.htm*
**Living in the Electronic Village**
  *http://www.rileyis.com/publications/phase1/usa.htm*

**Patrolling the Empire**
  *http://www.csrp.org/patrol.htm*
**United States Patent and Trademark Office**
  *http://www.uspto.gov/*
**World Intellectual Property Organization**
  *http://www.wipo.org/*

After the collapse of the Soviet Union, many Americans believed that democracy and a market economy would develop in short order. Commentators seemed to have taken a cue from Francis Fukuyama's imposingly entitled essay, "The End of History," that appeared in *The National Interest* in 1989. "What we may be witnessing," he wrote, is "not just the end of the Cold War, or the passing of a particular period of post-war history, but . . . the universalization of Western liberal democracy as the final form of human government." Fukuyama, deputy director of the State Department's planning staff in the elder Bush administration, hedged a bit. He was careful to argue that the victory of liberal capitalism "has occurred primarily in the realm of ideas or consciousness and is as yet incomplete in the real or material world."

We have grown wiser since those heady times. The events of September 11 showed Americans, in the most brutal fashion, that not everyone shares their values. More importantly, the political and economic chaos that has been so much a part of Russian life for the past decade, has led many commentators to conclude that liberal democracy and a market economy require more than "the realm of ideas or consciousness." They need, above all else, institutions that govern political and economic relationships. They require mechanisms for business contracts and land use, courts to adjudicate disputes, government agencies to record titles and regulate resources, and, not just a mechanism but a tradition of representative government. In a phrase, democracy and a market economy require the institutions of civil society.

We in the United States and Western Europe have long traditions of civil society, in some cases reaching back hundreds of years. The French sociologist, Emile Durkheim (1858–1917), hoped that as traditional societies gave way to urban industrial societies, rule by contract and law would provide the glue for social cohesion. To a very large extent this has been the case in the United States. The room in which I am writing is part of a house that sits on a small piece of property that belongs to me. I am confident that my title to this property is part of the public record. Were someone to appear on my doorstep with a claim to my property, a procedure exists to adjudicate our dispute. If I do not personally understand the rule, I can hire a lawyer, a specialist in civil procedures, to make my case before an independent judiciary.

But the rapid introduction of information technology over the past decade has proven problematic for the orderly resolution of disputes. It has been difficult for legislators to formulate laws for a set of relationships—those mediated by a computer—that are not well understood. Even if laws are successfully enacted, their existence, does not guarantee compliance, especially in the absence of an enforcement mechanism. As an article in the 08/09 edition of *Computers in Society* argues, laws to protect intellectual property exist, but it's expensive to enforce them

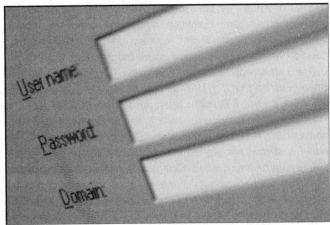

© Ingram Publishing/Fotosearch

(Band 2008). Still, the computer and recording industries try. The Digital Millennium Copyright Act of 1998 provides severe penalties for both piracy and for publicizing ways to circumvent security mechanisms. Not severe enough for students, it appears. Those who have read their university's computer use policies are more likely to violate them ("Piracy, Computer Crime, and IS Misues at the University").

No civil institution is more sacred in a democracy than the way it chooses public officials. Liberals have been envious ever since Richard Viguerie's computer-generated mailing lists—an innovation at the time—contributed to Ronald Reagan's victory in 1980. At a time when even Senate Majority Leader Harry Reid has a blog, some Democrats hope that the computer is finally on their side. According to Lakshmi Chaudry ("Can Blogs Revolutionize Progressive Politics"), "if television made politics more elitist and less substantive, blogs . . . have the potential to become engines of truly democratic, bottom-up, issue-rich political participation." The history of computing, for all that it has delivered, is littered with shards of broken promises. Only time will tell about this one.

A civil society is unimaginable without a free press. Yet in the United States, the readership of newspapers is declining, along with the numbers watching TV news, the very medium that did away with so many afternoon papers not long ago. While TV news has added the aggressive editorializing of Lou Dobbs and Bill O'Reilly, large newspapers have developed websites to generate readership and revenue. "Center Stage" tells the story of several on-line newsrooms. Here we learn that "with many people posting and without fixed schedules, it is impractical to funnel all content through a copy desk. So a fair amount of copy produced by the Web staff gets little or no editing, and few items get the multiple reads routine in print." Donna Shaw's piece ("Wikipedia in the Newsroom") illustrates another new issue that newspapers face, one that college students face as well. As much as all of us use *Wikipedia,* it's not quite proper to cite it in polite circles.

Strictly speaking, the military is not part of civil society. Yet, since civilians control the U.S. military by constitutional mandate, we can consider it a civil institution without stretching the meaning of the term terribly. On the eve of the Iraq war in April, 2003, *BusinessWeek Online* ran a pair of articles illustrating what one called the "doctrine of digital warfare," a doctrine that stresses air power, agile ground forces, and computer communication over lethal firepower and a large infantry. Sophisticated military systems take years to develop and deploy. Despite some tough-going in Iraq, the U.S. commitment to a high-tech battle field has not waned. Steve Featherstone ("The Coming Robot Army") describes the Army's Future Combat System "as the costliest program in history." The individual soldier is still part of the vision, "but he has been reconfigured as a sort of plug-and-play warrior, a node in what is envisioned as a sprawling network of robots, manned vehicles, ground sensors, satellites, and command sensors." Featherstone's piece makes it clear that military hardware is the result of a partnership between the engineering talent of the private sector and the very deep pockets of the American military.

Despite the robot soldiers that might be coming, for now, real live soldiers fight real live wars. David Talbot's piece ("A Technology Surges") describes a system that he calls, "Google Maps for the Iraq counterinsurgency." It could help keep these soldiers safe.

Education is yet another piece of civil society. American students in public schools study the mechanism of government, recite the Pledge of Allegiance, and learn to revere the sacred texts of American democracy, the Declaration of Independence, the Constitution, and the Bill of Rights. One task of American public education is to instill a common ideal of citizenship into a diverse and changing population. The contribution of computing to education—if not always uncontroversial—has been substantial. From educational software, to wired college campuses, to Internet-mediated distance education, computing has been a part of education since the introduction of personal computers in the early eighties. If you throw in mass, standardized testing, an enterprise nearly unthinkable without computers, computing has been a part of American education since the fifties. Over the past decade, students have become increasingly comfortable e-mailing their professors. As "E-Mail in Academia" argues, studies have shown that there is a relationship between a student's success and "the quality of one-on-one communication between teacher and student." This article reports on a formal study of academic e-mail use at the University of North Carolina.

# Reference

Band, Jonathan (2008). The Copyright Paradox. In P. De Palma (ed.), *Annual Editions: Computers in Society 08/09*. Boston: McGraw-Hill, pp. 107–108.

# Piracy, Computer Crime, and IS Misuse at the University

## Who commits software misuse? Knowing the answer to this question will help organizations protect their information systems.

TIMOTHY PAUL CRONAN, C. BRYAN FOLTZ, AND THOMAS W. JONES

*"Professor, can you help me? I installed software on my computer from my friend's CD and it doesn't work anymore. My friend is gone and I don't have the original CD. What should I do?"*

Does this statement sound familiar? If so, you are not alone. Many students openly admit to illegally installing software on home computers or otherwise misusing computer information systems. Other studies have examined characteristics of students (and non-students) who admit to committing information systems misuse, piracy, and computer crime. We used a survey to examine demographic characteristics of students as well as their awareness of university computer usage policies.

Thirty-four percent (34%) of students responding to this survey admit to committing some form of software misuse or piracy and 22% admit to committing data misuse during their lifetimes. Knowing that students commit information systems misuse is not new [10]. However, today's students are tomorrow's professionals. As such, an understanding of the demographic factors common to those students who commit misuse could help both university information systems departments and organizations better protect their information systems.

An amazing number of students in this study report committing some form of information systems misuse or computer crime. As mentioned, 34% and 22% of respondents admit committing software misuse and data misuse during their lifetimes, respectively. Software misuse in this study means destroying or copying software, using copied software, or distributing copied software without permission. Data misuse means accessing, modifying, or copying data stored on a computerized information system without authorization. Behaviors characteristic of misuse were located in the literature and condensed into these two areas. This study examines these responses by years of experience with computers, academic classification (underclassmen, upperclassmen), major, gender, and age.

*Familiarity with computers.* As expected, students who are more familiar with computers report committing more misuse. Upperclassmen, students with more experience, and students in computer-related majors all report committing more misuse than others. An interesting trend appears (Table 1) when broken down by academic classification. Underclassmen (freshmen and sophomores) report the least amount of software misuse (18%), while upperclassmen (juniors and seniors) report notably larger amounts (37%). Overall, 34% of respondents report software misuse; 7% report 10 or more occurrences. A similar pattern also is observed for data misuse, although fewer incidents of misuse are reported (underclassmen, 12%; upperclassmen, 25%). Overall, 22% of respondents report data misuse; 3% report 10 or more occurrences.

Further, of greater concern, individuals who indicate reading the computer usage policies also report more software misuse and data misuse. For example, of underclassmen who read the computer usage policies, 39% committed software misuse and 8% admit 10 or more occurrences. Of underclassmen who had not read the policies, 15% committed software misuse and 2% report this level of misuse. This unexpected and troubling result can be observed for both software misuse and data misuse in most academic classifications.

Years of experience with computers also are thought to influence misuse [10]. As seen in Table 2, respondents with greater experience report greater numbers of misuse. For example, all individuals with less than one year experience indicate no software misuse during their lifetimes, whereas 41% of individuals with more than 14 years experience make the same claim. Also, 78% of individuals with less than one year experience indicate never engaging in data misuse. This percentage drops to 61% for individuals with more than 14 years experience.

# Table 1 Classification and Familiarity with the University Computer Usage Policy

**Software Misuse:** How many times have you destroyed or copied *software*, used copied *software*, or distributed copied *software* without permission during your lifetime?

| Usage Policy | Class | Ten or More | Seven to Nine | Four to Six | One to Three | Never | N |
|---|---|---|---|---|---|---|---|
| | Under | 3.1% | | 1.5% | 13.8% | 81.5% | 65 |
| | Upper | 8.5% | 3.6% | 7.5% | 17.3% | 63.1% | 388 |
| All | Masters | 4.3% | 6.5% | 4.3% | 15.2% | 69.6% | 46 |
| | Other | 5.9% | | 5.9% | 41.2% | 47.1% | 17 |
| | Overall | 7.4% | 3.3% | 6.4% | 17.4% | 65.5% | 516 |
| | Under | 7.7% | | 7.7% | 15.4% | 69.2% | 13 |
| | Upper | 16.0% | 6.0% | 9.0% | 17.0% | 52.0% | 100 |
| Read Policy | Masters | | 20.0% | 10.0% | 30.0% | 40.0% | 10 |
| | Other | | | | 100.0% | | 1 |
| | Overall | 13.7% | 6.5% | 8.9% | 18.5% | 52.4% | 124 |
| | Under | 1.9% | | | 13.5% | 84.6% | 52 |
| | Upper | 5.9% | 2.8% | 6.9% | 17.4% | 67.0% | 288 |
| Did Not Read Policy | Masters | 5.6% | 2.8% | 2.8% | 11.1% | 77.8% | 36 |
| | Other | 6.3% | | 6.3% | 37.5% | 50.0% | 16 |
| | Overall | 5.4% | 2.3% | 5.6% | 17.1% | 69.6% | 392 |

**Data Misuse:** How many times have you accessed, modified, or copied *data* stored on a computerized information system without authorization during your lifetime?

| Usage Policy | Class | Ten or More | Seven to Nine | Four to Six | One to Three | Never | N |
|---|---|---|---|---|---|---|---|
| | Under | 1.5% | | 3.1% | 7.7% | 87.7% | 65 |
| | Upper | 3.4% | 2.6% | 4.4% | 14.5% | 75.2% | 387 |
| All | Masters | 4.3% | 2.2% | | 8.7% | 84.8% | 46 |
| | Other | 5.6% | | 5.6% | 11.1% | 77.8% | 18 |
| | Overall | 3.3% | 2.1% | 3.9% | 13.0% | 77.7% | 516 |
| | Under | | | 7.7% | 15.4% | 76.9% | 13 |
| | Upper | 7.1% | 5.1% | 5.1% | 17.2% | 65.7% | 99 |
| Read Policy | Masters | | 10.0% | | 20.0% | 70.0% | 10 |
| | Other | | | | | 100.0% | 1 |
| | Overall | 5.7% | 4.9% | 4.9% | 17.1% | 67.5% | 123 |
| | Under | 1.9% | | 1.9% | 5.8% | 90.4% | 52 |
| | Upper | 2.1% | 1.7% | 4.2% | 13.5% | 78.5% | 288 |
| Did Not Read Policy | Masters | 5.6% | | | 5.6% | 88.9% | 36 |
| | Other | 5.9% | | 5.9% | 11.8% | 76.5% | 17 |
| | Overall | 2.5% | 1.3% | 3.6% | 11.7% | 80.9% | 393 |

## Upperclassmen, students with more experience, and students in computer-related majors all report committing more misuse than others.

Misuse by major is presented in Table 3. As one might expect, computer information systems (CIS) majors report the most software misuse with 24% of CIS majors performing 10 or more instances within their lifetimes. This percentage does not exceed 8% for another major. Examining the percentages of individuals who report no misuse presents a similar view. Forty-nine percent of CIS majors indicate they never committed software misuse, while 57% of arts and science majors and 71% of business and economics majors make the same claim. Further, 73% of CIS majors, 78% of business and economics majors, and 83% of arts and sciences majors deny ever committing data misuse.

*Gender and age.* Other factors examined by this research include gender and age. As anticipated, males commit more misuse than females, while individuals in their twenties and thirties commit more misuse than other age groups. Gender often is associated with increased misuse [10]. Fifty-five percent of

# Table 2  Experience with Computers

**Software Misuse:** How many times have you destroyed or copied *software*, used copied *software*, or distributed copied *software* without permission during your lifetime?

| Years of Experience | Ten or More | Seven to Nine | Four to Six | One to Three | Never | N |
|---|---|---|---|---|---|---|
| less than 1 | | | | | 100.0% | 9 |
| 1 to 2 | 2.1% | 2.1% | 2.1% | 16.7% | 77.1% | 48 |
| 3 to 6 | 5.0% | 1.0% | 6.0% | 20.1% | 67.8% | 199 |
| 7 to 10 | 7.8% | 7.2% | 7.2% | 15.0% | 62.7% | 153 |
| 11 to 14 | 7.0% | 3.5% | 7.0% | 17.5% | 64.9% | 57 |
| more than 14 | 24.4% | 2.4% | 9.8% | 22.0% | 41.5% | 41 |
| not sure | | | | 14.3% | 85.7% | 7 |

**Data Misuse:** How many times have you accessed, modified, or copied *data* stored on a computerized information system without authorization during your lifetime?

| Years of Experience | Ten or More | Seven to Nine | Four to Six | One to Three | Never | N |
|---|---|---|---|---|---|---|
| less than I | | | 11.1% | 11.1% | 77.8% | 9 |
| 1 to 2 | | 4.2% | | 6.3% | 89.6% | 48 |
| 3 to 6 | 2.5% | | 3.5% | 14.5% | 79.5% | 200 |
| 7 to 10 | 3.3% | 3.9% | 4.6% | 12.4% | 75.8% | 153 |
| 11 to 14 | 1.8% | 3.6% | 3.6% | 14.3% | 76.8% | 56 |
| more than 14 | 14.6% | 2.4% | 7.3% | 14.6% | 61.0% | 41 |
| not sure | | | | | 100.0% | 7 |

males and 76% of females report no instances of software misuse, and 13% of males and only 2% of females report committing 10 or more software misuses. Further, 69% of males and 86% of females never committed data misuse, while 6% of males and less than 1% of females report committing 10 or more data misuses. However, the aforementioned percentages change dramatically when broken down by familiarity with computer usage policies. For example, of respondents who read the policies, the percentage committing 10 or more software misuses increases to 18% of males and 5% of females. Whereas, of those who do not read the policies, only 10% of males and 2% of females report this much software misuse. And, of those who read the policies, the percentage committing 10 or more data misuses increases to 7% of males and 2% of females. Of respondents who do not read the policies, these percentages are 5% of males and less than 1% of females.

The final demographic factor examined in this study is age. Thirty-five percent of respondents under 40 and 39% of respondents 40 and older report committing software misuse during their lifetimes, while 22% of respondents under 40 and 17% of respondents 40 and older report committing data misuse. However, the highest frequency of misuse occurs within the younger groups. Nine percent of respondents under 20 and 8% aged 21 to 29 report committing 10 or more lifetime software misuses, as compared to 4% each of respondents 30 to 39 and 40 and older. (Of the 509 usable responses to this question, only 23 respondents are 40 and older.) For data misuse, 3%, 3%, 2%, and 9% of respondents less than 20, 21 to 29, 30 to 39, and 40 and older, respectively, report 10 or more instances. However,

these results must be interpreted with caution as this survey was administered to college students, and thus is biased toward younger respondents.

# A Widespread Problem

Other studies have evaluated the prevalence of information systems misuse and computer crime by university students. A recent study notes 40% of students surveyed at two universities admitted to committing software piracy [3]. Further, none of these students were worried about punishment for their actions [3]. In a survey of 581 students at a southern university, 41% "knowingly used, made, or gave to another person a 'pirated' copy of commercially sold computer software" at some time in the past, while 34% did so during the past year [10]. Further, 18% "accessed another's computer account or files without his or her knowledge or permission just to look at the information or files," while 7% "added, deleted, changed, or printed" information from another's files without permission. Finally, 21% guessed passwords in attempting to access another student's accounts or files. In another study, 10% of respondents committed software misuse during the prior semester [5]. These misuse figures are very close to those generated within the present research, which indicate 34% of respondents committed software misuse during their lifetimes, while 22% committed data misuse sometime during their lifetimes.

The demographic results of the present study are also very similar to the results of past research. For example, males over 22 years old, enrolled as seniors or graduate students, were most likely to report committing misuse [5]. Further, misuse was especially common among majors dealing with forestry, engineering, business, liberal arts, and the sciences [5]; and misuse was more prevalent among computer science and engineering students, especially those in upper-level classes [3]. As previously noted, this research suggests males commit more misuse than females, as do students majoring in CIS.

Although the three universities discussed within this article publicly post computer usage policies (two of the universities insist students read these policies before email accounts are activated), only 24% of the respondents report having actually read the computer usage policies. Of these, 62% indicate reading the policies more than one year before the survey. Also, respondents who indicate reading the policies report higher levels of misuse.

These findings present an interesting challenge to universities: should additional resources be expended to familiarize all students with the university computer usage policies? The majority of students are unfamiliar with the university computer usage policies; however, students who are familiar with the policies report committing more misuse. Although an explanation of this unexpected result is beyond the scope of the current research, some possible explanations can be identified. For example, students who commit misuse could be more interested in reading the university computer usage policies than students not committing misuse. A second alternative might involve the university computer usage policies acting as a challenge to students and thus increasing the performance of misuse.

Until further research clarifies this matter, university computer security administrators must reconsider the methods used to educate students as to acceptable and unacceptable uses of university computing resources. This research clearly demonstrates that the majority of students are unfamiliar with the rules guiding their usage of university computing equipment. Perhaps repeated exposure would be more effective.

These unexpected results challenge the long-held belief that university computer usage policies prevent or limit the performance of misuse. Since organizations also utilize computer usage policies, the concern generated from these findings must be extended from the university setting to the organizational setting.

Although the use of student samples raises questions of representativeness and generalizability, in this case the students are valid users of the computing resources of these organizations. Users are defined as "individuals who interact with the system regularly" [11]; students utilizing university computers meet this definition of a user. From a technological standpoint, universities and other organizations share the same types of technology and the same risk factors. Universities must utilize the same methods as other organizations to protect themselves. In addition, universities may face even greater threats than the typical business organization. Since the computers in a classroom or lab are open for public use, tracking an instance of misuse usually leads back to the computer rather than the user. Further, university networks are often more vulnerable than corporate networks due to the need for collaboration and easy access to data [8].

The target population for this study is university students. The sample consists of 519 students enrolled in junior- and senior-level business courses at three Midwestern U.S. universities.

## Table 3 Misuse by Major

**Software Misuse:** How many times have you destroyed or copied *software*, used copied *software*, or distributed copied *software* without permission during your lifetime?

| Major | Ten or More | Seven to Nine | Four to Six | One to Three | Never | N |
|---|---|---|---|---|---|---|
| Arts and Science | 4.3% | 2.2% | 8.7% | 28.3% | 56.50% | 46 |
| Business and Economics | 3.9% | 3.3% | 6.1% | 15.6% | 71.1% | 360 |
| CIS | 24.4% | 2.6% | 3.8% | 20.5% | 48.7% | 78 |
| Other | 7.7% | 7.7% | 15.4% | 19.2% | 50.0% | 26 |
| Undecided | | | | 33.3% | 66.7% | 3 |

**Data Misuse:** How many times have you accessed, modified, or copied *data* stored on a computerized information system without authorization during your lifetime?

| Major | Ten or More | Seven to Nine | Four to Six | One to Three | Never | N |
|---|---|---|---|---|---|---|
| Arts and Science | 5.0% | | 2.5% | 10.0% | 82.5% | 40 |
| Business and Economics | 1.9% | 1.9% | 4.4% | 14.2% | 77.7% | 367 |
| CIS | 9.1% | 3.9% | 2.6% | 11.7% | 72.7% | 77 |
| Other | | 3.8% | 3.8% | 7.7% | 84.6% | 26 |
| Undecided | | | | | 100.0% | 3 |

The universities (and courses) were selected based upon the willingness of colleagues to participate in the study. Although this sample does not represent all students enrolled at these universities, this sample was deliberately chosen to maximize the potential for reported misuse conducted by the subject students. Students from arts and science colleges, business and economics colleges, and engineering colleges commit more misuse than other students [5].

All three universities utilize computer usage policies that outline acceptable and unacceptable use of computer systems. Each university also posts the policies on its Web site; two universities require their students to read these policies before email accounts are issued. The use of such policies has been linked to lower levels of misuse, while failing to use them has been linked to misunderstanding of correct use and thus to misuse [12].

The survey questionnaire was constructed by combining Straub's Computer Security Model Victimization Instrument [12] and items from instruments focusing on Ajzen's Theory of Planned Behavior [1]. The items based on Ajzen's Theory of Planned Behavior were customized to two specific areas of interest: software misuse and data misuse.

# Conclusion

Although concern with information systems misuse and computer crime is not new [10], it is of growing concern to commercial organizations [4] and the military [9]. Moreover, information systems misuse, piracy, and computer crime are international in scope. Reports suggest that the frequency of misuse is increasing rapidly [2]. Further, the cost of misuse is extremely high. A recent survey reports that respondents estimated losses of $141,496,560 during 2004. However, only 269 of 494 respondents were willing to report estimated dollar losses [4]. The actual loss is probably greater than stated since estimates only include recognized losses, and many organizations elect not to report losses for fear of negative publicity [4, 7].

Many organizations are so dependent upon their information systems that disruptions or failures often result in severe consequences that range from inconveniences to catastrophes such as complete organizational failure [6]. In addition, access to organizational information systems through networks and dial-in accounts leads to an extremely vulnerable environment [6]. This same situation may be found in universities around the country. Campus networks are becoming "an alluring target for hackers" and, possibly, terrorists [8].

Several researchers have reported that three-fourths or more of computer security violations by humans could be attributed to insiders or other trusted individuals, although current research suggests this trend may be changing. The 2004 CSI/FBI Computer Crime and Security Survey notes that about half of all reported incidents originate within the company, while half are external [4].

This research confirms past conclusions: students commit misuse and pirate software. Students possessing greater familiarity with computers report committing greater amounts of misuse. Individuals with certain majors, such as CIS, tend to commit more misuse than others. In addition, individuals with more computer experience tend to commit greater amounts of misuse than novices. Also, more misuse occurs by upperclassmen than by underclassmen. Finally, males commit more misuse than females, and individuals in their twenties and thirties report more misuse than other age groups.

However, the results of this research also suggest university computer usage policies are not effective in preventing students from committing misuse. First, the majority of respondents never read the computer usage policies at their universities. Second, students who read the policies report committing more misuses than those who do not read the policies. This unexpected result, which disagrees with past findings, suggests the need for continued research in this area.

Both of these results are particularly concerning as many organizations utilize written policy statements to explain proper and improper use of organizational information systems. It is thought such policies reduce the occurrence of misuse within an organization. Future research should address the issue of familiarity with computer usage policies. Given that the majority of respondents have not read the policies despite being required to do so by their respective universities, a method to enforce exposure to computer usage policies must be found.

Controlling misuse has been a concern in the MIS literature since the early 1960s [10], however, many organizations and critical systems are still vulnerable, especially as the modern computer environment incorporates ever-increasing amounts of networking and Internet connectivity. Existing research suggests organizations can defend themselves against such misuse by using computer usage policies. Unfortunately, the results herein, as well as simple observations of ever-increasing amounts of misuse, suggest these policies are ineffective. As a result, organizations need to consider other methods of protecting themselves. The first problem noted in the current research is a lack of familiarity with computer usage policies. Perhaps organizations need to enforce exposure, rather than relying on the user to read the policies. Further, repeated exposure could increase user retention of computer usage policies. The second problem noted in this research is the ineffectiveness of such policies at stopping misuse. While this could be a result of lack of familiarity with organizational computer usage policies, organizations must consider the possibility that such policies are simply ineffective in today's environment. This suggests other approaches should be explored, especially more active approaches, such as password protection and encryption.

**The results of this research also suggest university computer usage policies are not effective in preventing students from committing misuse.**

It is clear that additional means are necessary for every member of an organization to develop greater appreciation of, to understand, and to comply with computer usage policies. Unfortunately, simply having a company-wide computer usage policy in place does not correspondingly lead to the practice that the policy will be observed (or even enforced by the organization).

---

**These results are particularly concerning as many organizations utilize written policy statements to explain proper and improper use of organizational information systems.**

---

Future research should examine the impact of multiple exposures to those policies and should explore the relationship between repeated exposure to computer usage policies and reported instances of misuse as well as the implementation, communication, and enforcement of such policies. In order to reduce the cost and frequency of information systems misuse, piracy, and computer crime in today's environment, the authors recommend that an organization's (university's) employee (student) orientation program must include discussion of correct and incorrect computer usage, penalties imposed for violations, moral appeals, and methods of enforcement along with tougher enforcement policies.

# References

1. Ajzen, I. *Attitudes, Personality, and Behavior.* The Dorsey Press, Chicago, IL, 1988.
2. Anthes, G.H. Hack attack: Cyberthieves siphon millions from U.S. firms. *Computerworld 30*, 16 (1996), 81.
3. Carnevale, D. Software piracy seems rampant among students in a survey at 2 universities. *The Chronicle of Higher Education: Daily News* (March 4, 2002).
4. Gordon, L., Loeb, M., Lucyshyn, W., and Richardson, R. *2004 Ninth Annual CSI/FBI Computer Crime and Security Survey,* Computer Security Institute, 2004.
5. Hollinger, R.C. Crime by computer: Correlates of software piracy and unauthorized account access. *Security Journal 2*, 1 (1992), 2–12.
6. Loch, K.D., Carr, H.H., and Warkentin, M.E. Threats to information systems: Today's reality, yesterday's understanding. *MIS Quarterly 16*, 2 (1992), 173–186.
7. McAdams, A.C. Security and risk management: A fundamental business issue. *The Information Management Journal 38*, 4 (2004), 36–44.
8. Olsen, F. The growing vulnerability of campus networks. *The Chronicle of Higher Education 48*, 27 (March 15, 2002), A35–A36.
9. Schwartz, K.D. Hackers are ubiquitous, malicious, and taken far too lightly, experts say. *Government Computer News 16*, 23 (1997), 81–82.
10. Skinner, W.F. and Fream, A.M. A social learning theory analysis of computer crime among college students. *The Journal of Research in Crime and Delinquency 34*, 4 (1997), 495–518.
11. Stair, R.M. and Reynolds, G.W. *Principles of Information Systems: A Managerial Approach,* 3E. Course Technologies, Cambridge, MA, 1998.
12. Straub, D.W. Deterring computer abuse: The effectiveness of deterrent countermeasures in the computer security environment. Dissertation, Indiana University Graduate School of Business, 1986.

---

TIMOTHY PAUL CRONAN (cronan@uark.edu) is a professor and the M.D. Matthews Chair in Information Systems in the Sam M. Walton College of Business at the University of Arkansas. C. BRYAN FOLTZ (foltzc@utm.edu) is an assistant professor in the computer science and information systems department, College of Business, at the University of Tennessee, Martin, TN. THOMAS W. JONES (twjones@uark.edu) is a professor of Information Systems in the Sam M. Walton College of Business at the University of Arkansas.

---

From *Communications of the ACM*, 49(6), June 2006, pp. 85–89. Copyright © 2006 by Association for Computing Machinery, Inc. Reprinted by permission.

# Can Blogs Revolutionize Progressive Politics?

Lakshmi Chaudhry

"We have no interest in being anti-establishment," says Matt Stoller, a blogger at the popular Web site MyDD.com. "We're going to be the establishment."

That kind of flamboyant confidence has become the hallmark of blog evangelists who believe that blogs promise nothing less than a populist revolution in American politics. In 2006, at least some of that rhetoric is becoming reality. Blogs may not have replaced the Democratic Party establishment, but they are certainly becoming an integral part of it. In the wake of John Kerry's defeat in the 2004 presidential elections, many within the Democratic leadership have embraced blog advocates' plan for political success, which can be summed up in one word: netroots.

This all-encompassing term loosely describes an online grassroots constituency that can be targeted through Internet technologies, including e-mail, message boards, RSS feeds and, of course, blogs, which serve as organizing hubs. In turn, these blogs employ a range of features—discussion boards, Internet donations, live e-chat, social networking tools like MeetUp, online voting—that allow ordinary citizens to participate in politics, be it supporting a candidate or organizing around a policy issue. Compared to traditional media, blogs are faster, cheaper, and most importantly, interactive, enabling a level of voter involvement impossible with television or newspapers.

No wonder, then, that many in Washington are looking to blogs and bloggers to counter the overwhelming financial and ideological muscle of the right—especially in an election year. Just 18 months ago, the *New York Times Magazine* ran a cover story depicting progressive bloggers as a band of unkempt outsiders, thumbing their nose at party leadership. But now, it's the party leaders themselves who are blogging. Not only has Senate Minority leader Harry Reid started his own blog—Give 'em Hell Harry—and a media "war room" to "aggressively pioneer Internet outreach," he's also signed up to be the keynote speaker at the annual conference of the top political blog, Daily Kos.

Stoller predicts that as an organizing tool, "blogs are going to play the role that talk radio did in 1994, and that church networks did in 2002."

An Internet-fueled victory at the polls would certainly be impressive—no candidate backed by the most popular progressive blogs has yet won an election. But electoral success may merely confirm the value of blogs as an effective organizing tool to conduct politics as usual, cementing the influence of a select group of bloggers who will likely be crowned by the media as the new kingmakers.

Winning an election does not, however, guarantee a radical change in the relations of power. Technology is only as revolutionary as the people who use it, and the progressive blogosphere has thus far remained the realm of the privileged—a weakness that may well prove fatal in the long run.

In 2006, the biggest question facing blogs and bloggers is: Will their ascendancy empower the American people—in the broadest sense of the word—or merely add to the clout of an elite online constituency?

## The Birth of a Revolution

Alienation may not have been the mother of blogging technology, but it most certainly birthed the "political blogosphere." The galvanizing cause for the rapid proliferation of political blogs and their mushrooming audience was a deep disillusionment across the political spectrum with traditional media—a disillusionment accentuated by a polarized political landscape.

In the recent book *Blog! How the Newest Media Revolution Is Changing Politics, Business and Culture,* Web guru Craig Shirky links the rise of political blogs to the sharpening Red/Blue State divide. Both 9/11 and the Iraq war reminded people that "politics was vitally important," and marked the "moment people were looking for some kind of expression outside the bounds of network television," or, for that matter, cable news or the nation's leading newspapers.

Progressives were angry not just with the media but also with Democratic Party leaders for their unwillingness to challenge the Bush administration's case for war. That much-touted liberal rage found its expression on blogs like Eschaton, Daily Kos and Talking Points Memo, and continues to fuel the phenomenal growth of the progressive blogosphere. Like the rise of right-wing talk radio, this growth is directly linked to an institutional failure of representation. Finding no mirror for their views in the media, a large segment of the American public turned to the Internet to speak for themselves—often with brutal, uncensored candor.

As blogs have grown in popularity—at the rate of more than one new blog per second—they've begun to lose their vanguard edge. The very institutions that political bloggers often criticize have begun to adopt the platform, with corporate executives, media personalities, porn stars, lawyers and PR strategists all jumping into the fray. That may be why Markos Moulitsas Zúniga, the founder and primary voice of Daily Kos, thinks the word "blog" is beginning to outlive its usefulness. "A blog is merely a publishing tool, and like a tool, it can be used in any number of ways," he says.

But for many, to rephrase director Jean Renoir, a blogs are still a state of mind. To their most ardent advocates, blogs are standard-bearers of a core set of democratic values: participation, egalitarianism and transparency. Books like Dan Gillmor's *We the Media,* Howard Rheingold's *Smart Mobs,* James Surowiecki's *The Wisdom of Crowds,* and Joe Trippi's *The Revolution Will Not Be Televised* have become the bibles of progressive politics. Taken together, they express the dream of Internet salvation: harnessing an inherently democratic, interactive and communal medium, with the potential to instantaneously tap into the collective intellectual, political and financial resources of tens of millions of fellow Americans to create a juggernaut for social change.

According to Moulitsas, "The word 'blog' still implies a certain level of citizen involvement, of giving power to someone who is not empowered"—especially to progressives who, according to a study released last year by the New Politics Institute, have overtaken conservatives as the heavyweights of the political blogosphere.

## Vox Populi

Political blogs have often been most effective as populist fact-checkers, challenging, refuting and correcting perceived errors in news coverage.

"Independent bloggers have challenged the mainstream media and held them accountable, whether it's with Judy Miller or Bob Woodward," says Huffington Post founder Arianna Huffington. The most significant effect of this "we can fact-check your ass" credo has not been merely to put journalists on notice, but to change the way public knowledge is produced on a daily basis. "It's hard now for an important story to hit the front page of the *New York Times* and just die there," says Huffington. A news article is now merely the beginning of a public conversation in the blogosphere, where experts, amateurs and posers alike dissect its merits and add to its information, often keeping it alive long after journalists have moved on.

Popular understanding of what blogs are and what they can do has been muddled by an inevitably hostile relationship between political bloggers and traditional media. Writing in the Dec. 26 issue of *The New Republic,* Franklin Foer took bloggers to task for nursing "an ideological disdain for 'Mainstream Media'—or MSM, as it has derisively (and somewhat adolescently) come to be known." But Foer, like so many traditional journalists who criticize blogs, failed to grasp the very nature of his intended target.

Blogs are literally vox populi—or at the least the voice of the people who post entries and comments, and, to a lesser extent, of their devoted readers. Telling bloggers that they're wrong or to shut up is somewhat like telling respondents to an opinion survey to simply change their mind. When journalists reject bloggers as cranks or wingnuts, they also do the same to a large segment of the American public who see blogs as an expression of their views. Such dismissals feed the very alienation that makes blogs and bloggers popular.

The irony is that bloggers are most powerful when they work in tandem with the very media establishment they despise. "Bloggers alone cannot create conventional wisdom, cannot make a story break, cannot directly reach the vast population that isn't directly activist and involved in politics," says Peter Daou, who coordinated the Kerry campaign's blog outreach operations. Blogs instead exert an indirect form of power, amplifying and channeling the pressure of netroots opinion upwards to pressure politicians and journalists. "It's really a rising up," says Daou.

Can this online rebellion lead to real political change? The prognosis thus far is encouraging, but far from definitive.

## Can the Netroots Grow the Grassroots?

If television made politics more elitist and less substantive, blogs—and more broadly, netroots tools—have the potential to become engines of truly democratic, bottom-up, issue-rich political participation.

Blogs allow rank-and-file voters to pick the candidate to support in any given electoral race, influence his or her platform, and volunteer their time, money and expertise in more targeted and substantive ways. Democratic candidates in the midterm elections are already busy trying to position themselves as the next Howard Dean, vying for a digital stamp of approval that will bring with it free publicity, big money and, just maybe, a whole lot of voters.

When Rep. Sherrod Brown (D-Ohio) decided to take on Iraq veteran Paul Hackett in the Democratic primary for the Senate race in Ohio, he moved quickly to neutralize his opponent's advantage as the unquestioned hero of the progressive bloggers. The ace up Brown's sleeve: Jerome Armstrong, founder of the influential MyDD.com and veteran of Howard Dean's online campaign. Brown's next move was a blog entry on The Huffington Post titled, "Why I am a Progressive."

But not everyone is convinced that blogs can be as influential in a midterm election, when there are a large number of electoral contests spread across the country. "Raising money at a nationwide level for a special election is one thing," Pew scholar Michael Cornfield says, "but raising it and developing a core of activists and all the ready-to-respond messages when you have to run hundreds of races simultaneously—which is what will happen in 2006—is another thing." Moreover, the ability of the Internet to erase geographical distances can become a structural weakness in elections where district lines and eligibility are key.

**An effective netroots strategy in 2006 will have to master the failings of Howard Dean's campaign, which stalled because it couldn't grow his support base beyond his online constituency.**

An effective netroots strategy in 2006 will also have to master the shortcomings of the Dean's campaign, which stalled mainly because it failed to grow his support base beyond his online constituency—antiwar, white and high-income voters. In contrast, the Bush/Cheney operation used the Internet to coordinate on-the-ground events such as house parties, and rallies involving church congregations.

Cornfield describes the Republican model as, "one person who is online and is plugged into the blogosphere. That person becomes an e-precinct captain, and is responsible for reaching out offline or any means necessary for ten people."

This time around, Armstrong is determined to match the GOP's success. GrowOhio.org, which he describes as "a community blog for Democratic Party activists," will coordinate field operations for not just Brown but all Democratic candidates in each of Ohio's 88 counties. Its primary goal is to reach rural voters in areas where the campaign cannot field organizers on the ground.

"This isn't just about using the net for communications and fundraising, but for field organizing," Armstrong says.

What is also new in 2006 is the effort to redirect attention from the national to the local. "It's not just about focusing the national blogosphere on Ohio, but about building from the ground up in Ohio," Armstrong says. "Over 90 percent of our signups on GrowOhio.org are Ohio activists, and we will soon have Internet outreach coordinators in all 88 counties."

But many like Daou remain skeptical about the power of blogs to directly impact politics at the grassroots level. "You're not going to go out there and mobilize a million people and have them all come to the polls and donate money. Blogs will never do that," he says

And they may be even less effective in areas that are traditionally not as internet-savvy as the rest of the country, be it the rural red states or impoverished inner cities. Creating a virtual "community center" is unlikely to compensate for the Democrats' disadvantage on the ground. Due to the eroding presence of unions, Democrats no longer possess a physical meeting place where they can target and mobilize voters—unlike Republicans, who rely on a well-organized network of churches, gun clubs and chambers of commerce.

What is clear is that the 2006 elections will test the claim of blog evangelists that online activism can radically transform offline politics—a claim that is central to their far more ambitious vision for the future. In their book *Crashing the Gate* (to be released in April), Moulitsas and Armstrong envision blogs as the centerpiece of a netroots movement to engineer an imminent and sweeping transformation of the Democratic Party:

We are at the beginning of a comprehensive reformation of the Democratic Party—driven by committed progressive outsiders. Online activism on a nationwide level, coupled with offline activists at the local level . . . can provide the formula for a quiet, bloodless coup that can take control of the party. Money and mobilization are the two key elements of all political activity, and if the netroots have their way, the financial backbone of the Democratic Party will be regular people.

Whether a truly decentralized and "leaderless" netroots can function like a political party is debatable, but the latest wave of technological innovation does offer unprecedented opportunities for constructing a progressive movement for the digital age. Such an outreach effort would use the Internet very much like conservatives such as Richard Viguerie used direct mail to build a powerful political force. But in order to craft a genuinely democratic form of politics, the progressive blogosphere will have to overcome its greatest weakness: lack of diversity.

## The Rise of the Blogerati

In *Newsweek,* Simon Rosenberg, a beltway insider who lost the DNC chair to Dean, described the progressive blogosphere as the new "Resistance" within the Democratic Party, engaged in a civil war to wrest power from a craven and compromised beltway leadership. According to Rosenberg, the leaders of this "resistance" are the top progressive bloggers, more specifically the most popular and increasingly influential Moulitsas. Rosenberg told the *Washington Monthly,* "Frankly I don't think there's anyone who's had the potential to revolutionize the Democratic Party that Markos does."

Yet both the progressive blogosphere and the "revolutionaries" who dominate its ranks look a lot like the establishment they seek to overthrow.

The report by the New Politics Institute—which was launched by Rosenberg's New Democracy Network—notes: "Clearly, blogging is a world with a handful of haves, and a nearly uncountable number of have-nots. There are likely a few hundred thousand blogs in this country that talk about politics, but less than one-tenth of one percent of them account for more than 99 percent of all political blogging traffic."

For better or worse, traffic numbers have become an endorsement of the political agenda of specific individuals. While A-list bloggers repeatedly deny receiving any special treatment, the reality is that both the media and political establishment pay disproportionate attention to their views, often treating them as representative of the entire progressive blogosphere.

In a *Foreign Policy* article, political scientists Daniel Drezner and Henry Farrell cheerfully note, "The skewed network of the blogosphere makes it less time-consuming for outside observers to acquire information. The media only need to look at elite blogs to obtain a summary of the distribution of opinions on a given political issue." Why? Because the "elite blogs" serve as a filtering mechanism, deciding which information offered up by smaller blogs is useful or noteworthy. In effect, A-list blogs get to decide what issues deserve the attention of journalists and politicians, i.e., the establishment.

The past two years have also marked the emergence of a close relationship between top bloggers and politicians in Washington. A number of them—for example, Jesse Taylor at Pandagon, Tim Tagaris of SwingStateProject, Stoller and Armstrong—have been hired as campaign consultants. Others act as unofficial advisers to top politicos like Rep. Rahm Emmanuel (D-Ill.), who holds conference calls with preeminent bloggers to talk strategy. When the Senate Democrats invite Moulitsas to offer his personal views on netroots strategy—treating him, as a *Washington Monthly* profile describes, "a kind of part-time sage, an affiliate member"—the perks of success become difficult to deny.

Armstrong sees the rise of the blogger-guru—or "strategic adviser," as he puts it—as a positive development. Better to hire a blogger who is personally committed to the Democratic cause than a D.C.-based mercenary who makes money irrespective of who wins.

But the fact that nearly all these "advisers" are drawn from a close-knit and mostly homogenous group can make them appear as just a new boys' club, albeit one with better intentions and more engaged politics. Aside from notable exceptions like Moulitsas, who is part-Salvadoran, and a handful of lesser-known women who belong to group blogs, top progressive bloggers tend to be young, well-educated, middle class, male and white.

## Reach, Representation and Credibility

The lack of diversity is partly a function of the roots of blogging in an equally homogenous tech-geek community. Nevertheless, women and people of color constitute the fastest rising segment of those joining the blogosphere. Feminist and female-authored political blogs like Feministing, Bitch Ph.D, Echidne of the Snakes, and Salon's Broadsheet made considerable gains in traffic and visibility in 2005, as did Latino Pundit, Culture Kitchen, and Afro-Netizen. Better yet, they're forging networks and alliances to help each other grow. There is no doubt the membership of the blogosphere is changing, and will look very different five years from now. "We're just a step behind, just like any other area," says Pandagon's Amanda Marcotte.

But while the growth of the blogosphere may increase the actual traffic to a greater number of blogs, it also makes visibility far more scarce and precious for each new blogger. As one of the top women bloggers, Chris Nolan, noted on the PressThink blog, "The barrier to entry in this new business isn't getting published; anyone can do that. The barrier to entry is finding an audience."

Elite bloggers can play a key role in generating that audience. As Marcotte points out, "A lot more women are moving up in the Technorati rankings" (Technorati is a search engine for the blogosphere) because A-listers like Duncan Black and Kevin Drum in 2005 made it a priority to promote female bloggers. But when someone like Moulitsas decides to stop linking to other blogs—as he has recently done because he doesn't want to play "gatekeeper"—or when top bloggers repeatedly cite their fellow A-listers, it has enormous consequences. "It's pretty darn hard today to break in to the A-list if the other A-listers aren't linking to you," says Global Voices co-founder Rebecca MacKinnon.

If blogs derive their credibility from being the "voice of the people," surely we should be concerned about which opinions get attention over others. The question of representation affects not just who is blogging—and with great success—but also the audience of these blogs. What kind of democratic consensus does the blogosphere reflect when the people participating in it are most likely to be white, well-educated men?

Yet when it comes to issues of diversity, A-list bloggers like Moulitsas and Stoller can get defensive, and at times, dismissive. "Take a look at what you have today. Take a look at the folks who're leading the party, dominating the media, or even within corporations. Do you think the top ranks of any of those

## A Blog for the Other Six Billion of Us

Want to know about the upcoming cricket match between India and China? The recent arrests of human rights activists in Cambodia? Or why Bolivian president Evo Morales wears the same damned sweater for all his international photo-ops? You can find answers to these and other pressing questions on Global Voices, a gateway to the whole, wide virtual world that lies outside the confines of the American blogosphere. A project of the Berkman Center for Internet and Society at the Harvard Law School, the meta-blog is assembled by an international team of "blogger-editors" who serve as guides to conversations taking place on blogs in their corner of the world.

"If as an American you wanted to know what an ordinary Iranian or Bangladeshi or Chinese person thinks about what's happening in their country or their daily life, you had to wait for CNN to interview them or *New York Times* to quote them in an article," says Global Voices co-founder Rebecca MacKinnon. Now all you have to do is point on the country or region of your choice to find someone who can tell you, for example, just why the South African government is cozying up to Iran.

The Web site—which receives 10 to 12 thousand visitors a day—is in large part a response to the myopic reporting that passes for international news coverage in the mainstream media. The kind of reporting that MacKinnon was expected to deliver as the Asia correspondent for CNN USA, a job she quit in 2004. "I was told to cover my region more like a tourist, and that my expertise was getting in the way of doing the kind of story they wanted," she says.

But it's not just the media that are self-absorbed. Global Voices also offers an important corrective to the equally U.S.-centric focus of American political bloggers who seem as likely to forget that there are more pressing issues in this world than who wins what congressional seat in Colorado.

http://cyber.law.harvard.edu/globalvoices/

nstitutions is any more representative?" responds Stoller, his voice rising in indignation.

Where Stoller openly acknowledges the problem—describing blogs in one of his posts as "a new national town square for the white progressive base of the Democratic party"—and the need to take steps to tackle the disparity, Moulitsas is less generous. In his view, it's simply absurd to demand what he sarcastically describes as an "affirmative action of ideas" within an inherently meritocratic medium such as the blogosphere: "I don't see how you can say, 'Well, let's give more voice to African American lesbians.' Create a blog. If there's an audience, great. If there isn't, not so great." Besides, he suggests, if a Salvadoran war refugee—in his words, a "political nobody"—like him can make it on the Internet, there's nothing stopping anyone else from doing the same.

As for the relative paucity of top female progressive bloggers, Moulitsas is indifferent: "I haven't given it a lot of thought. I find it totally uninteresting. What I'm interested in is winning elections, and I don't give a shit what you look like." It's an odd and somewhat disingenuous response from an advocate of blogging as the ultimate tool of democratic participation.

Keith Jenkins, who authors Good Reputation Sleeping and works a day job as the picture editor at the *Washington Post,* says the low barriers to entry do not in themselves offer a sufficient guarantee of equal participation. "It's less about actively stopping and standing in the way and more about affirmatively enabling access, which was the underlying argument of civil rights movements and freedom movements across the board," he says. "It's about affirmatively making it possible for everybody to have a seat at the table, which benefits not only the people who are sitting down, but also the people who are already seated."

"We need to be encouraging a more diverse group of people to blog," agrees Global Voices' MacKinnon. "But we also need to be linking to them and giving them traffic so that they have a chance to make it to the A-list."

While the organic growth of the blogosphere may resolve issues of race and gender over time, it will do little to address its overwhelming bias toward urban professionals. And that can't be good news for a party that is already being punished at the polls for its weak connection to working-class Americans.

"For me the greatest problem is low-income people," Cornfield says. "The irony is that it's not because they don't have money to get a laptop—especially with the $100 laptop now. It's that people who are poor don't have the civic skill sets and motivation to go online and do these sorts of things. That will take a concerted effort."

At a time when the visible digital divide may be shrinking as increasing numbers of Americans come online, it may be replaced by an invisible version that benefits those who are well-educated, well-connected and organized.

Stoller does not think that it's important for blogs to reach a less-affluent audience: "Not everybody has to be part of that conversation. If someone wants to have access to those discussions, they should be able to do that. But for the most part, people—like that person working two shifts—will go on with their lives knowing that good people are making good decisions and policies on their behalf." Bloggers like Moulitsas—who is equally unconcerned that his blog will never reach "someone working at the DMV"—are likely betting that the cadre of activists they reach will be able to form connections across those differences within their community.

Perhaps sites like GrowOhio.org will prove them to be right if it manages to mobilize a constituency—e.g. rural voters—that is least likely to be wired, and in a region where the party's on-the-ground resources are weak. But any such strategy is unlikely to work if those in charge of crafting it—be they bloggers, politicians or so-called netizens—show little interest in expanding the reach of the progressive blogosphere to include the largest, most diverse audience possible. If the blogs are unable to bridge the class divide online, there is no reason to think they can create a grassroots movement that can do so in the real world.

"If you do make an active effort, it is easier to accomplish through the Internet than through pretty much any other medium including direct mail," Cornfield says. "But it will not happen on its own. It has to be a concerted effort." Social movements are built by people not ghosts in some virtual machine.

The *Washington Monthly* profile of Moulitsas included a revealing quote, in which he expressed disappointment at not being able to fulfill his dream of making it big in the tech industry back in 1998: "Maybe at some time, Silicon Valley really was this democratic ideal where the guy with the best idea made a billion dollars, but by the time I got there at least, it was just like anything else—a bunch of rich kids who knew each other running around and it all depended on who you knew."

The danger is that many may come to feel the same way about the blogosphere in the coming years.

---

**LAKSHMI CHAUDHRY** has been a reporter and an editor for independent publications for more than six years, and is a senior editor at *In These Times,* where she covers the cross-section of culture and politics.

# Center Stage

**The Internet has become an integral part of the way newspapers distribute their content, a phenomenon that's only going to increase. AJR's senior editor takes a firsthand look at four papers' Web operations.**

CARL SESSIONS STEPP

I t's only 9 A.M. and today's Houston Chronicle has barely hit people's doorsteps, but Sylvia Wood, the Chronicle's online local news editor, already is working a breaking, and heartbreaking, story.

A 15-year-old boy has been killed playing with a pistol with three friends. As seems so common, the boys thought the gun was unloaded. They pulled the trigger once. A harmless click. The second time, the ninth grader was shot in the chest.

Wood has posted a brief on chron.com. She has a Chronicle reporter on the way to the scene and is scrambling to locate a yearbook photo of the victim. She's also juggling two more spot stories while around her, in a newsroom as quiet as a library, print colleagues shuffle in sipping from their Starbucks cups and grunting their good mornings.

---

**The chance for error probably soars. On the other hand, you can correct those errors immediately and forever.**

---

It is a scene repeated more and more often as mainstream newsrooms adjust to becoming two worlds in one. The roller-coaster rhythm of print—the steady early climb followed by the precipitous plunge to deadline—is being joined, and may soon be overtaken, by the Web's all-out, all-day, all-night news cycle. Like the arrival of a gigantic planet next door, online newsrooms have begun exerting a culture-changing gravitational pull.

What do online newsrooms look like? How do they work? How are they affecting their print neighbors? I recently visited online newsrooms of various sizes and interviewed journalists within and outside the online world. The results were enlightening, and sometimes surprising.

First, at places large enough to have separate online newsrooms, they look similar to their print counterparts, except they are cleaner, quieter and younger. You see the usual rows of desks grouped into pods, with executives occupying glass offices. But things tend to look newer and sleeker, with carpet still unstained. There seem to be more twentysomethings. And because Web journalists mostly post copy gathered by others, there is less reporting going on and thus less noise.

Organizationally, online newsrooms are arranged by section. But you also find TV studios and mysterious hideaways where technical wizardry takes place (one at washingtonpost.com is known as The Cave). Titles vary. Online journalists are as likely to be called producers or news directors as editors.

A vital difference: With many people posting and without fixed schedules, it is impractical to funnel all content through a copy desk. So a fair amount of copy produced by the Web staff gets little or no editing, and few items get the multiple reads routine in print.

Design isn't a daily concern. Most homepages have a standard look, with a low-tech tool or template that lets editors post easily. Covering breaking news—especially crime, a role that had been appropriated by broadcast—is making a comeback. The running spot-news blog seems especially popular.

Most striking are two clear, probably transforming trends: a move toward merging online and print newsrooms, and a surge toward producing news almost around the clock. These changes may well revolutionize newsrooms, and they raise important questions. Who will produce the volumes of copy required? How will quality be monitored without the overlapping layers of editing? What will be stressed in hiring? How will all this affect the enduring and ingrained newsroom culture?

To explore all this, a good place to start is the sprawling operations of the Houston Chronicle and chron.com.

D ean Betz, chron.com's online news editor and in effect its managing editor, is hurrying to the newsroom's 4 P.M. meeting when he encounters, in an elevator, Dudley Althaus, a Mexico City correspondent on a home visit.

The reporter has heard the paper wants him to start a blog. Betz nods. The reporter wonders how you balance news and opinion in a blog. Let's discuss it with your editor, Betz replies. In the hallway, the Chronicle's reader representative, James Campbell, buttonholes Betz. He's already blogging. They chat about it as they enter the news meeting, a huge affair involving more than 35 people. Betz sets up an online connection projected onto a big screen.

He's called on right away by Editor Jeff Cohen. Betz describes what chron.com and its competitors have been posting.

Some key financial reports are due today, and Cohen presses for quick online publication. "We have got to be getting these stories up the second they come in," Cohen says. Then he announces, to predictable titters, that the Web site will be partnering in some unspecified way with a local Web-based dating service.

From blogs to business data to dating, Web activity is seizing center stage in Houston.

Betz, 44, says the goal is "making the newspaper and the Web site one thing. That's the only way newspapers have any chance of making things work—not thinking they are newspaper companies, but that they are news companies."

Editor Cohen, 51, is a convert. His print newsroom has about 350 staffers, and the paper's daily circulation is about 520,000. As at most newspapers, circulation and penetration have dropped, but Cohen says "we have more than made up for it on the Web." With 20 editorial staffers, the Web site draws some 2.9 million unique viewers a month and makes a profit. "It's obvious you have to start devoting more of your resources to the Web," Cohen says.

For now, most Web staffers work from the paper's 10th floor. Only Sylvia Wood sits in the fifth-floor city room. But all that is going to change.

Cohen opens a binder to show his online goals for 2006: to generate more content from readers, develop more Spanish content and "further integrate the Web and the newsroom."

He leads a brisk tour of space being remodeled to bring Web journalists onto the newsroom floor. "In order for it to be clear what we're doing," he says, "they've got to be close—in sight, in mind, not out of sight, out of mind."

Environmental reporter Dina Cappiello, 32, understands. "Psychologically, the physical presence says, 'This is important. This isn't going to be an afterthought.'"

The one Web editor inside the newsroom, Wood, sits with other assistant city editors at the center of the action. Here, she says, "You're pretty much clued in as to what the reporters are doing."

Wood, 39, works a 7 A.M. to 4 P.M. shift. She takes a handoff from an overnight editor, sits in on the morning news meeting, trolls early for updates and spot news, and tries to post about eight local items a day. "My goal," Wood says, "is to get as much as we can up before the 12 o'clock news."

The morning flurry stems in part from the fact that visits to chron.com spike as people arrive at work. The entire morning paper "rolls over" onto the Web around 12:30 A.M., but the site evolves all day. There are updates and Web-only features from sports and entertainment as well as news, plus numerous discussion forums and blogs by staff members and readers.

## TV News Online

The police chase breaks out at 2:20 P.M., just as Jim Thompson, KHOU-TV's Web site manager, is saying, "Our bread and butter is immediacy, breaking news, delivering content as it happens."

On cue, both Channel 11, a CBS affiliate, and its partner, KHOU.com, go straight to live chase video from the station's helicopter. Web Deputy Editor Michelle Homer streams it online, while KHOU reporters provide TV voice-over. The chase runs live for more than an hour until its dramatic end. The runaway driver crashes into a car occupied by a grandmother, mother and 8-month-old girl. As cameras roll and police close in, the mother leaps from her car and pounds furiously on the offending vehicle.

With about 350,000 unique visitors a month and a full-time staff of four, Belo-owned KHOU.com is smaller than its Houston Chronicle competitor. But it aggressively tracks local news, especially stories with hot video.

The KHOU newsroom resembles a small newspaper, with reporters' desks lining one side. The room is dominated by a power triangle: the TV assignment desk, the TV producers' pod and the Web pod, which benefits from the proximity. "Anyone who has worked in a newsroom knows," Thompson says, "that about 50 percent of what you get you overhear."

The police chase electrifies the room. All four assignment desk editors are simultaneously barking into phones and pounding keyboards. A news meeting comes to a standstill as Executive News Director Keith Connors follows the action. Thompson's group staffs the Web site six days a week, changing the lead story at least every three hours or so. The set-up is similar to newspaper sites, but far more preoccupied with video.

"If on TV we don't get video, we don't have a story," Thompson, 38, says. "So whenever a story breaks, our team is out the door. And that plays great for the Web site."

The Web also lends itself to footage that might not suit TV, Thompson says. "We don't want it to be a polished TV stand-up. We want it to be rough and raw. We want you the viewer to know what's it's like to be there. Sometimes it's not going to be pretty, but it's going to be the fastest, most accurate news you can get."

Connors plans to double the Web staff this year. "To be in this game, you have to get in totally," he says. "We are not wading in the kiddie pool. We need to jump totally in."

—Carl Sessions Stepp

Legal reporter Mary Flood, 52, a Web enthusiast who has covered Enron-related stories for three years, says she has filed as many as 12 updates a day from important court cases. "It's simultaneously made things more exciting and more exhausting," she says.

## Online Favorites

Most viewed newspaper Web sites in February

### Unique visitors

| | |
|---|---|
| nytimes.com | 12,702,000 |
| USAToday.com | 10,372,000 |
| washingtonpost.com | 8,244,000 |
| latimes.com | 4,865,000 |
| SFGate.com (San Francisco Chronicle) | 4,602,000 |
| wsj.com (Wall Street Journal) | 3,937,000 |
| Boston.com (Boston Globe) | 3,525,000 |
| nydailynews.com | 3,026,000 |
| chicagotribune.com | 2,942,000 |
| chron.com (Houston Chronicle) | 2,916,000 |

Source: *Nielsen//NetRatings*

Wood, Flood and practically everyone else acknowledge that with speed and continuous posting come risks. "The chance for error probably soars," says Flood, who urges sources to look for mistakes and alert her. "On the other hand, you can correct those errors immediately and forever."

Most Web content does get edited, although blurbs, headlines and short items may be posted directly by one person, and some contributors' blogs are unedited.

Cohen stresses that "I would prefer to have it completely accurate, vetted and dead-solid perfect rather than racing to get it up. If there are five editors that read every story before the newspaper version, there may be just two or three who vet it for the Web site. But still they are acutely aware of the accuracy issues."

Scott Clark, 46, the Web site's vice president and editor, says Web producers want better quality control. They consult wire service veterans about handling the fast pace. "We're jumping into stories in progress, and we get things wrong, the natural errors that come from the fog of news," Clark says. "We talk about knowing when to 'vague it up' and wait for the facts to settle. People on the Web recognize that they're seeing a flow and not the newspaper end product. They expect to come back and see that the story has changed. But the standards of journalism on the Web are the same as in print."

Almost everybody also agrees that the 24-7 cycle stretches resources.

Science writer Eric Berger, 32, is another big Web fan. As a reporter and SciGuy blogger, his is a familiar byline online. He tells about covering the launch of the shuttle Discovery last July. He rose before dawn and blogged from 4:55 A.M. through the 9:39 A.M. launch until 11 A.M., then wrote a print story for the next morning's front page. He isn't complaining, Berger stresses, but it's clear the Web adds work.

Reporter Cappiello underlines the point. "Industrywide, not just here, the Web requires more labor," she says. "I'm a little concerned how a reporter who covers cops is going to not only file, file, file for the Web, but report the print story and do the Sunday enterprise story."

Cohen does foresee his Web staff growing this year. Still, extra work and all, these journalists and others increasingly welcome the chance to revitalize their work. Blogging has been a big incentive; all those writers who wanted to be columnists now have the chance. You still encounter some skeptics, but it seems that a corner has been turned.

"There are people who think this is a ridiculous extension of their job," Flood says. "I look at this as my new job. It's the future of news. I love it."

This will also be the year of print-online integration at USA Today, where Editor Ken Paulson wants "a single 24-hour news organization." He's even moved the site's top executive, Kinsey Wilson, to the paper's masthead as an executive editor. For now, the online newsroom still occupies it own floor in USA Today's gleaming McLean, Virginia, skyscraper. But Paulson says that "culturally, we're merged," and over the coming months many sports, business, features and other online staffers will move side by side with their print counterparts.

On the day I visit, the Web staff is gathering for its 8:15 A.M. "cabinet meeting," so called because the nine editors huddle around a row of metal filing cabinets.

USAToday.com staffs its homepage around the clock, although less gets posted once the newspaper's contents are uploaded by midnight. Today's homepage editor, Brett Molina, 30, has been on duty since 6 A.M., updating stories about a mine fire and an Osama bin Laden tape.

The news meeting, one of several daily, resembles the typical print get-together, except more attention goes to multimedia and special effects. For example, Chet Czarniak, 55, the online managing editor who presides, expresses concern about live coverage of the mining disaster. "If raw video comes in," he warns, "be careful what we use."

Another exchange highlights the costs and benefits of immediacy. An editor has spotted what he calls a classic dumb headline, "Flawed coin was a mistake." Unlike in a print edition where it would live forever, the head is quickly rewritten.

With more than 10 million unique visitors a month, USAToday.com has 75 editorial staffers, with a funky combination of titles, some from print, some from broadcast. They face an unusual mission, since they don't produce local news. Their national audience spills over several time zones. Viewers come for assorted news, sports and the special packages and surprises associated with the USA Today brand.

USAToday.com puts less emphasis on breaking-news updates from its reporters than on special stories, imaginative packaging and Web-only features. "I'd rather have their 'breaking analysis' than chasing the basics," says Executive Producer Jody Brannon, 46. "What we're trying to do online," she adds, "is celebrate a new way of storytelling that leverages our expertise in visuals, graphics and multimedia." For example, video editor David Freer, 22, is fixing up an on-site TV studio and plans to "pump up this site" with video.

The action seems nonstop, with the homepage changing at least every 15 or 20 minutes. "The pace is just incredible," Czarniak says. "Saturday at 11 P.M. is just as important as Monday at 11 A.M. Speed to market is vital. It's not even a deadline a minute. There are constant deadlines. Our train is always leaving the station."

News Editor Randy Lilleston, 46, sees print people learning "broadcast sensibilities." "Stories are not permanent," he says. "They evolve. The story you read now is not the same as the one you'll read in two hours."

Lilleston, too, worries about balancing accuracy and speed. "Do you get the vetting you get in a newspaper? No, you do not," he says. But he adds crisply, "I reject the idea that online is an excuse for sloppiness. One of my goals is to knock down the idea that it is OK to be temporarily wrong. It is not OK."

Lilleston sees progress toward online safeguards. For example, most items posted directly are short, so typos and errors may be relatively easy to spot. Without a copy desk, editors are expected to turn to the person sitting next to them for a "second set of eyes." They constantly read behind one another, before and after postings.

News Director Patty Michalski, 33, who oversees the homepage, advises, "Get it right the first time. If it means taking two seconds longer, so be it." Michalski also stresses those small but all-important headlines, subheads (known as "chatter") and blurbs. Those few words often determine readership. She pushes posters to seek suggestions from others and to consider "anything to make it a teensy bit more specific."

Across the sites I visited, editors are emphasizing journalistic skills over technical know-how. A few years ago, Czarniak says, hiring priorities were something like 60 percent technical skills, 40 percent journalistic. "Now we're going the other way. The tools are much improved. It's easier to publish now. What we're looking for most are people who know good storytelling."

Even at USA Today, where the newspaper helped revolutionize design, the look of the homepage remains relatively constant. Too much change, says Brannon, "complicates the experience for the user." Except for mammoth stories, the homepage sticks to two or three "standard looks," with templates for easy posting.

Nor did I find many signs of the totally converged reporter, prowling for news with notebook, tape recorder and digital camera and wearing a videocam as headgear. Increasingly, reporters do take photos and provide audio, and some sites are experimenting with giving reporters, especially abroad, cell phones that allow video feeds. But few yet have the time, or capability, to function as multimedia do-it-alls. "I've seen their video," laughs video editor Freer, "and I don't like it."

For now, the big step is consolidation, a culture shock in itself. Czarniak says merging makes sense for production, quality and content. "The ultimate vision is that there are conversations about content among everyone," he says. "You're not concerned about the platform. You're concerned about how to tell the story."

Other major papers are moving toward consolidation, including the New York Times and the Los Angeles Times. But merging news operations can be complicated. In some places, the print newsroom is unionized while the online newsroom is not. Sometimes more than one corporate structure is involved. Besides, independence has its own advantages.

So not everyone is consolidating. A prime exception is washingtonpost.com, located across the Potomac River, in Virginia, four miles from its print sibling.

Technically, it's a separate company: Washington Post-Newsweek Interactive. Post Ombudsman Deborah Howell, in a column last December titled "The Two Washington Posts," quoted Post Co. CEO Donald Graham as saying that, while the two versions obviously must cooperate, each is a full-time, stand-alone operation.

## The action seems nonstop, with the homepage changing at least every 15 or 20 minutes.

Many Web staffers privately believe being closer would help. But there also is a sense that separate status lets the Web site flourish outside the shadow of the magisterial printed Post.

## Whether it is the Web or print or handhelds, the future is giving people news when they want it and how they want it.

In February, the Newspaper Association of America named washingtonpost.com as the best overall news site among large publications.

Staff members also point out that coordination by phone, e-mail and instant messaging is easy. In addition, a seven-person Continuous News Desk inside the Post's print newsroom provides copy and liaison.

Here, too, the online newsroom resembles that of a newspaper, except that the architecture is more modernistic, the tones more subdued. It's a jeans and sneakers environment, but less rowdy than many city rooms.

Executive Editor and Vice President Jim Brady, 38, says it sometimes feels like an insurance office, and he goads people to walk rather than e-mail across the room.

A big challenge, Brady says, is "getting a newsroom to move at lightning speed." But he sees somewhat less pressure here because, with stories constantly being posted, "there isn't the big run-up to deadline and then a sigh of relief."

The site, with about 65 full-time editorial staff and 20 to 24 part-timers, received 8.2 million unique visitors in February, according to Nielsen//NetRatings. About 80 percent are not from the Washington area, so the homepage is "bifurcated." A computer reads the ZIP codes of incoming viewers and directs them to either the local or the national homepage.

Dominating the room is the newsdesk, a semicircular command center occupied by a homepage editor, breaking news producer and photo editor. They work facing 10 monitors tuned to local and national news and weather. Two people have overnight duty, but the action picks up with the 5:30 A.M. arrival of a dayside homepage editor. Regular news meetings take place at 7 A.M., noon, 3 P.M. and 7 P.M.

Deputy Editor Meghan Collins Sullivan, 31, oversees the homepage and what she calls "the constant decision-making process." Rarely do more than a few minutes pass between updates, and the site gets frequent feeds from the Continuous News Desk's writers and other Post reporters. "There's a different sense of urgency here because we are on constant deadline," Sullivan says. "We don't have a limited amount of space. We have an infinite amount. So you can always be doing new things."

Sullivan and homepage editor Kenisha Malcolm, 28, convene the noon news meeting, similar to those at other Web sites. On this day, about 15 people take part, including, via conference call from the Post, Lexie Verdon, 51, from Continuous News. There's the usual discussion of upcoming stories, plus attention to audio, video, special features and the explosively popular blogs and online discussions.

Brady's second in command, Editor Howard Parnell, 45, grew up in nearby Falls Church, Virginia, and delivered the Post as a kid. He spent more than a decade working in print and the past 11 years online. Parnell agrees that the biggest difference online is the 24-7 pace. But he also sees across-the-board similarities.

"The managing people part is similar," he says, "and the emphasis on storytelling, on getting it right, and, just as it was in my newspaper days, the idea that this is a public trust."

C onsolidation's not that big an issue at the Daily Times in Salisbury, Maryland, where the "online newsroom" consists pretty much of City Editor Joe Carmean posting from his desk when he has time.

This morning's Web lead is about the newspaper itself, where a press breakdown has delayed delivery for hours. Papers are being printed at another Gannett paper up the road, and many won't be delivered until after lunch. With regular carriers unavailable, Executive Editor Greg Bassett and other honchos have been drafted to run delivery routes. The phone is ringing ceaselessly, and people wander into the lobby scouting for copies.

Ironically, the print version's front page can be found only one place this morning: on the Web site (delmarva.com), which regularly links to a pdf version of page one.

Bassett, 45, in the office since 4 A.M. and out on his route since 9, finally makes it back around 2 P.M., having just delivered his last 50 copies to subscribers at a local jail. He edits his hometown paper, which is unusual in this mobile age. In fact, he was born in the hospital directly across the street.

The paper has 28 editorial staffers, about 29,000 in circulation and 130,000 unique Web visitors a month. It's a small, community-oriented operation, but Bassett sees the future as clearly as anyone else, and he embraces the Web's potential.

"We write for online and update for print," he recites, echoing a refrain heard often around Gannett. "The only time I'm happy is when I have a newspaper in front of me and a tuna sandwich in my hand. But my 9-year-old son is going to get all his news from his cell phone."

When corporate executives solicited his training priorities for this year, Bassett specified "how to set up a 24-hour newsroom" and "how to write for online."

For now, only a handful of newsroom staffers can post, including Bassett, Carmean and Managing Editor Erick Sahler. More are being trained, and Bassett hopes to hire a full-time "online champion" this year.

Contents from the paper and several affiliated weeklies are automatically uploaded through Gannett's Digital Production Center, and Gannett provides additional Web packages. Wire news is also automatically updated. The Web site does relatively little with local sports, has no discussion groups or blogs (though one is planned), and offers only occasional audio. Its emphasis is on breaking news.

Like his counterparts at larger papers, Bassett pushes reporters toward feeding the Web quickly.

Around noon the day I visit, a reporter files a short piece on a morning meeting. City Editor Carmean scans it, then calls the writer. "Just one quick question," he says, and then peppers him with seven questions. (Editors are like that.) A few minutes later, Carmean calls up the Web template, types in a headline and subhead and posts the story.

Sahler, 39, sees the Web as a vehicle for once again competing with broadcast to cover wrecks, fires and early meetings.

"If there is a murder, before I could be content to wait for the cops to gather information because I was only thinking of publishing for tomorrow," says reporter Ben Penserga, 27. "Now I have to grab what I can for the Web."

**The managing people part is similar, and the emphasis on storytelling, on getting it right, and, just as it was in my newspaper days, the idea that this is a public trust.**

Carmean concedes that Web duties lengthen his day by about two hours, but he claims not to mind. "Sure it's long hours, and there are a lot of time-consuming elements," he says. "But I want to do it. I want this stuff on the Web. I want to reach a younger audience. There is no second place in journalism."

B ack at the Houston Chronicle, Sylvia Wood has, before noon, posted a yearbook photo of the ninth grader and a staff-written story on the shooting. Now she is racing after other stories.

It is easy to imagine the time, coming soon, when the 24-hour Web cycle dominates the newsroom tempo, work flow and culture. It will bring new excitement, but giant demands for resources in a time of cutbacks and thin reserves. It may also bring serious quality-control issues. Print journalism's credibility has long been connected to its layers of editing.

As for tomorrow's journalists, they will more likely be identified by their function than by their medium. As newsrooms turn into diversified information retailers, the biggest distinction may be between those who develop the content and those who distribute it, via print, broadcast, the Internet or other channels.

Eventually, many editors foresee consolidated newsrooms with a single chain of command and few distinctions between print and online. For now, most aren't leaping quite that far.

First comes the physical merger. That will bring both groups into side-by-side cooperation but maintain, at least at first, their separate identities. After that, who knows?

"The endgame," says Chronicle Editor Jeff Cohen, "is to have all our excellent journalists producing content, and air traffic controllers putting it on the various platforms."

Or, as Sylvia Wood says: "Whether it is the Web or print or handhelds, the future is giving people news when they want it and how they want it."

---

Senior Editor **CARL SESSIONS STEPP** (cstepp@jmail.umd.edu) teaches at the Philip Merrill College of Journalism at the University of Maryland. He wrote about newspapers' increased interest in short-form narratives in AJR's August/September 2005 issue.

# The Coming Robot Army

**Introducing America's future fighting machines.**

STEVE FEATHERSTONE

A small gray helicopter was perched on the runway, its rotors beating slowly against the shroud of fog and rain blowing in from the Chesapeake Bay. Visibility was poor, but visibility did not matter. The helicopter had no windows, no doors, and, for that matter, no pilot. Its elliptical fuselage looked as if it had been carved out of wood and sanded smooth of detail. It hovered above the runway for a moment, swung its blind face toward the bay, and then dissolved into the mist.

The helicopter was the first among a dozen unmanned aerial vehicles (UAVs) scheduled to fly during the annual Association for Unmanned Vehicle Systems International conference in Baltimore. The live demonstration area at Webster Field, a naval air facility located seventy miles south of Washington, D.C., was laid out along the lines of a carnival midway. Big defense contractors and small engineering firms exhibited the latest military robots under white tents staked out alongside an auxiliary runway. Armed soldiers kept watch from towers and strolled through the throng of military officers and industry reps. I took a seat among rows of metal chairs arrayed in front of a giant video screen, which displayed a live feed from the helicopter's surveillance camera. There was little to see except clouds, so the announcer attempted to liven things up.

"Yesterday we saw some boats out there," he said, with an aggressive enthusiasm better suited to a monster-truck rally. "They didn't know they were being targeted by one of the newest UAVs!" Next, two technicians from AeroVironment, Inc., jogged onto the airfield and knelt in the wet grass to assemble what appeared to be a remote-controlled airplane. One of them raised it over his shoulder, leaned back, and threw it into the air like a javelin. The airplane—called the Raven—climbed straight up, stalled, dipped alarmingly toward the ground, and then leveled off at two hundred feet, its tiny electric motor buzzing like a mosquito. The screen switched to show the Raven's video feed: a bird's-eye view of the airstrip, at one end of which a large American flag flapped limply on a rope strung between two portable cranes next to an inflatable Scud missile launcher.

"A lot of the principles we use here are taken from the model industry," an AeroVironment spokesman told the announcer

as the Raven looped around the field. The U.S. military has purchased more than 3,000 Ravens, many of which have been deployed in Iraq and Afghanistan, but apparently none of the military officers present had ever seen one land. At the end of the Raven's second flight, the crowd went silent as the tiny plane plummeted from the sky and careered into the ground, tearing off its wings. The technicians scrambled to the crash site, stuck the wings back on, and held the Raven triumphantly above their heads.

"It's designed that way," the spokesman explained.

"Hey, if you can't fix it with duct tape," the announcer said, "it's not worth fixing, am I right?"

Other teams took the field to demonstrate their company's UAVs. The sheer variety of aircraft and their launching methods—planes were slung from catapults and bungee cords, shot from pneumatic guns and the backs of pickup trucks, or simply tossed by hand into the air—testified to the prodigious growth in demand for military robots since the terrorist attacks of September 11, 2001, and the subsequent "global war on terrorism." In his opening conference remarks, Rear Admiral Timothy Heely compared the embryonic UAV market with aviation in the first decades of the twentieth century, when the Wright brothers built planes in their workshop and dirigibles carried passengers. "It's all out there," he said. "You don't want to throw anything away."

## Weaponized robots are the ultimate "force multiplier"—they can do the most damage with less people

It started to drizzle again. The military officers sought refuge under a catered VIP tent decorated with red, white, and blue bunting while the rest of us scattered in all directions. I headed to the unmanned ground vehicle (UGV) tent located at the far end of the runway. The tent's interior was dim; the air, sticky and hot. Tables stocked with brochures and laptops lined the vinyl walls. Robots rested unevenly on the grass. This was the first year UGVs were allowed demonstration time at the conference, and company reps were eager to show what their robots could do. A rep from iRobot, maker of the popular Roomba robotic vacuum cleaner, flipped open a shiny metal briefcase that contained an LCD monitor and a control panel studded with switches and buttons for operating the PackBots, a "man-packable" tracked robot not much bigger than a telephone book. Hundreds of PackBots have already been deployed in Iraq.

"If you can operate a Game Boy, you're good," the rep said.

A Raytheon engineer fired up an orange robot that looked like a track loader used in excavation. The only difference was a solid black box containing a radio receiver on top of the cage where the human driver normally sat. It rumbled out of the tent onto the airfield, followed by a camera crew.

"It's a Bobcat," the announcer shouted. "It's a *biiig* Bobcat!"

The Bobcat rolled up to a steel garbage bin containing a "simulated Improvised Explosive Device," hoisted it into the air with a set of pincers, and crumpled it like a soda can. A Raytheon spokesman listed all the things the tricked-out Bobcat could do, such as breach walls.

"You could also crush things like a car if you wanted to," he added.

"I never thought of crushing something," the announcer said. "But yeah, this would do very nicely."

After the Bobcat had dispatched the mangled garbage bin and returned to the tent, I asked a Raytheon engineer if the company had thought about arming it with machine guns. "Forget the machine guns," he said dismissively. "We're going lasers."

Military robots are nothing new. During World War II, Germans sent small, remote-controlled bombs on tank treads across front lines; and the United States experimented with unmanned aircraft, packing tons of high explosives into conventional bombers piloted from the air by radio (one bomber exploded soon after takeoff, killing Joseph Kennedy's eldest son, and the experiment was eventually shelved). But in a war decided by the maneuver of vast armies across whole continents, robots were a peculiar sideshow.

The practice of warfare has changed dramatically in the past sixty years. Since Vietnam, the American military machine has been governed by two parallel and complementary trends: an aversion to casualties and a heavy reliance on technology. The Gulf War reinforced the belief that technology can replace human soldiers on the battlefield, and the "Black Hawk down" incident in Somalia made this belief an article of faith. Today, any new weapon worth its procurement contract is customarily referred to as a "force multiplier," which can be translated as doing more damage with less people. Weaponized robots are the ultimate force multiplier, and every branch of the military has increased spending on new unmanned systems.

At $145 billion, the Army's Future Combat Systems (FCS) is the costliest weapons program in history, and in some ways the most visionary as well. The individual soldier is still central to the FCS concept, but he has been reconfigured as a sort of plug-and-play warrior, a node in what is envisioned as a sprawling network of robots, manned vehicles, ground sensors, satellites, and command centers. In theory, each node will exchange real-time information with the network, allowing the entire system to accommodate sudden changes in the "battle space." The fog of war would become a relic of the past, like the musket, swept away by crystalline streams of encrypted data. The enemy would not be killed so much as deleted.

FCS calls for seven new unmanned systems. It's not clear how much autonomy each system will be allowed. According to *Unmanned Effects (UFX): Taking the Human Out of the Loop*, a 2003 study commissioned by the U.S. Joint Forces Command, advances in artificial intelligence and automatic target recognition will give robots the ability to hunt down and kill the enemy with limited human supervision by 2015. As the study's title suggests, humans are the weakest link in the robot's "kill chain"—the sequence of events that occurs from the moment an enemy target is detected to its destruction.

At Webster Field, the latest link in the military's increasingly automated kill chain was on display: the Special Weapons Observation Reconnaissance Detection System, or SWORDS. I squatted down to take a closer look at it. Despite its theatrical name, SWORDS was remarkably plain, consisting of two thick rubber treads, stubby antennae, and a platform mounted with a camera and an M240 machine gun—all painted black. The robot is manufactured by a company named Foster-Miller, whose chief representative at the show was Bob Quinn, a slope-shouldered, balding man with bright blue eyes. Bob helped his engineer to get SWORDS ready for a quick demo. Secretary of the Army Francis Harvey, the VIP of VIPs, was coming through the UGV tent for a tour.

"The real demonstration is when you're actually firing these things," Bob lamented. Unfortunately, live fire was forbidden at Webster Field, and Bob had arrived too late to schedule a formal demonstration. At another conference two months before, he had been free to drive SWORDS around all day long. "I was going into the different booths and displays, pointing my gun, moving it up and down like the sign of the cross. People were going like this"—he jumped back and held up his hands in surrender—"then they would follow the robot back to me because they had no idea where I was. And that's the exact purpose of an urban combat capability like this."

Sunlight flooded into the tent as Secretary Harvey parted the canopy, flanked by two lanky Rangers in fatigues and berets. Bob ran his hand over his scalp and smoothed his shirt. It was sweltering inside the tent now. Beneath the brim of his tan baseball cap, Secretary Harvey's face was bright red and beaded with sweat. He nodded politely, leaning into the verbal barrage of specifications and payloads and mission packages the reps threw at him. When he got to SWORDS, he clasped his hands behind his back and stared down at the robot as if it were a small child. Someone from his entourage excitedly explained the various weapons it could carry.

Bob had orchestrated enough dog-and-pony shows to know that technology doesn't always impress men of Secretary Harvey's age and position. "We don't have it in the field yet," Bob interrupted, going on to say that SWORDS wasn't part of any official procurement plan. It was a direct result of a "bootstrap effort" by real soldiers at Picatinny Arsenal in New Jersey who were trying to solve real problems for their comrades in the field. "And soldiers love it," he added.

On the long bus ride back to Baltimore, I sat behind Master Sergeant Mike Gomez, a Marine UAV pilot. "All we are are battery-powered forward observers," he joked. Mike was biased against autonomous robots that could fire weapons or drop bombs with minimal, if any, human intervention. There were too many things that could go wrong, and innocent people could be killed as a result. At the same time, he wasn't opposed to machines that were "going to save Marines, save time, save manpower, save lives."

It wasn't the first time that day I'd heard this odd contradiction, and over the next three days I'd hear it again and again. It was as if everyone had rehearsed the same set of talking points. Robots will take soldiers out of harm's way. Robots will save lives. Allow robots to pull the trigger? No way, it'll never happen. But wasn't the logical outcome of all this fancy technology an autonomous robot force, no humans required save for those few sitting in darkened control rooms half a world away? Wasn't the best way to save lives—American lives, at least—to take humans off the battlefield altogether? Mike stared out the bus window at the passing traffic.

"I don't think that you can ever take him out," he said, his breath fogging the tinted glass. "What happens to every major civilization? At some point they civilize themselves right out of warriors. You've got sheep and you've got wolves. You've got to have enough wolves around to protect your sheep, or else somebody else's wolves are going to take them out."

Coming from a career soldier, Mike's views of war and humanity were understandably romantic. To him, bad wolves weren't the real threat. It was the idea that civilization might be able to get along without wolves, good or bad, or that wolves could be made of titanium and silicon. What would happen to the warrior spirit then?

Scores of scale-model UAVs dangled on wires from the ceiling of the exhibit hall at the Baltimore Convention Center, rotating lazily in currents of air-conditioning. Models jutted into the aisles, their wings canted in attitudes of flight. Company reps blew packing dust off cluster bombs and electronic equipment. They put out bowls of candy and trinkets. Everywhere I looked I saw ghostly black-and-white images of myself, captured by dozens of infrared surveillance cameras mounted inside domed gimbals, staring back at me from closed-circuit televisions.

In addition to cameras, almost every booth featured a large plasma monitor showing a continuous video loop of robots blowing up vehicles on target ranges, or robots pepper-spraying intruders, robots climbing stairs, scurrying down sewer pipes, circling above battlefields and mountain ranges. These videos were often accompanied by a narrator's bland voice-over, muttered from a sound system that rivaled the most expensive home theater.

I sat down in the concession area to study the floor map. An engineer next to me picked at a plate of underripe melon and shook his head in awe at the long lines of people waiting for coffee. "Four or five years ago it was just booths with concept posters pinned up," he said. "Now the actual stuff is here. It's amazing."

At the fringes of the exhibit hall, I wandered through the warrens of small companies and remote military arsenals squeezed side-by-side into $10 \times 10$ booths. I followed the screeching chords of thrash metal until I stood in front of a television playing a promotional video featuring a robot called Chaos. Chaos was built by Autonomous Solutions, a private company that had been spun out of Utah State University's robotics lab. In the video, it clambered over various types of terrain, its four flipper-like tracks chewing up dirt and rocks and tree bark. The real thing was somewhat less kinetic. A Chaos prototype lay motionless on the floor in front of the television. I nudged it with my foot and asked the company's young operations manager what it was designed to do.

"Kick the pants off the PackBot," he said, glancing around nervously. "No, I'm kidding."

A few booths down I encountered a group of men gathered around a robot the size of a paperback book. Apparently, it could climb walls by virtue of a powerful centrifuge in its belly. A picture showed it stuck to a building outside a second-story window, peering over the sill. But the rep holding the remote-control box kept ramming the robot into a cloth-draped wall at the back of his booth. The robot lost traction on the loose fabric and flipped over on its back, wheels spinning. A rep from the neighboring booth volunteered use of his filing cabinet. The little robot zipped across the floor, bumped the cabinet, and, with a soft whir, climbed straight up the side. When it got to the top it extended a metal stalk bearing a tiny camera and scanned the applauding crowd.

I continued along the perimeter, trying to avoid eye contact with the reps. Since it was the first day of the show, they were fresh and alert, rocking on their heels at the edges of their booths, their eyes darting from name badge to name badge in search of potential customers. I picked up an M4 carbine resting on a table in the Chatten Associates booth. The gun's grip had been modified to simulate a computer mouse. It had two rubber keys and a thumb stick for operating a miniature radio-controlled tank sporting an assault rifle in its turret.

"You'll need this," said Kent Massey, Chatten's chief operating officer. He removed a helmet from a mannequin's head and placed it on mine. Then he adjusted the heads-up display, a postage stamp-sized LCD screen that floated in front of my right eye. The idea behind the setup was that a soldier could simultaneously keep one eye on the battlefield while piloting the robot via a video feed beamed back to his heads-up display. He never had to take his finger off the trigger.

I blinked and saw a robot's-eye view of traffic cones arranged on a fluorescent green square of artificial turf. I turned my head first to the left, then to the right. The gimbal-mounted camera in the tank mimicked the motion, swiveling left, then right. I pushed the thumb stick on the carbine's pistol grip. The tank lurched forward, knocking down a cone.

"Try not to look at the robot," Kent advised.

I turned my back to him and faced the aisle. It was difficult for me to imagine how the soldier of the future would manage both the stress of combat and the information overload that plagues the average office worker. Simply driving the tank made me dizzy, despite Kent's claims that Chatten's head-aiming system increased "situational awareness" and "operational efficiency" by 400 percent. Then again, I wasn't Army material. I was too old, too analog. As a Boeing rep would later explain to me, they were "building systems for kids that are in the seventh and eighth grades right now. They get the PDAs, the digital things, cell phones, IM."

As I crashed the tank around the obstacle course, conventioneers stopped in the aisle to determine why I was pointing a machine gun at them. I aimed the muzzle at the floor.

"The one mission that you simply cannot do without us is armed reconnaissance," Kent said over my shoulder. "Poke around a corner, clear a house . . . We lost thirty-eight guys in Fallujah in exactly those kinds of circumstances, plus a couple hundred wounded. If [the robot] gets killed, there's no letter to write home."

Robots have always been associated with dehumanization and, more explicitly, humanity's extinction. The word "robot" is derived from the Czech word for forced labor, "robota," and first appeared in Karel Capek's 1920 play, R.U.R (*Rossum's Universal Robots*), which ends with the destruction of mankind.

This view of robots, popularized in such movies as the *Terminator* series, troubles Cliff Hudson, who at the time coordinated robotics efforts for the Department of Defense. I ran into Cliff on the second day of the show, outside Carnegie Mellton's National Robotics Engineering Center's booth. Like the scientists in R.U.R., Cliff saw robots as a benign class of mechanized serfs. Military robots will handle most of "the three Ds: dull, dangerous, dirty-type tasks," he said, such as transporting supplies, guarding checkpoints, and sniffing for bombs. The more delicate task of killing would remain in human hands.

"I liken it to the military dog," Cliff said, and brought up a briefing given the previous day by an explosive-ordnance disposal (EOD) officer who had just returned from Iraq. The highlight of the briefing was an MTV-style video montage of robots disarming IEDs. It ended with a soldier walking away from the camera, silhouetted against golden evening sunlight, his loyal robot bumping along the road at his heels. Cliff pressed his hands together. "It's that partnership, it's that team approach," he said. "It's not going to replace the soldier. It's going to be an added capability and enhancer."

Adjacent to where we stood talking in the aisle was a prototype of the Gladiator, a six-wheeled armored car about the size of a golf cart, built by Carnegie Mellon engineers for the Marines. It was one mean enhancer. The prototype was equipped with a machine gun, but missiles could be attached to it as well.

"If you see concertina wire, you send this down range," Cliff said, maintaining his theme of man/robot cooperation. "And then the Marines can come up behind it. It's a great weapon." Despite its capabilities, the Gladiator hadn't won the complete trust of the Marines. "It's a little unstable," Cliff admitted. "Most people are uncomfortable around it when the safety is removed."

Reps proffering business cards began circling around Cliff and his entourage, sweeping me aside. Jörgen Pedersen, a young engineer with thin blond hair and a goatee, watched the scene with bemused detachment, his elbows propped on the Gladiator's turret. Jörgen had written the Gladiator's fire-control software.

"How safe is this thing?" I asked him.

"We wanted it to err on the side of safety first," Jörgen said. "You can always make something more *un*safe." In the early stages of the Gladiator's development, Jörgen had discovered that its communications link wasn't reliable enough to allow machine-gun bursts longer than six seconds. After six seconds, the robot would stop firing. So he reprogrammed the fire-control system with a fail-safe.

"You may have great communications here," Jörgen said, touching the Gladiator with his fingertips. "But you take one step back and you're just on the hairy edge of where this thing can communicate well."

The integrity of data links between unmanned systems and their operators is a major concern. Satellite bandwidth, already in short supply, will be stretched even further as more robots and other sophisticated electronics, such as remote sensors, are committed to the battlefield. There's also the possibility that radio signals could be jammed or hijacked by the enemy. But these problems are inherent to the current generation of teleoperated machines: robots that are controlled by humans from afar. As robots become more autonomous, fulfilling missions according to pre-programmed instructions, maintaining constant contact with human operators will be unnecessary. I asked Jörgen if robots would someday replace soldiers on the battlefield. He reiterated the need for a man in the loop.

"Maybe that's because I'm short-sighted based on my current experiences," he said. "Maybe the only way that it could happen is if there's no other people out on that field doing battle. It's just robots battling robots. At that point, it doesn't matter. We all just turn on the TV to see who's winning."

It is almost certain that robot deployment will save lives, both military and civilian. And yet the prospect of robot-on-human warfare does present serious moral and ethical, if not strictly legal, issues. Robots invite no special consideration under the laws of armed conflict, which place the burden of responsibility on humans, not weapons systems. When a laser-guided bomb kills civilians, responsibility falls on everyone involved in the kill chain, from the pilot who dropped the bomb to the commander who ordered the strike. Robots will be treated no differently. It will become vastly more difficult, however, to assign responsibility for noncombatant deaths caused by mechanical or programming failures as robots are granted greater degrees of autonomy. In this sense, robots may prove similar to low-tech cluster bombs or land mines, munitions that "do something that they're not supposed to out of the control of those who deploy them, and in doing so cause unintended death and suffering," according to Michael Byers, professor of global politics and international law at the University of British Columbia.

## As robots become more autonomous, constant contact with human operators will be unnecessary.

The moral issues are perhaps similar to those arising from the use of precision-guided munitions (PGMs). There's no doubt that PGMs greatly limit civilian casualties and collateral damage to civilian infrastructure such as hospitals, electrical grids, and water systems. But because PGM strikes are more precise compared with dropping sticks of iron bombs from B-52s, the civilian casualties that often result from PGM strikes are considered necessary, if horribly unfortunate, mistakes. One need look no further than the PGM barrage that accompanied the ground invasion of Iraq in 2003. "Decapitation strikes" aimed at senior Iraqi leaders pounded neighborhoods from Baghdad to Basra. Due to poor intelligence, none of the fifty known strikes succeeded in finding their targets. In four of the strikes forty-two civilians were killed, including six members of a family who had the misfortune of living next door to Saddam Hussein's half brother.

It's not difficult to imagine a similar scenario involving robots instead of PGMs. A robot armed only with a machine gun enters a house known to harbor an insurgent leader. The robot opens fire and kills a woman and her two children instead. It's later discovered that the insurgent leader moved to a different location at the last minute. Put aside any mitigating factors that might prevent a situation like this from occurring and assume that the robot did exactly what it was programmed to do. Assume the commander behind the operation acted on the latest intelligence, and that he followed the laws of armed conflict to the letter. Although the deaths of the woman and children might not violate the laws of armed conflict, they fall into a moral black hole where no one, no human anyway, is directly responsible. Had the innocents of My Lai and Haditha been slain not by errant men but by errant machines, would we know the names of these places today?

More troubling than the compromised moral calculus with which we program our killing machines is how robots reduce even further the costs, both fiscal and human, of the choice to wage war. Robots do not have to be recruited, trained, fed, or paid extra for combat duty. When they are destroyed, there are no death benefits to disburse. Shipping them off to hostile lands doesn't require the expenditure of political capital either. There will be no grieving robot mothers pitching camp outside the president's ranch gates. Robots are, quite literally, an off-the-shelf war-fighting capability—war in a can.

This bloodless vision of future combat was best captured by a billboard I saw at the exhibition, in the General Dynamics booth. The billboard was titled "Robots as Co-Combatants," and two scenes illustrated the concept in the garish style of toy-model-box art. One featured UGVs positioned on a slope near a grove of glossy palm trees. In the distance, a group of mud-brick buildings resembling a walled compound was set against a barren mountain range. Bright red parabolas traced the trajectories of mortar shells fired into the compound from UGVs, but there were no explosions, no smoke.

The other scene was composed in the gritty vernacular of television news footage from Iraq. A squad of soldiers trotted down the cracked sidewalk of a city street, past stained concrete facades and terraces awash in glaring sunlight. A small, wingless micro-UAV hovered above the soldiers amid a tangled nest of drooping telephone lines, projecting a cone of white light that suggested an invisible sensor beam. And smack in the foreground, a UGV had maneuvered into the street, guns blazing. In both scenes, the soldiers are incidental to the action. Some don't even carry rifles. They sit in front of computer screens, fingers tapping on keyboards.

On the last day of the show, I sat in the concession area, chewing a stale pastry and scanning the list of the day's technical sessions. Most were dry, tedious affairs with such titles as "The Emerging Challenge of Loitering Attack Missiles." One session hosted by Foster-Miller, the company that manufactures the SWORDS robot, got my attention: "Weaponization of Small Unmanned Ground Vehicles." I filled my coffee cup and hustled upstairs.

I took a seat near the front of the conference room just as the lights dimmed. Hunched behind a podium, a Foster-Miller engineer began reading verbatim from a PowerPoint presentation about the history of SWORDS, ending with a dreary bullet-point list cataloguing the past achievements of the TALON robot, SWORDS's immediate predecessor.

"TALON has been used in most major, major . . ." The engineer faltered.

"Conflicts," someone in the audience stage-whispered. I turned to see that it was Bob Quinn. He winked at me in acknowledgment.

"Conflicts," the engineer said. He ended his portion of the talk with the same video montage that had inspired Cliff Hudson to compare robots to dogs. TALON robots were shown pulling apart tangles of wire connected to IEDs, plucking at garbage bags that had been tossed on the sides of darkened roads, extracting mortar shells hidden inside Styrofoam cups. Bob Quinn took the podium just as the final shot in the montage, that of the soldier walking down the road with his faithful TALON robot at his heels, faded on the screen behind him. The lights came up.

"The 800-pound gorilla, or the bully in the playpen, for weaponized robotics—for all ground-based robots—is Hollywood," Bob said. The audience stirred. Bob strolled off the dais and stood in the aisle, hands in his pockets. "It's interesting that UAVs like the Predator can fire Hellfire missiles at will without a huge interest worldwide. But when you get into weaponization of ground vehicles, our soldiers, our safety community, our nation, our world, are not ready for autonomy. In fact, it's quite the opposite."

Bob remained in the aisle, narrating a series of PowerPoint slides and video clips that showed SWORDS firing rockets and machine guns, SWORDS riding atop a Stryker vehicle,

'WORDS creeping up on a target and lobbing grenades at it. His point was simple: SWORDS was no killer robot, no Terminator. It was a capable weapons platform firmly in the control of the soldiers who operated it, nothing more. When the last video clip didn't load, Bob stalled for time.

"We've found that using Hollywood on Hollywood is a good strategy to overcome some of the concerns that aren't apparent with UAVs but are very apparent with UGVs," he said. Last February a crew from the History Channel had filmed SWORDS for an episode of *Mail Call*, a half-hour program hosted by the inimitable R. Lee Ermey, best known for his role as the profane drill sergeant in the movie *Full Metal Jacket*. Ermey's scowling face suddenly appeared onscreen, accompanied by jarring rock music.

"It's a lot smarter to send this robo-soldier down a blind alley than one of our flesh-and blood warriors," Ermey shouted. "It was developed by our troops in the field, not some suit in an office back home!"

Ermey's antic mugging was interspersed with quick cutaways of SWORDS on a firing range and interviews with EOD soldiers.

"The next time you start thinking about telling the kids to put away that video game, think again!" Ermey screamed. He jabbed his finger into the camera. "Some day they could be using those same kinds of skills to run a robot that will save their bacon!"

"That's a good way to get off the stage," Bob said. He was smiling now, soaking in the applause. "I think armed robots will save soldiers' lives. It creates an unfair fight, and that's what we want. But they will be teleoperated. The more as a community we focus on that, given the Hollywood perceptions, the better off our soldiers will be."

Downstairs in the exhibit hall, I saw that Boeing had also learned the value of Hollywood-style marketing. I had stopped by the company's booth out of a sense of obligation more than curiosity: Boeing is the lead contractor for FCS. While I was talking to Stephen Bishop, the FCS business-development manager, I noticed a familiar face appear on the laptop screen behind him.

"Is that—MacGyver?"

Stephen nodded and stepped aside so that I could get a better view of the laptop. The face did indeed belong to Richard Dean Anderson, former star of the television series *MacGyver* and now the star of a five-minute promotional film produced by Boeing. Judging by the digital special effects, the film probably cost more to make than what most companies had spent on their entire exhibits. Not coincidentally, the film is set in 2014, when the first generation of FCS vehicles are scheduled for full deployment. An American convoy approaches a bridge near a snowy mountain pass somewhere in Asia, perhaps North Korea. The enemy mobilizes to cut the Americans off, but they are detected and annihilated by armed ground vehicles and UAVs.

At the center of this networked firestorm is Richard Dean Anderson, who sits inside a command vehicle, furrowing his brow and tapping a computer touchscreen. As the American forces cross the bridge, a lone enemy soldier hiding behind a boulder fires a rocket at the lead vehicle and disables it. The attack falters.

"I do not have an ID on the shooter!" a technician yells. Anderson squints grimly at his computer screen. It's the moment of truth. Does he pull back and allow the enemy time to regroup, or does he advance across the bridge, exposing his forces to enemy fire? The rousing martial soundtrack goes quiet.

"Put a 'bot on the bridge," Anderson says.

A dune-buggy-like robot darts from the column of vehicles and stops in the middle of the bridge in a heroic act of self-sacrifice. The lone enemy soldier takes the bait and fires another missile, destroying the robot and unwittingly revealing his position to a micro-UAV loitering nearby. Billions of dollars and decades of scientific research come to bear on this moment, on one man hiding behind a snow-covered boulder. He is obliterated.

"Good job," Anderson sneers. "Now let's finish this."

The film ends as American tanks pour across the bridge into enemy territory. The digitally enhanced point of view pulls back to reveal the FCS network, layer by layer, vehicle by vehicle, eighteen systems in all, until it reaches space, the network's outer shell, where a spy satellite glides by.

"Saving soldiers' lives," Stephen said, glancing at his press manager to make sure he was on message. I commended the film's production values. Stephen seemed pleased that I'd noticed. "Three-stars and four-stars gave it a standing ovation at the Pentagon last November," he told me.

"You can't argue with MacGyver," I said.

"Because it's all about saving soldiers' lives," Stephen said. "Works for congressmen, works for senators, works for the grandmother in Nebraska."

Later that summer I visited Picatinny Arsenal, "Home of American Firepower," in New Jersey, to see a live-fire demonstration of the SWORDS robot. SWORDS was conceived at Picatinny by a small group of EOD soldiers who wanted to find a less dangerous way to "put heat on a target" inside caves in Afghanistan. Three years later, SWORDS was undergoing some final tweaks at Picatinny before being sent to Aberdeen Proving Ground for its last round of safety tests. After that, it would be ready for deployment.

"As long as you don't break my rules you'll be fine," said Sergeant Jason Mero, motioning for us to gather around him. Sgt. Mero had participated in the initial invasion of Iraq, including the assault on Saddam International Airport. He had buzzed sandy brown hair, a compact build, and the brusque authority common to non-commissioned officers. He told us exactly where we could stand, where we could set up our cameras, and assured us that he was there to help us get what we needed. Other than the "very, very loud" report of the M240 machine gun, there was little to worry about.

"The robot's not going to suddenly pivot and start shooting everybody," he said, without a hint of irony.

A crew from the Discovery Networks' Military Channel dragged their gear onto the range. They were filming a special on "Warbots," and the producer was disappointed to learn that the SWORDS robot mounted with a formidable-looking M202 grenade launcher wasn't operable. He would have to make do with the less telegenic machine-gun variant. The producer, Jonathan Gruber, wore a canvas fishing hat with the brim pulled down to the black frames of his stylish eyeglasses. Jonathan gave stage directions to Sgt. Mero, who knelt in the gravel next to SWORDS and began describing how the loading process works.

"Sergeant, if you could just look to me," Jonathan prompted. "Good. So, is a misfeed common?"

"No, not with this weapon system," Sgt. Mero said. "It's very uncommon." "My questions are cut out," Jonathan said. "So if you could repeat my question in the answer? So, you know, 'Misfeeds are not common . . .'"

"Mis—" Sgt. Mero cleared his throat. His face turned red. "However, misfeeds are not common with the M240 bravo."

"Okay, great, I'm all set for now, thanks."

The firing range was scraped out of the bottom of a shallow gorge, surrounded on all sides by trees and exposed limestone. Turkey vultures circled above the ridge. The weedy ground was littered with spent shell casings and scraps of scorched metal. Fifty yards from where I sat, two human silhouettes were visible through shoulder-high weeds in front of a concrete trap filled with sand. Sgt. Mero hooked a cable to SWORDS's camera, then flipped a red switch on the control box. I felt the M240's muzzle blast on my face as SWORDS lurched backward on its tracks, spilling smoking shells on the ground.

A cloud of dust billowed behind the silhouettes. Sgt. Mero fired again, then again. With each burst, recoil pushed SWORDS backward, and Sgt. Mero, staring at the video image on the control box's LCD screen, readjusted his aim. I could hear servos whining. When Sgt. Mero finished the ammunition belt, he switched off SWORDS and led us downrange to the targets.

"So, um, Sergeant?" Jonathan said. "As soon as you see our camera you can just start talking."

"As you see, the M240—"

"And Sergeant?" Jonathan interrupted. "I don't think you have to scream. You can just speak in a normal voice. We're all close to you."

"The problem with a heavy machine gun is, obviously, there's going to be a lot of spray," Sgt. Mero said, bending down to pick up one of the silhouettes that had fallen in the weeds. "Our second guy over here that we actually knocked down—he didn' get very many bullets, but he actually got hit pretty hard."

Through the weeds I spotted the SWORDS robot squatting i the dust. My heart skipped a beat. The machine gun was pointe straight at me. I'd watched Sgt. Mero deactivate SWORDS. saw him disconnect the cables. And the machine gun's feed tra was empty. There wasn't the slightest chance of a misfire. M fear was irrational, but I still made a wide circle around th robot when it was time to leave.

Within our lifetime, robots will give us the ability to wage war without committing ourselves to the human cost of actually fighting a war. War wil become a routine, a program. The great nineteenth-century military theorist Carl von Clausewitz understood that although wa may have rational goals, the conduct of war is fundamentall irrational and unpredictable. Absent fear, war cannot be calle war. A better name for it would be target practice.

Back on the firing line, Sgt. Mero booted up SWORDS an began running it around the range for the benefit of the cameras It made a tinny, rattling noise as it rumbled over the rocks. A Discovery crewman waddled close behind it, holding his camera low to the ground. He stumbled over a clump of weeds, an for a second I thought he was going to fall on his face. But h regained his balance, took a breath, and ran to catch up wit the robot.

"I think I'm good," Jonathan said after the driving demonstration. "Anything else you want to add about this?"

"Yeah," Sgt. Mero said, smiling wryly. "It kicks *ass*. It' *awesome*." In repentance for this brief moment of sarcasm Sgt. Mero squared his shoulders, looked straight into the camera, and began speaking as if he were reading from cue cards "These things are amazing," he said breathlessly. "They don' complain, like our regular soldiers do. They don't cry. They're not scared. This robot here has no fear, which is a good supplement to the United States Army."

"That's great," Jonathan said.

---

STEVE FEATHERSTONE is a writer and photographer in Syracuse New York. His last article for *Harper's Magazine*, "The Line Is Hot," appeared in the December 2005 issue.

# A Technology Surges

**In Iraq, soldiers conducting frontline street patrols finally get software tools that let them share findings and plan missions.**

DAVID TALBOT

First Lieutenant Brian Slaughter wanted his comrades to learn from the insurgent attack that could have killed him on May 21, 2004. Before dawn, the 30-year-old had been leading 12 men in three armored Humvees along a canal in Baghdad's al-Dora district when a massive blast from an improvised explosive device (IED) lifted his vehicle off the ground. Concealed attackers followed with a volley of rocket-propelled grenades and machine-gun fire. But the IED had been buried too deep to kill, a second IED detonated too early to hit the patrol, and a third failed to explode. When the brief battle ended, two insurgents were dead, and ten were prisoners. On the American side, one man had been injured, with a bullet to the leg.

Slaughter knew that information about the encounter could help his fellow soldiers—especially green replacements arriving from Fort Stewart, GA—avoid getting killed or maimed. It might help them capture insurgents, too. So when dawn broke, he explored the blast site with a digital camera. He took pictures of the mound of brown earth concealing the still-unexploded second IED, and of a red-and-white detonator cord that led to the device. He took pictures of a berm and a copse of palm trees that had concealed the enemy. He took pictures of the improvised weapon: a 155-millimeter artillery shell that had been drilled out and fitted with a fuse.

But his attempts to share the information ran into a technological roadblock. Back at Camp Falcon, a facility on the southern outskirts of Baghdad that's one of a handful of so-called forward operating bases around the city, he typed up a document in Microsoft Word and appended his photos. The report went to a battalion intelligence officer swamped by two or three dozen such reports daily. The intelligence officer's summaries went into a database called ASAS-L. A product of Cold War thinking, the database allows top commanders to monitor and coordinate troop movements—but it's not easily accessible to patrol leaders like Slaughter.

So for practical purposes, his report didn't exist. Even the version that stayed on his computer at Camp Falcon eventually vanished. "It went home with my unit. There was no server. No continuity. Nothing," he says. The pictures survive—on his laptop in Nashville, TN. He showed them to me, along with lots of other pictures that might have had some value to his fellow soldiers, including one of the smiling principal of a girls' school in Baghdad and one of an Iraqi translator—later killed, Slaughter says—interviewing someone who Slaughter says was believed to be an imam with ties to al-Qaeda in Iraq.

But the days of patrol leaders operating half-blind on the deadly streets of Iraq are drawing to a close. After a two-year rush program by the Pentagon's research arm, the U.S. Defense Advanced Research Projects Agency, or DARPA, troops are now getting what might be described as Google Maps for the Iraq counter-insurgency. There is nothing cutting-edge about the underlying technology: software that runs on PCs and taps multiple distributed databases. But the trove of information the system delivers is of central importance in the daily lives of soldiers.

The new technology—called the Tactical Ground Reporting System, or TIGR—is a map-centric application that junior officers (the young sergeants and lieutenants who command patrols) can study before going on patrol and add to upon returning. By clicking on icons and lists, they can see the locations of key buildings, like mosques, schools, and hospitals, and retrieve information such as location data on past attacks, geotagged photos of houses and other buildings (taken with cameras equipped with Global Positioning System technology), and photos of suspected insurgents and neighborhood leaders. They can even listen to civilian interviews and watch videos of past maneuvers. It is just the kind of information that soldiers need to learn about Iraq and its perils.

For some units, anyway, the database is becoming the technological fulcrum of the counterinsurgency. More than 1,500 junior officers—about a fifth of patrol leaders—are already using the technology, which was first deployed in early 2007. The first major unit to use it—the First Brigade Combat Team, First Cavalry Division—returned to the United States in late January. A few days before leaving Camp Taji, northwest of Baghdad, one soldier in this unit, Major Patrick Michaelis—who had many better things to do—paused to write an effusive 1,000-word e-mail to *Technology Review*. He said that the technology had saved the lives of soldiers by allowing them to avoid IEDs, and that it enabled them to make better use of intelligence, capture insurgents, and improve their relationships with local people. "The ability . . . to draw the route . . . of your patrol that day and then to access the collective reports, media, analysis of the entire organization, is pretty powerful," Michaelis wrote. "It is a bit revolutionary from a military perspective when you think about it, using peer-based information to drive the next move. . . . Normally we are used to our higher headquarters telling the patrol leader what he needs to think."

## A Granular Environment

The Pentagon has long talked about empowering soldiers with information. Some new networking technologies were deployed during the Iraq invasion, albeit with mixed results (see *"How Tech Failed in Iraq,"* November 2004). And back in the United States, the Pentagon has been pursuing multibillion-dollar R&D programs with names like Future Combat Systems. These programs anticipate a day when aircraft, ground vehicles, robots, and soldier-mounted sensors collect masses of information; new software makes sense of it all, detecting changes and identifying targets; and wireless networking technologies link fighting units and even individual soldiers, who might have digital displays mounted to their helmets. Such technologies are part of the military's long-term plan to introduce what is sometimes called "network-centric warfare."

Generally, however, these high-tech visions have not meant much to the soldiers and marines patrolling dangerous streets in Iraq. U.S. troops conduct more than 300 street patrols around the country every day; those patrols make up one of the war's principal fronts. But for the most part, the leaders of the patrols have found it difficult to access digital information about their routes. Intelligence dissemination was stuck for years in another era. "We have a tendency in the army and marines and air force to build systems, first of all, that are platform-centric [built to ride on, say, a tank or a plane] and second, to build them for the higher echelons," says Pat O'Neal, a retired brigadier general who acts as an advisor to DARPA—and whose son is currently serving in Iraq. "Because that's where we felt, in the Cold War, the emphasis had to be, for the coördination of forces on a very large scale. That didn't set us up for success when we found ourselves in Iraq. It is a very granular environment, a very block-to-block environment."

Soldiers had no consistent way to submit reports; many carried old-fashioned "green books" for handwritten notes, while some tried to set up homegrown databases. And report writing varied from camp to camp. The need for something better was obvious. In 2005, DARPA started tackling the problem at Fort Hood, TX, with the help of returning soldiers from the First Brigade Combat Team. Programmers from companies that contracted with DARPA (including Ascend Intel, where Slaughter is now director of business development) interviewed soldiers to learn what they needed.

A prototype of the system was shown to soldiers for the first time during a training exercise at Fort Hood in April 2006, and in January 2007, it was introduced in Iraq. There, programmers observed how the troops used it; they collected feedback and quickly made changes. Finally—with help from the Rapid

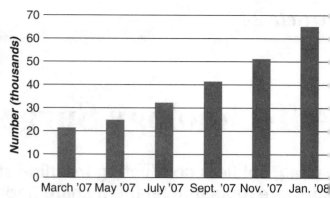

**Iraq War Data.** Cumulative number of entries, including event (such as attacks, site visits, meetings, and discovery of weap ons caches) and places (such as mosques, checkpoints, and boundaries), in the Tactical Ground Reporting System (TIGR database available to patrol leaders.

Equipping Force, an army unit devoted to quickly moving new gear into the field—the system reached the 1,500 patrol lead ers using it now. Deploying it widely required dealing with two main challenges raised by Iraq's spotty data connections: how to synchronize scattered copies of the same database, any one of which a returning patrol leader might modify, and how to give soldiers multimedia information without crashing the system. One solution was a network that carefully rations out bandwidth. For example, the default mode for any photograph is a thumbnail version. A soldier has to click on the thumbnail to see a larger version and will get a response only if bandwidth allows.

"This is something I've heard from a couple of generals there are lots of technologies that get pushed out to Iraq because engineers want to help, but they are niche applications," says Mari Maeda, the DARPA program manager in charge of the effort. "This application is broadly used by patrol leaders, on a day-to-day basis. I think the impact is very, very large." O'Neal offers an even less restrained assessment: "Best technology I've seen for small units in the past 40 years."

Walter Perry, a senior researcher at the Rand think tank in Arlington, VA, and a Vietnam-era army signals officer, also wel comes the new system. Perry works with a Pentagon-wide task force that has been trying to combat the scourge of IEDs through advanced intelligence gathering and new kinds of sensors and detectors. "One of the very first things we did in looking at the IED problem was to recognize that the army is trying to fight an insurgency with a pretty blunt instrument," Perry says. "This is about 90 percent police work and 10 percent violent conflicts. Patrols—the cop on a beat—fill out a report saying, Here is what I did. You get situational awareness." And that is of key importance in fighting IEDs, he says.

## Technology Gap

With the new DARPA technology, soldiers are getting more and better information. But some experts say that for the sol diers to be truly empowered, military doctrine and organization will need to change too. "I have seen one after another of these interesting networking technologies come along, and none of hem has made a dent in the institutional resistance to organizational change or doctrinal innovation," says John Arquilla, a professor of defense analysis at the Naval Postgraduate School in Monterey, CA, who is a progenitor of the concept of network organization in the military. Yes, he says, patrol leaders can now enter information into the system more easily. But "we still have divisional-, brigade-, and battalion-level structures, mostly on supersized forward operating bases, with the number of smaller outposts relatively few. If we are going to talk about a networked warfare, we need to put the network front and center in our thinking." One way to do that is to deploy soldiers in smaller groups with more authority to make decisions.

That's what happened in 2001, when special-operations forces were chasing al-Qaeda and the Taliban in the mountains of Afghanistan. When a team identified a target, it did not have to send a report up the chain of command and wait for a decision before acting. It could call on comrades and even call in air strikes. "If you believe that the real implication of the Information Age is the empowerment of small groups—and if there is any lesson from 9/11, that is it—we are really talking about information that allows small groups of people to do striking things," says Arquilla. The Iraq counterinsurgency should fight the same way the special forces fought in Afghanistan, he says.

Still, even without the kinds of organizational changes that Arquilla is advocating (see *"Network Warfare,"* p. 12), DARPA's new software system is empowering frontline soldiers and shaping operations. For example, in a telephone interview from Camp Falcon, 28-year-old Captain David Lively described how TIGR once helped soldiers track down a pair of mortar attackers. One night, Lively recalled, soldiers on patrol radioed back to base that they were being shelled. At the base, other soldiers tapped into the database and quickly found earlier reports of mortars coming from an intersection of two canals in the vicinity. "TIGR provided some real-time history to where we could look back where a common source was coming from," Lively said. The soldiers at the base radioed the findings to their comrades and to a circling Apache helicopter. The pilot headed for the spot and was able to pursue a fleeing pickup truck with mortar tubes in its bed.

Michaelis says such anecdotes are not uncommon. "I can't name the number of times that patrol leaders and company commanders have turned to me and stated [that] their most important tool they have to fight this fight has been TIGR," he wrote. "I've had . . . time-sensitive operations that were able to make associations between the target being handed to them and local residents, [allowing the soldiers to find insurgents who otherwise would have escaped]. I've had patrol leaders avoid potential IED hot spots or pass on IED tactics to their fellow patrol leaders."

And the technology is poised to expand. For now, it is accessible only at military bases. The next step, says Maeda, is to install it in Humvees and other military vehicles, allowing soldiers to download and act on new information in real time. Some of these vehicles already have some low-bandwidth connections, and Maeda says DARPA is working on ways to make the software work using these thin pipes. In addition, the system may soon deliver new kinds of information. In the next two to three years, it could offer surveillance pictures from circling unmanned aerial vehicles (UAVs) or other sensor systems. It could store biometric information, so that a soldier could see if a civilian being interviewed was a known insurgent suspect. "There is a whole list of enhancements that users have requested that we want to fill," Maeda says.

If those enhancements are realized, the result will look a lot like a deployed version of what the Pentagon's big R&D programs have been pursuing. But TIGR is growing organically, in response to the needs of soldiers on the ground. It might be going too far to say that this technology will be the one to force doctrinal and organizational change; perhaps not everyone will embrace it. "No doubt it causes discomfort in those comfortable in traditional intel development," Michaelis writes. As O'Neal points out, however, everyone involved in fighting the Iraq insurgency is motivated to save soldiers' lives by every means possible. In some cases, it's quite personal. "I'm focused on contemporary technology for the current force," O'Neal says. "It's all for my son."

**David Talbot** is *Technology Review*'s chief correspondent.

# Wikipedia in the Newsroom

**While the line "according to Wikipedia" pops up occasionally in news stories, it's relatively rare to see the user-created online encyclopedia cited as a source. But some journalists find it very valuable as a road map to troves of valuable information.**

DONNA SHAW

When the Las Vegas Review-Journal published a story in September about construction cranes, it noted that they were invented by ancient Greeks and powered by men and donkeys.

Michigan's Flint Journal recently traced the origins of fantasy football to 1962, and to three people connected to the Oakland Raiders.

And when the Arizona Republic profiled a controversial local congressman in August, it concluded that his background was "unclear."

What all three had in common was one of the sources they cited: Wikipedia, the popular, reader-written and -edited online encyclopedia. Dismissed by traditional journalism as a gimmicky source of faux information almost since it debuted in 2001, Wikipedia may be gaining some cautious converts as it works its way into the mainstream, albeit more as a road map to information than as a source to cite. While "according to Wikipedia" attributions do crop up, they are relatively rare.

To be sure, many Wikipedia citations probably sneak into print simply because editors don't catch them. Other times, the reference is tongue-in-cheek: The Wall Street Journal, for example, cited Wikipedia as a source for an item on "turducken" (a bizarre concoction in which a chicken is stuffed into a duck that is stuffed into a turkey) in a subscriber e-mail update just before Thanksgiving. In the e-mail, the Journal reporter wrote that some of his information was "courtesy of Wikipedia's highly informative turducken entry. As my hero Dave Barry says, "I'm not making this up. Although, I'll admit that somebody on Wikipedia might have."

And when Time Inc. Editor-in-Chief John Huey was asked how his staffers made sure their stories were correct, he jokingly responded, "Wikipedia."

It's unclear if many newsrooms have formal policies banning Wikipedia attribution in their stories, but many have informal ones. At the Philadelphia Inquirer, which cited Wikipedia in an article about the death of television personality Tom Snyder last July, Managing Editor Mike Leary recently sent an e-mail to staff members reminding them they are never to use Wikipedia "to verify facts or to augment information in a story." A news database search indicates that "according to Wikipedia" mentions are few and far between in U.S. papers, and are found most frequently in opinion columns, letters to the editor and feature stories. They also turn up occasionally in graphics and information boxes.

Such caution is understandable, as for all its enticements, Wikipedia is maddeningly uneven. It can be impressive in one entry (the one on the Naval Battle of Guadalcanal includes 138 endnotes, 18 references and seven external links) and sloppy in another (it misspells the name of AJR's editor). Its topics range from the weighty (the Darfur conflict) to the inconsequential (a list of all episodes of the TV series "Canada's Worst Handyman"). Its talk pages can include sophisticated discussions of whether fluorescent light bulbs will cause significant mercury pollution or silly minutiae like the real birth date of Paris Hilton's Chihuahua. Some of its commentary is remarkable but some contributors are comically dense, like the person who demanded proof that 18th-century satirist Jonathan Swift wasn't serious when he wrote that landlords should eat the children of their impoverished Irish tenants.

Hubble Smith, the Review-Journal business reporter who wrote the crane story, says he was simply looking for background on construction cranes for a feature on the Las Vegas building boom when the Wikipedia entry popped up during a search. It was among the most interesting information he found, so he used it. But after his story went to the desk, a copy editor flagged it.

"He said, 'Do you realize that Wikipedia is just made up of people who contribute all of this?'" Smith recalls. "I had never used it before." The reference was checked and allowed to remain in the story.

Indeed, the primary knock against Wikipedia is that its authors and editors are also its users—an unpaid, partially anonymous army, some of whom insert jokes, exaggeration and even outright lies in their material. About one-fifth of the editing is done by anonymous users, but a tight-knit community of 600 to 1,000 volunteers does the bulk of the work, according to Wikipedia cofounder Jimmy Wales. Members of this group can delete material or, in extreme cases, even lock particularly outrageous entries while they are massaged.

The extent of the potential for misinformation became clearer in August, when a new tool called WikiScanner (wikiscanner .virgil.gr/) began providing an ingenious database to identify propagandists and hoaxers. It gave Wikipedia critics plenty of new ammunition, as it revealed that among those surreptitiously rewriting entries were employees of major corporations, politicians and the CIA trying to make their bosses look better. And then there was the John Seigenthaler Sr. episode, in which someone edited the prominent retired journalist's Wikipedia biography to insinuate that he briefly had been a suspect in the assassinations of John and Robert F. Kennedy. In an op-ed piece for USA Today in 2005, Seigenthaler, who once worked for Bobby Kennedy and was one of his pallbearers, railed against Wikipedia, calling it "a flawed

nd irresponsible research tool." (A Nashville man later admitted insert-
ig the material as a joke aimed at a coworker, and apologized.)

No one is more aware of such pitfalls than the leadership of
Wikipedia, whose online disclaimer reminds users that "anyone with an Internet connection" can alter the content and
autions, "please be advised that nothing found here has necessarily
een reviewed by people with the expertise required to provide you
vith complete, accurate or reliable information." An even more blunt
ssessment appears in the encyclopedia's "Ten things you may not
now about Wikipedia" posting: "We do not expect you to trust us.
t is in the nature of an ever-changing work like Wikipedia that, while
ome articles are of the highest quality of scholarship, others are admit-
edly complete rubbish." It also reminds users not to use Wikipedia as
primary source or for making "critical decisions."

Wales says it doesn't surprise him to hear that some journalists are
autiously trying it out. "I think that people are sort of slowly learn-
ng how to use Wikipedia, and learning its strengths and its weak-
esses," he says. "Of course, any reasonable person has to be up front
hat there are weaknesses. . . . On the other hand, there are lots of
ources that have weaknesses." Wales thinks the encyclopedia's best
ournalistic use is for background research rather than as a source to
e quoted.

Wales, a board member and chairman emeritus of the nonprofit Wiki-
media Foundation Inc., which owns Wikipedia, says the company con-
tantly strives to improve its product. "Right now we're tightly focused
n making sure that, for example, the biographies are well sourced," he
ays. The foundation is also developing new tools "to block people who
re misbehaving," including one for new German-language Wikipedia
users that will vet their contributions. If it works, Wales says, it can be
olled out for Wikipedia encyclopedias in other languages.

He also defends the right of Wikipedia—and perhaps even reporters—
o have a little fun. "I subscribe to Google alerts and I saw that turducken
item in the Wall Street Journal e-mail] and I thought, well, what other
ource would you use? Britannica doesn't cover this nonsense," he says.

There are still plenty of journalists who aren't convinced of
Wikipedia's worth, among them the denizens of testycopyeditors
.org, where contributors to the online conversation have names like
"crabby editor" and "wordnerdy." Asked his opinion of Wikipedia,
Phillip Blanchard, the Washington Post copy editor who started testycopyeditors, responds, "I'm not sure what I could add, beyond 'don't
use it' and 'it's junk.'"

While the Post has no written policy against it, "I can't imagine a
circumstance under which a fact would be attributed to Wikipedia,"
says Blanchard, who works on the financial desk. "'According to Wikipedia' has appeared only a couple of times in the Washington Post,
once in a humor column and once in a movie review."

Gilbert Gaul, a Pulitzer Prize-winning reporter at the Post, describes
himself as a "dinosaur in the changing world" when it comes to rules
about sourcing stories. Wikipedia, he says, doesn't meet his personal
test—for one thing, "there is no way for me to verify the information
without fact-checking, in which case it isn't really saving me any time."
He prefers to do his own research, so he can "see and touch everything,"
rather than rely on the mostly anonymous content of Wikipedia.

"I like much of the new technology. . . . But to me rules, borders,
guidelines and transparency matter a lot," Gaul said in an e-mail interview. "I need and want to be able to trust the people I am reading or
chatting with. If I can't, what is the point?"

Other journalists, though, are at least somewhat won over by what
can be an impressive feature: those sometimes lengthy Wikipedia
citations that lead to other, more authoritative sources. David Cay
Johnston, a Pulitzer-winning reporter for the New York Times, says

he recently looked up "thermodynamics" to see where it led him, and
found that Wikipedia's entry listed numerous references from reliable
sources.

"I have a solid understanding of the concept, but once we get into
fine points, I have nothing beyond my skepticism as a reporter to judge
the accuracy, validity and reliability of what is there," he says. "However, this entry appears to be useful as a source guide. It has names
of researchers whose books were published by eminent organizations,
and you can take that as a quick way to find sources. So as a tip sheet,
as a road map to reliable sources, Wikipedia seems valuable."

Jim Thomsen, a copy editor at the Kitsap Sun in Bremerton,
Washington, has no problem with attributing information to the online
encyclopedia in certain cases. "If I see something in Wikipedia I might
want to cite for background and context for a story, I trace back the
cites to their original sources," Thomsen said in an e-mail interview.
"If I feel the origins are solid, I'll use the info.

## For a student who just uses a search engine and they use the first thing that pops up . . . this undermines the kind of thing we're trying to teach them.

"I know there's been a lot of hullabaloo about people with agendas
seeding Wikipedia with slanted or even false information, but as I see
it, that sort of stuff can be easily sniffed out—by looking at the cites,
and tracking them back. No cites? Fuhgeddaboudit. The bottom line
is that Wikipedia can be a great tool as a central Clearinghouse for
contextual information. But not a single syllable there should be taken
at face value."

The Los Angeles Times is one of many newspapers that have
allowed an occasional "according to Wikipedia" in their pages in the
last several months. One was in a commentary piece about Barack
Obama; another appeared in a staff-written story about a professional
"man in the street" who managed to be interviewed repeatedly. The
reference in the latter story drew rapid fire on testycopyeditors.org,
with comments including "Shame on the Los Angeles Times" and "No,
no, a thousand times no."

Melissa McCoy, the Times' deputy managing editor in charge of
copy desks, says the paper occasionally allows Wikipedia attribution.
"We're certainly not going to use Wikipedia as a standalone news
source, but we're not going to exclude it if it takes us somewhere," she
says. "If a reporter spots something in there and it makes them do an
extra phone call, it's silly" not to use it.

There's no unanimity about Wikipedia among academic experts,
who have engaged in vigorous debates about the online encyclopedia. While many professors refuse to allow students to
cite it, it has attracted some prominent defenders, including historians
and scientists who have analyzed its content.

"If a journalist were to find something surprising on Wikipedia
and the journalistic instincts suggested it was correct, the journalist
might add that as an unsubstantiated Wiki-fact and invite Comment,"
says Cathy Davidson, a professor at Duke University and cofounder
of HASTAC (Humanities, Arts, Science, and Technology Advanced
Collaboratory, www.hastac.org), a network of researchers developing
new ways to collect and share information via technology. "Perhaps an
online version of the printed piece, for example, might include a blog
inviting people to comment on the Wiki-fact. It may be that there would
be Wikifacts online that were not in the printed piece. In other words,

why not use the new technologies available to expand knowledge in all kinds of ways?"

Journalists also should consider, Davidson says, whether some of the sources they deem reliable have their own inadequacies. For example, when she recently researched the origins of calculus, she found that standard Western histories generally credited England's Isaac Newton and Germany's Gottfried Wilhelm Leibniz. But Wikipedia went much further, tracing the discovery of basic calculus functions back to the Egyptians in 1800 BC, and then to China, India and Mesopotamia—all hundreds of years before the Europeans.

So while journalists should be cautious no matter what resources they use, "What Wikipedia does reveal to those in the Euro-American world is knowledge which most of our sources, even the most scholarly, have, in the past, neglected because it did not fit in our intellectual genealogies, in our history of ideas," Davidson says.

In December 2005, the science journal Nature published a survey of several experts about the content of comparable Wikipedia and online Encyclopedia Britannica entries. In a conclusion hotly disputed by Britannica, Nature said that Wikipedia "comes close to Britannica in terms of the accuracy of its science entries," in that the average Wikipedia article contained four errors to Britannica's three. Britannica's 20-page response said that "almost everything about the journal's investigation . . . was wrong and misleading . . . the study was so poorly carried out and its findings so error-laden that it was completely without merit." The company further asserted that Nature had misrepresented its own data—its numbers, after all, showed that Wikipedia had a third more inaccuracies than Britannica—and asked for "a full and public retraction of the article." Nature stood by its story.

"The Nature piece profoundly undermined the authority upon which Britannica depends," says Gregory Crane, editor in chief of the Perseus Digital Library at Tufts University. He is a recent convert to the pro-Wikipedia camp, calling it "the most important intellectual phenomenon of the early 21st century."

He recognizes its faults, especially when Wikipedians write about controversial topics. So "people have to do some critical thinking," Crane says, by evaluating their sources, "whether it's Wikipedia or the New York Times."

In an article he wrote in 2005, Crane acknowledged that Wikipedia "is an extreme case whose success so far has shocked skeptical scholars." But he noted as well that other, more mainstream reference works had similar foundations—for example, the Oxford English Dictionary was written over a period of 70 years by thousands of people, including "an inmate at an asylum for the criminally insane."

A 2006 analysis by another scholar and Wikipedia fan, George Mason University historian Roy Rosenzweig, found some inaccuracies, omissions, uneven writing and even plagiarism in selected entries. But his comparison of several Wikipedia biographies against comparable entries in two other encyclopedias found that Wikipedia "roughly matches" Microsoft's Encarta in accuracy while still falling short of the Oxford University Press' American National Biography Online. "This general conclusion is supported by studies comparing Wikipedia to other major encyclopedias," wrote Rosenzweig, who was director of the university's Center for History and New Media until his death last year.

Still, many if not most in the academic community think that Wikipedia, if used at all, should be no more than a secondary source, and they frequently tell their students as much. For Cornell University professor Ross Brann, that position was reinforced in early 2007, after the outing of a salaried Wikipedia employee and editor who called himself "Essjay" and claimed to be a tenured professor with doctorates in theology and canon law. Turns out he had seriously padded his résumé. The New Yorker discovered after interviewing Essjay that he was actually a 24-year-old community college dropout. To Brann, a professor of Judeo-Islamic Studies and director of graduate studies for the Department of Near Eastern Studies, the incident confirmed that Wikipedia could not be trusted as a primary source.

"I just tell students, 'Do not use Wikipedia, do not cite it, do not go there for my classes.' We're trying to teach them how to use sources, how to evaluate different sources, and I think that in general, although obviously a wonderful resource, for a student who just uses a search engine and they use the first thing that pops up . . . this undermines the kind of thing we're trying to teach them," Brann says.

Brann notes that Wikipedia's popularity probably has a lot to do with the fact that its entries so frequently pop up first, because that's the nature of search engines. "Many of them just work by the multiplicity of uses, others by virtue of ad arrangements—somebody is deciding for you what you're going to look at," he says.

And what about college journalists, a group that has never known life without computers? A news database search suggests that they are just as reluctant to cite Wikipedia as their professional colleagues. In August, for example, the University of Iowa newspaper, the Daily Iowan, used the WikiScanner database to determine that thousands of Wikipedia entries had been made or modified by people using the campus computer network. Some involved obvious but harmless enough vandalism: "Hawkeyes Rule" was inserted into text about the college's football stadium; less generously, a former university president was called a "eater of monkey brains," according to the paper's story.

Jason Brummond, editor in chief of the Daily Iowan, says he considers Wikipedia a good initial source, "but you go from there to find what most people would consider a more reputable source." Reporters in his newsroom generally understand that, he adds.

Brummond thinks the age of the journalist doesn't necessarily have that much to do with accepting Wikipedia: "It's more a personal awareness of how Wikipedia works."

In September, the University of Kansas student newspaper ran an editorial calling upon Wikipedia to do a better job of restoring "adulterated pages," noting that "despite a thousand recitations by our professors that Wikipedia is not a genuine source, students trust the site to give them accurate information." Nevertheless, Erick Schmidt, editor of the University Daily Kansan, says he doesn't rely much on Wikipedia, in part because his reporters write mostly about college and community issues. Plus, "we're taught to be cautious of things and skeptical," he says.

Schmidt rejects the notion that college students uncritically accept Wikipedia because they are infatuated with all things Internet. "We don't want to move things to technology because we think it's cool or paper is lame," he says. "But honestly, we are pressed for time, and if technology speeds things up . . . that's why we're being drawn to it."

For his part, Wales maintains that the more people use Wikipedia, the more they'll come to understand and accept it. His conclusion, he says, "comes from people who have used the site for a long time and know, 'I have to be careful'. . . which is what good reporting is supposed to be about anyway."

But whatever the verdict on Wikipedia, one thing should not change, says the New York Times' Johnston: "No matter who your sources are, when you sign your name, you are responsible for every word, every thought, every concept."

Contributing writer **DONNA SHAW** (shaw@tcnj.edu) has written about front-page ads, hyperlocal Web sites and Pulitzer Prizes for *AJR*.

# E-Mail in Academia
## Expectations, Use, and Instructional Impact

**An exploration of e-mail communication between faculty and students at UNC Chapel Hill identified issues surrounding the use of e-mail to advance instructional outcomes.**

MEREDITH WEISS AND DANA HANSON-BALDAUF

"The more elaborate our means of communication, the less we communicate," claimed theologian and educator Joseph Priestly.[1] Born in 1733, Priestly could hardly have imagined the Internet, e-mail, and instant messaging, although his prophetic statement presaged a dilemma now faced on college campuses worldwide. The popularity of and reliance on emergent computer-mediated communication technologies such as instant messaging, blogs, and social networks have arguably widened the generation gap between faculty and traditional undergraduate students. Marc Prensky defined this generational technology divide by coining the terms *digital natives* and *digital immigrants*. He wrote,

> The single biggest problem facing education today is that our Digital Immigrant instructors, who speak an outdated language (that of the pre-digital age), are struggling to teach a population that speaks an entirely new language.[2]

The purpose of the study reported here was to explore differences between professors (digital immigrants) and undergraduate students (digital natives) at the University of North Carolina at Chapel Hill regarding their expectations and use of e-mail and its perceived impact on instructional outcomes and student success. The ubiquitous nature of e-mail presents an ideal opportunity to investigate its use along this generational divide. Additionally, the study of e-mail practice and perception in the context of higher education might foster more meaningful scholarly communication between teacher and student and, in turn, positively impact instructional outcomes and student success.

## Literature Review

Regardless of the context and medium, the process of communication is complicated and multifaceted. Over the years, many have sought to better understand and explain the phenomenon. Ernest Pascarella, for example, has spent much of his career exploring faculty and student communication and its impact on academic achievement and the college experience. Although not set within the context of the digital environment, his studies reveal a strong association between student outcomes and the degree and quality of one-on-one communication between teacher and student.[3] These outcomes reflect positive trends in academic achievement, personal growth (both intellectual and developmental), the degree of effort extended to studies, student connection and satisfaction with academic coursework and the institute, attrition, and attainment of educational and career goals.[4]

How does Pascarella's work fit within the context of a digital instructional environment? Recently, Robert Duran, Lynne Kelly, and James Keaten[5] investigated faculty use and perception of communication via e-mail in correspondence with students. They found that faculty ($n = 257$) received more than two times the number of e-mails they produced (faculty received an average of 15.15 e-mails per week compared to 6.72 e-mails per week they sent). Excuses for late work or missed class sessions were the most cited reasons for student-initiated e-mail communication. Despite some faculty dissatisfaction ($n = 13$, or 21 percent) with the amount of time and effort spent on e-mail communication, faculty overall perceived benefits (a mean of 3.05 on a 5-point scale) and liabilities (2.95) as roughly equal. Faculty found they could communicate better with reticent students (3.25) and relay pertinent and timely course information to classes using e-mail.

A 2003 study conducted by Michael Russell and his colleagues found that teachers use technology, including e-mail, more for preparation and work-related communication, and less often for instructional purposes.[6] Interestingly, this finding seemed especially true among less experienced teachers, despite their self-reported high levels of comfort using technology. In John Savery's 2002 study, however, 90 percent of faculty surveyed reported using e-mail five times or more per semester for instructional use.[7]

Unfortunately, terms such as "instructional purposes" and "instructional use" are not consistently defined across studies. Studies in 2001 and 2004 identified the concept of *cognitive presence* in computer-mediated instruction,[8] which we propose should be present for an instructional use of e-mail. Cognitive presence is defined as an atmosphere of inquiry and higher-order learning that supports critical thinking, reflection, knowledge construction, collaboration, and discourse.

Numerous studies further address the general use of e-mail, particularly in the corporate environment. These studies focus on e-mail etiquette,[9] appropriate behavior, norms, and conventions,[10] development of user expectations,[11] e-mail management and system design,[12] user productivity,[13] and e-mail training.[14] Though these studies investigated how e-mail is used and managed, studies related to e-mail use in the specific context of faculty-student communication and enhanced learning are limited and warrant further investigation.

# Purpose of the Study

This study aimed to explore e-mail practice in academia between professors and undergraduate students in relation to their expectations and use of e-mail, along with its perceived impact on instructional outcomes and student success. Additional areas of investigation included survey participants' emotions regarding e-mail use and their formal e-mail training experiences.

The study addressed three questions:

1. What do faculty and students perceive as appropriate e-mail use in their communications with one another?
2. How do faculty and students actually use e-mail in communicating with one another?
3. Does e-mail communication have a perceived positive impact on learning, grades, and faculty-student familiarity?

# Methodology

The study employed an exploratory quantitative and qualitative research design using an electronic survey tool. Two surveys were developed and administered to faculty and undergraduate students, respectively, in the fall of 2006. Each survey had approximately 74 parallel questions, presented in a mostly closed-question format. Participants had opportunities to provide comments regarding their responses on select survey questions.

Use of an electronic survey tool enabled gathering information from a large population in a systematic, efficient (both time and cost), and comparable manner. Additionally, participants could complete the survey at a convenient time and place. Prior to administering the survey, a pilot survey checked for clarity of wording and time it would take participants to complete the actual survey.

Each survey consisted of four components:

- Introduction,
- Demographics,
- Style (referring to self-reported e-mail behaviors), and
- Perceived style (referring to a respondent's impression of another's e-mail behavior).

The introduction functioned as a filtering tool to eliminate participants who did not meet study specifications. Part-time students and faculty were not included in this study, for example, nor were faculty with titles other than assistant, associate, or full professor. In addition, participants were instructed to respond only in terms of their e-mail communications surrounding on-campus undergraduate courses (distance education interactions were excluded).

The student survey demographic section collected information about gender, age, ethnicity, residency status, class status, and major. The faculty survey demographic section collected information about gender, age, ethnicity, professorship status level, years teaching, and academic discipline.

The final two sections of both surveys collected core information regarding e-mail attitudes, perceptions, expectations, and behaviors. The style section investigated participant e-mail use in regard to the construction of e-mails, frequency of use, behaviors, responsiveness, attitudes, and expectations. The section on perceived style collected information about how participants viewed their counterparts' attitudes and expectations.

## Survey Implementation

The survey was administered through a computer-mediated tool and promoted through the UNC Mass E-mail System, which distributes e-mail messages to the entire university community. The incentive for participating in the survey was the chance to win a $20 gift certificate to a local shopping mall. Means of participant identification were limited to IP addresses (collected as standard procedure with the survey tool) and an optional submission of an e-mail address to participate in the drawing to win the gift certificate.

## Participants

Participants were recruited from a pool of UNC Chapel Hill undergraduate students and faculty from all disciplines. Access to this pool of participants was achieved through the UNC Mass E-mail System.

Only full-time undergraduate students and full-time on-campus faculty serving in an on-campus instructional role to undergraduate students were included in the study. This allowed the samples to more accurately reflect a clear distinction between what Prensky refers to as digital natives and digital immigrants, given that the majority of undergraduates are between the ages of 17 and 21.

## Procedure

An introductory e-mail outlining the intent of the study directed participants to the survey link. Individuals who consented to participate and who met the specified requirements were asked to respond to a total of 73 questions (74 for faculty). With the exception of the introductory questions, which were designed to ensure that participants met the guidelines for the study, participants had the option of not responding to questions. Many of the questions also permitted comments.

Access to the survey remained open for one week. Participants were informed that the results of the study would be made available to the UNC Chapel Hill community.

## Analysis of Data

After closing access to the survey site, we compiled data from both the faculty and student surveys and organized it by category and parallel questions. Coding of data occurred on questions in which respondents could indicate multiple answers. Data was cross-tabulated using descriptive statistics, performing a chi square analysis and using Fisher's exact test, when appropriate, to determine statistical significance.

# Results

The UNC Chapel Hill undergraduate faculty population of 1,818 represents more than 60 disciplines. Of the 97 faculty who participated in the study, 56 met the study's specifications; 25 respondents did not teach undergraduate students, and 16 were not ranked as assistant, associate, or full professor. Roughly 43 percent of faculty participants identified themselves as full professors, 38 percent as associate professors, and 20 percent as assistant professors. The average age for a UNC faculty member is approximately 50 years,[15] which is consistent with our survey participants because the majority of our faculty responders were between the ages of 41 and 60.

Of the UNC undergraduate student population, 178 participated in the study. Of those, 166 met study specifications, with roughly 4 percent freshmen, 30 percent sophomores, 24 percent juniors, and 41 percent seniors. Approximately 87 percent were under 22 years of age, and 12 percent were between the ages of 22 and 25. In regard to residency, 79 percent of student participants were in-state, 20 percent out-of-state, and 1 percent international. Table 1 summarizes the demographics of the study participants.

## Appropriate E-Mail Use

Research question 1 asked, what do faculty and students perceive as appropriate e-mail use in communicating with one another? As Table 2 shows, both faculty and students generally agree on appropriate use of e-mail correspondence, although faculty are less likely to view lecture clarification as an appropriate use. Faculty additionally reported that providing career advice over e-mail was appropriate.

Faculty respondents provided additional information in open-ended questions regarding their perception of how e-mail can best be used. Comments included:

It is not a substitute for office hours, nor am I willing to answer long substantive questions in e-mail. It is an efficient way to communicate with simple questions and schedule/remind/inform about in-depth opportunities for learning.

I prefer e-mails for some purposes (like excuses for absences) and not for others (like answers that will take a long time to formulate in writing).

I think students should primarily use e-mail to inform the instructor of valid excuses for missing class/assignments, getting clarifications on assignments, or setting up appointments. I think students should meet with instructors during office hours for lecture clarifications, questions about grading, advising, and meeting with prospective instructors.

The comments above seem to offer a possible explanation for student dissatisfaction. Students complained about incomplete explanations and brevity:

The professor not taking the time to thoughtfully read my e-mail. Often they will read parts, and assume one thing and respond to what they assume my concern/question is.

Professors usually send very short e-mails in response to my long ones and don't answer all of my questions.

Too often professors will pop back a quick response when I have sent a well thought out but e-mailed [set of] questions. The habit of writing quick e-mails overrides the original goal of communication. When I e-mail a professor, I don't expect to have a 3 or 4 e-mail conversation; I think out my question in detail hoping they will do the same with their response.

It seems the two groups have different expectations for the appropriate use of e-mail.

Note that while these comments suggest a faculty preference for face-to-face meetings in regard to substantive information inquiry, students might not know this. Furthermore, although survey results indicate that majorities of students (93 percent) and faculty (82 percent) feel that e-mail is an appropriate venue for lesson clarification, communication expectations surrounding substantive e-mail conversations need clarification.

## Actual E-Mail Use

Research question 2 asked, how do faculty and students actually use e-mail in communicating with one another? Both faculty (72 percent) and students (78 percent) concur that e-mail use is encouraged as appropriate for coursework correspondence. Forty-one percent of faculty indicated that they provide e-mail behavior expectations to their students at the beginning of the semester; another 39 percent indicated that although they did not extend these expectations to their students, they are open to the possibility; and 20 percent felt that providing e-mail behavior expectations was unnecessary. Fifty-seven percent of student respondents indicated that they would prefer to know faculty e-mail behavior expectations in advance. One student respondent noted,

**Table 1** E-Mail Study Participants

| | Faculty | Students |
|---|---|---|
| Gender | | |
| Female | 50% | 80% |
| Male | 50% | 20% |
| Ethnicity* | | |
| American Indian or Alaska Native | 2% | 3% |
| Asian | 2% | 11% |
| Black or African American | 2% | 14% |
| Hispanic | 0% | 5% |
| White | 96% | 73% |
| Other | 2% | 2% |
| Range in Age | | |
| Less than 22 | 0% | 87% |
| 22–25 | 0% | 12% |
| 26–30 | 0% | 1% |
| 31–40 | 14% | 1% |
| 41–50 | 25% | 1%** |
| 51–60 | 34% | ** |
| 61+ | 25% | ** |

\* Participants could choose multiple ethnicities.
\*\* One percent of student participants were over 41 years old.

**Table 2** Perceived Appropriate Use of E-mail

| | Faculty believe it is appropriate for students to use e-mail for: | Students believe it is appropriate for faculty to use e-mail for: |
|---|---|---|
| Assignment clarification | 94% | 99% |
| Question asking/answering | 92% | 93% |
| Excuses (missed classes, assignments, etc.) | 94% | N/A |
| Lecture clarification | 82% | 93% |
| Relationship building | 58% | 66% |

I think it is fine that every professor has different standards/expectations about e-mail formality, but they should all make it clear at the beginning of the semester.

Both faculty and students agree that the primary purpose for using e-mail to communicate with one another relates to general housekeeping functions such as assignment clarification, explanations for missed classes or assignments, and question asking and answering. In open-text responses, faculty also reported using e-mail to send out course announcements, items of possible interest, guidance for research, reminders, and feedback on drafts of student work. Students responded that they also used e-mail to set appointments with professors, discuss assignment performance, and request grade clarification (see Table 3).

## Table 3 Faculty and Student Use of E-mail Communication

| | Faculty use e-mail for: | Students use e-mail for: |
|---|---|---|
| Assignment clarification | 87% | 83% |
| Excuses (missed classes, assignments, etc.) | 78%* | 58% |
| Question asking/answering | 83% | 83% |
| Lecture clarification | 46% | 28% |
| Relationship building | 26% | 13% |

* Responding to student excuses

In regard to the amount of e-mail, a number of student respondents expressed some frustration:

I respond to all my e-mails the first time I receive them. I will forget to respond if I read them and log out of the session.

I just have to return e-mails as soon as I check them so that I don't forget; also so that my inbox isn't flooded (which it always is).

Faculty respondents had similar frustrations:

I think you should have asked if the increasing volume of e-mails from students is posing a problem for the faculty, who are having to spend hours extra a week in answering e-mails, but get no credit for this in their departments or in the university—the answer is a resounding YES!!!

I would like students to ask themselves if the question can wait until my next office hours. I'm simply too busy to reply to all of the e-mails I get from students.

I would like for them not to ask questions that require long, thoughtful answers. I get hundreds of e-mails a day and am swamped with work. If they need that kind of answer they should talk to me after class or come to office hours (which almost no one does any more).

Results from the study seem to validate faculty frustration in regard to the large amount of e-mail messages they receive. Ninety-four percent of student respondents indicated that they e-mail their professors between one and 10 times a month. With an average class size of 30 students, that equates to a minimum of 30 e-mails a month per class, with the potential for 300 e-mails a month per class. Note also that approximately 5 percent of undergraduate classes at UNC have an enrollment of more than 100 students per instructor.[16]

## Perceived Impact of E-Mail

Research question 3 asked, does e-mail communication have a perceived positive impact on learning, grades, and the faculty-student relationship? As Table 4 shows, both students and faculty agree that increased e-mail communication contributes to learning and teacher-student relationships. Students, however, more often believe that it leads to higher grades.

Little narrative information was available regarding improved learning and grades as a result of increased e-mail communication between faculty and students. Respondents had much to say, however, about the idea of e-mail communication and relationship building. As students noted:

Faculty should express some interest in getting to know the student academically/personally more often, and I think e-mail is a good way to get started.

I wish that they would become more personal with students, ask questions and try to get to know the student.

On the flip side, professors indicated:

Relationship building and career advice should be done in person, but setting up appointments for this by e-mail is fine.

I think e-mail communication is great, convenient, and helpful in many ways, but I am concerned that it replaces face-to-face contact with me in too many instances. Fewer students come to office hours because of e-mail, and I think that is a potential problem, especially for students who aren't doing as well in the class as they could be.

It was not clear from survey results whether the increased amount of e-mail communication correlates with a decrease in faculty office hour visits.

When questioned about their views on whether student-faculty e-mail communication was formal or informal, the majority of faculty and students believe it can be either. Analysis of data, however, found a significant difference ($p = 0.0$) in the beliefs held by faculty and students in regard to the other being "too friendly" in communicating via e-mail. Fifty-three percent of faculty members believe that students are often or sometimes too friendly, while only 5 percent of students feel this way about faculty. Perhaps students—as digital natives brought up in an Internet world filled with opportunities for online relationship building—are simply more seasoned in developing online relationships and more apt to view computer-mediated conversations as a means to that end.

Two additional survey components captured interesting results: apprehension about using e-mail to communicate with faculty and reactions to the idea of formal e-mail training.

**Apprehension.** Clearly, faculty at UNC underestimate student apprehension about initiating e-mail communications with professors. While 35 percent of faculty indicated they perceive students to be apprehensive, 66 percent of student respondents indicated that they were apprehensive. In contrast, 100 percent of faculty responders said they did not feel apprehensive the first time they e-mail a student, while 13 percent of student responders reported believing their professors are at least sometimes apprehensive in initiating e-mail communication. Nonetheless, several students noted comfort using e-mail over other forms of communication. For example:

Because I am shy and don't like to speak on the phone first, I prefer e-mails so I can really think out my message and construct what I want to say so I can avoid miscommunication or sending a garbled message on my part. So I typically use e-mail as a communication mode more than office hours or anything.

Another student noted that the more casual an e-mail conversation, the less intimidating it is for the student to respond:

I noticed my computer science professors are much more casual in their e-mails to me. (Don't always use a lot of formality, sometimes don't use complete sentences, address me by my first name, and sign with their first name.) I like this better than the more formal e-mails I have received from other professors because it makes it less intimidating for me to write them back, and it makes me more comfortable with communicating with them via e-mail.

A student also noted that e-mail is often used when a student is anxious about speaking in front of his/her peers:

E-mail is a method of communication that can reduce anxiety for a student who needs additional help or who wants to express an idea without the judgment of peers.

## Table 4 Perceived Positive Impact of Increased E-mail

|  | Faculty | Students |
|---|---|---|
| Learning | 50% | 67% |
| Grades | 6% | 30% |
| Relationships | 49% | 68% |

**E-Mail Training.** Both students (43 percent) and faculty (64 percent) believe e-mail training would benefit others, but neither group indicates a strong desire for their own personal training in e-mail use. Only 14 percent of faculty and 31 percent of students indicated interest. Faculty's major objection seemed to be time:

Nice idea. Yet another of those desirable things (like training on using PowerPoint or other computer programs) that I'd love but absolutely don't have time for.

One student was enthusiastic about the possibility:

Please!!!! I'm so bad at e-mail etiquette, and I can't handle the sheer number of e-mails. I would love to attend training on using e-mail productively.

Other students noted,

I do not think that real training is necessary; if professors do receive a lot of lazily-composed e-mails, perhaps a few guidelines on the matter, presented at the beginning of the course, would suffice.

It sounds interesting, but I would have to be convinced that it is relevant and necessary in my life.

# Limitations and Implications for Future Research

This exploratory study examined e-mail communication between faculty and students. The primary limitation of the study is sample size. Before results can be generalized to other institutions, further research conducted in multiple academic institutions is necessary to confirm, expand, or revise findings and propagate development of a model of best practice for instructional e-mail use in academia to enhance learning.

We also believe that future studies would benefit from a more-even gender distribution, relative to enrollment, among student responders. It is not clear why female students responded at higher rates than male students in this initial study.

Another limitation of the study was the exclusion of other instructional members of the academic community such as graduate students, adjunct professors, and practitioner instructors, as well as those participating in distance education courses.

It is also prudent to consider the possibility of survey bias in terms of those who chose to participate in the survey. If, as Presky notes, digital immigrants (in this situation, professors) lack a proclivity toward technology use, many might not have read the e-mail calling for participation or might have chosen not to participate in the web-based survey. Future studies, therefore, might benefit from including an alternate method of information gathering for those who are averse to e-mail or Internet interaction.

# Discussion

Without question, e-mail has grown to be a viable and indispensable means of information exchange in academia. Results of this initial study unfortunately indicate that e-mail has yet to reach its full potential as a meaningful instructional tool for inquiry and higher-order learning. Survey results and narrative responses, however, offer insight into possibilities for expanding the role and functionality of e-mail as an instructional tool.

We propose that professors can greatly improve e-mail communication and alleviate frustration simply by taking a few minutes at the beginning of each semester to set clear expectations and guidelines for e-mail use. Survey responses indicate that both faculty and students believe this initiative would be helpful. Topics to address during this discussion might include apprehension about using e-mail, appropriate use of e-mail communication, hours during which faculty will respond to e-mail, formality of the communication, grammar standards for the messages, information necessary to include in messages, ways faculty prefer to be addressed and to address students in return, expectations of responsiveness, and appropriate subject lines (see Table 5).

We believe e-mail communication has the potential to greatly enhance learning. As survey results indicate, faculty and students agree that increased e-mail communication can have a positive impact on learning. To realize this impact, though, e-mail communication between professor and student must be seen as an extension of instruction. A paradigm shift from viewing e-mail communication solely as suited for housekeeping functions to viewing it as a means to further scholarly discourse and cognitive challenge is needed.

We suggest that appropriate e-mail use be reframed into an instructional conversation. Students, for example, might be encouraged to ask substantive questions over e-mail without expecting answers. A professor might instead respond with a series of questions or suggest a different angle from which the student could begin to research the answer. The professor might also bring a student's e-mail question to the classroom for discussion or post it on an online discussion board for class collaboration. If this type of exchange is a clearly set expectation at the beginning of the semester, both parties will benefit. Faculty will not feel burdened to answer all questions, and students would not expect them to. Instead, students will be challenged to find their own answers, leading to a truly scholarly exploration that extends the classroom experience.

Finally, as our study revealed, many students feel uneasy or intimidated when initiating face-to-face conversations with faculty; they prefer using e-mail to ask questions or relay information. It is important for faculty to recognize this. Addressing these issues, conveying a sense of openness and availability, and engaging students in positive one-on-one conversations may alleviate some of these feelings and create richer and more meaningful scholarly interactions in the classroom and digital environment.

# Conclusion

The ubiquitous use of e-mail in academia coupled with the strong relationship between student achievement and faculty-student one-on-one communication necessitates continued exploration of the influence of instructional e-mail correspondence. It is also a compelling reason for faculty to proficiently, thoughtfully, and strategically craft their e-mail messages to students. In doing so, faculty may increase the scope of their influence, establish a cognitive online presence, and extend scholarly dialogue and thought. Additionally, we propose that the development, communication, and adherence to agreed-upon e-mail expectations, norms, and guidelines would improve communications, lessen faculty and student frustrations, and alleviate student anxiety.

## Table 5  Suggested Expectations and Guidelines for E-Mail Use

| Topic | Expectations and Guidelines |
| --- | --- |
| Apprehension | Shared expectations and guidelines can ease student apprehension about communicating with the professor over e-mail. |
| | Assuage student fears about approaching the professor with questions in person, during or outside of class. |
| Appropriate uses | Housekeeping, such as assignment clarification, excuses, question asking/answering, announcements. |
| | Instructional, such as lecture clarification and question asking/answering. Explain guidelines for such requests. |
| | Mentoring, such as relationship building and career advice. |
| Inappropriate uses | Debating grades. Under what circumstances if any is this appropriate over e-mail? |
| | Long, substantive question asking with the expectation of an e-mail "answer."* |
| | When is e-mail an inappropriate substitute for office hours or in-class discussion? |
| Concluding an e-mail | Should students always end with a thank you or some acknowledgment? |
| | Would faculty prefer students only respond when further action is requested (to avoid e-mail overload)? |
| E-mail hours | When the professor will or will not respond to e-mail. |
| Emoticons** | Does the professor appreciate and feel comfortable with their use? |
| | Will faculty use them when communicating with students? Does this help students understand tone? |
| Formality | How formal or informal the professor believes e-mail communications should be. |
| | Does this depend on the context of the message? Or how well the professor and student know each other? |
| | What does the professor perceive as "too informal" or "too formal" when it comes to e-mail communication with students? |
| | Appropriate tone. |
| Grammar, etc. | Are proper grammar, spelling, and complete sentences expected all the time? |
| | Are one-word answers acceptable? |
| Information to include | Full name, course, section, semester, etc. |
| Proper address | How the professor prefers to be addressed. |
| | How the professor plans to address students. |
| Responsiveness expectations | The amount of time a student should expect to wait before receiving a response. |
| | The amount of time the professor expects to wait to receive a student's response. |
| Subject line | What constitutes an acceptable subject line? One word? Complete description? |

* It might be appropriate to set the expectation that the professor will either respond in such a way to aid the student in researching the answer or bring the question to the classroom or online discussion board for class collaboration.

** Groups of keyboard characters that typically represent a facial expression or emotion.

Achieving these goals requires instruction in e-mail use, however. Despite objections to attending e-mail training, both faculty and students agree that it would be beneficial—for each other. By raising awareness of the association between student success and one-on-one communication with faculty in an environment where e-mail serves as one of the primary methods of contact, we hope that both faculty and students will begin to see the value of e-mail training and become more willing to attend. Moreover, we believe it is critical for faculty to realize that learning how to better use e-mail can save them time, assuage a number of their current frustrations, and alleviate student communication concerns.

Clearly, unless training options are flexible in method of delivery, efficient, and relevant to each audience, high attendance will be a challenge. We believe, however, that faculty trained in the optimal use of e-mail can better expand and reframe the use of e-mail communication to enhance teaching and learning and thereby improve student outcomes.

# Endnotes

1. John W. Severinghaus, "Priestley, the Furious Free Thinker of the Enlightenment, and Scheele, the Taciturn Apothecary of Uppsala," *Acta Anaesthesiologica Scandinavica,* vol. 46, no. 1 (January 2002), pp. 2–9, http://www.blackwell-synergy.com/toc/aas/46/1.

2. Marc Prensky, "Digital Natives, Digital Immigrants," *On the Horizon,* vol. 9, no. 5 (October 2001), pp. 1–6, http://www.marcprensky.com.

3. Ernest T. Pascarella and Patrick T. Terenzini, *How College Affects Students: Findings and Insights from Twenty Years of Research* (San Francisco, CA: Jossey-Bass, 1991).

4. For a review of the literature of a number of Pascarella's studies, see Mark A. Lamport, "Student-Faculty Informal Interaction and the Effect on College Student Outcomes:

A Review of the Literature," *Adolescence,* vol. 28, no. 112 (Winter 1993), pp. 971–991.

5. Robert L. Duran, Lynne Kelly, and James A. Keaten, (2005). "College Faculty Use and Perceptions of Electronic Mail to Communicate with Students," *Communication Quarterly,* vol. 53, no. 2 (2005), pp. 159–176.

6. Michael Russell, Damian Bebell, Laura O'Dwyer, and Kathleen O'Connor, "Examining Teacher Technology Use: Implications for Preservice and Inservice Teacher Preparation," *Journal of Teacher Education,* vol. 54, no. 4 (September 2003), pp. 297–311, http://jte.sagepub.com/content/vol54/issue4/.

7. John R. Savery, "Faculty and Student Perceptions of Technology Integration in Teaching," *Journal of Interactive Online Learning,* vol. 1, no. 2 (Fall 2002), http://www.ncolr .org/jiol/issues/showissue.cfm?volID=1&IssueID=3.

8. See the studies by D. Randy Garrison, Terry Anderson, and Walter Archer, "Critical Thinking, Cognitive Presence, and Computer Conferencing in Distance Education," *American Journal of Distance Education,* vol. 15, no. 1 (2001), pp. 7–23, http://www.ajde.com/Contents/vol15_1.htm; and Heather Kanuka and D. Randy Garrison, "Cognitive Presence in Online Learning," *Journal of Computing in Higher Education,* vol. 15, no. 2 (March 2004), pp. 30–49, http://www.jchesite.org/vol152 .html.

9. Virginia Shea, *Netiquette* (San Francisco: Albion Books, 1994).

10. Uta Pankoke-Babtz and Phillip Jeffrey, "Documented Norms and Conventions on the Internet," *International Journal of Human-Computer Interaction,* vol. 14, no. 2 (2002), pp. 219–235, http://www.informatik.uni-trier.de/ ley/db/journals/ ijhci/ijhci14.html.

11. Joshua R. Tyler and John C. Tang, "When Can I Expect an E-Mail Response: A Study of Rhythms in E-Mail Usage," *Proceedings of the 2003 Eighth European Conference on Computer-Supported Cooperative Work,* held September 14–18, 2003, in Helsinki, Finland (Springer Publishing, 2003), pp. 239–258, http://www.ecscw.org/2003.htm; and Laura A.

Dabbish, Robert E. Kraut, Susan Fussell, and Sara Kiesler, "Understanding E-Mail Use: Predicting Action on a message," *Proceedings of the SIGCHI Conference on Human Factors in Computing Systems,* held April 2–7, 2005, in Portland, Oregon (New York: ACM Press, 2005), pp. 691–700, http://portal.acm .org/citation.cfm?id=1055068.

12. Victoria Bellotti, Nicholas Ducheneaut, Mark Howard, and Ian Smith, "Taking E-Mail to Task: The Design and Evaluation of a Task Management Centered E-Mail Tool," *Proceedings of the SIGCHI Conference on Human Factors in Computing Systems,* held April 5–10, 2003, in Ft. Lauderdale, Florida (New York: ACM Press, 2003), pp. 345–352, http://portal.acm.org/citation .cfm?id=642672.

13. Guy Vollmer and Katrin Gabbner, "Quality Improvement of E-Mail Communication in Work Groups and Organizations by Reflection," *Proceedings of the 2005 International ACM SIGGROUP Conference on Supporting Group Work,* held at Sanibel Island, Florida (New York: ACM Press, 2005), pp. 124–127, http://portal.acm.org/citation.cfm?id=1099225.

14. Anthony Burgess, Thomas Jackson, and Janet Edwards, "E-Mail Training Significantly Reduces E-Mail Defects," *International Journal of Information Management,* vol. 25, no. 1 (2005), pp. 71–83, http://www.elsevier.com/wps/find/ journaldescription.cws_home/30434/description#description.

15. University of North Carolina, "UNC: Academic: Facts and Figures," 2006, accessed November 20, 2006, at http:// admissions.unc.edu/academics/factsandfigures.htm.

16. University of North Carolina, "Undergraduate Admissions: FAQs," 2007, accessed November 4, 2007, at http://www .admissions.unc.edu/faq/studying.htm#average.

**MEREDITH WEISS** (mlweiss@e-mail.unc.edu) is Associate Dean for Administration, Finance, and Information Technology in the UNC School of Law. Both she and **DANA HANSON-BALDAUF** (hansonda@ e-mail.unc.edu) are PhD candidates in the School of Information and Library Science, University of North Carolina at Chapel Hill.

# UNIT 6
# Risk and Avoiding Risk

## Unit Selections

27.  **Why Spyware Poses Multiple Threats to Security,** Roger Thompson
28.  **The Virus Underground,** Clive Thompson
29.  **False Reporting on the Internet and the Spread of Rumors: Three Case Studies,** Paul Hitlin
30.  **The New Right-Wing Smear Machine,** Christopher Hayes
31.  **A Growing Watch List,** Karen DeYoung

## Key Points to Consider

- The overview to this unit mentions Michael Crichton's latest novel, *Prey.* The physicist Freeman Dyson reviews this novel in the February 13, 2002, issue of *The New York Review of Books.* Do you agree with what he has to say about the threats that technology holds for us?

- Who is Kevin Mitnick? Where does he work now? What does this say about the way we view white-collar crime in the United States?

- Who is Robert Tappan Morris? His family history is interesting. Why?

- Do you feel safe giving your credit card number to merchants over the Web? Find out how (or if) your number is protected from criminals who might intercept traffic between you and the merchants.

- This unit includes an article on the use of the Internet to spread rumors. Do you agree with the editor's decision to include this articles under the heading "Risk and Avoiding Risk"?

- How many of the rumors described in article 39 have you heard?

- Are you comforted or frightened by the Terrorist Identities Datamart Environment database?

## Student Web Site
www.mhcls.com

## Internet References

**AntiOnline: Hacking and Hackers**
*http://www.antionline.com/index.php*

**Copyright & Trademark Information for the IEEE Computer Society**
*http://computer.org/copyright.htm*

**Electronic Privacy Information Center (EPIC)**
*http://epic.org*

**Internet Privacy Coalition**
*http://www.epic.org/crypto/*

**Center for Democracy and Technology**
*http://www.cdt.org/crypto/*

**Survive Spyware**
*http://www.cnet.com/internet/0-3761-8-3217791-1.html*

**An Electronic Pearl Harbor? Not Likely**
*http://www.nap.edu/issues/15.1/smith.htm*

If literature and film are guides, we in the United States and Western Europe have tangled feelings about technology. On the one hand, we embrace each technical marvel that enters the market place. On the other, a world in which machines have gained the upper hand is a cultural staple. Not long ago, Michael Crichton's novel, *Prey,* frightened us with killer robots that evolved by natural selection to inhabit bodies, snatch souls, and take over the world. Teenagers around the country are still watching the handsome couple from *The Matrix,* Neo and Trinity, take on technology run amuck. This time, our creations farm humankind and harvest their capacity to produce energy. More recently, *Children of Men* creates a world, torn by war, in which there has not been a human birth in twenty years.

As it happens, we have good reason to worry about technology, especially computer technology, but the risks are more prosaic. They include privacy intrusions, software that cannot be made error free, and deliberate sabotage. We even have grounds to fear that much of our cultural heritage, now digitized, will be inaccessible when the software used to encode it becomes obsolete. These are issues that concern practicing computer scientists and engineers. *The Communications of the ACM,* the leading journal in the field, has run a column in recent years called Inside Risks, dedicated to exploring the unintended consequences of computing. Another ACM journal, *Software Engineering Notes,* devotes a large part of each issue to chronicling software failures.

Spyware—software downloaded unknowingly—is receiving increasing attention. Harm caused by spyware ranges from gobbling up computer speed on your PC to enlisting your machine in attacks that can disrupt major businesses or the government ("Why Spyware Poses Multiple Threats to Security").

With all of this potential mayhem in the news, it's nice to learn that the good guys have some tricks of their own in the form of fraud detection software.

Anyone who has spent time looking at Internet news sources knows that they can sometimes be unreliable. Paul Hitlin's "False Reporting on the Internet and the Spread of Rumors" examines Internet coverage of the Vince Foster suicide along with other stories to understand just why this is so. Christopher Hays, in "The New Right-Wing Smear Machine," makes the case that the "vast majority of Internet-disseminated rumors have come from the right." During this 2008 campaign season, circulating e-mails have claimed that Barak Obama is a Muslim who studied in a fundamentalist Muslim school while a child in Jakarta, and that Hillary Clinton snubbed a group of women whose children have died in combat. The difference between these and orchestrated attacks, like those on John Kerry's military service, is that their source is unknown.

When a great part of the tide of information that arrives in our mail boxes each day is simply false, what are we to do? The idea that an informed citizenry is essential to a functioning

© Martin Poole/Getty Images

democracy has been around since the middle of the 18th century. How those citizens are to be informed is the crux of the matter. Jefferson himself was sometimes distrustful of newspapers and no less a figure than Thomas Paine said that there is a "difference between error and licentiousness" (Brown 1997: 89). The question then as now is who judges which is which. This leads to the most important question of all. Would our free-wheeling culture be better-served by a constrained media, including e-mail. Read the articles and decide for yourself.

Just as Internet news sources cut two ways, so also does the government's ability to amass data. On the one hand, had various government agencies communicated more efficiently, the terrorist attacks of 2001 might have been prevented. On the other hand, read "A Growing Watch List" to learn about Maher Arar, a Canadian imprisoned in Syria at the behest of the U.S. government. Though Ahar has since been cleared of terrorism charges and awarded compensation of $9 million, he is still not free to fly to the United States. His name seems to appear on the Terrorist Identities Datamart Environment, a list that is "a storehouse for data about individuals that the intelligence community believes might harm the United States." Why it appears there is a secret.

Those who remember the "Year-2000 Bug" remember countless news stories about the interconnectedness of computers and our increasing dependence upon them. The global communication network is vastly larger now. Since 1995, the number of Internet users around the world has grown from "nearly zero to over a billion," almost one fifth of the world's population. Interconnected computer systems are not just more pervasive than they were a few years ago, their dispersion and our dependence on them make them more vulnerable.

What is a reasonable person to make of all of this? People around the world are actively trying to disrupt Internet traffic.

Thieves get hold of computer generated lists of names, list presumably compiled so that government agencies could bette serve their clients. Our digital records are disintegrating eve as we digitize more and more of them. Political debate appear to be reaching new lows, as unattributed allegations swarr through the Internet. The government compiles massive data bases about terrorism and catches the innocent in its nets Disruption of the global communications network could be cata strophic as financial markets and global supply chains collapse One strives for the equanimity of Neil Postman: "Technology giveth and technology taketh away."

## Reference

Brown, R. (1997). *The Strength of a People: The Ideal of an Informed Citizenry in America 1650–1970.* Chapel Hill, NC: The University of North Carolina Press.

# Why Spyware Poses Multiple Threats to Security

Roger Thompson

S pyware is becoming a relentless onslaught from those seeking to capture and use private information for their own ends. Spyware is annoying and negatively impacts the computing experience. Even worse, there are real and significant threats to corporate and even national security from those who use and abuse spyware.

There is much debate in Congress, state legislatures, and industry about what constitutes spyware. While that debate is an important one in terms of possible remedies, we can count the cost that unfettered spyware is having on individual users as well as on corporate networks. Regardless of whether we agree to divide the term spyware into various subsets such as adware or malware, the truth is any software application, if downloaded unknowingly or unwittingly, and without full explanation, is unacceptable and unwelcome.

With that understanding as a backdrop, the following is a working definition of spyware: Any software intended to aid an unauthorized person or entity in causing a computer, without the knowledge of the computer's user or owner, to divulge private information. This definition applies to legitimate business as much as to malicious code writers and hackers who are taking advantage of spyware to break into users' PCs.

Many PC users have unwittingly loaded, or unknowingly had spyware downloaded onto their computers. This happens when a user clicks "yes" in response to a lengthy and often extremely technical or legalistic end user licensing agreement. Or it happens when a user simply surfs the Web, where self-activating code is simply dropped onto their machines in what is known as a "drive-by download."

## Spyware Dangers Real and Pervasive

The dangers of spyware are not always known and are almost never obvious. Usually, you know when you have a virus or worm—they are quite obvious. Spyware silently installs itself on a PC, where it might start to take any number of different and unwanted actions, including:

- "Phone home" information about an individual, their computer, and their surfing habits to a third party to use to spam a computer user or push pop-up ads to their screen;
- Open a computer to a remote attacker using a Remote Access Trojan (RAT) to remotely control a computer;
- Capture every keystroke a user types—private or confidential email, passwords, bank account information—and report it back to a thief or blackmailer;
- Allow a computer to be hijacked and used to attack a third party's computers in a denial-of-service attack that can cost enterprises millions and expose them to legal liability; and
- Probe a system for vulnerabilities that can enable a hacker to steal files or otherwise exploit a computer system.

**Theft through spyware could be the most important and least understood espionage tactic in use today.**

## Spyware Harms Computer Performance

The misuse of technology and hijacking of spyware is a real and present danger to security and privacy. The ill effects of spyware do not stop there. Spyware seriously degrades computer performance and productivity.

Testing at our company's research laboratory earlier this year revealed that the addition of just one adware pest slowed a computer's boot time by 3.5 minutes. Instead of just under two minutes to perform this operation, it took the infected PC close to seven minutes. Multiply that by a large number of PCs and you have a huge productivity sinkhole. Add another pest and the slowdown doubles again.

We also tested Web page access, and again it took much longer once a pest was added to a clean machine. Almost five times longer in fact for a Web page to load on an infected PC. The pest also caused three Web sites to be accessed, rather than the one requested, and caused the PC to transmit and receive much greater amounts of unknown data—889 bytes transmitted compared to 281 transmitted from the clean machine, and 3,086 bytes received compared to 1,419 bytes received by the clean machine. This translates into significant increases in bandwidth utilization. Managing bandwidth costs money.

Increased costs due to unnecessary consumption of bandwidth on individual PCs, and the necessary labor costs in rebuilding systems to ensure they are no longer corrupt are virtually unquantifiable. System degradation is time consuming for the individual PC user and even more so for network administrators managing corporate networks. Even new PCs straight from the factory come loaded with thousands of pieces of spyware, all busy "phoning home" information about the user and slowing down computing speeds.

## National Security Threats

As noted here, keystroke loggers and other programs embedded with spyware can be used to steal critical data. Literally thousands of spyware applications are downloaded every day in large organizations whose employees use the Internet. The probability is high that at least some of those applications are designed to steal passwords and other critical data. Theft through spyware could be the most important and least understood espionage tactic in use today.

Another disturbing threat posed by spyware goes directly to the ability of terrorists or others to disable computer networks in times of crisis. In the past year, spyware has been used to essentially hijack large numbers of personal computers and organize them into "Bot Armies." Some of the organizers of these armies use them to send millions of spam email messages without user knowledge. Advertisements offering this service have even appeared in Europe and Asia.

The potential exists to move beyond annoyance to something much worse—targeted distributed denial-of-service (DDoS) attacks aimed at disrupting major business or government activity. A DDoS attack coordinated through thousands of individual PCs, owned by innocent and even unwitting users, could be a very difficult threat to address quickly, effectively, and fairly.

Individual PC users are never aware their machine is being used to disrupt Internet traffic. There is currently little or no recourse to a legal solution even if the occurrence can be monitored.

## Possible Solutions

Only a combination of education and protection, disclosure through legislation, active prosecution, and planning will provide the answer needed to address the spyware threat. None of these solutions by themselves is enough.

The first line of defense is education and protection. Any individual, business, or government agency currently connected to the Internet must realize they are part of a complex network that is inextricably intertwined. Creators of spyware take advantage of that fact, plus the knowledge that most PC users are not

sophisticated technologists. The technology industry has begun to make computer users aware of the spyware threat by the creation of and active outreach by several groups and organizations, including the Consortium of Anti-Spyware Technology (COAST).

Consumer education about spyware and promotion of comprehensive anti-spyware software aimed at detecting and removing unwanted pests is fundamental to this outreach, which is modeled after the decade-long effort by anti-virus software companies to raise awareness about virus threats. However, individual computer users, precisely because of the insidious nature of spyware, can only do so much to protect themselves, and are not personally responsible for controlling the spread of spyware.

Which brings us to the second line of defense—disclosure legislation. All applications, including those bundled and downloaded along with free software and with legitimate commercial applications, should be readily identifiable by users prior to installation and made easy to remove or uninstall. It is this transparent disclosure, and the ability of individual users to decide what does and does not reside on their systems, that must be legislated. Individuals should have the ability to make fully informed decisions about what they choose to download onto their machines, while understanding the implications of doing so.

The third line of defense is aggressive prosecution. The deceptive practices employed by many spyware developers are already illegal under existing laws against consumer fraud and identity theft. Law enforcement agencies at the federal and state level should be encouraged to aggressively pursue and prosecute those who clandestinely use spyware to disrupt service, steal data, or engage in other illegal activity. Appropriate agencies should work closely with their counterparts in other countries to address this issue.

The final line of defense is planning. A spyware Bot Army DDoS targeted at key federal, state, or local agencies is well within the realm of possibility. Such an attack could be very damaging, especially if it was designed to conceal a more conventional attack, or disrupt a response to such an attack. Overcoming this type of DDoS attack could itself be highly disruptive to both individuals and businesses. It is critical that responsible bodies plan for both spyware-related DDoS attacks and responses to those attacks. If necessary, those plans should be coordinated with businesses and others. Again, this coordination should include working with responsible bodies in other countries.

Spyware is a significant threat to the effective functioning and continued growth of the Internet. It also poses threats to national security. Given the dangers it represents, it is important that business and government work together to address the issue and safeguard the productivity and security of the Internet computing environment.

**ROGER THOMPSON** is director of malicious content research at Computer Associates.

# The Virus Underground

**Philet0ast3r, Second Part to Hell, Vorgon and guys like them around the world spend their Saturday nights writing fiendishly contagious computer viruses and worms. Are they artists, pranksters or techno-saboteurs?**

CLIVE THOMPSON

This is how easy it has become.

Mario stubs out his cigarette and sits down at the desk in his bedroom. He pops into his laptop the CD of Iron Maiden's "Number of the Beast," his latest favorite album. "I really like it," he says. "My girlfriend bought it for me." He gestures to the 15-year-old girl with straight dark hair lounging on his neatly made bed, and she throws back a shy smile. Mario, 16, is a secondary-school student in a small town in the foothills of southern Austria. (He didn't want me to use his last name.) His shiny shoulder-length hair covers half his face and his sleepy green eyes, making him look like a very young, languid Mick Jagger. On his wall he has an enormous poster of Anna Kournikova—which, he admits sheepishly, his girlfriend is not thrilled about. Downstairs, his mother is cleaning up after dinner. She isn't thrilled these days, either. But what bothers her isn't Mario's poster. It's his hobby.

When Mario is bored—and out here in the countryside, surrounded by soaring snowcapped mountains and little else, he's bored a lot—he likes to sit at his laptop and create computer viruses and worms. Online, he goes by the name Second Part to Hell, and he has written more than 150 examples of what computer experts call "malware": tiny programs that exist solely to self-replicate, infecting computers hooked up to the Internet. Sometimes these programs cause damage, and sometimes they don't. Mario says he prefers to create viruses that don't intentionally wreck data, because simple destruction is too easy. "Anyone can rewrite a hard drive with one or two lines of code," he says. "It makes no sense. It's really lame." Besides which, it's mean, he says, and he likes to be friendly.

But still—just to see if he could do it—a year ago he created a rather dangerous tool: a program that autogenerates viruses. It's called a Batch Trojan Generator, and anyone can download it freely from Mario's Web site. With a few simple mouse clicks, you can use the tool to create your own malicious "Trojan horse." Like its ancient namesake, a Trojan virus arrives in someone's e-mail looking like a gift, a JPEG picture or a video, for example, but actually bearing dangerous cargo.

Mario starts up the tool to show me how it works. A little box appears on his laptop screen, politely asking me to name my Trojan. I call it the "Clive" virus. Then it asks me what I'd like the virus to do. *Shall the Trojan Horse format drive C:?* Yes, I click. *Shall the Trojan Horse overwrite every file?* Yes. It asks me if I'd like to have the virus activate the next time the computer is restarted, and I say yes again.

Then it's done. The generator spits out the virus onto Mario's hard drive, a tiny 3k file. Mario's generator also displays a stern notice warning that spreading your creation is illegal. The generator, he says, is just for educational purposes, a way to help curious programmers learn how Trojans work.

But of course I could ignore that advice. I could give this virus an enticing name, like "britney_spears_wedding_clip.mpeg," to fool people into thinking it's a video. If I were to e-mail it to a victim, and if he clicked on it—and didn't have up-to-date antivirus software, which many people don't—then disaster would strike his computer. The virus would activate. It would quietly reach into the victim's Microsoft Windows operating system and insert new commands telling the computer to erase its own hard drive. The next time the victim started up his computer, the machine would find those new commands, assume they were part of the normal Windows operating system and guilelessly follow them. Poof: everything on his hard drive would vanish—e-mail, pictures, documents, games.

I've never contemplated writing a virus before. Even if I had, I wouldn't have known how to do it. But thanks to a teenager in Austria, it took me less than a minute to master the art.

Mario drags the virus over to the trash bin on his computer's desktop and discards it. "I don't think we should touch that," he says hastily.

Computer experts called 2003 "the Year of the Worm." For 12 months, digital infections swarmed across the Internet with the intensity of a biblical plague. It began in January, when the Slammer worm infected nearly 75,000 servers in 10 minutes, clogging Bank of America's A.T.M. network and causing sporadic flight delays. In the summer, the Blaster worm struck, spreading by exploiting a flaw in Windows; it carried taunting messages directed at Bill Gates, infected hundreds of thousands of computers and tried to use them to bombard a Microsoft Web site with data. Then in August, a worm called Sobig.F exploded with even more force, spreading via e-mail that it generated by stealing addresses from victims' computers. It propagated so rapidly that at one point, one out of every 17 e-mail messages traveling through the Internet was a copy of Sobig.F. The computer-security firm mi2g estimated that the worldwide cost of these attacks in 2003, including clean-up and lost productivity, was at least $82 billion (though such estimates have been criticized for being inflated).

The pace of contagion seems to be escalating. When the Mydoom.A e-mail virus struck in late January, it spread even faster than Sobig.F; at its peak, experts estimated, one out of every five e-mail messages was a copy of Mydoom.A. It also carried a nasty payload: it reprogrammed victim computers to attack the Web site of SCO, a software firm vilified by geeks in the "open source" software community.

You might assume that the blame—and the legal repercussions—for the destruction would land directly at the feet of people like Mario. But as the police around the globe have cracked down on cybercrime in the past few years, virus writers have become more cautious, or at least more crafty. These days, many elite writers do not spread their works at all. Instead, they "publish" them, posting their code on Web sites, often with detailed descriptions of how the program works. Essentially, they leave their viruses lying around for anyone to use.

Invariably, someone does. The people who release the viruses are often anonymous mischief-makers, or "script kiddies." That's a derisive term for aspiring young hackers, usually teenagers or curious college students, who don't yet have the skill to program computers but like to pretend they do. They download the viruses, claim to have written them themselves and then set them free in an attempt to assume the role of a fearsome digital menace. Script kiddies often have only a dim idea of how the code works and little concern for how a digital plague can rage out of control.

### The modern virus epidemic is born of a symbiotic relationship between the people smart enough to write a virus and the people dumb enough—or malicious enough—to spread it.

Our modern virus epidemic is thus born of a symbiotic relationship between the people smart enough to write a virus and the people dumb enough—or malicious enough—to spread it. Without these two groups of people, many viruses would never see the light of day. Script kiddies, for example, were responsible for some of the damage the Blaster worm caused. The original version of Blaster, which struck on Aug. 11, was clearly written by a skilled programmer (who is still unknown and at large). Three days later, a second version of Blaster circulated online, infecting an estimated 7,000 computers. This time the F.B.I. tracked the release to Jeffrey Lee Parson, an 18-year-old in Minnesota who had found, slightly altered and re-released the Blaster code, prosecutors claim. Parson may have been seeking notoriety, or he may have had no clue how much damage the worm could cause: he did nothing to hide his identity and even included a reference to his personal Web site in the code. (He was arrested and charged with intentionally causing damage to computers; when his trial begins, probably this spring, he faces up to 10 years in jail.) A few weeks later, a similar scene unfolded: another variant of Blaster was found in the wild. This time it was traced to a college student in Romania who had also left obvious clues to his identity in the code.

This development worries security experts, because it means that virus-writing is no longer exclusively a high-skill profession. By so freely sharing their work, the elite virus writers have made it easy for almost anyone to wreak havoc online. When the damage occurs, as it inevitably does, the original authors just shrug. *We may have created the monster,* they'll say, *but we didn't set it loose.* This dodge infuriates security professionals and the police, who say it is legally precise but morally corrupt. "When they publish a virus online, they *know* someone's going to release it," says Eugene Spafford, a computer-science professor and security expert at Purdue University. Like a collection of young Dr. Frankensteins, the virus writers are increasingly creating forces they cannot control—and for which they explicitly refuse to take responsibility.

"Where's the beer?" Philet0ast3r wondered. An hour earlier, he had dispatched three friends to pick up another case, but they were nowhere in sight. He looked out over the controlled chaos of his tiny one-bedroom apartment in small-town Bavaria. (Most of the virus writers I visited live in Europe; there have been very few active in the United States since 9/11, because of fears of prosecution.) Philet0ast3r's party was crammed with 20 friends who were blasting the punk band Deftones, playing cards, smoking furiously and arguing about politics. It was a Saturday night. Three girls sat on the floor, rolling another girl's hair into thick dreadlocks, the hairstyle of choice among the crowd. Philet0ast3r himself—a 21-year-old with a small silver hoop piercing his lower lip—wears his brown hair in thick dreads. (Philet0ast3r is an online handle; he didn't want me to use his name.)

Philet0ast3r's friends finally arrived with a fresh case of ale, and his blue eyes lit up. He flicked open a bottle using the edge of his cigarette lighter and toasted the others. A tall blond friend in a jacket festooned with anti-Nike logos put his arm around Philet0ast3r and beamed.

"This guy," he proclaimed, "is the *best* at Visual Basic."

In the virus underground, that's love. Visual Basic is a computer language popular among malware authors for its simplicity; Philet0ast3r has used it to create several of the two dozen viruses he's written. From this tiny tourist town, he works as an assistant in a home for the mentally disabled and in his spare time runs an international virus-writers' group called the "Ready Rangers Liberation Front." He founded the group three years ago with a few bored high-school friends in his even tinier hometown nearby. I met him, like everyone profiled in this article, online, first e-mailing him, then chatting in an Internet Relay Chat channel where virus writers meet and trade tips and war stories.

Philet0ast3r got interested in malware the same way most virus authors do: his own computer was hit by a virus. He wanted to know how it worked and began hunting down virus-writers' Web sites. He discovered years' worth of viruses online, all easily downloadable, as well as primers full of coding tricks. He spent long evenings hanging out in online chat rooms, asking questions, and soon began writing his own worms.

One might assume Philet0ast3r would favor destructive viruses, given the fact that his apartment is decorated top-to-bottom with anticorporate stickers. But Philet0ast3r's viruses, like those of many malware writers, are often surprisingly mild things carrying goofy payloads. One worm does nothing but display a picture of a raised middle finger on your computer screen, then sheepishly apologize for the gesture. ("Hey, this is not meant to you! I just wanted to show my payload.") Another one he is currently developing will install two artificial intelligence chat-agents on your computer; they appear in a pop-up window, talking to each other nervously about whether your antivirus software is going to catch and delete them. Philet0ast3r said he was also working on something sneakier: a "keylogger." It's a Trojan virus that monitors every keystroke its victim types—including passwords and confidential e-mail messages—then secretly mails out copies to whoever planted the virus. Anyone who spreads this Trojan would be able to quickly harvest huge amounts of sensitive personal information.

Technically, "viruses" and "worms" are slightly different things. When a virus arrives on your computer, it disguises itself. It might look like an OutKast song ("hey_ya.mp3"), but if you look more closely, you'll see it has an unusual suffix, like "hey_ya.mp3.exe." That's because it isn't an MP3 file at all. It's a tiny program, and when you click on it, it will reprogram parts of your computer to do something new, like display a message. A virus cannot kick-start itself; a human needs to be fooled into clicking on it. This turns virus writers into armchair psychologists, always hunting for new tricks to dupe someone into activating a virus. ("All virus-spreading," one virus writer said caustically, "is based on the idiotic behavior of the users.")

Worms, in contrast, usually do not require any human intervention to spread. That means they can travel at the breakneck pace of computers themselves. Unlike a virus, a worm generally does not alter or destroy data on a computer. Its danger lies in its speed: when a worm multiplies, it often generates enough traffic to brown out Internet servers, like air-conditioners bringing down the power grid on a hot summer day. The most popular worms today are "mass mailers," which attack a victim's computer, swipe the addresses out of Microsoft Outlook (the world's most common e-mail program) and send a copy of the worm to everyone in the victim's address book. These days, the distinction between worm and virus is breaking down. A worm will carry a virus with it, dropping it onto the victim's hard drive to do its work, then e-mailing itself off to a new target.

## Computer code blurs the line between speech and act. Posting a virus on a Web site, one expert says, is "like taking a gun and sticking bullets in it and sitting it on the counter and saying, 'Hey, free gun!'"

The most ferocious threats today are "network worms," which exploit a particular flaw in a software product (often one by Microsoft). The author of Slammer, for example, noticed a flaw in Microsoft's SQL Server, an online database commonly used by businesses and governments. The Slammer worm would find an unprotected SQL server, then would fire bursts of information at it, flooding the server's data "buffer," like a cup filled to the brim with water. Once its buffer was full, the server could be tricked into sending out thousands of new copies of the worm to other servers. Normally, a server should not allow an outside agent to control it that way, but Microsoft had neglected to defend against such an attack. Using that flaw, Slammer flooded the Internet with 55 million blasts of data per second and in only 10 minutes colonized almost all vulnerable machines. The attacks slowed the 911 system in Bellevue, Wash., a Seattle suburb, to such a degree that operators had to resort to a manual method of tracking calls.

Philet0ast3r said he isn't interested in producing a network worm, but he said it wouldn't be hard if he wanted to do it. He would scour the Web sites where computer-security professionals report any new software vulnerabilities they discover. Often, these security white papers will explain the flaw in such detail that they practically provide a road map on how to write a worm that exploits it. "Then I would use it," he concluded. "It's that simple."

Computer-science experts have a phrase for that type of fast-spreading epidemic: "a Warhol worm," in honor of Andy Warhol's prediction that everyone would be famous for 15 minutes. "In computer terms, 15 minutes is a really long time," says Nicholas Weaver, a researcher at the International Computer Science Institute in Berkeley, who coined the Warhol term. "The worm moves faster than humans can respond." He suspects that even more damaging worms are on the way. All a worm writer needs to do is find a significant new flaw in a Microsoft product, then write some code that exploits it. Even Microsoft admits that there are flaws the company doesn't yet know about.

Virus writers are especially hostile toward Microsoft, the perennial whipping boy of the geek world. From their (somewhat self-serving) point of view, Microsoft is to blame for the worm epidemic, because the company frequently leaves flaws in its products that allow malware to spread. Microsoft markets its products to less expert computer users, cultivating precisely the sort of gullible victims who click on disguised virus attachments. But it is Microsoft's success that really makes it such an attractive target: since more than 90 percent of desktop computers run Windows, worm writers target Microsoft in order to hit the largest possible number of victims. (By relying so exclusively on Microsoft products, virus authors say, we have created a digital monoculture, a dangerous thinning of the Internet's gene pool.)

Microsoft officials disagree that their programs are poor quality, of course. And it is also possible that their products are targeted because it has become cool to do so. "There's sort of a natural tendency to go after the biggest dog," says Phil Reitinger, senior security strategist for Microsoft. Reitinger says that the company is working to make its products more secure. But Microsoft is now so angry that it has launched a counterattack. Last fall, Microsoft set up a $5 million fund to pay for information leading to the capture of writers who target Windows machines. So far, the company has announced $250,000 bounties for the creators of Blaster, Sobig.F and Mydoom.B.

The motivations of the top virus writers can often seem paradoxical. They spend hours dreaming up new strategies to infect computers, then hours more bringing them to reality. Yet when they're done, most of them say they have little interest in turning their creations free. (In fact, 99 percent of all malware never successfully spreads in the wild, either because it expressly wasn't designed to do so or because the author was inept and misprogrammed his virus.) Though Philet0ast3r is proud of his keylogger, he said he does not intend to release it into the wild. His reason is partly one of self-protection; he wouldn't want the police to trace it back to him. But he also said he does not ethically believe in damaging someone else's computer.

So why write a worm, if you're not going to spread it?

For the sheer intellectual challenge, Philet0ast3r replied, the fun of producing something "really cool." For the top worm writers, the goal is to make something that's brand-new, never seen before. Replicating an existing virus is "lame," the worst of all possible insults. A truly innovative worm, Philet0ast3r said, "is like art." To allow his malware to travel swiftly online, the virus writer must keep its code short and efficient, like a poet elegantly packing as much creativity as possible into the tight format of a sonnet. "One condition of art," he noted, "is doing good things with less."

When he gets stuck on a particularly thorny problem, Philet0ast3r will sometimes call for help from other members of the Ready Rangers Liberation Front (which includes Mario). Another friend in another country, whom Philet0ast3r has never actually met, is helping him complete his keylogger by writing a few crucial bits of code that will hide the tool from its victim's view. When they're done, they'll publish their invention in their group's zine, a semiannual anthology of the members' best work.

The virus scene is oddly gentlemanly, almost like the amateur scientist societies of Victorian Britain, where colleagues presented papers in an attempt to win that most elusive of social currencies: street cred. In fact, I didn't meet anyone who gloated about his own talent until I met Benny. He is a member of 29A, a super-elite cadre within the virus underground, a handful of coders around the world whose malware is so innovative that even antivirus experts grudgingly admit they're impressed. Based in the Czech Republic, Benny, clean-cut and wide-eyed, has been writing viruses for five years, making him a veteran in the field at age 21. "The main thing that I'm most proud of, and that no one else can say, is that I always come up with a new idea," he said, ushering me into a bedroom so neat that it looked as if he'd stacked his magazines using a ruler and level. "Each

worm shows something different, something new that hadn't been done before by anyone."

Benny—that's his handle, not his real name—is most famous for having written a virus that infected Windows 2000 two weeks before Windows 2000 was released. He'd met a Microsoft employee months earlier who boasted that the new operating system would be "more secure than ever"; Benny wrote (but says he didn't release) the virus specifically to humiliate the company. "Microsoft," he said with a laugh, "wasn't enthusiastic." He also wrote Leviathan, the first virus to use "multithreading," a technique that makes the computer execute several commands at once, like a juggler handling multiple balls. It greatly speeds up the pace at which viruses can spread. Benny published that invention in his group's zine, and now many of the most virulent bugs have adopted the technique, including last summer's infamous Sobig.F.

For a virus author, a successful worm brings the sort of fame that a particularly daring piece of graffiti used to produce: the author's name, automatically replicating itself in cyberspace. When antivirus companies post on their Web sites a new "alert" warning of a fresh menace, the thrill for the author is like getting a great book review: something to crow about and e-mail around to your friends. Writing malware, as one author e-mailed me, is like creating artificial life. A virus, he wrote, is "a humble little creature with only the intention to avoid extinction and survive."

Quite apart from the intellectual fun of programming, though, the virus scene is attractive partly because it's very social. When Philet0ast3r drops by a virus-writers chat channel late at night after work, the conversation is as likely to be about music, politics or girls as the latest in worm technology. "They're not talking about viruses—they're talking about relationships or ordering pizza," says Sarah Gordon, a senior research fellow at Symantec, an antivirus company, who is one of the only researchers in the world who has interviewed hundreds of virus writers about their motivations. Very occasionally, malware authors even meet up face to face for a party; Philet0ast3r once took a road trip for a beer-addled weekend of coding, and when I visited Mario, we met up with another Austrian virus writer and discussed code for hours at a bar.

The virus community attracts a lot of smart but alienated young men, libertarian types who are often flummoxed by the social nuances of life. While the virus scene isn't dominated by those characters, it certainly has its share—and they are often the ones with a genuine chip on their shoulder.

"I am a social reject," admitted Vorgon (as he called himself), a virus writer in Toronto with whom I exchanged messages one night in an online chat channel. He studied computer science in college but couldn't find a computer job after sending out 400 résumés. With "no friends, not much family" and no girlfriend for years, he became depressed. He attempted suicide, he said, by walking out one frigid winter night into a nearby forest for five hours with no jacket on. But then he got into the virus-writing scene and found a community. "I met a lot of cool people who were interested in what I did," he wrote. "They made me feel good again." He called his first virus FirstBorn to celebrate his new identity. Later, he saw that one of his worms had been written up as an alert on an antivirus site, and it thrilled him. "Kinda like when I got my first girlfriend," he wrote. "I was god for a couple days." He began work on another worm, trying to recapture the feeling. "I spent three months working on it just so I could have those couple of days of godliness."

Vorgon is still angry about life. His next worm, he wrote, will try to specifically target the people who wouldn't hire him. It will have a "spidering" engine that crawls Web-page links, trying to find likely e-mail addresses for human-resource managers, "like careers@microsoft.com, for example." Then it will send them a fake résumé infected with the worm. (He hasn't yet decided on a payload, and he hasn't ruled out a destructive one.) "This is a revenge worm," he explained—for "not hiring me, and hiring some loser that is not even half the programmer I am."

Many people might wonder why virus writers aren't simply rounded up and arrested for producing their creations. But in most countries, writing viruses is not illegal. Indeed, in the United States some legal scholars argue that it is protected as free speech. Software is a type of language, and writing a program is akin to writing a recipe for beef stew. It is merely a bunch of instructions for the computer to follow, in the same way that a recipe is a set of instructions for a cook to follow. A virus or worm becomes illegal only when it is activated—when someone sends it to a victim and starts it spreading in the wild, and it does measurable damage to computer systems. The top malware authors are acutely aware of this distinction. Most every virus-writer Web site includes a disclaimer stating that it exists purely for educational purposes, and that if a visitor downloads a virus to spread, the responsibility is entirely the visitor's. Benny's main virus-writing computer at home has no Internet connection at all; he has walled it off like an airlocked biological-weapons lab, so that nothing can escape, even by accident.

**Vorgon is angry about life. His next worm, he says, will try to specifically target the people who wouldn't hire him. "This is a revenge worm," he explained.**

Virus writers argue that they shouldn't be held accountable for other people's actions. They are merely pursuing an interest in writing self-replicating computer code. "I'm not responsible for people who do silly things and distribute them among their friends," Benny said defiantly. "I'm not responsible for those. What I like to do is programming, and I like to show it to people—who may then do something with it." A young woman who goes by the handle Gigabyte told me in an online chat room that if the authorities wanted to arrest her and other virus writers, then "they should arrest the creators of guns as well."

One of the youngest virus writers I visited was Stephen Mathieson, a 16-year-old in Detroit whose screen name is Kefi. He also belongs to Philet0ast3r's Ready Rangers Liberation Front. A year ago, Mathieson became annoyed when he found

members of another virus-writers group called Catfish_VX plagiarizing his code. So he wrote Evion, a worm specifically designed to taunt the Catfish guys. He put it up on his Web site for everyone to see. Like most of Mathieson's work, the worm had no destructive intent. It merely popped up a few cocky messages, including: *Catfish_VX are lamers. This virus was constructed for them to steal.*

Someone did in fact steal it, because pretty soon Mathieson heard reports of it being spotted in the wild. To this day, he does not know who circulated Evion. But he suspects it was probably a random troublemaker, a script kiddie who swiped it from his site. "The kids," he said, shaking his head, "just cut and paste."

Quite aside from the strangeness of listening to a 16-year-old complain about "the kids," Mathieson's rhetoric glosses over a charged ethical and legal debate. It is tempting to wonder if the leading malware authors are lying—whether they do in fact circulate their worms on the sly, obsessed with a desire to see whether they will really work. While security officials say that may occasionally happen, they also say the top virus writers are quite likely telling the truth. "If you're writing important virus code, you're probably well trained," says David Perry, global director of education for Trend Micro, an antivirus company. "You know a number of tricks to write good code, but you don't want to go to prison. You have an income and stuff. It takes someone unaware of the consequences to release a virus."

But worm authors are hardly absolved of blame. By putting their code freely on the Web, virus writers essentially dangle temptation in front of every disgruntled teenager who goes online looking for a way to rebel. A cynic might say that malware authors rely on clueless script kiddies the same way that a drug dealer uses 13-year-olds to carry illegal goods—passing the liability off to a hapless mule.

"You've got several levels here," says Marc Rogers, a former police officer who now researches computer forensics at Purdue University. "You've got the guys who write it, and they know they shouldn't release it because it's illegal. So they put it out there knowing that some script kiddie who wants to feel like a big shot in the virus underground will put it out. They know these neophytes will jump on it. So they're grinning ear to ear, because their baby, their creation, is out there. But they didn't officially release it, so they don't get in trouble." He says he thinks that the original authors are just as blameworthy as the spreaders.

Sarah Gordon of Symantec also says the authors are ethically naïve. "If you're going to say it's an artistic statement, there are more responsible ways to be artistic than to create code that costs people millions," she says. Critics like Reitinger, the Microsoft security chief, are even harsher. "To me, it's online arson," he says. "Launching a virus is no different from burning down a building. There are people who would never toss a Molotov cocktail into a warehouse, but they wouldn't think for a second about launching a virus."

What makes this issue particularly fuzzy is the nature of computer code. It skews the traditional intellectual question about studying dangerous topics. Academics who research nuclear-fission techniques, for example, worry that their research could help a terrorist make a weapon. Many publish their findings anyway, believing that the mere knowledge of how fission works won't help Al Qaeda get access to uranium or rocket parts.

But computer code is a different type of knowledge. The code for a virus is itself the weapon. You could read it in the same way you read a book, to help educate yourself about malware. Or you could set it running, turning it instantly into an active agent. Computer code blurs the line between speech and act. "It's like taking a gun and sticking bullets in it and sitting it on the counter and saying, 'Hey, free gun!'" Rogers says.

Some academics have pondered whether virus authors could be charged under conspiracy laws. Creating a virus, they theorize, might be considered a form of abetting a crime by providing materials. Ken Dunham, the head of "malicious code intelligence" for iDefense, a computer security company, notes that there are certainly many examples of virus authors assisting newcomers. He has been in chat rooms, he says, "where I can see people saying, 'How can I find vulnerable hosts?' And another guy says, 'Oh, go here, you can use this tool.' They're helping each other out."

There are virus writers who appreciate these complexities. But they are certain that the viruses they write count as protected speech. They insist they have a right to explore their interests. Indeed, a number of them say they are making the world a better place, because they openly expose the weaknesses of computer systems. When Philet0ast3r or Mario or Mathieson finishes a new virus, they say, they will immediately e-mail a copy of it to antivirus companies. That way, they explained, the companies can program their software to recognize and delete the virus should some script kiddie ever release it into the wild. This is further proof that they mean no harm with their hobby, as Mathieson pointed out. On the contrary, he said, their virus-writing strengthens the "immune system" of the Internet.

These moral nuances fall apart in the case of virus authors who are themselves willing to release worms into the wild. They're more rare, for obvious reasons. Usually they are overseas, in countries where the police are less concerned with software crimes. One such author is Melhacker, a young man who reportedly lives in Malaysia and has expressed sympathy for Osama bin Laden. Antivirus companies have linked him to the development of several worms, including one that claims to come from the "Qaeda network." Before the Iraq war, he told a computer magazine that he would release a virulent worm if the United States attacked Iraq—a threat that proved hollow. When I e-mailed him, he described his favorite type of worm payload: "Stolen information from other people." He won't say which of his viruses he has himself spread and refuses to comment on his connection to the Qaeda worm. But in December on Indovirus. net, a discussion board for virus writers, Melhacker urged other writers to "try to make it in the wild" and to release their viruses in cybercafes, presumably to avoid detection. He also told them to stop sending in their work to antivirus companies.

Mathieson wrote a critical post in response, arguing that a good virus writer shouldn't need to spread his work. Virus authors are, in fact, sometimes quite chagrined when someone puts a dangerous worm into circulation, because it can cause a public backlash that hurts the entire virus community. When the

Melissa virus raged out of control in 1999, many Internet service providers immediately shut down the Web sites of malware creators. Virus writers stormed online to pillory the Melissa author for turning his creation loose. "We don't need any more grief," one wrote.

If you ask cyberpolice and security experts about their greatest fears, they are not the traditional virus writers, like Mario or Philet0ast3r or Benny. For better or worse, those authors are a known quantity. What keeps antivirus people awake at night these days is an entirely new threat: worms created for explicit criminal purposes. These began to emerge last year. Sobig in particular alarmed virus researchers. It was released six separate times throughout 2003, and each time the worm was programmed to shut itself off permanently after a few days or weeks. Every time the worm appeared anew, it had been altered in a way that suggested a single author had been tinkering with it, observing its behavior in the wild, then killing off his creation to prepare a new and more insidious version. "It was a set of very well-controlled experiments," says Mikko Hypponen, the director of antivirus research at F-Secure, a computer security company. "The code is high quality. It's been tested well. It really works in the real world." By the time the latest variant, Sobig.F, appeared in August, the worm was programmed to install a back door that would allow the author to assume control of the victim's computer. To what purpose? Experts say its author has used the captured machines to send spam and might also be stealing financial information from the victims' computers.

No one has any clue who wrote Sobig. The writers of this new class of worm leave none of the traces of their identities that malware authors traditionally include in their code, like their screen names or "greetz," shout-out hellos to their cyber-friends. Because criminal authors actively spread their creations, they are cautious about tipping their hand. "The F.B.I. is out for the Sobig guy with both claws, and they want to make an example of him," David Perry notes. "He's not going to mouth off." Dunham of iDefense says his online research has turned up "anecdotal evidence" that the Sobig author comes from Russia or elsewhere in Europe. Others suspect China or other parts of Asia. It seems unlikely that Sobig came from the United States, because American police forces have been the most proactive of any worldwide in hunting those who spread malware. Many experts believe the Sobig author will release a new variant sometime this year.

Sobig was not alone. A variant of the Mimail worm, which appeared last spring, would install a fake pop-up screen on a computer pretending to be from PayPal, an online e-commerce firm. It would claim that PayPal had lost the victim's credit-card or banking details and ask him to type it in again. When he did, the worm would forward the information to the worm's still-unknown author. Another worm, called Bugbear.B, was programmed to employ sophisticated password-guessing strategies at banks and brokerages to steal personal information. "It was specifically designed to target financial institutions," said Vincent Weafer, senior director of Symantec.

The era of the stealth worm is upon us. None of these pieces of malware were destructive or designed to cripple the Internet with too much traffic. On the contrary, they were designed to be unobtrusive, to slip into the background, the better to secretly harvest data. Five years ago, the biggest danger was the "Chernobyl" virus, which deleted your hard drive. But the prevalence of hard-drive-destroying viruses has steadily declined to almost zero. Malware authors have learned a lesson that biologists have long known: the best way for a virus to spread is to ensure its host remains alive.

"It's like comparing Ebola to AIDS," says Joe Wells, an antivirus researcher and founder of WildList, a long-established virus-tracking group. "They both do the same thing. Except one does it in three days, and the other lingers and lingers and lingers. But which is worse? The ones that linger are the ones that spread the most." In essence, the long years of experimentation have served as a sort of Darwinian evolutionary contest, in which virus writers have gradually figured out the best strategies for survival.

Given the pace of virus development, we are probably going to see even nastier criminal attacks in the future. Some academics have predicted the rise of "cryptoviruses"—malware that invades your computer and encrypts all your files, making them unreadable. "The only way to get the data back will be to pay a ransom," says Stuart Schechter, a doctoral candidate in computer security at Harvard. (One night on a discussion board I stumbled across a few virus writers casually discussing this very concept.) Antivirus companies are writing research papers that worry about the rising threat of "metamorphic" worms—ones that can shift their shapes so radically that antivirus companies cannot recognize they're a piece of malware. Some experimental metamorphic code has been published by Z0mbie, a reclusive Russian member of the 29A virus-writing group. And mobile-phone viruses are probably also only a few years away. A phone virus could secretly place 3 A.M. calls to a toll number, sticking you with thousand-dollar charges that the virus's author would collect. Or it could drown 911 in phantom calls. As Marty Lindner, a cybersecurity expert at CERT/CC, a federally financed computer research center, puts it, "The sky's the limit."

The profusion of viruses has even become a national-security issue. Government officials worry that terrorists could easily launch viruses that cripple American telecommunications, sowing confusion in advance of a physical 9/11-style attack. Paula Scalingi, the former director of the Department of Energy's Office of Critical Infrastructure Protection, now works as a consultant running disaster-preparedness exercises. Last year she helped organize "Purple Crescent" in New Orleans, an exercise that modeled a terrorist strike against the city's annual Jazz and Heritage Festival. The simulation includes a physical attack but also uses a worm unleashed by the terrorists designed to cripple communications and sow confusion nationwide. The physical attack winds up flooding New Orleans; the cyberattack makes hospital care chaotic. "They have trouble communicating, they can't get staff in, it's hard for them to order supplies," she says. "The impact of worms and viruses can be prodigious."

This new age of criminal viruses puts traditional malware authors in a politically precarious spot. Police forces are under more pressure than ever to take any worm seriously, regardless of the motivations of the author.

A young Spaniard named Antonio discovered that last fall. He is a quiet 23-year-old computer professional who lives near Madrid. Last August, he read about the Blaster worm and how it exploited a Microsoft flaw. He became intrigued, and after poking around on a few virus sites, found some sample code that worked the same way. He downloaded it and began tinkering to see how it worked.

Then on Nov. 14, as he left to go to work, Spanish police met him at his door. They told him the anti-virus company Panda Software had discovered his worm had spread to 120,000 computers. When Panda analyzed the worm code, it quickly discovered that the program pointed to a site Antonio had developed. Panda forwarded the information to the police, who hunted Antonio down via his Internet service provider. The police stripped his house of every computer—including his roommate's—and threw Antonio in jail. After two days, they let him out, upon which Antonio's employer immediately fired him. "I have very little money," he said when I met him in December. "If I don't have a job in a little time, in a few months I can't pay the rent. I will have to go to my parents."

The Spanish court is currently considering what charges to press. Antonio's lawyer, Javier Maestre, argued that the worm had no dangerous payload and did no damage to any of the computers it infected. He suspects Antonio is being targeted by the police, who want to pretend they've made an important cyberbust, and by an antivirus company seeking publicity.

Artificial life can spin out of control—and when it does, it can take real life with it. Antonio says he did not actually intend to release his worm at all. The worm spreads by scanning computers for the Blaster vulnerability, then sending a copy of itself to any open target. Antonio maintains he thought he was playing it safe, because his computer was not directly connected to the Internet. His roommate's computer had the Internet connection, and a local network—a set of cables connecting their computers together—allowed Antonio to share the signal. But what Antonio didn't realize, he says, was that his worm would regard his friend's computer as a foreign target. It spawned a copy of itself in his friend's machine. From there it leapfrogged onto the Internet—and out into the wild. His creation had come to life and, like Frankenstein's monster, decided upon a path of its own.

**CLIVE THOMPSON** writes frequently about science and technology. His last article for the magazine was about mobile-phone culture.

# False Reporting on the Internet and the Spread of Rumors
## *Three Case Studies*

PAUL HITLIN

Following the tragic events of September 11, 2001, a significant number of unsubstantiated rumors circulated around the Internet. One email pointed to the existence of prophecies by Nostradamus written hundreds of years earlier that predicted the attacks. Another accused Israel of masterminding the strikes and that thousands of Jews were told in advance to stay home from work that morning. The Internet allowed for a vast audience to spread these rumors along with the technology to facilitate their transmission, even though there was little evidence to support them and the rumors were later proven incorrect. Considering this spread of rumors, Stephen O'Leary (2002) writes:

> What may be hard for mainstream journalists to understand is that, in crisis situations, the social functions of rumor are virtually indistinguishable from the social functions of 'real news.' People spread rumors via the Net for the same reason that they read their papers or tune into CNN: they are trying to make sense of their world. (pg. 3)

O'Leary claims that these rumors fill a need for consumers of news that is very similar to the void that 'real news' fills. However, are the consequences the same? These Internet rumors help people to make sense of their world following a tragedy, although the lasting consequences are potentially much more harmful.

The Internet is certainly not responsible for errors in journalism. Every medium of news has a history of misreported stories. However, the nature of the Internet has created a new method for consumers to get their news and allowed for far greater numbers of people to become involved with the production and dissemination of news. As a consequence, cyberjournalism and the Internet have had real effects on both the process of reporting and subsequent public discourse.

How are errors in Internet journalism corrected online? What are the overarching consequences of errors that appear on Internet web sites? Jim Hall (2001) believes that one problem with instant news appearing on the Internet is that the way errors are handled does not adequately address the fact that an error was made. He writes, "The problem with instant news is that when it is wrong it tends to be buried, sedimenting into and reinforcing its context, rather than corrected" (p. 133). Errors of Internet reporting do not often get identified and corrected as they do in newspapers. Instead, even if the editors of the Web site where the error first appeared change their site to remove the error, often the same false information will have already spread throughout other Web sites and emails. These rumors can become part of a public folklore even if there are no facts to support the original reports.

This paper will first consider Hall's assertion that errors are buried rather than corrected, and will examine the reasons Internet reporting leads to false reports. Then, three case studies of significant false reports on the Internet will be compared to the theories behind cyberjournalism in order to understand why the errors occurred and the impacts of these stories. Investigating these three examples will help us to begin to understand how we can decrease the influence of false reports in the future.

The first case study is the plane crash of TWA flight 800 in 1996. Even before full investigations were conducted, the Internet was full of reports of missiles or other causes behind the crash, the impacts of which would reach as far as the White House. The second case study will examine Matt Drudge's report that former White House special assistant Sidney Blumenthal physically abused his wife. The third case study will take a look at the pervasive rumors that the death of former Bill Clinton aide Vince Foster was a murder, not a suicide, even though numerous investigations have concluded that these accusations are unsupported. This incident is a clear example of how partisan politics can play a role in the spread of false reports on the Internet.

There has been much discussion about what distinguishes a 'journalist' working for a mainstream news source from a self-titled 'reporter' who never leaves his/her computer and instead just links to reports on other sites. While these distinctions are important and worth discussing, it will not be within the realm of this study to draw out these distinctions. Instead, this paper will consider news reports that appear on the Internet regardless

f whether or not the site displaying the report considers itself a
ews source. As we will see, public opinion can often be influ-
nced as much from rumors on sites with little credibility as it
an from more mainstream sources.

# Reasons for Cyberjournalism Errors

Before considering the specific cases of false reporting, it is
mportant to understand why the nature of the Internet may
ncourage reporting errors. Philip Seib (2001) points out that
he Internet is not alone in containing factual errors. He writes,
"the Web really is little different from other media in terms
of its potential to abuse and be abused and its capability for
elf-governance" (pp. 129–130). The Internet itself, the actual
echnology, can not be held responsible for false reports since
hose reports have existed in all forms of media. However, there
re qualities of the Internet and the manner in which news is
eported on the Web that create differences in how frequently
rrors appear and what results as a consequence.

The causes of most cyberjournalism errors can be separated
nto four main categories. Let us now turn to each cause and
xamine it in turn.

## 1. The Need for Speed

The first and probably most significant reason for false report-
ng on the Internet is the 24-hour a day news cycle that the
Internet promotes. With the development of newspapers, the
news cycle was a daylong process that ended with having a
story included in the next day's edition of the paper. This
cycle changed with the expansion of cable television channels devoted entirely to news such as CNN and later MSNBC
and Fox News. The cycle was expanded even further by the
development of the Internet which is available to consumers
24-hours a day. Because of the constant need to keep both
cable television and the Internet supplied with new informa-
ion, expectations of news deadlines have shifted. As Seib
notes, in the current information age, the deadline for reporters is always 'now' (p. 142).

Competitive pressures have also contributed to an emphasis being placed more on timeliness than accuracy. A number
of Internet sites, such as Matt Drudge's *Drudge Report,* are
one-person operations that issue reports on gossip and rumor
without being constrained by traditional standards of reporting. These sites apply pressure to other news organizations
to be the first to report a story or risk being scooped. Drudge
himself believes that "absolute truth matters less than absolute
speed" (Seib, 2001, p. 143). He also suggests that since we live
in an information economy, complete accuracy is not possible
or even necessary. Drudge focuses instead on immediacy and
believes that the Web encourages this type of reporting (Hall,
2002, p. 148).

The pressure on reporters to be the first with a story has
detracted from more traditional methods of journalism. Because
the goal used to be to get a report into the next day's newspaper
or that evening's nightly news television broadcast, reporters

had more time for fact-checking. The 24-hour-a-day news cycle
has decreased the time reporters have to assure accuracy and as
a result, many errors found on the Internet can be attributed to
the competitive pressure for journalists to be the first to break a
specific news story.

## 2. The Desire to Attract 'Hits'

Competition among Web sites is also a cause for some false
reports. Web sites have financial incentives to attract visitors
to their sites, whether it is through advertising or a desire to
widen the site's influence. Hall argues that journalism on the
Web has promoted the idea that news is 'infotainment' and
more at the mercy of the demands of the marketplace than to its
audiences (Hall, 2001, p. 155). Web sites must fill the desires
of consumers, or risk losing those consumers to other sites that
either get the information first or are even more sensational in
their reporting.

Furthermore, with the ability of Internet users to visit almost
any news source in the world, as opposed to being confined to
their local newspapers or television stations, the competition
on the Web exacerbates the desire of sites to get the story first.
Most news sites are updated several times a day, and competition forces those sites to get the story first or risk being thought
of as irrelevant or out-of-date.

## 3. Political Gains

The specific source of many Internet rumors is often difficult to
ascertain. However, certain rumors on the Internet are clearly
promoted for partisan political gain and to advance a particular
ideology.

Even after four investigations came to the same conclusions
about Vince Foster's death, certain political groups were still
spreading false reports in order to promote their own cause. For
example, a fund-raising letter sent out by anti-Clinton groups
asked for $1,000 donations in order to support the "Clinton
Investigation Commission" which would investigate the claim
that Foster was murdered (Piacente, 1997). Opponents of the
Clinton administration perpetuated this false report to the exclusion of evidence in the case. These anti-Clinton groups were
less concerned with accuracy than with forwarding a partisan
agenda and the persistence of this specific rumor can be attributed to their political motives.

## 4. Attraction to Scandal

News, and specifically news on the Web, is often led by scandal
and the concept of the spectacular rather than issues of depth
(Hall, 2001, p. 137). For example, reports that TWA flight 800
was brought down by a missile were much more exciting than
a report that a technical problem in the plane caused the crash.
While some sites did wait for investigations into the cause of
the crash to make conclusions about what actually brought the
plane down, other sites used more dramatic rumors of missile
fire to headline their reports. The competition between sites on
the Web and the ability for consumers to move rapidly between
those sites furthers the need for reporters to lead with scandal in order to catch consumers' attention. This desire for the

spectacular, along with an emphasis on scandal, often leads to other false reports on the Internet.

# Correction Policy, Social Cascades, and Online Credibility

Now that we have seen the four main reasons errors are found on the Internet, another key issue to understand is how those mistakes are corrected. There is still no singular method that Web sites use to correct errors, but as Seib (2001) writes:

> The easiest way to fix a mistake is simply to erase it and replace it with the correct information. That is a temptation unique to electronic publication, since there is no "original" version in the print or video archives . . . This is fine for readers who come to the site after the correction has been made. But failure to post a formal notice of correction implies that there was never an error, and that is less than honest. (pp. 154–155)

The question of how to correct a mistake once it is discovered that causes Hall to suggest that the nature of Internet journalism reinforces the error's context rather than corrects the false information. While some retractions are clearly posted, as was the case with Matt Drudge following the accusations against Sidney Blumenthal, often the error has already spread to other sources. As a result, whether or not the original source is corrected no longer matters because the information will have already moved onto other places on the Web.

The result of this spread of Internet rumors is a phenomenon described by Cass Sunstein as one of 'social cascades.' Sunstein suggests that groups of people often move together in a direction of one set of beliefs or actions. He refers to this as a cascade effect (Sunstein, 2002, p. 80). Information can travel and become entrenched even if that information is incorrect. Sunstein argues that the Internet, with its wide reach and seemingly unending amount of Web sites and emails, greatly increases the likelihood of social cascades. Rumors can be passed to many users and spread quickly. The result is that the information appears believable solely due to the fact that the information has been repeated so many times. Richard Davis (1999) sums up the potential danger of this phenomenon:

> Anyone can put anything on the Internet and seemingly does. Often, one cannot be sure of the reliability of the information provided. Reliability diminishes exponentially as the information is passed from user to user and e-mail list to e-mail list until it acquires a degree of legitimacy by virtue of its widespread dissemination and constant repetition. (p. 44)

A number of other factors also contribute to the believability of information passed on the Internet. Richard Davis and Diana Owen (1998) discuss many of the reasons why 'new media,' consisting of the Internet, talk radio, and interactive television, often engage users in different ways than previous forms of news. They claim that much of new media relies on active participation by users rather than a more passive relationship between users and newspapers or earlier television programs. Davis and Owen describe the influence of this connection:

> The degree of involvement or interactivity with media is linked to the level of an audience member's media consumption and the strength of the effects of the communication. People who have a highly active relationship with a particular medium, such as callers to talk radio programs, may be more likely to establish a regular habit of attending to the medium and are more likely to be influenced by content than those whose acquaintance with the communication source is more casual. (p. 160)

Internet users who participate in online activities are not only more likely to be influenced by content they see online but new media has a capacity to create strong psychological bonds between users and the media source. Davis and Owen add, "Individuals form personal relationships with their television sets and their computers. They treat computers as if they are people, talking to them, ascribing personalities to them and reacting to them emotionally when computers hand out praise or criticism during an interactive sessions" (p. 160). Users have greater influence over the content of media on the Web than in previous forms of media, whether it results from emailing articles of interest or responding to online polls and questionnaires. These interactions contribute to the perceived credibility that Internet users ascribe to information they receive over the Web. Stories that might be disregarded as false had they been disseminated through other forms of media often facilitate social cascade effect if that information is spread online.

Having considered both why errors appear on the Internet and the difficulty in effectively correcting false information, let us now consider three cases of prominent false reports on the Internet and how those instances were handled.

# Case Study One: The Crash of TWA Flight 800 in 1996

A clear example of how constant repetition of an erroneous report can result in widespread belief can be seen in the wake of the crash of TWA Flight 800. On July 17, 1996, the passenger flight left JFK International Airport in New York en route to Paris, but tragically crashed into the Long Island Sound. All 230 passengers and crew on board died.

Almost immediately, the National Transportation Safety Board (NTSB) began investigating the causes of the crash and rumors started to spread throughout the Internet as to what led to the tragedy. Three main theories quickly surfaced as to what caused the crash: the crash was an act of terrorism conducted from onboard the flight; a mechanical malfunction was responsible for bringing down the plane; or the plane was shot down by a surface-to-air missile (Cobb & Primo, 2003, p. 104).

Some evidence initially indicated the crash could be a result of terrorism, either an onboard bomb or a projectile fired at the plane from the ground. The accident took place several days before the beginning of the 1996 Summer Olympics in Atlanta.

which later become a target of a bombing attack. Some observers felt the timing of the plane crash indicated that it was somehow connected to international terrorism. In addition, numerous eyewitnesses reported having seen a streak of light approaching the plane before the explosion (Charles, 2001, p. 218). As the NTSB and the FBI began to investigate, numerous signals from the federal government indicated that all three potential theories were in play. As much as six months into a very public investigation, the NTSB was still declaring that all three theories remained as possibilities (Negroni, 2001). This did not change until March of 1997, when federal investigators began to dismiss theories of a missile bringing TWA Flight 800 down, claiming there was "no physical evidence" of such an attack (CNN.com, 1997).

As the investigation into the crash progressed and began to rule out terrorism, rumors persisted throughout the Internet that a government cover-up was concealing the real causes. At the forefront of those rumors was Pierre Salinger, a former press secretary to John F. Kennedy and correspondent for ABC News. Salinger insisted that he had a letter from French intelligence proving that a U.S. Navy missile ship shot down TWA Flight 800, and the FBI was covering up the act. Salinger's claims were reported in numerous news outlets. In addition, Salinger and several other journalists published a report in *Paris Match* stating that radar images existed that proved that a missile hit the plane (Harper, 1998, p. 85).

Salinger's credentials and his unwillingness to give up on his theory lent great credibility to the missile story. Many people on the Internet who believed the government was trying to hide something picked up on his writings. Interestingly enough, the letter that Salinger claimed had come from French intelligence was instead a memo that had been circulating on the Internet for several months written by a former United Air Lines pilot named Richard Russell. As Mark Hunter writes in his Salon .com article, Salinger's insistence on promoting his conspiracy theory of both the missile and the FBI cover-up, even with scare evidence, actually harmed the real investigation by causing a significant distraction for investigators. It also caused further psychological stress on the family members of the victims of the crash who were forced to revisit the circumstances as a result of these repeated allegations.

By the time the NTSB issued its final report on the crash in August of 2000, much of the talk of conspiracy theories relating to the crash had disappeared. In 2001, the Federal Aviation Agency (FAA) acted in response to what was believed to be the actual cause of the crash and issued safety rules to minimize flammable vapors and decrease the risk of a tank igniting (Cobb & Primo, 2003, p. 117). However, the consequences of the crash rumors can be seen both in continuing public discourse and actions taken by upper levels of the federal government.

The immediate rumors following the crash about a possible bomb or missile attack led to direct government action. In the days that followed the accident, before much hard evidence was discovered, President Clinton issued a tightening of security at airports throughout the country in order to try to prevent

any acts of terrorism (Cobb & Primo, 2003, p. 106). Clinton later created the White House Commission on Aviation Safety, led by Vice President Al Gore, which issued recommendations for improving airline safety (Cobb & Primo, 2003, pp. 110–111). Just the possibility of a terrorist or missile attack was enough for the federal government to react strongly and tighten security.

What role did the Internet play in promoting and maintaining the false rumors about the crash of TWA Flight 800? Internet sites were not alone in reporting the rumors about the crash. Many newspapers, including the *Washington Post* and *New York Times,* also reported the possibilities of a bomb or terror attack (Cobb & Primo, 2003, pp. 107–108). However, the Internet did allow for certain aspects of the story to persist even when the evidence against the rumors was mounting. For one thing, a letter written by Richard Russell that circulated by email throughout the Internet played a key role in Salinger's claims about a government cover-up. Whether or not Salinger knew the true source of the letter, the circulation of the note alone added some perceived credibility to the rumor. This Internet 'error' was not corrected and removed. Instead, as Hall suggested, the nature of the Internet embedded the rumor. The circulation continued even after the NTSB determined it was false: a clear example of a social cascade facilitated by the Internet, moving many to believe the government was hiding information and not telling the full story about the crash.

To further this notion about the impact of these rumors, one only has to look to the Internet today, more than seven years after the crash, to see how public discourse has been influenced. While the Internet is full of conspiracy theories and anti-government rhetoric, a simple search can still find many Web sites that maintain that the TWA crash was a government cover-up. A clear example is the Web site whatreallyhappened .com. One can still go to this site at any time and read about how the government is hiding secrets and promoting beliefs that the "witnesses who saw a missile hit the jumbo jet are all drunks" (whatreallyhappened.com, 2002). To any person deciding to conduct research into the causes of this plane crash today, the Internet is a rich resource consisting of both facts about the accident and significant rumor and innuendo.

## Case Study Two: Sidney Blumenthal vs. Matt Drudge and Internet Libel

While some Internet rumors persist on numerous Web sites, others can be linked more closely with one specific site, as is the case with a report that appeared on Matt Drudge's Web site, drudgereport.com, in 1997. Matt Drudge's one-man newsroom is most well known for breaking the story about President Bill Clinton's Oval Office affair with a White House intern. Along with breaking that story, Drudge has had 'exclusives' with a number of other stories, some of which turned out not to be true at all. Included among these was the report that Bill Clinton had fathered an illegitimate black son, a report that was later proven to be false (Hall, 2001, p. 129).

On August 8, 1997, Drudge chose to report on his Web site allegations about White House special assistant Sidney Blumenthal. Writing about a Republican operative who was facing allegations of spousal abuse, Drudge issued the 'exclusive' on his Web site that included the following:

The *Drudge Report* has learned that top GOP operatives who feel there is a double-standard of only reporting [sic] shame believe they are holding an ace card: New White House recruit Sidney Blumenthal has a spousal abuse past that has been effectively covered up.

The accusations are explosive.

"There are court records of Blumenthal's violence against his wife," one influential Republican [sic], who demanded anonymity, tells the *Drudge Report*. (Blumenthal, 2003, pp. 239–240)

Drudge goes on to write that one White House source claimed the allegations were entirely false and that Drudge had been unsuccessful in his attempts to contact Blumenthal regarding these charges.

Three problems existed for Drudge in relation to this story. First, no court records existed that claimed Blumenthal abused his wife. Second, Drudge had not in fact made any attempts to contact Blumenthal. And third, Sidney Blumenthal decided to sue Matt Drudge and the Internet carrier of his column, American Online (AOL), for libel after other conservative news sources such as the *New York Post* and talk radio programs picked up the story (Blumenthal, 2003, p. 241).

This false Internet report was unique in that the origin of the rumor on the Web was clear along with who was responsible for spreading the rumor. Because of this, Blumenthal did have an opportunity to confront his accuser, which he did the day after the report first appeared. Blumenthal and his lawyer sent a letter to Drudge demanding to know the sources of the report. If Drudge did not comply, Blumenthal threatened to take "appropriate action" (Blumenthal, 2003, p. 244). In direct response to the threat, Drudge printed a retraction on his Web site that read, "I am issuing a retraction of my information regarding Sidney Blumenthal that appeared in the Drudge Report on August 11, 1997" (Blumenthal, 2003, p. 247). Drudge never officially apologized for the specific claim, although he was quoted as saying, "I apologize if any harm has been done. The story was issued in good faith. It was based on two sources who clearly were operating from a political motivation" (Kurtz, 1997).

While the lawsuit proceeded against Drudge with the blessing of President Clinton and the White House, the final result was not nearly as dramatic as the initial report. In May of 2001, Drudge and Blumenthal settled the suit out of court, and Blumenthal agreed to pay $2,500 to Drudge to reimburse travel expenses (Kurtz, 2001). Blumenthal claimed that he settled the suit because Drudge had endless financial backing from conservative groups and the suit was doing little more than providing additional exposure for Drudge (Blumenthal, 2003, p. 784). One interesting side note to this case is that early in the process,

a U.S. District judge had ruled that the Internet service provider, AOL, could not be a defendant in the libel case even though they had paid Drudge for his work. This decision was a significant victory for Internet service providers in protecting them from lawsuits concerning the content that appears on their own Web sites (Swartz, 1998).

Unlike the rumors about the TWA crash, this case study is much clearer in terms of who was responsible for placing the rumor online. Defamation of character is common in the Internet world, but Blumenthal viewed his lawsuit as an opportunity to make a larger point, "bringing the Internet under the same law that applied to the rest of the press" (Blumenthal, 2003, p. 471). Judging exactly how successful he was in doing so and whether future Internet sites will be as willing to publish unsubstantiated rumors is difficult. Drudge, for one, continues to publish numerous stories with seemingly little fear about being incorrect. However, this example does illustrate one occurrence where a retraction was issued on the same Internet site as the original error. Did the retraction correct the harm that resulted from a false story? Clearly Sidney Blumenthal did not feel so and continued his libel lawsuit even after the retraction was issued.

In addition, this news report was more a result of a partisan political agenda than it was an issue of Drudge trying to beat his competition by issuing an exclusive story not available on any other site. Drudge has been accused by many of having strong ties to conservative political groups who may have planted the Blumenthal story, but there seem to be no indications that other news sites were in competition with Drudge to be the first to issue this report. He would not thus have been facing a shortened time to check sources and facts. Drudge himself acknowledged that his sources for this story were acting on their own political agenda.

## Case Study Three: The Suicide of White House Aide Vince Foster

Unlike the previous case study, the origins of the rumors involving the suicide of White House Aide Vince Foster are less clear. On July 20, 1993, the body of Vince Foster was discovered in a park in Washington, D.C. Foster had apparently committed suicide, and much of the initial evidence pointed to a self-inflicted gunshot wound as the cause of death. He had been showing tremendous signs of stress as he found himself the subject of political battles in Washington and a number of accusations against the Clinton administration. Foster had reportedly been very upset about the attention he was receiving in the "Travelgate" scandal and his role in questions about billing records involving Hillary Clinton and Whitewater investments (Tisdall, 1994). However, immediately after his body was found, rumors began circulating the Internet suggesting that Foster's death had not been a suicide. These reports claimed that the death was a murder that was covered-up by members of the Clinton administration who felt Foster knew too much about the Whitewater investigation being conducted by Independent Counsel Kenneth Starr.

Rumors of unresolved questions within the investigation of Foster's death began to spread throughout the Internet by members of conservative activist groups who made no secret of their hatred of President Clinton. Why was there no suicide note? Why were the keys on Foster's body not found at the scene, but only later, once the body was moved? What did the torn note say that was found near the body? Why were records missing from Vince Foster's office after the body was found? Those looking for sensational stories and rumors involving this story did not have to look hard on the Internet to find them.

The cascade effect of this story reached remarkable levels. Numerous Web sites published the rumor that Foster's death was a murder, including Matt Drudge's site (Scheer, 1999). Presidential candidate Pat Buchanan received criticism in 1996 by Jewish groups after an article published on his official campaign Web site claimed that Foster's death was ordered by Israel and that Hillary Clinton was secretly working as a Mossad agent (O'Dwyer, 1996). Rush Limbaugh, a conservative radio talk-show host, mentioned the accusations on his radio program and Representative John Linder, Republican of Georgia, even inserted the accusation into the record at Congressional hearings involving the Whitewater scandal (*Atlanta Journal and Constitution,* 1994). In fact, the rumors of murder were so persistent on the Internet and other mediums that a Time/CNN poll taken in 1995 during the Senate hearings of the aftermath of Foster's death showed that only 35 percent of respondents believed Foster's death was a suicide. Twenty percent believed he had been murdered (Weiner, 1995).

Rumors of a Clinton-led cover-up have continued to exist even after four separate investigations, conducted by the U.S. Park Police, the FBI, Special Counsel Robert Fiske, and Independent Counsel Ken Starr, all came to the same conclusion: Foster's death was a suicide. The persistent refusal to accept the conclusions of these investigations is demonstrated in a 1998 editorial in *The Augusta Chronicle* written five years after Foster's death. "Imagine [Ken Starr] ruling the Vince Foster killing a suicide when not one item of evidence would indicate suicide, but numerous items indicate obvious murder!" (*The Augusta Chronicle,* 1998).

Much of the persistent nature of these specific rumors can be traced to partisan political groups. Richard Scaife, a wealthy financier of many anti-Clinton groups, has been quoted as saying, "The death of Vincent Foster: I think that's the Rosetta Stone to the whole Clinton Administration" (Weiner, 1995). Scaife has supported groups, such as the Western Journalism Center, that have included work by Christopher Ruddy, a reporter who was dismissed by the *New York Post* for pursuing cover-up theories relating to the death. Ruddy, who refers to himself as part of the 'vast right-wing conspiracy' described by Hillary Clinton, has written and published numerous articles attacking both the Clinton administration and the Foster investigations. Even today, reports written by Ruddy questioning the investigations' findings can be found online (www.newsmax .com/ruddy/). In addition, fund-raising letters for conservative groups, including a 1997 letter from a group called "Clinton Investigation Committee," have been used to raise money to continue various investigations against Clinton, including the Foster case (Piacente, 1997). These organizations, Web sites, newspaper articles, and fund-raising letters, have all helped to

perpetuate the rumors that Vince Foster's death was a murder, and somehow the Clinton administration was involved.

Because these rumors have persisted for years, their existence cannot be attributed to the timing pressure of the Internet news cycle. Instead, the theories involving Foster's death are a result of the desire for the sensational and partisan political efforts, in this instance from groups who opposed Bill Clinton. The possibility of a printed retraction seems impractical and would likely have no effect, since, unlike the Blumenthal case, there was no one specific site that started the rumors on the Internet, and because the rumors have extended far beyond the Internet into newspapers and even among members of Congress. The cascade effect of all of these rumors is that a certain contingent, in this case opponents of Bill Clinton, continues to believe that the Clintons were responsible for Vince Foster's death. The political consequences for such accusations, even after they have been disproved, can be far reaching because false information has to potential to unreasonably decrease the public's faith in public officials and the competency of their government.

## Conclusion

The expansion of the Internet has great potential for promoting political discourse and allowing for far more citizens to be involved with the production and dissemination of news. Davis and Owen (1998) describe this positive potential:

Increasingly, computer networks have become tools for political communication as well. Users gather political information, express their opinions, and mobilize other citizens and political leaders. The information superhighway is fast becoming an electronic town hall where anyone with a personal computer and a modem can learn about the latest bill introduced in Congress, join an interest group, donate money to a political candidate, or discuss politics with people they have never seen who may live half a world away. (pg. 110)

However, as these three case studies have shown, the potential for the Internet to be a conduit of false information or the spreading of rumors is also significant. The dilemma for those who are concerned about the role the Internet will play in the future of democracy will be to discover how to balance the positive democratizing aspects with the potentially harmful aspects that include the spread of false reports and misleading information.

The main goal of this investigation was to examine how errors of Internet reporting are handled online. These three case studies demonstrate that there is no single method as to how Internet errors are corrected. When one source for a rumor exists, as was the case with the Blumenthal story, a retraction is possible on that initial source which can somewhat lessen the impact of the false story. However, even that example was picked up by other mainstream newspaper and radio sources.

This study then supports Hall's assertion that the nature of the Internet reinforces the context of errors rather than corrects them. As seen with the Vince Foster case, significant numbers of people believed that his death was a murder even after several investigations had concluded otherwise. Public discourse was not shifted entirely even after the early reports were disproved or corrected. In fact, in all three of the cases presented here, the Internet rumors and false reports were picked up by other sources and continued to spread even after evidence pointed to contrary facts.

Another substantial conclusion that can be ascertained from this investigation is that Sunstein's assessment of social cascades is valid in regards to errors on the Internet. For those people who are interested in finding evidence to support their views, even if the evidence itself is questionable, the Internet can be a tremendous facilitator. And the reach of the influence of these reports is not just to conspiracy theorists. Their impact can be seen even in actions taken by government officials, such as President Clinton after the crash of TWA flight 800. These social cascades can have important political consequences, whether on airline safety regulations or in the perceptions of political figures. A connection appears to exist between the capabilities of the Internet and the vastness of the social cascading that can occur as a result of rumor and innuendo.

How, then, should the potential for social cascading as a result of misleading information be balanced with the positive potential of the Internet? Not all scholars agree that the implications of an 'anything goes' attitude of Internet reporting is entirely negative. Davis and Owen (1998) make an argument relating to old media that an increase of tabloid journalism may not be entirely destructive because it "can foster a sense of intimacy with the public," and also attract viewers to news sources (pg. 209). This same line of reasoning can be applied to the Internet sites such as Matt Drudge's that spread rumor while using standards for verification that are less than those that are utilized by traditional media. Consequently, it is possible that the lowering of journalistic norms that is apparent online will not have entirely negative consequences if the result encourages more people to search for news and connect with other Internet users.

Even if it is true that the Internet's impact on journalism and the increase of false reports is not entirely negative, this investigation has demonstrated that harmful effects can result from the cascade effects of misinformation. The question that arises from this investigation is regarding how to control or combat the prevalence of errors on the Internet. Sidney Blumenthal acknowledged that one of the goals of his lawsuit against Drudge was to bring the Internet under the same type of libel laws that newspaper and television journalists must follow. However, Blumenthal's attempt at forcing the Internet "reporter" to face negative consequences as a result of his false report was unsuccessful, and further attempts by the government to regulate the content of the Internet seem likely to be impractical, costly, and ineffective overall. There is simply too much online content for the government to be able to enforce the same types of journalistic laws that other news mediums must follow, not to mention the potential for excessive government censorship.

At the same time, it is incredibly unlikely that the four reasons mentioned earlier in this discussion that cause errors in reporting, that is, the need for speed, the desire to attract hits, the goal of advancing a partisan agenda, and the attraction to scandal, will lessen and lower the competitive pressures on Internet journalists in the next few years. If anything, those pressures are likely to increase as more and more people turn to the Internet for their news. The only probable method for improving the accuracy of online reporting would be for news producers themselves to make better attempts at following voluntary guidelines that are closer to the standards used by old media sources. Offering guidelines for reporters to follow is not new. Sabato, Stencel, and Lichter (2000) describe a number of guidelines reporters should follow in reporting political scandals in their book entitled *Peepshow* and journalism schools have been teaching professional norms for decades. Other sets of standards that are usually applied to traditional news outlets could be applied to Internet sources as well. These standards, such as the need for multiple sources for issuing a report, do not guarantee complete accuracy in reporting, as can be seen with the recent scandals of newspaper reporters Jayson Blair of the *New York Times* and Jack Kelley of *USA Today*. However, attempts to follow these more traditional guidelines would lessen the frequency and impact of Internet reporting errors.

Seib agrees with the need for online reporters to voluntarily follow traditional ethics of reporting. In his predictions for the future of Internet journalism, he notes that it will be increasingly important for reporters to aim at fairness and accuracy. He writes, "The 'Drudge effect'—shoot-from-the-hip sensationalism—will give online journalism a bad name if the public perceives it to be a dominant characteristic of this medium" (p. 162). The best way for journalists to deal with this perceived 'Drudge effect' and the potentially harmful impact of Internet rumors is to deliver a consistently fair and accurate news product. The marketplace will in time come to rely on the high-quality product more than the hastily put together news site that does not have a good track record of accuracy. Seib's faith in the public's desire for quality reporting is the most hopeful and promising view as to how to lessen the impact of social cascades based on misleading or false information.

Along with offering positive aspects of the Internet, Davis and Owen (1998) also write, "new technologies have enhanced opportunities for the mass dissemination of misinformation" (p. 200). As this study has shown, this rapidly expanding technology can have potentially harmful effects if false reports are spread without supporting evidence. In order for us to reap the positive effects of the Internet, which include added convenience and the possibility of increased political discourse, the dangers of false information must also be confronted. The most effective method to lessen the amount and impact of false Internet errors will be for news producers on the Web to follow traditional journalistic standards of fact-checking and sourcing. False reporting will not disappear, but, we must make ourselves aware of the various types of reporting that can be found on the Web and hope that market forces will encourage high-quality reporting as opposed to unsubstantiated rumors passing as news. Awareness of the potential for both types of reporting is a central condition for encouraging effective and accurate online reporting.

# References

*The Atlanta Journal and Constitution* (1994, July 29). "Hatemongers Who Cry Wolf . . . " Editorial, p. A14.

*The Augusta Chronicle (Georgia)* (1998, December 11). "Calls for Investigation, Not Cover-Up." Editorial, p. A4.

Blumenthal, Sidney (2003). *The Clinton Wars.* New York: Farrar, Straus and Giroux.

Charles, Michael T. (2001). "The Fall of TWA Flight 800." In Uriel Rosenthal, R. Arjen Boin, & Louise K. Comfort (Eds.), *Managing Crises: Threats, Dilemmas, Opportunities* (pp. 216–234). Springfield, IL.: Charles C. Thomas Publisher, Ltd.

CNN.com (1997, March 11). *NTSB: "No Physical Evidence" Missile Brought Down TWA 800.* Atlanta, GA: CNN.com. Retrieved October 18, 2003, from the CNN Interactive Web site: http://www.cnn.com/US/9703/11/twa.missile/

Cobb, Roger W., & Primo, David M. (2003*). The Plane Truth: Airline Crashes, the Media, and Transportation Policy.* Washington, D.C.: Brookings Institution Press.

Davis, Richard (1999). *The Web of Politics: The Internet's Impact on the American Political System.* New York: Oxford University Press.

Davis, Richard & Owen, Diana (1998). *New Media and American Politics.* New York: Oxford University Press.

Hall, Jim (2001). *Online Journalism: A Critical Primer.* London: Pluto Press.

Harper, Christopher (1998). *And That's the Way It Will Be: News and Information in a Digital World.* New York: New York University Press.

Hunter, Mark (1997). *The Buffoon Brigade: Pierre Salinger and His Conspiracy-Minded Colleagues Are Stopping Investigators from Finding Out What Really Happened to TWA Flight 800.* San Francisco: Salon.com. Retrieved October 18, 2003, from the Salon.com Web site: http://www.salon.com/march97/ news/news970326.html

Kurtz, Howard (1997, August 12). "Blumenthals Get Apology, Plan Lawsuit: Web Site Retracts Story of Clinton Aide." *The Washington Post,* p. A11.

Kurtz, Howard (2001, May 2). "Clinton Aide Settles Libel Suit Against Matt Drudge—At a Cost." *The Washington Post,* p. C1

Negroni, Christine (1997, January 17). *Six Months Later, Still No Answer to TWA Flight 800 Mystery.* Atlanta, GA: CNN.com. Retrieved October 18, 2003, from the CNN Interactive Web site: http://www.cnn.com/US/9701/17/twa/index.html

O'Dwyer, Thomas (1996, February 18). "Buchanan Web Site Blames Mossad for Clinton Aide's Death; Calls Hillary an Agent." *The Jerusalem Post,* p. 1.

O'Leary, Stephen (2002). *Rumors of Grace and Terror.* Los Angeles, CA: The Online Journalism Review. Retrieved September 29, 2003, from the Online Journalism Review Web site: http://www.ojr.org/ojr/ethics/1017782038.php

Piacente, Steve (1997, April 16). "Letter Claims Foster was Killed." *The Post and Courier*(Charleston, SC)*,* p. A9.

Ruddy, Christopher (1999). "A Memo: The Unanswered Questions in the Foster Case." West Palm Beach, FL: The Christopher Ruddy Web site. Retrieved November 27, 2003, from Newsmax.com: http://www.newsmax.com/articles/?a=1999/2/8/155138

Sabato, Larry J., Stencel, Mark, & Lichter, S. Robert (2000). *Peepshow: Media and Politics in an Age of Scandal.* Lanham, MD: Rowman & Littlefield Publishers, Inc.

Scheer, Robert (1999, January 14). "More Sludge From Drudge: The Story that Clinton Fathered an Illegitimate Son Turns Out to Be a Hoax." *Pittsburgh Post-Gazette,* p. A15.

Seib, Philip (2001). *Going Live: Getting the News Right in a Real-Time, Online World.* Lanham, MD: Rowman & Littlefield Publishers, Inc.

Sunstein, Cass (2002). *Republic.com.* Princeton: Princeton University Press.

Swartz, Jon (1998, June 23). "Free-Speech Victory For Internet; AOL Off the Hook in Landmark Libel Case." *The San Francisco Chronicle,* p. A1.

Tisdall, Simon (1994, February 7). "The Body in the Park." *The Guardian*(London)*,* p. 2.

Weiner, Tim (1995, August 13). "One Source, Many Ideas in Foster Case." *The New York Times,* pp. 1–19.

whatreallyhappened.com (2002, June 10). *Was TWA Flight 800 Shot Down by a Military Missile?* Retrieved October 18, 2003, from the whatreallyhappened.com Web site: http://www.whatreallyhappened.com/RANCHO/ CRASH/TWA/twa.html

# Note

1. For complete text of the Internet letter written by Russell, see (Harper, 1998, pp. 85–86).

From *gnovis,* April 26, 2004 (Original manuscript), pp. 1–26. Copyright © 2004) by Communication, Culture and Technology Program (CCT), Georgetown University. Reprinted by permission. www.gnovis.georgetown.edu

# The New Right-Wing Smear Machine

## E-mail turns out to be the ideal medium for the spreading of misinformation.

CHRISTOPHER HAYES

On February 27, 2001, two members of the American Gold Star Mothers, an organization of women who've lost sons or daughters in combat, dropped by the temporary basement offices of the new junior senator from New York, Hillary Clinton. They didn't have an appointment, and the office, which had been up and running for barely a month, was a bit discombobulated. The two women wanted to talk to the senator about a bill pending in the Senate that would provide annuities for the parents of those killed, but they were told that Clinton wasn't in the office and that the relevant staff members were otherwise engaged. The organization later submitted a formal request in writing for a meeting, which Clinton granted, meeting and posing for pictures with four members of the group.

But the story doesn't end there. In May of that year, the right-wing website *NewsMax,* a clearinghouse for innuendo and rumor, ran a short item with the headline "Hillary Snubs Gold Star Mothers." Reporting via hearsay—a comment relayed to someone who then recounted it to the column's author—the article claimed that Clinton and her staff "simply refused" to meet with the Gold Star Mothers, making hers the "only office" in the Senate that snubbed the group.

At first the item didn't attract much attention, but it quickly morphed into an e-mail that started ricocheting across the Internet. "Bet this never hits the TV news!" began one version. "According to NewsMax.com there was only one politician in DC who refused to meet with these ladies. Can you guess which politician that might be? . . . None other than the Queen herself—the Hildebeast, Hillary Clinton."

Before long, the Gold Star Mothers and the Clinton office found themselves inundated by inquiries about the "snub," prompting the Gold Star Mothers to post a small item debunking the claim on their website. When that didn't stem the tide, they posted a lengthier notice. "These allegations were not initiated by the Gold Star Mothers. . . . This is a fabricated report picked up by an individual using the Gold Star Mothers as an instrument to discredit Senator Clinton. . . . We do not need mischeivous gossip and unfounded lies to promote our organization. Please help stop it now."

That plea notwithstanding, the e-mail continues to circulate to this day. Anyone who's been following politics for the past fifteen years won't be surprised to find Hillary Clinton the subject of a false and damning right-wing smear. We've all become familiar with the ways the Republican noise machine transmits lurid bits of misinformation and tendentious attacks from the conservative fringe into the heart of American political discourse, the process by which a slightly misdelivered joke by John Kerry attracts the ire of Rush Limbaugh and ends up on the front page of the *New York Times.*

But in some senses, the kind of under-the-radar attack embodied in the Gold Star e-mail—which never made the jump to Fox or Drudge—is even harder to deal with. "It's a Pandora's box," says Jim Kennedy, who served as Clinton's communications director during her first Senate term. "Once [the charges] are out in the ether, they are very hard to combat. It's very unlike a traditional media, newspaper or TV show, or even a blog, which at least has a fixed point of reference. You know they're traveling far and wide, but there's no way to rebut them with all the people that have seen them."

Such is the power of the right-wing smear forward, a vehicle for the dissemination of character assassination that has escaped the scrutiny directed at the Limbaughs and Coulters and O'Reillys but one that is as potent as it is invisible. In 2004 putative firsthand accounts of Kerry's performance in Vietnam traveled through e-mail in right-wing circles, presaging the Swift Boat attacks. Last winter a forward began circulating accusing Barack Obama of being a secret Muslim schooled in a radical madrassa (about which more later). While the story was later fed through familiar right-wing megaphones, even making it onto Fox, it has continued to circulate via e-mail long after being definitively debunked by CNN. In other words, the few weeks the smear spent in the glare of the mainstream media was just a tiny portion of a long life cycle, most of which has been spent darting from inbox to inbox.

**What kind of havoc could be wreaked in 2008 by a few political operatives armed with little more than Outlook and a talent for gossip?**

In that respect, the e-mail forward doesn't fit into our existing model of the right-wing noise machine's structure (hierarchical) or its approach (broadcast). It is, instead, organic and peer-to-peer. If the manufactured outrage over Kerry's botched joke about George Bush's study habits was the equivalent of a Hollywood blockbuster, the Gold Star Mother smear was like one of those goofy viral videos of a dog on a skateboard on YouTube. Of course, some of those videos end up with 25 million page views. And now that large media companies understand their potential, they've begun trying to create their own. Which prompts the obvious question: if a handful of millionaires and disgruntled Swift Boat Veterans were able to sabotage Kerry's campaign in 2004, what kind of havoc could be wreaked in 2008 by a few political operatives armed with little more than Outlook and a talent for gossip?

The smear forward has its roots in two distinct forms of Internet-age communication. First, there's the electronically disseminated urban legend ("Help find this missing child!"; "Bill Gates is going to pay people for every e-mail they send!"), which has been a staple of the Internet since the mid-'90s. Then there's the surreal genre of right-wing e-mail forwards. These range from creepy rage-filled quasi-fascist invocations ("The next time you see an adult talking during the playing of the National Anthem—kick their ass") to treacly aphorisms of patriotic/religious uplift ("remember only two defining forces have ever offered to die for you, Jesus Christ . . . and the American Soldier" ).

For a certain kind of conservative, these e-mails, along with talk-radio, are an informational staple, a means of getting the real stories that the mainstream media ignore. "I get a million of them!" says Gerald DeSimone, a 74-year-old veteran from Ridgewood, New Jersey, who describes his politics as "to the right of Attila the Hun." "If I forwarded every one on, everyone would hate me. . . . I'm trying to cut back. I try to send no more than two or three a day. I must get thirty or forty a day."

Mike D'Asto, a 29-year-old assistant cameraman living in New York, received so many forwards from his conservative father he started a blog called MyRightWingDad.net, where he shares them with other unwitting recipients. "I suddenly have connected to all these people who receive these right-wing forwards from their brothers-in-law," D'Asto told me. "Surprisingly, a very large number of people receive these."

And that, of course, is the problem.

Rumormongering and whisper campaigns are as old as politics itself (throughout Thomas Jefferson's presidency opposition newspapers and pamphlets spread the word of his affair with Sally Hemings), but never has there been a medium as perfectly suited to the widespread anonymous diffusion of misinformation as e-mail. David Mikkelson, who, along with his wife, Barbara, founded and runs the website Snopes.com, knows this better than anyone. Devoted exclusively to debunking (and occasionally confirming) urban legends and e-mail-circulated apocrypha, Snopes attracts 4–5 million unique visitors a month, making it one of the Internet's most popular sites. In the early days, Mikkelson says, there were hardly any political

urban legends, but that changed in 2000. "A lot of the things that were circulating in the world at large, things like ridiculing Al Gore for supposedly inventing the Internet," started to be passed along via e-mail, as well as "a photograph of Gore holding a gun intended to mock him for not holding it safely."

From the beginning, the vast majority of these Internet-disseminated rumors have come from the right. (Snopes lists about fifty e-mails about George W. Bush, split evenly between adulatory accounts of him saluting wounded soldiers or witnessing to a wayward teenager, and accounts of real and invented malapropisms. In contrast, every single one of the twenty-two e-mails about John Kerry is negative.) For conservatives, these e-mails neatly reinforce preconceptions, bending the facts of the world in line with their ideological framework: liberals, immigrants, hippies and celebrities are always the enemy; soldiers and conservatives, the besieged heroes. The stories of the former's perfidy and the latter's heroism are, of course, never told by the liberal media. So it's left to the conservative underground to get the truth out. And since the general story and the roles stay the same, often the actual characters are interchangeable.

"A lot of the chain letters that were accusing Al Gore of things in 2000 were recycled in 2004 and changed to Kerry," says John Ratliff, who runs a site called BreakTheChain.org, which, like Snopes, devotes itself to debunking chain e-mails. One e-mail falsely described a Senate committee hearing in the 1980s where Oliver North offered an impassioned Cassandra-like warning about the threat of Osama bin Laden, only to be dismissed by a condescending Democratic senator. Originally it was Al Gore who played the role of the senator, but by 2004 it had changed to John Kerry. "You just plug in your political front-runner du jour," Ratliff says.

Even if many of the tropes were consistent, the tenor of the e-mails grew more aggressive between 2000 and 2004. "It got really nasty," says Ratliff. "You started seeing things reported as real news that, if you looked into it, you realized was opinion or supposition or someone trying to discredit another candidate through character assassination. You saw a lot of chain letters that purported to be from members of the Swift Boat group or firsthand accounts of people who supposedly had experience with Kerry in Vietnam. A lot of them didn't check out."

Aside from specious allegations about his military service, many of the e-mails attacking Kerry either emphasized his wealth (photos of each of his five residences) or relayed putative firsthand accounts of the senator acting like an imperious prick. Hal Cranmer, a former Air Force pilot, wrote a widely circulated account of his experience flying Kerry around Vietnam and Cambodia in 1991 in which Kerry scarfs pizza meant for the crew, forces the pilots to sit for an hour in an un-air-conditioned plane and boasts that he "never sail[s] on anything less than 135 feet." (Since it's a matter of historical record that Kerry has sailed boats smaller than 135 feet, this quote seems highly dubious.)

When I tracked down Cranmer during his lunch break at the aerospace manufacturing firm he works for in Minnesota, I was surprised to hear him ruefully recall his brush with Internet fame. "It gave me a real lesson. My wife says one of the reasons she married me is that I don't talk badly about people," he said with a laugh. "I really didn't mean to do that here."

In spring 2004, as John Kerry began to emerge as the probable nominee, Cranmer e-mailed his account to the libertarian website LewRockwell.com, where readers were sharing their personal experiences about meeting Kerry. "I said, OK, I'll put in my two cents. . . . I thought maybe I'd get one or two e-mails about it and it would just disappear." That was not to be. "All of a sudden I was getting fifty e-mails a day. I had an annual meeting with the Air Force pilots, and a friend said, 'Tell your story about John Kerry,' and everyone in the room was going, 'I got that e-mail! That was you?' I had neighbors walking in and saying, 'Hey, I got an e-mail about you.' I was trying to keep this low-key, not try to ruin an election here. I was just relating an experience that happened to me. People drew all kinds of crazy conclusions from it other than I had a bad experience with him." Added Cranmer, "Maybe he's the nicest guy in the world, and he was in a bad mood going into Vietnam. . . . I really didn't mean this to be as huge as it was."

Cranmer told me he was a libertarian and a big fan of Ron Paul. "I voted for Bush in 2000 and have regretted it ever since. I didn't even vote in 2004." He now wishes he'd kept his impressions to himself. Some anecdote of casual thoughtlessness "shouldn't be what defines the presidency."

But of course, that's exactly the kind of thing that did define the last presidential election. Cranmer's e-mail, and those of a similar ilk, were perfectly in line with the broader narrative of the Bush campaign, in which the major knock on Kerry was that he was an elitist, disingenuous jerk—a "bad man," in Lynne Cheney's phrasing. Like the other popular e-mails that circulated in 2004, Cranmer's includes not a single substantive criticism of Kerry's platform or policy preferences, but the unflattering picture it offers has an effect that's immediate and visceral. It lingers in the back of one's head.

It was similar gossip that helped spell doom for John McCain during the South Carolina primary in 2000, when a whisper campaign spread rumors that he had a black daughter out of wedlock. "John McCain was done in by leaflets put on cars in church parking lots," says Democratic campaign consultant Chris Lehane. Forwarded e-mails, he says, "are the digital version of this and potentially more pernicious and far-reaching because of the obvious efficiencies of the online world. I would fully expect to see it manifesting in the GOP primary." Sure enough, a few weeks after I spoke to Lehane, Mike Huckabee's Iowa state campaign chair, Bob Vander Plaats, issued a statement denying that he'd written an e-mail that voters had received bearing his name. In that hoax e-mail, someone impersonating Vander Plaats announced that he was dropping Huckabee because of low fundraising numbers and backing Mitt Romney instead and urging others to do the same.

Faced with dubious attacks, circulating below the radar, campaigns find themselves in a familiar bind, one that handcuffed Kerry in 2004 when the Swift Boat charges first cropped up in ads, talk-radio and e-mail. If you respond, you run the risk of

bringing the original false accusation to a wider audience. This is particularly true when the e-mails don't even have a putative author attached. "For lots of these e-mails, there's never any definable source," says Mikkelson. "They just seem to come out of nowhere."

That leads to the $64,000 question: are these anonymous attacks organic emanations of the diffuse political consciousness, or are they deliberately seeded by professional political operators? Mikkelson is skeptical that anyone could intentionally write the kind of e-mail that would take off virally. "Even people who are steeped in it, it's very, very difficult to start some thing deliberately that will catch on." Still, there's some evidence it's been done. Snopes determined that a gushing pro-Bush e-mail from 2004 about watching the President worship in the pews of St. John's Church in Washington was actually written by the press spokeswoman for Republican Senator Lamar Alexander. Her name is Laura Lefler, and she now works for Senator Bob Corker. I tried to contact Lefler to get a sense of what inspired her to write the e-mail and how exactly, she disseminated it, but she wouldn't return my calls or e-mails.

The most notorious smear forward of this cycle is the Obama madrassa canard, which represents the cutting edge of electronic rumor. At least two weeks before the Obama/madrassa smear appeared in the online magazine *Insight,* on January 17, it had been circulating widely in an e-mail forward that laid out the basics of Obama's bio in a flat, reportorial tone before concluding thus:

> Obama takes great care to conceal the fact that he is a Muslim. . . . Lolo Soetoro, the second husband of Obama's mother . . . introduced his stepson to Islam. Osama was enrolled in a Wahabi school in Jakarta. Wahabism is the radical teaching that is followed by the Muslim terrorists who are now waging Jihad against the western world. Since it is politically expedient to be a Christian when seeking major public office in the United States, Barack Hussein Obama has joined the United Church of Christ in an attempt to downplay his Muslim background.
>
> Let us all remain alert concerning Obama's expected presidential candidacy.

Did you catch that typo in the crucial sentence? And the strategic deployment of Obama's middle name? It's a coldly effective bit of slander: a single damning lie (the school Obama attended was a run-of-the mill public elementary school) snuggled tightly within a litany of mundane facts, followed by dark insinuation.

Who wrote it? The unsatisfying answer is, we'll probably never know. "The thing to keep in mind about e-mail is that there is absolutely zero built-in security or data integrity," my friend Paul Smith, a software developer with EveryBlock.com, explained to me when I asked him if there was any way I could trace the Obama e-mail to its original author. "That's why there is spam. I could construct an e-mail from scratch and deliver it and have it seem like it was coming from Steve Jobs, and for all intents and purposes the receiver would have no way of knowing it wasn't from Cupertino."

But even if the identity of the e-mail's author was un-recoverable, it was still possible to trace back the roots of its content. The origin proved even more bizarre than I could have guessed.

On August 10, 2004, just two weeks after Obama had given his much-heralded keynote speech at the DNC in Boston, a perennial Republican Senate candidate and self-described "independent contrarian columnist" named Andy Martin issued a press release. In it, he announced a press conference in which he would expose Obama for having "lied to the American peo-ple" and "misrepresent[ed] his own heritage."

Martin raised all kinds of strange allegations about Obama but focused on him attempting to hide his Muslim past. "It may well be that his concealment is meant to endanger Israel," read Martin's statement. "His Muslim religion would obviously raise serious questions in many Jewish circles where Obama now enjoys support."

A quick word about Andy Martin. During a 1983 bankruptcy case he referred to a federal judge as a "crooked, slimy Jew, who has a history of lying and thieving common to members of his race." Martin, who in the past was known as Anthony Martin-Trigona, is one of the most notorious litigants in the his-tory of the United States. He's filed hundreds, possibly thou-sands, of lawsuits, often directed at judges who have ruled against him, or media outlets that cover him unfavorably. A 1993 opinion by the US Court of Appeals for the Eleventh Cir-cuit, in Atlanta, described these lawsuits as "a cruel and effective weapon against his enemies," and called Martin a "notoriously vexatious and vindictive litigator who has long abused the American legal system." He once even attempted to intervene in the divorce proceedings of a judge who'd ruled against him, petitioning the state court to be appointed as the guardian of the judge's children.

When I asked Martin for the source of his allegations about Obama's past, he told me they came from "people in London, among other places." Why London, I asked? "I started talking to them about Kenyan law. Every little morsel led me a little farther along."

Within a few days of Martin's press conference, the con-servative site *Free Republic* had picked it up, attracting a long comment thread, but after that small blip the specious "questions" about Obama's background disappeared. Then,

in the fall of 2006, as word got out that Obama was consider-ing a presidential run, murmurs on the Internet resumed. In October a conservative blog called Infidel Bloggers Alliance reposted the Andy Martin press release under the title "Is Barack Obama Lying About His Life Story?" A few days later the online *RumorMillNews* also reposted the Andy Martin press release in response to a reader's inquiry about whether Obama was a Muslim. Then in December fringe right-wing activist Ted Sampley posted a column on the web raising the possibility that Obama was a secret Muslim. Sampley, who co-founded Vietnam Veterans Against John Kerry and once accused John McCain of having been a KGB asset, quoted heavily from Martin's original press release. "When Obama was six," Sampley wrote, "his mother, an atheist, married Lolo Soetoro, an Indonesian Muslim, and moved to Jakarta, Indonesia. . . . Soetoro enrolled his stepson in one of Jakarta's Muslim Wahabbi schools. Wahabbism is the radical teaching that created the Muslim terrorists who are now waging Jihad on the rest of the world."

On December 29, 2006, the very same day that Sampley posted his column, Snopes received its first copy of the e-mail forward, which contains an identical charge in strikingly similar language. Given the timing, it seems likely that it was a distilla-tion of Sampley's work.

Despite the fact that CNN and others have thoroughly debunked the smear, the original false accusation has clearly sunk into people's consciousness. One Obama organizer told me recently that every day, while calling prospective voters, he gets at least one or two people who tell him they won't be vot-ing for Obama because he's a Muslim. According to Google, "Barack Obama Muslim" is the third most-searched term for the Illinois senator. And an August CBS poll found that when voters were asked to give Obama's religion, as many said Muslim as correctly answered Protestant.

Oh yeah. And the e-mail continues to circulate.

"Everybody started calling me" when the e-mail first made the rounds, Andy Martin told me. "They said, 'Hey, did you write this?' My answer was 'they are all my children.'"

CHRISTOPHER HAYES, a Nation contributing writer and a Puffin Foundation Writing Fellow at The Nation Institute, is a senior editor of *In These Times*.

# A Growing Watch List

**Data on both U.S. citizens and foreigners flow from a massive clearinghouse.**

KAREN DEYOUNG

Each day, thousands of pieces of intelligence information from around the world—field reports, captured documents, news from foreign allies and sometimes idle gossip—arrive in a computer-filled office in McLean, Va., where analysts feed them into the nation's central list of terrorists and terrorism suspects.

Called TIDE, for Terrorist Identities Datamart Environment, the list is a storehouse for data about individuals that the intelligence community believes might harm the United States. It is the wellspring for watch lists distributed to airlines, law enforcement, border posts and U.S. consulates, created to close one of the key intelligence gaps revealed after Sept. 11, 2001: the failure of federal agencies to share what they knew about al-Qaeda operatives.

But in addressing one problem, TIDE has spawned others. Ballooning from fewer than 100,000 files in 2003 to about 435,000, the growing database threatens to overwhelm the people who manage it. "The single biggest worry that I have is long-term quality control," says Russ Travers, in charge of TIDE at the National Counterterrorism Center in McLean. "Where am I going to be, where is my successor going to be, five years down the road?"

TIDE has also created concerns about secrecy, errors and privacy. The list marks the first time foreigners and U.S. citizens are combined in an intelligence database. The bar for inclusion is low, and once someone is on the list, it is virtually impossible to get off it. At any stage, the process can lead to "horror stories" of mixed-up names and unconfirmed information, Travers acknowledges.

The watch lists fed by TIDE, used to monitor everyone entering the country or having even a casual encounter with federal, state and local law enforcement, have a higher bar. But they have become a source of irritation—and potentially more serious consequences—for many U.S. citizens and visitors.

In 2004 and 2005, misidentifications accounted for about half of the tens of thousands of times a traveler's name triggered a watch-list hit, the Government Accountability Office reported in September. Congressional committees have criticized the process, some charging that it collects too much information about Americans, others saying it is ineffective against terrorists. Civil rights and privacy groups have called for increased transparency.

"How many are on the lists, how are they compiled, how is the information used, how do they verify it?" asks Lillie Coney, associate director of the Washington-based Electronic Privacy Information Center. Such information is classified, and individuals barred from traveling are not told why.

Republican Sen. Ted Stevens of Alaska said last year that his wife had been delayed repeatedly while airlines queried whether Catherine Stevens was the watch-listed Cat Stevens. The listing referred to the Britain-based pop singer who converted to Islam and changed his name to Yusuf Islam. The reason Islam is not allowed to fly to the United States is secret.

So is the reason Maher Arar, a Syrian-born Canadian, remains on the State Department's consular watch list. Detained in New York while enroute to Montreal in 2002, Arar was sent by the U.S. government to a year of imprisonment in Syria. Canada, the source of the initial information about Arar, cleared him of all terrorism allegations last September—three years after his release—and has since authorized $9 million in compensation.

TIDE is a vacuum cleaner for both proven and unproven information, and its managers disclaim responsibility for how other agencies use the data. "What's the alternative?" Travers says. "I work under the assumption that we're never going to have perfect information—fingerprints, DNA—on 6 billion people across the planet. . . . If someone actually has a better idea, I'm all ears."

The electronic journey a piece of terrorism data takes from an intelligence outpost to an airline counter is interrupted at several points for analysis and condensation. President Bush ordered the intelligence community in 2003 to centralize data on terrorism suspects, and U.S. agencies at home and abroad now send everything they collect to TIDE. It arrives electronically as names to be added or as additional information about people already in the system.

The 80 TIDE analysts get "thousands of messages a day," Travers says, much of the data "fragmentary," "inconsistent" and "sometimes just flat-out wrong." Often the analysts go back to the intelligence agencies for details. "Sometimes you'll get sort of corroborating information," he says, "but many times you're not going to get much. What we use here, rightly or wrongly, is a reasonable-suspicion standard."

Each TIDE listee is given a number, and statistics are kept on nationality and ethnic and religious groups. Some files include aliases and sightings, and others are just a full or partial name, perhaps with a sketchy biography. Sunni and Shiite Muslims are the fastest-growing categories in a database whose entries include Saudi financiers and Colombian revolutionaries. U.S. citizens—who Travers says make up less than 5 percent of listings—are included if an "international terrorism nexus" is established. A similar exception for the administration's warrantless wiretap program came under court challenge from privacy and civil rights advocates.

Every night at 10, TIDE dumps an unclassified version of that day's harvest—names, dates of birth, countries of origin and passport information—into a database belonging to the FBI's Terrorist Screening Center. TIDE's most sensitive information is not included. The FBI adds data about U.S. suspects with no international ties for a combined daily total of 1,000 to 1,500 new names.

Between 5 and 6 A.M., a shift of 24 analysts drawn from the agencies that use watch lists begins a new winnowing process at the center's Crystal City, Va., office. The analysts have access to case files at TIDE and the original intelligence sources, says the center's acting director, Rick Kopel.

Decisions on what to add to the Terrorist Screening Center master list are made by midafternoon. The bar is higher than TIDE's; total listings were about 235,000 names as of last fall, according to Justice Department Inspector General Glenn A. Fine. The bar is then raised again as agencies decide which names to put on their own watch lists: the Transportation Security Administration's "no-fly" and "selectee" lists for airlines; Consular Lookout and Support System at the State Department; the Interagency Border and Inspection System at the Department of Homeland Security; and the Justice Department's National Crime Information Center. The criteria each agency use are classified, Kopel says.

Some information may raise a red flag for one agency but not another. "There's a big difference between CLASS and no-fly," Kopel says, referring to State's consular list. "About the only criteria CLASS has is that you're not a U.S. person. . . . Say 'a Mohammed from Syria.' That's useless for me to watch-list here in the United States. But if I'm in Damascus processing visas . . . that might be enough for someone to . . . put a hold on the visa process."

All of the more than 30,000 individuals on the TSA's no-fly list are prohibited from entering an aircraft in the United States. People whose names appear on the longer selectee list—those the government believes merit watching but does not bar from travel—are supposed to be subjected to more intense scrutiny.

With little to go on beyond names, airlines find frequent matches. The screening center agent on call will check the file for markers such as sex, age and prior "encounters" with the list. The agent might ask the airlines about the passenger's eye color, height or defining marks, Kopel says. "We'll say, 'Does he have any rings on his left hand?' and they'll say, 'Uh, he doesn't have a left hand.' Okay. We know that [the listed person] lost his left hand making a bomb."

If the answers indicate a match, that "encounter" is fed back into the FBI screening center's files and ultimately to TIDE. Kopel says the agent never tells the airline whether the person trying to board is the suspect. The airlines decide whether to allow the customer to fly.

TSA receives thousands of complaints each year, such as this one released to the Electronic Privacy Information Center in 2004 under the Freedom of Information Act: "Apparently, my name is on some watch list because everytime I fly, I get delayed while the airline personnel call what they say is TSA," wrote a passenger whose name was blacked out. Noting that he was a high-level federal worker, he asked what he could do to remove his name from the list.

The answer, Kopel says, is little. A unit at the screening center responds to complaints, he says, but will not remove a name if it is shared by a terrorism suspect. Instead, people not on the list who share a name with someone listed can be issued letters instructing airline personnel to check with the TSA to verify their identity. The GAO reported that 31 names were removed in 2005.

A recent review of the entire terrorist Screening Center database was temporarily abandoned when it proved too much work even for the night crew, which generally handles less of a workload. But the no-fly and selectee lists are being scrubbed to emphasize "people we think are a danger to the plane, and not for some other reason they met the criteria," Kopel says.

A separate TSA system that would check every passenger name against the screening center's database has been shelved over concern that it could grow into a massive surveillance program. The Department of Homeland Security was rebuked by Congress in December for trying to develop a risk-assessment program to profile travelers entering and leaving the United States based on airline and financial data.

Kopel insisted that private information on Americans, such as credit-card records, never makes it into the screening center database and that "we rely 100 percent on government-owned information."

The center came in for ridicule last year when CBS's "60 Minutes" noted that 14 of the 19 Sept. 11 hijackers were listed—five years after their deaths. Kopel defends the listings, saying that "we know for a fact that these people will use names that they believe we are not going to list because they're out of circulation—either because they're dead or incarcerated. . . . It's not willy-nilly. Every name on the list, there's a reason that it's on there."

# UNIT 7

# International Perspectives and Issues

## Unit Selections

32. **China's Tech Generation Finds a New Chairman to Venerate,** Kevin Holden
33. **Restoring the Popularity of Computer Science,** David A. Patterson
34. **China's Computer Wasteland,** Benjamin Joffe-Walt
35. **In Search of a PC for the People,** Bruce Einhorn
36. **In Korea, a Boot Camp Cure for Web Obsession,** Martin Fackler
37. **New Tech, Old Habits,** Moon Ihlwan and Kenji Hall

## Key Points to Consider

- "In Search of a PC for the People" mentions Nicholas Negroponte, an MIT professor and founder of the nonprofit organization One Laptop Per Child. Use the Internet to find out more about this group. What do they have to say about the recent decision of a New York school district to drop its "laptop for students" program?

- Find out more about proxy servers. What is to prevent an authoritarian government from shifting the monitoring of traffic within its borders to a proxy server? Suppose an authoritarian government sets up a web site claiming to be anonymous.org. How could it be distinguished from the real thing? What if a volunteer within a proxy server group sells a list of names and searched web sites to authoritarian regimes. Do the proxy server websites you have visited address these issues?

- Do you know anyone who you think is addicted to online gaming? Use the Internet to learn about the status of gamers and gaming in South Korea.

## Student Web Site
www.mhcls.com

## Internet Reference

**Information Revolution and World Politics Project**
*http://www.ceip.org/files/projects/irwp/irwp_descrip.ASP*

For the past several years, we have been hearing a great deal about a global economy, the exchange of goods, services, and labor across national boundaries. Yet human beings have been trading across long distances for centuries. The discovery of Viking artifacts in Baghdad and sea shells in the Mississippi Valley are two of many, many examples. The beginnings of capitalism in the 15th century accelerated an existing process (Merrett 2008). When most commentators speak of globalization, though, they refer increasingly to the interdependent trade we have witnessed since the collapse of the former Soviet Union, and the global availability of the Internet and satellite communications. Without the new information technologies, the global marketplace would not be possible. We can withdraw money from our bank accounts using ATMs in Central Turkey, make cell phones calls from nearly anywhere on the planet, and check our e-mail from a terminal located in an Internet café in Florence or Katmandu. They also make it possible for businesses to transfer funds around the world and, if you happen to be a software developer, to employ talented—and inexpensive—software engineers in growing tech centers like Bangalore, India.

Or China. Those of us old enough to remember the Chinese Red Guard waving copies of Chairman Mao's Little Red Book might be surprised to find that "Bill Gates has become the new idol of youths across China" ("China's Tech Generation Finds a New Chairman to Venerate").

One area where the United States still has the indisputable lead is in squeezing every ounce of productivity out of information technology. Some of what we have read about the length of the Korean and Japanese workweek may be due to the unwillingness of employers in those countries to give their employees laptops. See "New Tech, Old Habits," for an account of the more creative side of American business.

Not all international consequences of computer technology are economic. One of the most exciting developments in theoretical computer science in recent years has been strong cryptography, the art of enciphering messages. For practical purposes, freely available cryptographic software can produce unbreakable codes. Governments, including our own, have worried about this for a decade. Whatever you might think about making wiretap-proof software available to criminals in the United States, it is being put to good use in countries with repressive governments. Authoritarian governments find themselves in a fix, at least with respect to encrypted email.

U.S. newspaper readers are occasionally astonished at stories about South Koreans dying at the gaming console. With ninety percent of homes having a broadband connection,

© Don Bishop/Getty Images

online gaming has become a professional sport. The dark side is classic addiction, along with classic withdrawal symptoms. Martin Fackler's *New York Times* piece describes South Korean boot camps for adolescents who can't tear themselves away from their computers.

We in the United States, especially students on well-endowed university campuses, have grown accustomed to a cornucopia of computing devices that were not available anywhere a generation ago. They are still unavailable in the developing world. The computer industry is beginning to see that designing computers appropriate to the needs and resources of this emerging market is more than a good deed, it might well be good business. See "In Search of a PC for the People" and learn why "selling computers in the developing world is more complex than simply adding Mandarin, Hindi, or Arabic software to existing PCs."

The global interconnectedness that Marshall McLuhan observed forty years ago has only increased in complexity with developments in computer technology. Now instead of merely receiving one-way satellite feeds, as in McLuhan's day, we can talk back through e-mail, web sites, and blogs. It is not surprising that all of this communication is having unanticipated effects across the planet. Who, for instance, during the Tiananmen Square uprising of 1989 could have predicted that a newly market-centered China would become the source of significant competition to the United States? Or, who could ever have predicted that Bill Gates would replace Chairman Mao in the hearts of the young Chinese? No one, in fact, which is why the study of computer use internationally is so fascinating.

## Reference

Merrett, C. (2008). The Future of Rural Communities in a Global Economy. The University of Iowa Center for International Finance and Development. Retrieved 9/13/08 from: http://www.uiowa.edu/ifdebook/issues/globalization/perspectives/merrett.shtml.

# China's Tech Generation Finds a New Chairman to Venerate

KEVIN HOLDEN

Since the passing of Chairman Mao Zedong, a new chairman has come to represent the aims and aspirations of millions of Chinese youth—the chairman of Microsoft, Bill Gates.

"Chairman Mao was the great symbol of revolutionary China, but Bill Gates has become the new idol of youths across China," said a researcher with China's ministry of propaganda. "Gates has become more popular in China than any government leader."

Books by or about Microsoft's chairman are massive best sellers across China, even in the IT-impoverished countryside, and Gates has been cited as the ultimate role model by everyone, from the founders of internet startups to Chinese cyberdissidents.

"I read about Bill Gates before I had ever even seen a computer," said Dong Ruidong, who abandoned his rural village for the bright lights and cybercafes of the Chinese capital. "Even in the remotest villages of China, Gates is one of the most popular figures alive."

The Chinese edition of Gates' *The Road Ahead* "was one of the most successful books in our history," said Wang Mingzhou, who edited the Chinese edition. It is "among the most important works published since the founding of the People's Republic of China."

Wang, who rode the success of Gates' book to be named president of the Peking University Press, said *The Road Ahead* "helped launch the internet revolution across China, and gave it power and speed."

"Bill Gates is without doubt now one of the most influential foreigners in China," Wang said.

Chairman Gates is everything Chairman Mao was not. Mao crushed capitalists, closed newspapers and universities, and isolated China from the world. But Chairman Gates celebrates free enterprise and is busy forging partnerships with Chinese entrepreneurs, creating cybercolleges and integrating China's best and brightest into the web-linked world.

Gates has disbursed grants from his $30-billion philanthropic Gates Foundation to bring computers to rural China and health care to the poor, and in the process has acquired the aura of an internet-age angel.

Chinese youths stand to gain from the virtual universities Gates is helping create, and from student software packages Microsoft has begun offering for $3 (1/50th the retail price) each to governments buying computers for K–12 kids.

Microsoft Vice President Will Poole, who is helping spearhead the race to double the globe's cybercitizenry to 2 billion people by 2015, said Microsoft's software packages could be provided in tandem with the ultra-cheap XO machines being produced in China by the One Laptop Per Child group.

China's Ministry of Education, which paints Gates with an almost superhuman glow in books like *Junior English for China,* might use this software in its quest to churn out more internet-generation graduates.

China's internet population jumped by 23 percent to reach 130 million people in 2006, but nine-tenths of China's 1.3 billion citizens are still on the dark side of the digital divide.

At a recent Asian leadership forum in Beijing with Chinese technocrats and U.N. leaders, Gates outlined his latest goal—to extend internet access beyond the globe's 1 billion online elite to its 5 billion digitally dispossessed—many of whom are in China.

"Microsoft is now over 30 years old, and the original dream was about computers for everyone," he said. "As we go after this next 5 billion, it is really going back to the original roots, the original commitment of what Microsoft is all about."

Of course, meeting that goal would also position Microsoft to multiply, by a factor of 10, its current base of 600 million Windows users worldwide, and further expand Gates' global influence.

Microsoft's chairman is extending lots of incentives to new Windows users here, and has become a symbol of global fame and fortune, and of American-style freedoms. While hosting Chinese President Hu Jintao at an aristocratic feast at the Gates' private residence in Seattle last spring, Gates echoed Microsoft's testimony during U.S. congressional hearings on "The Internet in China: A Tool for Freedom or Suppression."

In remarks repeated across Chinese chat rooms, Gates told Hu: "Industry and government around the world should work even more closely to protect the privacy and security of internet users, and promote the exchange of ideas."

During his recent tour of China, Gates predicted the next global leader might be born here: "There was a survey done in the U.S. that asked where the next Bill Gates will come from," he said. "Sixty percent of the U.S. said the next stunning success would come from Asia."

Yet few Chinese believe that a clone of Gates, if born in China, could become *the* Bill Gates.

"Piracy is so widespread here that Microsoft would never generate such massive profits," said author Huang Wen.

Despite the massive, institutionalized piracy that has led the United States to file a complaint against China with the World Trade Organization, Gates has been amazingly tolerant of China's counterfeiters. This has created a paradoxical image of an internet-age Robin Hood and gained him universal admiration.

"Bill Gates deserves to win the Nobel Peace Prize," said the Chinese propaganda officer. "He gives people across the globe not only material help, but also inspiration that if they work very, very hard, they might one day become more important than a president."

# Restoring the Popularity of Computer Science

## Inaccurate impressions of the opportunities of 21st century CS are shrinking the next generation of IT professionals. You can help by dispelling incorrect beliefs about employment and by helping improve pre-college education.

DAVID A. PATTERSON

Although universities were recently struggling to cope with an avalanche of computer science majors—some going so far as to erecting academic barriers to deflect the masses—they may soon need to reverse course and remove obstacles to the major, and even to recruiting to broaden participation in CS. Figure 1 tracks the change in popularity of the CS major among incoming freshmen over time in the U.S., which has been be a good predictor of graduates four to five years later [1].

Clearly, the CS major is now in a downward cycle in the U.S., especially for women. While the percentage of men intending to major in CS is no worse than the mid-1990s, the number of female CS majors is at a historic low. This drop is occurring while their academic numbers are increasing, as the majority of college students today are female. Colleagues outside North America suggest a similar decline in Europe. As an extreme example, a few CS departments were even closed in the U.K.

Everyone has an opinion as to why the CS numbers are down in this age group, so let me share mine: The expected negative impact of offshoring IT jobs in North America and Europe, and the current negative view of the CS profession by pre-college students, especially females. What can we do about these issues?

ACM's Job Migration Task Force has examined the impact of outsourcing extensively and is working to publish its findings, which we hope to complete this fall. I believe the truth will surely be better for our field than the worst fears of pre-college students and their parents. For example, Figure 2 shows the annual U.S. IT employment though May 2004. (The U.S. Bureau of Labor Statistics is about 15 months behind.)[1] Moreover, most of us believe things have gotten much better in the year since the survey was completed. Does anyone besides me know that U.S. IT employment was 17% higher than in 1999—5% higher than the bubble in 2000 and showing an 8% growth

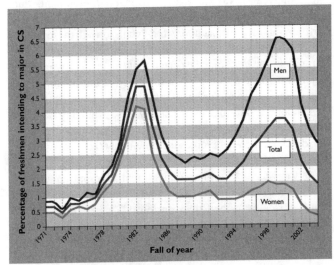

**Figure 1 Computer science listed as probable major among incoming freshman.**

Source: HERI at UCLA.

in the most recent year—and that the compound annual growth rate of IT wages has been about 4% since 1999 while inflation has been just 2% per year? Such growth rates swamp predictions of the outsourcing job loss in the U.S., which most studies estimate to be 2% to 3% per year for the next decade.[2]

Regarding the negative CS impressions held by students not yet in college, we hope ACM's new Computer Science Teachers Association (CSTA) will help in this regard. CSTA is a membership organization that supports and promotes the teaching of CS and other computing disciplines. CSTA provides opportunities for pre-college teachers and students to better understand the computing disciplines and to more successfully prepare themselves to teach and learn. Remarkably, before ACM

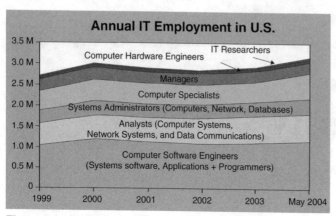

**Figure 2   Annual IT employment in the U.S.**

formed CSTA nine months ago, computer science was the only academic discipline within the U.S. high school curriculum without national professional representation.

To give you an idea what CSTA is trying to do to further the CS cause, here is the list of its existing committees: Curriculum, Equity, Finance, Funding Development, Governance, Membership, Policy and Advocacy, Professional Development, Publications and Communications, Research, and Standards and Certification (see csta.acm.org for details on all these groups and much more). I am particularly interested in the Equity committee, for I've long suspected that the drop in women CS majors was related to the initial unattractive impression of our field when high schools started teaching CS in the 1980s.

Although it only began in January, CSTA already has more than 2,000 members, and these members come from all over the world. CSTA members represent more than 60 countries and all 50 states in the U.S.

At the recent National Educational Computing Conference, panel speakers from Canada, Israel, Scotland, and South Africa described their current CS curriculum for students ages 12 to 18 and the issues that surround its implementation. They all emphasized the importance of supporting CS education as a means for ensuring the economic futures of their countries.

While all of the countries noted their efforts to implement a new national curriculum were initially hampered by issues such as lack of funding or insufficient time for teacher training, no point about the need for well-trained teachers was made more poignantly than by Michael Chiles from South Africa. He told the audience that the HIV/AIDS pandemic is taking the lives of so many teachers that it is becoming almost impossible to replace them. Not only are the teachers themselves dying, so many people in business are dying that industries looking for

technically skilled workers are luring the healthy CS teachers away from the classroom.

This panel discussion led to a CSTA project to create a white paper that will provide an international perspective on successful models for CS curriculum development and implementation. Judith Gal-Ezer, the panel speaker representing Israel, serves as an international director to the CSTA Board.

What can you do to help? First, please try to counteract the widespread impression that the CS field is not a good one for the future. For example, you can help publicize real employment data and the results of ACM's upcoming outsourcing study.

Second, if you know pre-college teachers, please suggest they consider joining CSTA. Studies of teachers belonging to such organizations suggest they gain important knowledge and psychological support as well as establish networking relationships that provide opportunities to share curricula. The resulting reform is also more widespread and long lasting.

CSTA could also use specific help on some of their committees. The Research committee is looking for volunteers to assist on statistical analysis of surveys. The Standards and Certification committee needs volunteers to create a database of teacher certification requirements in different regions. It could also use more practicing teachers on its Curriculum committee. Finally, if you really care about the issue of pre-college education, join CSTA.

It's difficult to imagine a more important topic for our future than trying to change public opinion about career opportunities in CS and to improve pre-college education, so thanks in advance for your help.

## Notes

1. Private communication, John Sargent, Office of Technology, Policy Technology Administration, U.S. Department of Commerce, July 2005. For clarity, Figure 2 combines the 12 official U.S. Department of Labor titles into seven related categories.

2. Private communication, William Asprey, Indiana University, July 2005.

## Reference

1. Vegso, J. Interest in CS as a major drops among incoming freshmen. *Computing Research News 17,* 3 (May 2005); www.cra.org/CRN/articles/may05/vegso.

**DAVID A. PATTERSON** (pattsn@eecs.berkeley.edu) is president of the ACM and the Pardee Professor of Computer Science at the University of California at Berkeley.

From *Communications of the ACM,* Vol. 48, No. 9, September 2005, pp. 25–26, 28. Copyright © 2005 by Association for Computing Machinery, Inc. Reprinted by permission.

# China's Computer Wasteland

Benjamin Joffe-Walt

"Shhh. Shhhhhhhhh!" the driver in Guangdong province whispers to us. He stares at the photographer out of the corner of his eye. When we stop, he won't even get out of the car. The photographer's every movement makes him jump a bit, and he receives the snap of her camera like the crack of a machine gun. "Careful!" he says. "They really will kill you."

We drive clandestinely, heads ducked, bodies curled up, eyes downward. "There, there it is!" the driver points. "They burn along the river." In front of us sprawl colossal piles of smoldering green computer circuit boards.

At first, Guiyu seems like any other rural Chinese town—flooded rice fields, streets swamped with produce vendors, migrant workers carrying bamboo on mopeds. But then you open the window. There is no smell more violent. The air is fierce, infected, as if the atmosphere itself had been viscously conquered by toxic paint, scorched bread, and burning plastic. An immediate noxious thickness enters your mouth, a toxic attack on all skin.

"I'm just trying to get some money," says Luo Yuan Chang, a newly arrived migrant from Hunan province who is burning old computers along the river. "Farming computers is more profitable than growing rice."

Computer waste from the West has made this poor mainland farming region an ecological disaster area. A large town along the Lianjiang River in southeastern China, Guiyu is the secret epicenter of illegal e-waste (electronic waste) processing in China. Workers there don't refurbish and sell the computers. They don't use them. Instead, they take hammers, chisels, and cutting torches to computers, keyboards, speakers, and other sorts of e-waste and smash them to bits for scrap metal, toner, gold, and reusable chips.

Chang stands shirtless atop scorched medical equipment, printing toner, and audio speakers. "I used to drive trucks, but I couldn't find a job so I had to come here and burn the rubbish," the forty-year-old says. "My family is here, and if I have no work we couldn't live, so I don't care how dangerous it is." When asked, though, he doesn't know much about the dangers involved.

It's plenty dangerous.

According to the Worldwatch Institute, workers breathe in all types of toxins: cadmium in chip resistors and semiconductors; beryllium on motherboards and connectors; brominated flame retardants in circuit boards and plastic casings; and lead, phosphor, barium, and hexavalent chromium in computer monitors.

The average CRT computer monitor contains four to eight pounds of lead, and the average LCD monitor contains four milligrams of mercury. Less than one-fourth of a teaspoon of mercury can contaminate more than 400 acres of a lake, making the fish unsafe to eat.

"There are many cases of lung problems, and the burning releases pollutants that cause diseases like silicosis, heart attacks, and pulmonary edema," says Dr. Chen at a local health clinic.

International watchdog groups estimate that the United States alone exported more than $1 billion worth of electronic waste to China last year while receiving virtually none from China. Though particularly pronounced in China, the e-waste of the Western world is being dumped all over Asia. *The Times of India* reports that "electronic waste is giving the country a big headache" and that India has become a "favorite dumping ground for countries like the U.S., Malaysia, Sweden, Canada, and Singapore."

Toxics Link, an Indian environmental group, claims that recycling a computer in India costs $2 on average, compared to $20 in the United States. Policymakers in the United States also understand the dynamics of dumping in Asia. After a pilot project to recycle computer monitors, the U.S. Environmental Protection Agency estimated that it is ten times cheaper to ship them to Asia than to recycle them in the United States.

China is not only a computer dumping ground. It also produces many of the 150 million computers that head out yearly on a peculiar round trip. For instance, IBM, Apple, Hewlett-Packard, Dell, and Sony all manufacture electronic goods in China. They then sell these products to Western countries. Finally, China gets them back as rubbish.

"Most of it is coming from recycling programs in countries that are trying to prevent pollution of their own territory," says Lai Yun, a Chinese environmentalist.

Today, more than 50 percent of U.S. households own a computer and have, on average, two to three old computers stored away in the basement or garage. Studies estimate that 315 million to 600 million computers in the United States will be obsolete by 2006.

"That's the same as a twenty-two-story pile of e-waste covering the entire 472 square miles of the City of Los Angeles," says the Computer TakeBack Campaign, an effort by a consortium of thirteen environmental organizations.

## Farming computers is more profitable than growing rice.

Two member groups, the Basel Action Network and the Silicon Valley Toxics Coalition, say in a report that 80 percent of e-waste collected in the United States is exported to Asia.

The United States is using "hidden escape valves to export the crisis to developing countries of Asia," the report states. "The poor of the world," it adds, are forced to "bear a disproportionate share of the e-waste environmental burden. This current reality is the dirty little secret of the electronics industry."

"The real crime," says Jim Puckett of the Basel Action Network, "is the unwillingness of countries like the United States and Japan to take responsibility for preventing the global dumping of their own toxic waste."

Guiyu is a cyber desert. Desolate mountains of electronic trash are everywhere, as hundreds of trucks drive over burnt circuit boards, the intricate crunch audible from almost a mile away. Dogs with diseased eyes are chained to e-waste "farmhouses" of moldy concrete walls. Circuit boards are used to hole up corrugated iron shacks housing migrants right next to heaps of junk along the river. The streams running through the migrants' riverside tenements are a blinding, shiny silver due to mercury and other toxins. Private traders import millions of gallons of water to the town and sell it at a premium to residents.

"Even if the work would kill me, I'd continue," says He Ti Guang, a wire cutter in an e-waste factory downtown. "I have no choice. My family is poor, so I came here to earn money." A thirty-five-year-old migrant from Sichuan province, Guang has warts, burns, and rashes up and down his arms.

"This waste is too hot, and it burns. My skin itches all the time," he says. "I think the wires are toxic, but I don't know."

His wife works in a plastics e-waste factory, melting old wires, computer monitors, TVs, and cellphones to be used for plastic chairs and thermoses.

"I've had many health problems," Li Sheng Cui says. "My body is weak and my stomach hurts when I laugh." She cringes and blinks erratically. "Your tongue tastes like sugar, and your skin is itchy," she says, holding her finger in her mouth. "It's impossible to wear a white shirt. You wash it and it turns yellow."

China's e-waste crisis is a byproduct of its unequal development. "China's opening to international markets and capital has greatly exacerbated the divide between urban middle class wealth and the rural poor," says Yun Xien, a local environmental activist. "E-waste is just one profitable coping mechanism for rural China."

E-waste sweatshops often sit in secluded areas off the street. Inside are migrant workers, usually women, stripping wires, banging circuits, and disassembling broken motors. Workers say the average salary for sweatshop work is $3 to $4 per day for men, and about half that for women.

"The law has no effect here," says He Hai, who smuggled circuit boards to Guiyu as the e-waste boom took off. "Everyone here gets money from this kind of thing, so no one can afford to let it stop."

Hai says bribery is prevalent, as is intimidation. "Everything seems peaceful, but this place is very dangerous," he says. "The migrant workers fear the local people will beat them if they talk about it to anyone."

This is the underbelly of China's economic boom.

"The more developed areas won't do it," says Zhao Jun, who migrated to Guiyu twelve years ago as a teenager to work in e-waste. "This area was so poor, and it was hard to grow rice, so about a decade ago people began picking up rubbish to look for valuables. Gradually, they realized computer rubbish is better than other rubbish and started getting into e-waste. When I came, it was a one-story village with all dirt roads; now it's a city with big buildings and rich people."

Local residents got rich scouring the trash and brought in migrants to start scouring it for them. "The most dangerous and hardest jobs they give to the migrant workers," says Jun. "The locals who used to do the e-waste work are now wealthy e-waste bosses."

James Songqing is one such boss. His office is in a large building that makes up part of the new Guiyu skyline. He sits on his posh furniture next to a buddy holding a slingshot. Young women enter to pour them tea as Chinese soap operas play in the background.

Since my guide warned me that e-waste bosses want to keep all journalists out and would even kill me if they knew what I was doing, I pretend I'm interested in buying ten tons of bronze a month for a South African company.

"It is outside," Songqing says. On his front patio lie about two tons of untreated bronze in large white sacks. It sells for $1.50 a kilo, he says. "It takes me two weeks to produce twenty tons of the stuff."

By my calculations, his street-side sweatshop is making upwards of $30,000 per month in profit.

Hai does not approve of this trade. "It's in the interests of our country to stop e-waste," he says. "We should stop e-waste altogether because it is foreign countries' rubbish."

Sound computer recycling programs are available. But, given the volume of e-waste produced each year, domestic reuse and recycling is wishful thinking for the time being.

Computers are not built to be recycled, environmentalists say, and their dismantling is extremely dangerous, labor-intensive, and costly.

The Computer TakeBack Campaign seeks to pressure "consumer electronics manufacturers and brand owners to take full responsibility for the lifecycle of their products." The groups in the campaign call on consumers to use their buying power to promote greater corporate responsibility, computer recycling, and a reduction in hazardous e-waste.

Outside the United States, there have been some successes. In May of 2001, the European Union adopted a directive that requires producers of electronics to take financial responsibility for the recovery and recycling of e-waste and to phase out the use of hazardous materials.

But reforms are lagging in the United States. "Brand owners and manufacturers in the U.S. have dodged their responsibility for management of products at the end of their useful life, while public policy has failed to promote producer take back, clean design, and clean production," says the Computer TakeBack Campaign.

We head back to the river to thank Chang. He is meandering on top of crumbled, smoking circuit boards, in a burning pile of e-waste. Chang must work late. He competes with eight other migrants, and he has a month-old baby.

We try to ask him more about his life, but his tune has changed. He is tight-lipped, redder in the face, unyielding. He gets frustrated immediately and says he has to go.

"I don't care for these questions of health and responsibility," he says. "Life is better here because I can get more money."

He turns away from us, coughs a bit, and bikes home along the banks of the Lianjiang River.

BENJAMIN JOFFE-WALT is a freelance writer based in South Africa. Research for this article was supported by a grant from the Fund for Investigative Journalism, Inc.

*The Digital Divide*

# In Search of a PC for the People

**The race is on to serve "the next billion" in emerging markets. Whose low-cost model will win?**

Bruce Einhorn

In Silicon Valley, "the next billion" is shorthand for the vast potential market in the developing world, where few people have access to PCs. For Mark J. Beckford, it's almost an obsession. The 39-year-old Intel Corp. general manager has spent most of the past decade trying to create computers for that next billion. From his office in Shanghai, he oversees a team of about two dozen engineers in China, Brazil, Egypt, and India, all designing PCs suited to the needs and wallets of customers in emerging markets. "The next billion isn't going to come by pushing the same things," he says. "It requires new levels of affordability, access methods, ease of use, connectivity, and power."

These days lots of companies are trying to serve that same billion. Intel's biggest rival, Advanced Micro Devices Inc., is working on various possibilities, including a PC in India that sells for about $200. Taiwan's VIA Technologies Inc., the world's No. 3 designer of microprocessors, has launched a business group focusing on low-cost computers for emerging markets. Microsoft Corp. in late May introduced a low-cost solution. And Nicholas Negroponte, a professor at Massachusetts Institute of Technology, is leading a group called One Laptop Per Child, which aims to produce a machine for $140 or so by year end, and as little as $50 by 2010. "I think of digital access for kids as a human right," Negroponte said in an e-mail interview.

But as they target emerging markets, the world's info-tech powers are grappling with a host of difficult issues. How do you design a PC that's affordable to almost anyone? What traditional features do you ditch to do that? Will users in developing countries be satisfied with these computers, or will they resent the idea of getting dumbed-down machines? Do they want global brands, or are they happy to accept no-name alternatives?

## Leaner and Greener

Just about everybody agrees selling computers in the developing world is more complex than simply adding Mandarin, Hindi, or Arabic software to existing PCs. In many places, PCs must withstand desert heat and sand—and cope with frequent electricity outages. That requires more rugged designs that are also energy-efficient. "In emerging markets we see a huge appetite for PCs," says Richard Brown, a VIA vice-president who heads the new PC-1 business unit, set up early this year to sell computers in developing countries. "But they need to be smaller, cooler, quieter, and greener."

Microsoft, meanwhile, has come up not with computers, but with an innovative way to finance them. On May 22, the software giant announced FlexGo, software that keeps machines from working until users type in a number from a pre-paid card. The idea is that consumers in developing countries, who might not be able to shell out $500 or more in one go, can afford perhaps half the cost of a PC up front, then pay for the actual hours they use the machine via the cards. After a certain number of hours—and payments—the computer becomes the property of the consumer. In the developing world, computers are "simply out of reach for people who would like a PC in the home," says Will Poole, senior vice-president of Microsoft's Market Expansion Group. "What do we do to change the equation?"

Most companies are seeking to solve that equation through innovative design. For instance, Intel in March launched its "Community PC," targeted at Indian villages where those who can't afford computers of their own share a common machine. The Community PC, which costs about $550, has a filter to keep out dust, can run on a car battery when blackouts occur, and is equipped with a one-button "recover" feature in case of crashes. Also in March, Intel introduced a $250 to $350 miniaturized desktop computer (with the clunky name of Low Cost Full Featured PC); Mexican officials have ordered 400,000 for delivery by November. And the company in May revealed a prototype of a new notebook called the ClassMate PC that carries a price tag below $400.

Designing machines for developing countries can be taxing for engineers accustomed to building PCs from off-the-shelf, commodity parts. "Before, it was just cut and paste, follow the guidelines," says Kent Geeng, president of iDot Computers Inc.,

# Laptops for All

More low-cost computers are being developed for emerging markets

### INTEL

Has hardy "Community PCs" for India, systems for Net cafes in China, and the ClassMate, a $400 notebook for students.

### MICROSOFT

On May 22, the software giant announced a pay-as-you-go computer for low- and middle-income countries.

### AMD

Offers a PC in India with local partner HCL for around $200. Also sells the low-cost Personal Internet Communicator.

### VIA

This Taiwanese chipmaker is building PCs powered by car batteries or solar cells, with sand-resistant cases for use in Africa.

### One Laptop Per Child

Founded by Nicholas Negroponte of MIT's Media Lab, this nonprofit aims to build a laptop for $100 or less.

which designs VIA's low-cost PCs. To reach the target price of $230, his engineers had to start from scratch. "A cost-effective machine is much more difficult than doing the high end," says

Geeng. "It's like building a Nissan to drive at the same speed as a Porsche."

That's just what bothers some critics, who don't believe people in poor countries need to compute at Autobahn speeds. Stephen Dukker, who founded low-cost computing pioneer eMachines Inc. in 1998, now runs Seoul-based Ncomputing Ltd. His goal is to sell not PCs but "thin clients," diskless machines that work only if connected to a server. Since a single PC can run 10 of these devices, schools and libraries in impoverished areas could get computers in front of many more people far more cheaply than by buying actual PCs for everyone. Dukker's device—little more than a chip surrounded by plastic—costs just $70 or so. "Why are we trying to force people to use a computing technology that's not appropriate for them?" says Dukker.

## Do Third World users need to compute at Autobahn speeds?

PC alternatives, though, don't have a great track record. Oracle Corp. and Sun Microsystems Inc. tried to push thin clients in the late 1990s, without much success. Negroponte has attracted a lot of attention, but skeptics say that children—and their parents—may not really want a machine that cheap. "You have a low-cost device, but it's very limited," says Beckford's colleague, Intel Vice-President Bill M. Siu.

The real demand, says Microsoft's Poole, is for "a solid, midrange PC." With so many companies targeting emerging markets, there's a lot riding on the right answer.

With Jay Greene, in Seattle and Peter Burrows, in San Mateo, Calif.

## Article 36

# In Korea, a Boot Camp Cure for Web Obsession

MARTIN FACKLER

Mokcheon, South Korea—The compound—part boot camp, part rehab center—resembles programs around the world for troubled youths. Drill instructors drive young men through military-style obstacle courses, counselors lead group sessions, and there are even therapeutic workshops on pottery and drumming.

But these young people are not battling alcohol or drugs. Rather, they have severe cases of what many in this country believe is a new and potentially deadly addiction: cyberspace.

They come here, to the Jump Up Internet Rescue School, the first camp of its kind in South Korea and possibly the world, to be cured.

South Korea boasts of being the most wired nation on earth. In fact, perhaps no other country has so fully embraced the Internet. Ninety percent of homes connect to cheap, high-speed broadband, online gaming is a professional sport, and social life for the young revolves around the "PC bang," dim Internet parlors that sit on practically every street corner.

But such ready access to the Web has come at a price as legions of obsessed users find that they cannot tear themselves away from their computer screens.

Compulsive Internet use has been identified as a mental health issue in other countries, including the United States. However, it may be a particularly acute problem in South Korea because of the country's nearly universal Internet access.

It has become a national issue here in recent years, as users started dropping dead from exhaustion after playing online games for days on end. A growing number of students have skipped school to stay online, shockingly self-destructive behavior in this intensely competitive society.

Up to 30 percent of South Koreans under 18, or about 2.4 million people, are at risk of Internet addiction, said Ahn Dong-hyun, a child psychiatrist at Hanyang University in Seoul who just completed a three-year government-financed survey of the problem.

They spend at least two hours a day online, usually playing games or chatting. Of those, up to a quarter million probably show signs of actual addiction, like an inability to stop themselves from using computers, rising levels of tolerance that drive them to seek ever longer sessions online, and withdrawal symptoms like anger and craving when prevented from logging on.

To address the problem, the government has built a network of 140 Internet-addiction counseling centers, in addition to treatment programs at almost 100 hospitals and, most recently, the Internet Rescue camp, which started this summer. Researchers have developed a checklist for diagnosing the addiction and determining its severity, the K-Scale. (The K is for Korea.)

In September, South Korea held the first international symposium on Internet addiction.

"Korea has been most aggressive in embracing the Internet," said Koh Young-sam, head of the government-run Internet Addiction Counseling Center. "Now we have to lead in dealing with its consequences."

Though some health experts here and abroad question whether overuse of the Internet or computers in general is an addiction in the strict medical sense, many agree that obsessive computer use has become a growing problem in many countries.

Doctors in China and Taiwan have begun reporting similar disorders in their youth. In the United States, Dr. Jerald J. Block, a psychiatrist at Oregon Health and Science University, estimates that up to nine million Americans may be at risk for the disorder, which he calls pathological computer use. Only a handful of clinics in the United States specialize in treating it, he said.

"Korea is on the leading edge," Dr. Block said. "They are ahead in defining and researching the problem, and recognize as a society that they have a major issue."

The rescue camp, in a forested area about an hour south of Seoul, was created to treat the most severe cases. This year, the camp held its first two 12-day sessions, with 16 to 18 male participants each time. (South Korean researchers say an overwhelming majority of compulsive computer users are male.)

The camp is entirely paid for by the government, making it tuition-free. While it is too early to know whether the camp can wean youths from the Internet, it has been receiving four to five applications for each spot. To meet demand, camp administrators say they will double the number of sessions next year.

During a session, participants live at the camp, where they are denied computer use and allowed only one hour of cellphone calls a day, to prevent them from playing online games via the phone. They also follow a rigorous regimen of physical exercise and group activities, like horseback riding, aimed at

...ilding emotional connections to the real world and weakening ...ose with the virtual one.

"It is most important to provide them experience of a lifestyle ...ithout the Internet," said Lee Yun-hee, a counselor. "Young ...oreans don't know what this is like."

Initially, the camp had problems with participants sneaking ...way to go online, even during a 10-minute break before lunch, ...s. Lee said. Now, the campers are under constant surveil-...nce, including while asleep, and are kept busy with chores, ...ke washing their clothes and cleaning their rooms.

One participant, Lee Chang-hoon, 15, began using the com-...ater to pass the time while his parents were working and he ...as home alone. He said he quickly came to prefer the virtual ...orld, where he seemed to enjoy more success and popularity ...an in the real one.

He spent 17 hours a day online, mostly looking at Japanese ...mics and playing a combat role-playing game called Sudden ...ttack. He played all night, and skipped school two or three ...mes a week to catch up on sleep.

When his parents told him he had to go to school, he reacted ...olently. Desperate, his mother, Kim Soon-yeol, sent him to ...e camp.

"He didn't seem to be able to control himself," said Mrs. Kim, ... hairdresser. "He used to be so passionate about his favorite ...bjects" at school. "Now, he gives up easily and gets even more ...bsorbed in his games."

Her son was reluctant at first to give up his pastime.

"I don't have a problem," Chang-hoon said in an interview three days after starting the camp. "Seventeen hours a day online is fine." But later that day, he seemed to start changing his mind, if only slightly.

As a drill instructor barked orders, Chang-hoon and 17 other boys marched through a cold autumn rain to the obstacle course. Wet and shivering, Chang-hoon began climbing the first obstacle, a telephone pole with small metal rungs. At the top, he slowly stood up, legs quaking, arms outstretched for balance. Below, the other boys held a safety rope attached to a harness on his chest.

"Do you have anything to tell your mother?" the drill instructor shouted from below.

"No!" he yelled back.

"Tell your mother you love her!" ordered the instructor.

"I love you, my parents!" he replied.

"Then jump!" ordered the instructor. Chang-hoon squatted and leapt to a nearby trapeze, catching it in his hands.

"Fighting!" yelled the other boys, using the English word that in South Korea means the rough equivalent of "Don't give up!"

After Chang-hoon descended, he said, "That was better than games!"

Was it thrilling enough to wean him from the Internet?

"I'm not thinking about games now, so maybe this will help," he replied. "From now on, maybe I'll just spend five hours a day online."

# New Tech, Old Habits

**Despite world-class IT networks, Japanese and Korean workers are still chained to their desks.**

MOON IHLWAN AND KENJI HALL

Masanori Goto was in for a culture shock when he returned to Japan after a seven-year stint in New York. The 42-year-old public relations officer at cellular giant NTT DoCoMo logged many a late night at his Manhattan apartment, using his company laptop to communicate with colleagues 14 time zones away. Now back in Tokyo, Goto has a cell phone he can use to send quick e-mails after hours, but he must hole up at the office late into the night if he needs to do any serious work. The reason: His bosses haven't outfitted him with a portable computer. "I didn't realize that our people in Japan weren't using laptops," he says. "That was a surprise."

A few hundred miles to the west, in Seoul, Lee Seung Hwa also knows what it's like to spend long hours chained to her desk. The 33-year-old recently quit her job as an executive assistant at a carmaker because, among other complaints, her company didn't let lower-level employees log on from outside the office. "I could have done all the work from home, but managers thought I was working hard only if I stayed late," says Lee.

These days, information technology could easily free the likes of Goto and Lee. Korea and Japan are world leaders in broadband access, with connection speeds that put the U.S. to shame. And their wireless networks are state of the art, allowing supercharged Web surfing from mobile phones and other handhelds, whether at a café, in the subway, or on the highway. But when it comes to taking advantage of connectivity for business, Americans are way ahead.

For a study in contrasts, consider the daily commute. American trains are packed with business people furiously tapping their BlackBerrys or Treos, squeezing a few extra minutes into their work days. In Tokyo or Seoul, commuters stare intently at their cell phone screens, but they're usually playing games, watching video clips, or sending Hello Kitty icons to friends. And while advertising for U.S. cellular companies emphasizes how data services can make users more productive at work, Asian carriers tend to stress the fun factor.

Why? Corporate culture in the Far East remains deeply conservative, and most businesses have been slow to mine the opportunities offered by newfangled communications technologies. One big reason is the premium placed on face time at the office. Junior employees are reluctant to leave work before the boss does for fear of looking like slackers. Also, Confucianism places greater stock on group effort and consensus-building than on individual initiative. So members of a team all feel they must stick around if there is a task to complete. "To reap full benefits from IT investment, companies must change the way they do business," says Lee In Chan, vice-president at SK Research Institute, a Seoul management think tank funded by cellular carrier SK Telecom. "What's most needed in Korea and Japan is an overhaul in business processes and practices."

## Time, Not Task

In these countries, if you're not in the office, your boss simply assumes you're not working. It doesn't help that a lack of clear job definitions and performance metrics makes it difficult for managers to assess the productivity of employees working off site. "Performance reviews and judgments are still largely time-oriented here, rather than task-oriented as in the West," says Chi Bum Coo, a Seoul-based executive partner at business consulting firm Accenture Ltd.

Even tech companies in the region often refuse to untether workers from the office. Camera-maker Canon Inc. for instance dispensed with flextime four years ago after employees said it interfered with communications, while Samsung stresses that person-to-person contact is far more effective than e-mail. In Japan, many companies say they are reluctant to send workers home with their laptops for fear that proprietary information might go astray. Canon publishes a 33-page code of conduct that includes a cautionary tale of a worker who loses a notebook computer loaded with sensitive customer data on his commute. At Korean companies SK Telecom, Samsung Electronics, and LG Electronics, employees must obtain permission before they can carry their laptops out of the office. Even then, they often are barred from full access to files from work. And while just about everyone has a cell phone that can display Web pages or send e-mails, getting into corporate networks is complicated and unwieldy.

# Bound by Tradition

Despite fast wireless and broadband networks, Korean and Japanese companies aren't getting the most out of technology. Here's why:

**FUN FACTOR** Smart phones are viewed more as toys than tools.

**FACE TIME** If you're not in the office, no one thinks you're working.

**INFO-FEAR** Companies worry that laptop-toting commuters could misplace sensitive data.

The result: Korean and Japanese white-collar workers clock long days at the office, often toiling till midnight and coming in on weekends. "In my dictionary there's no such thing as work/life balance as far as weekdays are concerned," says a Samsung Electronics senior manager who declined to be named. Tom Coyner, a consultant and author of *Mastering Business in Korea: A Practical Guide,* says: "Even your wife would think you were not regarded as an important player in the office if you came home at five or six."

These factors may be preventing Japan and Korea from wringing more productivity out of their massive IT investments. Both countries place high on lists of global innovators. For instance, Japan and Korea rank No. 2 and No. 6, respectively, out of 30 nations in terms of spending on research and development, according to the Organization for Economic Cooperation and Development. And the Geneva-based World Intellectual Property Organization says Japan was second and Korea fourth in international patent filings. But when it comes to the productivity of IT users, both countries badly lag the U.S., says Kazuyuki Motohashi, a University of Tokyo professor who is an expert on technological innovation. "Companies in Japan and Korea haven't made the structural changes to get the most out of new technologies," he says.

Still, a new generation of managers rising through the ranks may speed the transformation. These workers are tech-savvy and often more individualistic, having come from smaller families. Already, some companies are tinkering with changes to meet their needs. SK Telecom abolished titles for all midlevel managers in the hopes that this would spur workers to take greater initiative. Japan's NEC Corp. is experimenting with telecommuting for 2,000 of its 148,000 employees. And in Korea, CJ 39 Shopping, a cable-TV shopping channel, is letting 10% of its call-center employees work from home.

Foreign companies are doing their bit to shake things up. In Korea, IBM has outfitted all of its 2,600 employees with laptops and actively encourages them to work off site. The system, which was first introduced in 1995, has allowed the company to cut back on office space and reap savings of $2.3 million a year. One beneficiary is Kim Yoon Hee. The procurement specialist reports to the office only on Tuesdays and Thursdays. On other days, calls to her office phone are automatically routed to her laptop, so she can work from home. "It would have been difficult for me to remain employed had it not been for the telecommuting system," says Kim, 35, who quit a job at a big Korean company seven years ago because late nights at the office kept her away from her infant daughter. "This certainly makes me more loyal to my company."

# UNIT 8

# The Frontier of Computing

## Unit Selections

38. **A Nascent Robotics Culture: New Complicities for Companionship,** Sherry Turkle
39. **Toward Nature-Inspired Computing,** Jiming Liu and K. C. Tsui
40. **Google and the Wisdom of Clouds,** Stephen Baker

## Key Points to Consider

- 2003 marked the 30th anniversary of the publication of an essay entitled "Animals, Men and Morals" by Peter Singer in the *New York Review of Books.* This essay is often credited with beginning the animal rights movement. Singer argues that because animals have feelings, they can suffer. Because they can suffer, they have interests. Because they have interests, it is unethical to conduct experiments on them. Suppose scientists succeed in developing machines that feel pain and fear. What obligations will we have toward them? If this is difficult to imagine, watch the movie *Blade Runner* with Harrison Ford. What do you think now?

- The overview to this unit says that the dollar value of the output of the meat and poultry industries exceeds the dollar value of the output of the computer industry. The overview mentions one reason why we hear so much more about software than chickens. Can you think of others?

- Suppose you were provided with a robot whose task is to filter spam from your e-mail. Now suppose you are provided with a real secretary to do the same task. Both of these assistants will make judgment calls. That is, based on what you have told them, each will make best guesses as to whether the e-mail is spam or not. How do you feel about your robot making the occasional error? How do you feel about your secretary making a mistake?

- Professor Turkle poses a disturbing question that is quoted in the To The Reader section of this book: "Are you really you if you have a baboon's heart inside, had your face resculpted by Brazil's finest plastic surgeons, and are taking Zoloft to give you a competitive edge?" Are you?

## Student Web Site
www.mhcls.com

## Internet References

**Introduction to Artificial Intelligence (AI)**
*http://www-formal.stanford.edu/jmc/aiintro/aiintro.html*
**Kasparov vs. Deep Blue: The Rematch**
*http://www.chess.ibm.com/home/html/b.html*
**PHP-Nuke Powered Site: International Society for Artificial Life**
*http://alife.org/*

According to the U.S. Census Bureau statistics not long ago, the output of the meat and poultry industry was worth more than the output of the computer and software industries. Though this is not exactly a fair comparison—computers are used to build still other products—it does get at something significant about computers: they figure more importantly in our imaginations than they do in the economy. Why is this? Part of the answer has to do with who forms opinions in developed nations. The computer is an indispensable tool for people who staff the magazine, newspaper, publishing, and education sectors. If meat packers were the opinion makers, we might get a different sense of what is important. Recall "Five Things We Need to Know about Technological Change." Postman says that "Embedded in every technology there is a powerful idea . . . To a person with a computer, everything looks like data."

We can concede Postman's point but still insist that there is something special about computing. Before computers became a household appliance, it was common for programmers and users alike to attribute human-like properties to them. Joseph Weizenbaum, developer of Eliza in the 1970s, a program that simulated a Rogerian psychotherapist, became a severe critic of certain kinds of computing research, in part because he noticed that staff in his lab had begun to arrive early to ask advice from the program. In 1956, a group of mathematicians interested in computing gathered at Dartmouth College and coined the term "Artificial Intelligence." AI, whose goal is to build into machines something that we can recognize as intelligent behavior, has become perhaps the best-known and most criticized area of computer science. Since intelligent behavior, like the ability to read and form arguments, is often thought to be the defining characteristic of humankind (we call ourselves "homo sapiens," after all), machines that might exhibit intelligent behavior have occupied the dreams and nightmares of western culture for hundreds of years.

All of our ambiguous feelings about technology are congealed in robots. The term itself is surprisingly venerable, having been invented by the Czech playwright Karel Copek in 1921. They can be loveable like R2D2 from *Star Wars* or Robbie from *The Forbidden Planet* of a generation earlier. They can be forbidding but loyal, like Gort from *The Day the Earth Stood Still.* They can even be outfitted with logical safety mechanisms that render them harmless to humans. This last, an invention of Isaac Asimov in *I, Robot,* is a good thing, too, since so many of our robotic imaginings look like *The Terminator.* Sherry Turkle of MIT has been studying the relationship between humans and their machines for twenty years. In "A Nascent Robotics Culture," she asks the jarring question, "What is a robot kind of love?"

As mentioned in the overview to Unit 7, the development of public-key cryptography in the late seventies was a significant achievement in computer science. Since classical times, cryptographers have grappled with a serious weak point in any cryptographic system. Suppose Alice encrypts a message and sends it to Bob. She also needs to send Bob instructions, known as the key, telling him how to decrypt the message. This is a problem, since the key can be intercepted. In the late seventies, a Stanford engineer and an itinerant mathematician developed a mechanism that avoids it, called public-key cryptography. If all

© Corbis/PictureQuest

this seems a little obscure, look at your browser the next time you purchase something on-line. The web address should begin with *http,* indicating that it is making use of public-key techniques to encrypt your credit card number.

Researchers from around the world met in Atlanta this past summer for GECCO, 2008, the Genetic and Evolutionary Computing Conference. In the mid-seventies, John Holland at the University of Michigan proposed a mechanism for problem solving based loosely on the idea of Darwinian natural selection. Since that time, researchers have use genetic algorithms, as Holland called them, to solve problems too difficult to be solved using conventional computing techniques. The genetic algorithm is one of several computing techniques based on a "paradigm that draws on the principles of self-organization of complex systems." The article, "Toward Nature-Inspired Computing," is an excellent introduction.

Fifteen years ago, the study of database systems was an important but unheralded part of computer science. For all its importance, how an insurance company organizes its data could seem a little dull. But that was before Google began to tame the chaos of the Internet through sophisticated storage and retrieval techniques and, above all, through clusters of computers it calls "the cloud." See "Google and the Wisdom of Clouds," for a glimpse at how one creative researcher at Google is teaching researchers around the world to extract patterns from large collections of data.

Robots, quantum cryptography, digital memories; the articles in this unit have ranged widely but with this common theme: the technologies described are neither fully-formed nor have their impact on society been large. Computing history is filled with bad predictions. Perhaps the most spectacularly wrong is widely attributed to Thomas Watson, head of IBM, who in 1943 is supposed to have said, "I think there is a world market for maybe five computers." But there have been many, many others. Will robots get no further than furbies? Will the distance limitations of quantum cryptography not be overcome? Do we really want to record everything we've thought and everyplace we've been? It's hard to know. But no one wants to be the next Thomas Watson.

# Article 38

# A Nascent Robotics Culture
## New Complicities for Companionship

Encounters with humanoid robots are new to the everyday experience of children and adults. Yet, increasingly, they are finding their place. This has occurred largely through the introduction of a class of interactive toys (including Furbies, AIBOs, and My Real Babies) that I call "relational artifacts." Here, I report on several years of fieldwork with commercial relational artifacts (as well as with the MIT AI Laboratory's Kismet and Cog). It suggests that even these relatively primitive robots have been accepted as companionate objects and are changing the terms by which people judge the "appropriateness" of machine relationships. In these relationships, robots serve as powerful objects of psychological projection and philosophical evocation in ways that are forging a nascent robotics culture.

SHERRY TURKLE

## Introduction

The designers of computational objects have traditionally focused on how these objects might extend and/or perfect human cognitive powers. But computational objects do not simply do things *for* us, they do things *to* us as people, to our ways of being the world, to our ways of seeing ourselves and others (Turkle 2005[1984], 1995). Increasingly, technology also puts itself into a position to do things *with* us, particularly with the introduction of "relational artifacts," here defined as technologies that have "states of mind" and where encounters with them are enriched through understanding these inner states (Turkle 2004a, 2004b). Otherwise described as "sociable machines (Breazeal 2000, 2002, Breazeal and Scasselati 1999, 2000, Kidd 2004), the term relational artifact evokes the psychoanalytic tradition with its emphasis on the meaning of the person/machine encounter.

In the late 1970s and early 1980s, children's style of programming reflected their personality and cognitive style. And computational objects such as Merlin, Simon, and Speak and Spell provoked questions about the quality of aliveness and about what is special about being a person. (Turkle 2005[1984]) Twenty years later, children and seniors confronting relational artifacts as simple as Furbies, AIBOs and My Real Babies (Turkle 2004a) or as complex as the robots Kismet and Cog (Turkle et al. 2004) were similarly differentiated in their style of approach and similarly provoked to ask fundamental questions about the objects' natures.

Children approach a Furby or a My Real Baby and explore what it means to think of these creatures as alive or "sort of alive"; elders in a nursing home play with the robot Paro and grapple with how to characterize this creature that presents itself as a baby seal (Taggart, W. et al. 2005, Shibata 1999, 2005). They move from inquiries such as "Does it swim?" and "Does it eat?" to "Is it alive?" and "Can it love?"[1]

These similarities across the decades are not surprising. Encounters with novel computational objects present people with category-challenging experiences. The objects are liminal, betwixt and between, provoking new thought. (Turner 1969; Bowker and Star 1999). However, there are significant differences between current responses to relational artifacts and earlier encounters with computation. Children first confronting computer toys in the late 1970s and early 1980s were compelled to classification. Faced with relational artifacts, children's questions about classification are enmeshed in a new desire to *nurture and be nurtured by* the artifacts rather than simply categorize them; in their dialogue with relational artifacts, children's focus shifts from cognition to affect, from game playing to fantasies of mutual connection. In the case of relational artifacts for children and the elderly, nurturance is the new "killer app." We attach to what we nurture (Turkle 2004, 2005b).

## We Attach to What We Nurture

In *Computer Power and Human Reason*, Joseph Weizenbaum wrote about his experiences with his invention, ELIZA, a computer program that seemed to serve as self object as it engaged people in a dialogue similar to that of a Rogerian psychotherapist (1976). It mirrored one's thoughts; it was always supportive. To the comment: "My mother is making me angry," the program might respond, "Tell me more about your mother," or "Why do you feel so negatively about your mother." Weizenbaum was disturbed that his students, fully knowing that they were talking with a computer program, wanted to chat with it, indeed, wanted to be alone with it. Weizenbaum was my colleague at MIT at the time; we taught courses together on computers and society. And at the time that his book came out, I felt moved to reassure him. ELIZA seemed to me like a Rorschach through which people expressed themselves. They became involved with ELIZA, but the spirit was "as if." The gap between program and person was vast. People bridged it with attribution and desire. They thought: "I will talk to this program 'as if' it were a person; I will vent, I will rage, I will get things off my chest." At the time, ELIZA seemed to me no more threatening than an interactive diary. Now, thirty years later, I ask myself if I had underestimated the quality of the connection.

A newer technology has created computational creatures that evoke a sense of mutual relating. The people who meet relational artifacts feel a desire to nurture them. And with nurturance comes the fantasy of reciprocation. They wanted the creatures to care about them in return. Very little about these relationships seemed to be experienced "as if." The experience of "as if" had morphed into one of treating robots "as though." The story of computers and their evocation of life had come to a new place.

Children have always anthropomorphized the dolls in their nurseries. It is important to note a difference in what can occur with relational artifacts. In the past, the power of objects to "play house" or "play cowboys" with a child has been tied to the ways in which they enabled the child to project meanings onto them. They were stable "transitional objects." (Winnicott 1971) The doll or the teddy bear presented an unchanging and passive presence. But today's relational artifacts take a decidedly more active stance. With them, children's expectations that their dolls want to be hugged, dressed, or lulled to sleep don't only come from the child's projection of fantasy or desire onto inert playthings, but from such things as the digital dolls' crying inconsolably or even saying: "Hug me!" or "It's time for me to get dressed for school!" *In the move from traditional transitional objects to contemporary rela-*

*tional artifacts, the psychology of projection gives way to a relational psychology, a psychology of engagement. Yet, old habits of projection remain: robotic creatures become enhanced in their capacities to enact scenarios in which robots are Rorschachs, projective screens for individual concerns.*

From the perspective of several decades of observing people relating to computational creatures, I see an evolution of sensibilities.

- Through the 1980s, people became deeply involved with computational objects—even the early computer toys became objects for profound projection and engagement. Yet, when faced with the issue of the objects' affective possibilities, a modal response might be summed up as "Simulated thinking may be thinking; simulated feeling is never feeling. Simulated love is never love."
- Through the 1990s, the development of a "culture of simulation" brought the notion of simulation (largely through participation in intensive game spaces) into the everyday. The range and possibilities of simulation became known to large numbers of people, particularly young people.
- By the late 1990s, the image of the robot was changing in the culture. A robotics presence was developing into a robotics culture increasingly shaped by the possibility if not the reality of robots in the form of relational artifacts. Alongside a tool model, people are learning about a notion of cyber-companionship. Acceptance of this notion requires a revisiting of old notions of simulation to make way for a kind of companionship that feels appropriate to a robot/person relationship.

## The Evolution of Sensibilities: Two Moments

A first moment: I take my fourteen-year-old daughter to the Darwin exhibit at the American Museum of Natural History. The exhibit documents Darwin's life and thought, and with a somewhat defensive tone (in light of current challenges to evolution by proponents of intelligent design), presents the theory of evolution as the central truth that underpins contemporary biology. The Darwin exhibit wants to convince and it wants to please. At the entrance to the exhibit is a turtle from the Galapagos Islands, a seminal object in the development of evolutionary theory. The turtle rests in its cage, utterly still. "They could have used a robot," comments my daughter. She considers it a shame to bring the turtle all this way and put it in a cage for a performance that draws so little on the turtle's "aliveness." I am startled by her comments, both solicitous of the imprisoned turtle because it is alive and unconcerned about its authenticity. The museum has been advertising these turtles as wonders, curiosities, marvels—among the plastic models of life at the museum, here is the life that Darwin saw. I begin to talk with others at the exhibit, parents and children. It is Thanksgiving weekend. The line is long, the crowd frozen in place. My question, "Do you care that the turtle is alive?" is welcome diversion. A ten-year-old girl would prefer a robot turtle because aliveness comes with aesthetic inconvenience: "its water looks dirty. Gross." More usually, votes for the robots echo my daughter's sentiment that in this setting, aliveness doesn't seem worth the trouble. A twelve-year-old girl opines: "For what the turtles do, you didn't have to have the live ones." Her father looks at her, uncomprehending: "But the point is that they are real, that's the whole point."

The Darwin exhibit gives authenticity major play: on display are the actual magnifying glass that Darwin used, the actual notebooks in which he recorded his observations, indeed, the very notebook in which he wrote the famous sentences that first described his theory of evolution *But in the children's reactions to the inert but alive Galapagos turtle, the idea of the "original" is in crisis.* I recall my daughter's reaction when she was seven to a boat ride in the postcard blue Mediterranean. Already an expert in the world of simulated fish tanks, she saw a creature in the water, pointed to it excitedly and said: "Look mommy, a jellyfish! It looks so realistic!" When I told this story to a friend who was a research scientist at the Walt Disney Company, he was not surprised. When Animal Kingdom opened in Orlando, populated by "real," that is, biological animals, its first visitors complained that these animals were not as "realistic" as the animatronic creatures in Disney World, just across the road. The robotic crocodiles slapped their tails, rolled their eyes, in sum, displayed "essence of crocodile" behavior. The biological crocodiles, like the Galapagos turtle, pretty much kept to themselves. What is the gold standard here?

I have written that now, in our culture of simulation, the notion of authenticity is for us what sex was to the Victorians—"threat and obsession, taboo and fascination" (Turkle, 2005[1984]). I have lived with this idea for many years, yet at the museum, I find the children's position strangely unsettling. For them, in this context, aliveness seems to have no intrinsic value. Rather, it is useful only if needed for a specific purpose. "If you put in a robot instead of the live turtle, do you think people should be told that the turtle is not alive?" I ask. Not really, say several of the children. Data on "aliveness" can be shared on

a "need to know" basis, for a purpose. But what *are* the purposes of living things? When do we need to know if something is alive?

A second moment: an older woman, 72, in a nursing home outside of Boston is sad. Her son has broken off his relationship with her. Her nursing home is part of a study I am conducting on robotics for the elderly. I am recording her reactions as she sits with the robot Paro, a seal-like creature, advertised as the first "therapeutic robot" for its ostensibly positive effects on the ill, the elderly, and the emotionally troubled. Paro is able to make eye contact through sensing the direction of a human voice, is sensitive to touch, and has "states of mind" that are affected by how it is treated—for example, it can sense if it is being stroked gently or with some aggressivity. In this session with Paro, the woman, depressed because of her son's abandonment, comes to believe that the robot is depressed as well. She turns to Paro, strokes him and says: "Yes, you're sad, aren't you. It's tough out there. Yes, it's hard." And then she pets the robot once again, attempting to provide it with comfort. And in so doing, she tries to comfort herself.

Psychoanalytically trained, I believe that this kind of moment, if it happens between people, has profound therapeutic potential. What are we to make of this transaction as it unfolds between a depressed woman and a robot? When I talk to others about the old woman's encounter with Paro, their first associations are usually to their pets and the solace they provide. The comparison sharpens the questions about Paro and the quality of the relationships people have with it. I do not know if the projection of understanding onto pets is "authentic." That is, I do not know whether a pet could feel or smell or intuit some understanding of what it might mean to be with an old woman whose son has chosen not to see her anymore. What I do know is that Paro has understood nothing. Like other "relational artifacts" its ability to inspire relationship is not based on its intelligence or consciousness, but on the capacity to push certain "Darwinian" buttons in people (making eye contact, for example) that cause people to respond *as though* they were in relationship. For me, relational artifacts are the new uncanny in our computer culture, as Freud (1960) put it, "the long familiar taking a form that is strangely unfamiliar."

Confrontation with the uncanny provokes new reflection. Do plans to provide relational robots to children and the elderly make us less likely to look for other solutions for their care? If our experience with relational artifacts is based on a fundamentally deceitful interchange (artifacts' ability to persuade us that they know and care about our existence) can it be good for us? Or might it be good for us in the "feel good" sense, but bad for us in our lives as moral beings? The answers to such questions are not dependent on what computers can do today or what they are likely to be able to do in the future. These questions ask what *we* will be like, what kind of people are *we* becoming as we develop increasingly intimate relationships with machines.

# Rorschach and Evocation

We can get some first answers by looking at the relationship of people—here I describe fieldwork with children and seniors—with these new intimate machines. In these relationships it is clear that the distinction between people using robots for projection of self (as Rorschach) and using robots as philosophically evocative objects, is only heuristic. They work together: children and seniors develop philosophical positions that are inseparable from their emotional needs. Affect and cognition work together in the subjective response to relational technologies. This is dramatized by a series of case studies, first of children, then of seniors, in which the "Rorschach effect" and the "evocative object effect" are entwined.[2]

## *Case Studies of Children*

I begin with a child, Orelia, ten, whose response to the robot AIBO serves as commentary on her relationship to her mother, a self-absorbed woman who during her several sessions with her daughter and the robot does not touch, speak to, or make eye contact with her daughter. One might say that Orelia's mother acts robotically and the daughter's response is to emphasize the importance and irreducibility of the human heart. In a life characterized by maternal chill, Orelia stressed warmth and intuition as ultimate human values.

### Orelia: Keeping a Robot in Its Place

I met Orelia at a private Boston-area middle school where we were holding group sessions of fifth graders with a range of robotic toys. Orelia received an AIBO to take home; she kept a robot "diary." We met several times with Orelia and her parents in their Charlestown home. (Turkle 2004a)

Orelia is bright and articulate and tells us that her favorite hobby is reading. She makes determined distinctions between robots and biological beings. "AIBO is not alive like a real pet; it does not breathe." There is no question in her mind that she would choose a real dog over an AIBO. She believes that AIBO can love but only because "it is programmed to." She continues: "If [robots] love, then it's artificial love. [And] if it's an artificial love, then there really isn't anything true . . . I'm sure it would be

programmed to [show that it likes you], you know, the computer inside of it telling it to show artificial love, but it doesn't love you."

Orelia is sure that she could never love an AIBO. "They [robots] won't love you back if you love them." In order to love an AIBO, Orelia says it would need "a brain and a heart." Orelia feels that it is not worth investing in something that does not have the capacity to love back, a construction that is perhaps as much about the robot as about her relationship with her mother.

Orelia's brother Jake, nine, the baby of the family, is more favored in his mother's eyes. Unlike his sister, Jake assumes that AIBO has feelings. Orelia speaks to the researchers *about* AIBO; Jake addresses AIBO directly. He wants to stay on AIBO's good side, asking, "Will he get mad if you pick him up?" When Jake's style of addressing AIBO reveals that Jake finds the robot's affective states genuine, Orelia corrects her brother sharply: "It [AIBO] would just be mad at you because it's programmed to know 'if I don't get the ball, I'll be mad.'" The fact that AIBO is programmed to show emotions make these artificial and not to be trusted.

Orelia expands on real versus programmed emotion:

A dog, it would actually feel sorry for you. It would have sympathy, but AIBO, it's artificial. I read a book called *The Wrinkle in Time,* where everyone was programmed by this thing called "It." And all the people were completely on routine. They just did the same thing over and over. I think it'd be the same thing with the [artificial] dog. The dog wouldn't be able to do anything else.

For Orelia, only living beings have real thoughts and emotions:

With a real dog if you become great friends with it, it really loves you, you know, it truly . . . has a brain, and you know somewhere in the dog's brain, it loves you, and this one [AIBO], it's just somewhere on a computer disk . . . If a real dog dies, you know, they have memories, a real dog would have memories of times, and stuff that you did with him or her, but this one [AIBO] doesn't have a brain, so it can't.

Orelia wants the kind of love that only a living creature can provide. She fears the ability of any creature to behave 'as if' it could love. She denies a chilly emotional reality by attributing qualities of intuition, transparency, and connectedness to all people and animals. A philosophical position about robots is linked to an experience of the machine-like equalities of which people are capable, a good example of the interdependence of philosophical position and psychological motivation.

# Melanie: Yearning to Nurture a Robotic Companion

The quality of a child's relationship with a parent does not determine a *particular* relationship to robotic companions. Rather, feelings about robots can represent different strategies for dealing with one's parents, and perhaps for working through difficulties with them. This is illustrated by the contrast between Orelia and ten-year-old Melanie. Melanie, like Orelia, had sessions with AIBO and My Real Baby at school and was given both to play with at home. In Melanie's case, feelings that she did not have enough of her parent's attention led her to want to nurture a robotic creature. Melanie was able to feel more loved by loving another; the My Real Baby and AIBO were "creature enough" for this purpose.

Melanie is soft-spoken, intelligent, and well mannered. Both of her parents have busy professional lives; Melanie is largely taken care of by nannies and baby-sitters. With sadness, she says that what she misses most is spending time with her father. She speaks of him throughout her interviews and play sessions. Nurturing the robots enables her to work through feelings that her parents, and her father in particular, are not providing her with the attention she desires.

Melanie believes that AIBO and My Real Baby are sentient and have emotions. She thinks that when we brought the robotic dog and doll to her school "they were probably confused about who their mommies and daddies were because they were being handled by so many different people." She thinks that AIBO probably does not know that he is at her particular school because the school is strange to him, but "almost certainly does knows that he is outside of MIT and visiting another school." She sees her role with the robots as straightforward; it is maternal.

One of Melanie's third-grade classmates is aggressive with My Real Baby and treats the doll like an object to explore (poking the doll's eyes, pinching its skin to test its "rubberness," and putting her fingers roughly inside its mouth). Observing this behavior, Melanie comes over to rescue the doll. She takes it in her arms and proceeds to play with it as though it were a baby, holding it close, whispering to it, caressing its face. Speaking of the My Real Baby doll that she is about to take home, Melanie says, "I think that if I'm the first one to interact with her then maybe if she goes home with another person [another study participant] she'll cry a lot . . . because she doesn't know, doesn't think that this person is its Mama." For Melanie, My Real Baby's aliveness is dependent on its animation and relational properties. Its lack of biology is not in play. Melanie understands that My Real Baby is a machine. This is clear in her description of its possible "death."

Hum, if his batteries run out, maybe [it could die]. I think it's electric. So, if it falls and breaks, then it would die, but if people could repair it, then I'm not really sure. [I]f it falls and like totally shatters I don't think they could fix it, then it would die, but if it falls and one of its ear falls off, they would probably fix that.

Melanie combines a mechanical view of My Real Baby with confidence that it deserves to have her motherly love. At home, Melanie has AIBO and My Real Baby sleep near her bed and believes they will be happiest on a silk pillow. She names My Real Baby after her three-year old cousin Sophie. "I named her like my cousin . . . because she [My Real Baby] was sort of demanding and said most of the things that Sophie does." She analogies the AIBO to her dog, Nelly. When AIBO malfunctions, Melanie does not experience it as broken, but as behaving in ways that remind her of Nelly. In the following exchange that takes place at MIT, AIBO makes a loud, mechanical, wheezing sound and its walking becomes increasingly wobbly. Finally AIBO falls several times and then finally is still. Melanie gently picks up the limp AIBO and holds it close, petting it softly. At home, she and a friend treat it like a sick animal that needs to be rescued. They give it "veterinary care."

In thinking about relational artifacts such as Furbys, AIBOs, My Real Babies, and Paros, the question is posed: how these objects differ from "traditional" (non-computational) toys, teddy bears, and Raggedy-Ann dolls. Melanie, unbidden, speaks directly to this issue. With other dolls, she feels that she is "pretending." With My Real Baby, she feels that she is really the dolls's mother: "[I feel] like I'm her real mom. I bet if I really tried, she could learn another word. Maybe Da-da. Hopefully if I said it a lot, she would pick up. It's sort of like a real baby, where you wouldn't want to set a bad example."

For Melanie, not only does My Real Baby have feelings, Melanie sees it as capable of complex, mixed emotions. "It's got similar to human feelings, because she can really tell the differences between things, and she's happy a lot. She gets happy, and she gets sad, and mad, and excited. I think right now she's excited and happy at the same time."

Our relationship, it grows bigger. Maybe when I first started playing with her she didn't really know me so she wasn't making as much of these noises, but now that she's played with me a lot more she really knows me and is a lot more outgoing. Same with AIBO.

When her several weeks with AIBO and My Real Baby come to an end, Melanie is sad to return them. Before leaving them with us, she opens the box in which they are housed and gives them an emotional good bye. She hugs each one separately, tells them that she will miss them very much but that she knows we [the researchers] will take good care of them. Melanie is concerned that the toys will forget her, especially if they spend a lot of time with other families.

Melanie's relationship with the AIBO and My Real Baby illustrates their projective qualities: she nurtures them because getting enough nurturance is an issue for her. But in providing nurturance to the robots, Melanie provided it to herself as well (and in a way that felt more authentic than developing a relationship with a "traditional" doll). In another case, a seriously ill child was able to use relational robots to speak more easily in his own voice.

## Jimmy: From Rorschach to Relationship

Jimmy, small, pale, and thin, is just completing first grade. He has a congenital illness that causes him to spend much time in hospitals. During our sessions with AIBO and My Real Baby he sometimes runs out of energy to continue talking. Jimmy comes to our study with a long history of playing computer games. His favorite is Roller Coaster Tycoon. Many children play the game to create the wildest roller coasters possible; Jimmy plays the game to maximize the maintenance and staffing of his coasters so that the game gives him awards for the safest park. Jimmy's favorite toys are Beanie Babies. Jimmy participates in our study with his twelve-year-old brother, Tristan.

Jimmy approaches AIBO and My Real Baby as objects with consciousness and feelings. When AIBO slams into the red siding that defines his game space, Jimmy interprets his actions as "scratching a door, wanting to go in . . . I think it's probably doing that because it wants to go through the door . . . Because he hasn't been in there yet." Jimmy thinks that AIBO has similar feelings toward him as his biological dog, Sam. He says that AIBO would miss him when he goes to school and would want to jump in to the car with him. In contrast, Jimmy does not believe that his Beanie Babies, the stuffed animal toys, have feelings or 'aliveness,' or miss him when he is at school. Jimmy tells us that other relational artifacts like Furbies 'really do' learn and are the same 'kind of alive' as AIBO.

During several sessions with AIBO, Jimmy talks about AIBO as a super dog that show up his own dog as a limited creature. Jimmy says: "AIBO is probably as smart as Sam and at least he isn't as scared as my dog [is]." When we ask Jimmy if there are things that his dog can do that AIBO can't do, Jimmy answers not in terms of his dog's strengths but in terms of his deficiencies: "There are some things that *Sam can't do and AIBO can.* Sam can't fetch a ball. AIBO can. And Sam definitely can't kick a ball." On several other occasions, when AIBO completed a trick, Jimmy commented "My dog couldn't do that!" AIBO is the "better" dog. AIBO is immortal, invincible. AIBO cannot get sick or die. In sum, AIBO represents what Jimmy wants to be.

During Jimmy's play sessions at MIT, he forms a strong bond with AIBO. Jimmy tells us that he would probably miss AIBO as much as Sam if either of them died. As we talk about the possibility of AIBO dying, Jimmy explains that he believes AIBO could die if he ran out of power. Jimmy wants to protect AIBO by taking him home.

If you turn him off he dies, well, he falls asleep or something . . . He'll probably be in my room most of the time. And I'm probably going to keep him downstairs so he doesn't fall down the stairs. Because he probably, in a sense he would die if he fell down the stairs. Because he could break. And. Well, he could break and he also could . . . probably or if he broke he'd probably . . . he'd die like.

Jimmy's concerns about his vulnerable health are expressed with AIBO in several ways. Sometimes he thinks the dog is vulnerable, but Jimmy thinks he could protect him. Sometimes he thinks the dog is invulnerable, a super-hero dog in relation to his frail biological counterpart. He tests AIBO's strength in order to feel reassured.

Jimmy "knows" that AIBO does not have a real brain and a heart, but sees AIBO as a mechanical kind of alive, where it can function as if it had a heart and a brain. For Jimmy, AIBO is "alive in a way," because he can "move around" and "[H]e's also got feelings. He shows . . . he's got three eyes on him, mad, happy, and sad. And well, that's how he's alive." As evidence of AIBO's emotions, Jimmy points to the robot's lights: "When he's mad, then they're red. [And when they are green] he's happy."

Jimmy has moments of intense physical vulnerability, sometimes during our sessions. His description of how AIBO can strengthen himself is poignant. "Well, when he's charging that means, well he's kind of sleepy when he's charging but when he's awake he remembers things more. And probably he remembered my hand because I kept on poking in front of his face so he can see it. And he's probably looking for me."

AIBO recharging reassures Jimmy by providing him with a model of an object that can resist death. If AIBO can be alive through wires and a battery then this leaves hope that people can be "recharged" and "rewired" as well. His own emotional connection to life through technology motivates a philosophical position that robots are "sort of alive."

At home, Jimmy likes to play a game in which his Bio Bugs attack his AIBO. He relishes these contests in which he identifies with AIBO. AIBO lives through technology and Jimmy sees AIBO's survival as his own. AIBO symbolizes Jimmy's hopes to someday be a form of life that defies death. The Bio Bugs are the perfect embodiment of threat to the body, symbolizing the many threats that Jimmy has to fight off.

Jimmy seems concerned that his brother, Tristan, barely played with AIBO during the time they had the robot at home. Jimmy brings this up to us in a shaky voice. Jimmy explains that his brother didn't play with AIBO because "he didn't want to get addicted to him so he would be sad when we had to give him back." Jimmy emphasizes that he did not share this fear. Tristan is distant from Jimmy. Jimmy is concerned that his brother's holding back from him is because Tristan fears that he might die. Here, AIBO becomes the "stand in" for the self.

When he has to return his AIBO, Jimmy says that AIBO he will miss the robot "a little bit" but that it is AIBO that will probably miss him more.

Researcher: Do you think that you'll miss AIBO?

Jimmy: A little bit. He'll probably miss me.

## Seniors: Robots as a Prism for the Past

In bringing My Real Babies into nursing homes, it was not unusual for seniors to use the doll to re-enact scenes from their children's youth or important moments in their relationships with spouses. Indeed, seniors were more comfortable playing out family scenes with robotic dolls than with traditional ones. Seniors felt social "permission" to be with the robots, presented as a highly valued and "grownup" activity. Additionally, the robots provided the elders something to talk about, a seed for a sense of community.

As in the case of children, projection and evocation were entwined in the many ways seniors related to the robots. Some seniors, such as Jonathan, wanted the objects to be transparent as a clockwork might be and became anxious when their efforts to investigate the robots' "innards" were frustrated. Others were content to interact with the robot as it presented itself, with no window onto how it 'worked' in any mechanical sense. They took the relational artifact 'at interface value' (Turkle 1995). In each case, emotional issues were closely entwined with emergent philosophies of technology.

## Jonathan: Exploring a Relational Creature, Engineer-Style

Jonathan, 74, has movements that are slow and precise; he is well spoken, curious, and intelligent. He tells us that throughout his life he has been ridiculed for his obsessive ways. He tends to be reclusive and has few friends at the nursing home. Never married, with no children, he has always been a solitary man. For most of his life, Jonathan worked as an accountant, but was happiest when he worked as a computer programmer. Now, Jonathan approaches AIBO and My Real Baby with a desire to analyze them in an analytical, engineer's style.

From his first interaction with the My Real Baby at a group activity to his last interview after having kept the robot for four months in his room, Jonathan remained fascinated with how it functioned. He handles My Real Baby with detachment in his methodical explorations.

When Jonathan meets My Real Baby the robot is cooing and giggling. Jonathan looks it over carefully, bounces it up and down, pokes and squeezes it, and moves its limbs. With each move, he focuses on the doll's reactions. Jonathan tries to understand what the doll says and where its voice comes from. Like Orelia, Jonathan talks to the researchers about the robot, but does not speak to the robot itself. When he discovers that My Real Baby's voice comes from its stomach, he puts his ear next to the stomach and says: "I think that this doll is a very remarkable toy. I have never seen anything like this before. But I'd like to know, how in the entire universe is it possible to construct a doll that talks like this?"

Despite his technical orientation to the robot, Jonathan says that he would be more comfortable speaking to a computer or robot about his problems than to a person.

> Because if the thing is very highly private and very personal it might be embarrassing to talk about it to another person, and I might be afraid of being ridiculed for it . . . And it wouldn't criticize me . . . Or let's say that if I wanted to blow off steam, it would be better to do it to a computer than to do it to a living person who has nothing to do with the thing that's bothering me. [I could] express with the computer emotions that I feel I could not express with another person, to a person.

Nevertheless, Jonathan cannot imagine that his bond with My Real Baby could be similar to those he experiences with live animals, for example the cats he took care of before coming to the nursing home:

> Some of the things I used to enjoy with the cat are things I could never have with a robot animal. Like the cat showing affection, jumping up on my lap,

letting me pet her and listening to her purr, a robot animal couldn't do that and I enjoyed it very much.

Jonathan makes a distinction between the affection that can be offered by something alive and an object that acts as if it were alive.

## Andy: Animation in the Service of Working Through

Andy, 76, at the same nursing home as Jonathan, is recovering from a serious depression. At the end of each of our visits to the nursing home, he makes us promise to come back to see him as soon as we can. Andy feels abandoned by family and friends. He wants more people to talk with. He participates in a day-program outside the home, but nevertheless, often feels bored and lonely. Andy loves animals and has decorated his room with scores of cat pictures; he tells us that some of his happiest moments are being outside in the nursing home's garden speaking to birds, squirrels, and neighborhood cats. He believes they communicate with him and considers them his friends. Andy treats robotic dolls and pets as sentient; they become stand-ins for the people he would like to have in his life. Like Jonathan, we gave Andy a My Real Baby to keep in his room for four months. He never tired of its company.

The person Andy misses most is his ex-wife Rose. Andy reads us songs he has written for her and letters she has sent him. My Real Baby helps him work on unresolved issues in his relationship with Rose. Over time, the robot comes to represent her.

Andy: Rose, that was my ex-wife's name.

Researcher: Did you pretend that it was Rose when you talked to her?

Andy: Yeah. I didn't say anything bad to her, but some things that I would want to say to her, it helped me to think about her and the time that I didn't have my wife, how we broke up, think about that, how I miss seeing her . . . the doll, there's something about her, I can't really say what it is, but looking at her reminds me of a human being. She looks just like her, Rose, my ex-wife, and her daughter . . . something in her face is the same, looking at her makes me feel more calm, I can just think about her and everything else in my life.

Andy speaks at length about his difficulty getting over his divorce, his feelings of guilt that his relationship with Rose did not work out, and his hope that he and his ex-wife might someday be together again. Andy explains how having the doll enables him to try out different scenarios that might lead to a reconciliation with Rose. The doll's presence enables him to express his attachment and vent his feelings of regret and frustration.

Researcher: How does it make you feel to talk to the doll?

Andy: Good. It lets me take everything inside me out, you know, that's how I feel talking to her, getting it all out of me and feel not depressed . . . when I wake up in the morning I see her over there, it makes me feel so nice, like somebody is watching over you.

Andy: It will really help me [to keep the doll] because I am all alone, there's no one around, so I can play with her, we can talk. It will help me get ready to be on my own.

Researcher: How?

Andy: By talking to her, saying some of the things that I might say when I did go out, because right now, you know I don't talk to anybody right now, and I can talk much more right now with her than, I don't talk to anybody right now.

Andy holds the doll close to his chest, rubs its back in a circular motion, and says lovingly, "I love you. Do you love me?" He makes funny faces at the doll, as if to prevent her from falling asleep or just to amuse her. When the doll laughs with perfect timing as if responding to his grimaces, Andy laughs back, joining her. My Real Baby is nothing if not an "intimate machine."

## Intimate Machines: A Robot Kind of Love

The projective material of the children and seniors is closely tied to their beliefs about the nature of the relational artifacts in their care. We already know that the "intimate machines" of the computer culture have shifted how children talk about what is and is not alive (Turkle 2005[1984]). For example, children use different categories to talk about the aliveness of "traditional" objects than they do when confronted with computational games and toys. A traditional wind-up toy was considered "not alive" when children realized that it did not move of its own accord. Here, the criterion for aliveness was in the domain of physics: autonomous motion. Faced with computational media, children's way of talking about aliveness became psychological. Children classified computational objects as alive (from the late 1970s and the days of the electronic toys Merlin, Simon, and Speak and Spell) if they could *think* on their own. Faced with a computer toy that could play tic-tac-toe, what counted to a child was not the object's physical but psychological autonomy.

Children of the early 1980s came to define what made people special in opposition to computers, which they saw as our "nearest neighbors." Computers, the children reasoned, are rational machines; people are special because they are emotional. Children's use of the category "emotional machines" to describe what makes people special was a fragile, unstable definition of human uniqueness. In 1984, when I completed my study of a first generation of children who grew up with electronic toys and games, I thought that other formulations would arise from generations of children who might, for example, take the intelligence of artifacts for granted, understand how it was created, and be less inclined to give it philosophical importance. But as if on cue, robotic creatures that presented themselves as having both feelings and needs entered mainstream American culture. By the mid-1990s, as emotional machines, people were not alone.

With relational artifacts, the focus of discussion about whether computational artifacts might be alive moved from the psychology of projection to the psychology of engagement, from Rorschach to relationship, from creature competency to creature connection. Children and seniors already talk about an "animal kind of alive" and a "Furby kind of alive." The question ahead is whether they will also come to talk about a "people kind of love" and a "robot kind of love."

What is a robot kind of love?

In the early 1980s, I met a thirteen-year-old, Deborah, who responded to the experience of computer programming by speaking about the pleasures of putting "a piece of your mind into the computer's mind and coming to see yourself differently." Twenty years later, eleven-year-old Fara reacts to a play session with Cog, a humanoid robot at MIT that can meet her eyes, follow her position, and imitate her movements, by saying that she could never get tired of the robot because "it's not like a toy because can't teach a toy; it's like something that's part of you, you know, something you love, kind of like another person, like a baby."

In the 1980s, debates in artificial intelligence centered on the question of whether machines could "really" be intelligent. These debates were about the objects themselves, what they could and could not do. Our new debates about relational and sociable machines—debates that will have an increasingly high profile in mainstream culture—are not about the machines' capabilities but about our vulnerabilities. In my view, decisions about the role of robots in the lives of children and seniors cannot turn simply on whether children and the elderly "like" the robots. What does this deployment of "nurturing technology" at the two most dependent moments of the life cycle say about us? What will it do to us? What kinds of relationships are appropriate to have with machines? And what is a relationship?

My work in robotics laboratories has offered som images of how future relationships with machines ma look, appropriate or not. For example, Cynthia Breazea was leader on the design team for Kismet, the roboti head that was designed to interact with humans "socia bly," much as a two-year-old child would. Breazeal wa its chief programmer, tutor, and companion. Kisme needed Breazeal to become as "intelligent" as it did anc then Kismet became a creature Breazeal and others coulc interact with. Breazeal experienced what might be callec a maternal connection to Kismet; she certainly describes a sense of connection with it as more than "mere" machine When she graduated from MIT and left the AI Laboratory where she had done her doctoral research, the tradition o academic property rights demanded that Kismet be lef behind in the laboratory that had paid for its development What she left behind was the robot "head" and its attendant software. Breazeal described a sharp sense of loss Building a new Kismet would not be the same.

In the summer of 2001, I studied children interacting with robots, including Kismet, at the MIT AI Laboratory (Turkle et. al. 2006). It was the last time that Breazea would have access to Kismet. It is not surprising that separation from Kismet was not easy for Breazeal, but more striking, it was hard for the rest of us to imagine Kisme without her. One ten-year-old who overheard a conversation among graduate students about how Kismet would be staying in the AI lab objected: "But Cynthia is Kismet's mother."

It would be facile to analogize Breazeal's situation to that of Monica, the mother in Spielberg's A.I., a film in which an adopted robot provokes feelings of love in his human caretaker, but Breazeal is, in fact, one of the first people to have one of the signal experiences in that story, separation from a robot to which one has formed an attachment based on nurturance. At issue here is not Kismet's achieved level of intelligence, but Breazeal's experience as a "caregiver." My fieldwork with relational artifacts suggests that being asked to nurture a machine that presents itself as an young creature of any kind, constructs us as dedicated cyber-caretakers. Nurturing a machine that presents itself as dependent creates significant attachments. We might assume that giving a sociable, "affective" machine to our children or to our aging parents will change the way we see the lifecycle and our roles and responsibilities in it.

Sorting out our relationships with robots bring us back to the kinds of challenges that Darwin posed to his generation: the question of human uniqueness. How will interacting with relational artifacts affect people's way of thinking about what, if anything, makes people special? The sight of children and the elderly exchanging tendernesses with robotic pets brings science fiction into everyday life and techno-philosophy down to earth. The question here is not whether children will love their robotic pets more than their real life pets or even their parents, but rather, what will loving come to mean?

One woman's comment on AIBO, Sony's household entertainment robot, startles in what it might augur for the future of person-machine relationships: "[AIBO] is better than a real dog . . . It won't do dangerous things, and it won't betray you . . . Also, it won't die suddenly and make you feel very sad." Mortality has traditionally defined the human condition; a shared sense of mortality has been the basis for feeling a commonality with other human beings, a sense of going through the same life cycle, a sense of the preciousness of time and life, of its fragility. Loss (of parents, of friends, of family) is part of the way we understand how human beings grow and develop and bring the qualities of other people within themselves (Freud 1989).

Relationships with computational creatures may be deeply compelling, perhaps educational, but they do not put us in touch with the complexity, contradiction, and limitations of the human life cycle. They do not teach us what we need to know about empathy, ambivalence, and life lived in shades of gray. To say all of this about our love of our robots does not diminish their interest or importance. It only puts them in their place.

## Notes

1. A note on method: the observations presented here are based on open-ended qualitative fieldwork. This is useful in the study of human/robot interaction for several reasons. Case studies and participant-observation in natural settings enable the collection of empirical data about how people think about and use technology outside the laboratory. Qualitative methods are well-positioned to bring cultural beliefs and novel questions to light. Open-ended qualitative work puts the novelty of the technology at the center of things and says, "When you are interested in something new: *observe, listen, ask.*" Additionally, qualitative approaches to human-robot interaction provide analytical tools that help us better understand both the technologies under study and the social and cultural contexts in which these technologies are deployed. Differences in individual responses to technology are a window onto personality, life history, and cognitive style. Seeing technology in social context helps us better understand social complexities.

2. My case studies of robots and seniors with AIBO and My Real Baby are drawn from work conducted through weekly visits to schools and nursing homes from 2001 to 2003, studies that encompassed several hundred participants. In my discussion of Paro, I am reporting on studies of the same two nursing homes during the spring of 2005, a study that took place during twelve site visits

and recruited 23 participants, ranging in age from 60–104, six males, and seventeen females. Researchers on these projects include Olivia Dasté, for the first phase of work, and for the second phase, Cory Kidd and Will Taggart.

## References

Bowker, G.C., and Star, S.L. 1999. *Sorting Things Out: Classification and Its Consequences,* Cambridge, Mass.: MIT Press.

Breazeal, C. "Sociable Machines: Expressive Social Exchange Between Humans and Robots." 2000. PhD Thesis, Massachusetts Institute of Technology.

Breazeal, C. 2002. *Designing Sociable Robots,* Cambridge: MIT Press.

Breazeal, C., and Scassellati, B. 1999. "How to Build Robots that Make Friends and Influence People," in *Proceedings of the IEEE/RSJ International Conference on Intelligent Robots and Systems (IROS-99),* pp. 858–863.

Breazeal, C., and Scassellati, B., 2000. "Infant-like Social Interactions Between a Robot and a Human Caretaker," *Adaptive Behavior,* 8, pp. 49–74.

Freud, S. 1960. "The Uncanny," in *The Standard Edition of the Complete Psychological Works of Sigmund Freud,* vol. 17, J. Strachey, trans. and ed. London: The Hogarth Press, pp. 219–252.

Freud, S. 1989. "Mourning and Melancholia," in *The Freud Reader.* P. Gay, ed. New York: W.W. Norton & Company, p. 585.

Kahn, P., Friedman, B., Perez-Granados, D.R., and Freier, N.G. 2004. "Robotic Pets in the Lives of Preschool Children," in *CHI Extended Abstracts,* ACM Press, 2004, pp. 1449–1452.

Kidd, C.D. "Sociable Robots: The Role of Presence and Task in Human-Robot Interaction." 2004. Master's Thesis, Massachusetts Institute of Technology.

Shibata, T., Tashima, T., and Tanie, K. 1999. "Emergence of Emotional Behavior through Physical Interaction between Human and Robot," in *Proceedings of the IEEE International Conference on Robotics and Automation,* 1999, pp. 2868–2873.

Shibata, T. (accessed 01 April 2005). "Mental Commit Robot," Available online at: http://www.mel.go.jp/soshiki/robot/biorobo/shibata/

Taggard, W., Turkle, S., and Kidd, C.D. 2005. "An Interactive Robot in a Nursing Home: Preliminary Remarks," in *Proceedings of CogSci Workshop on Android Science,* Stresa, Italy, pp. 56–61.

Turkle, S. 2005 [1984]. The Second Self: Computers and the Human Spirit. Cambridge, Mass.: MIT Press.

Turkle, S, *Life on the Screen.* 1995. New York: Simon and Schuster.

Turkle, S. 2004. "Relational Artifacts," NSF Report, (NSF Grant SES-0115668).

Turkle, S. 2005a. "Relational Artifacts/Children/Elders: The Complexities of CyberCompanions," in *Proceedings of the CogSci Workshop on Android Science,* Stresa, Italy, 2005, pp. 62–73.

Turkle, S. 2005b. "Caring Machines: Relational Artifacts for the Elderly." Keynote AAAI Workshop, "Caring Machines." Washington, D.C.

Turkle, S., Breazeal, C., Dasté, O., and Scassellati, B. 2006. "First Encounters with Kismet and Cog: Children's Relationship with Humanoid Robots," in *Digital Media: Transfer in Human Communication,* P. Messaris and L. Humphreys, eds. New York: Peter Lang Publishing.

Turner, V. 1969. The Ritual Process. Chicago: Aldine.

Weizenbaum, J. 1976. *Computer Power and Human Reason: From Judgment to Calculation.* San Francisco, CA: W. H. Freeman. Winnicott. D. W. (1971). *Playing and Reality.* New York: Basic Books.

# Toward Nature-Inspired Computing

## NIC-based systems utilize autonomous entities that self-organize to achieve the goals of systems modeling and problem solving.

JIMING LIU AND K. C. TSUI

Nature-inspired computing (NIC) is an emerging computing paradigm that draws on the principles of self-organization and complex systems. Here, we examine NIC from two perspectives. First, as a way to help explain, model, and characterize the underlying mechanism(s) of complex real-world systems by formulating computing models and testing hypotheses through controlled experimentation. The end product is a potentially deep understanding or at least a better explanation of the working mechanism(s) of the modeled system. And second, as a way to reproduce autonomous (such as lifelike) behavior in solving computing problems. With detailed knowledge of the underlying mechanism(s), simplified abstracted autonomous lifelike behavior can be used as a model in practically any general-purpose problem-solving strategy or technique.

Neither objective is achievable without formulating a model of the factors underlying the system. The modeling process can begin with a theoretical analysis from either a macroscopic or microscopic view of the system. Alternatively, the application developer may adopt a blackbox or whitebox approach. Blackbox approaches (such as Markov models and artificial neural networks) normally do not reveal much about their working mechanism(s). On the other hand, whitebox approaches (such as agents with bounded rationality) are more useful for explaining behavior [7].

The essence of NIC formulation involves conceiving a computing system operated by population(s) of autonomous entities. The rest of the system is referred to as the environment. An autonomous entity consists of a detector (or set of detectors), an effector (or set of effectors), and a repository of local behavior rules (see Figure 1) [5,8].

A detector receives information related to its neighbors and to the environment. For example, in a simulation of a flock of birds, this information would include the speed and direction the birds are heading and the distance between the

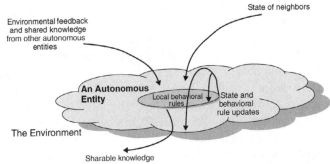

**Figure 1** Modeling an autonomous entity in a NIC-based system.

birds in question. The details of the content and format of the information must be defined according to the system to be modeled or to the problem to be solved. The notion of neighbors may be defined in terms of position (such as the bird(s) ahead, to the left, and to the right), distance (such as a radial distance of two grids), or both (such as the birds up to two grids ahead of the nominal viewpoint bird).

Environmental information conveys the status of a certain feature of interest to an autonomous entity. The environment can also help carry sharable local knowledge. The effector of an autonomous entity refers collectively to the device for expressing actions. Actions can be changes to an internal state, an external display of certain behaviors, or changes to the environment the entity inhabits. An important role of the effector, as part of the local behavior model, is to facilitate implicit information sharing among autonomous entities.

Central to an autonomous entity are the rules of behavior governing how it must act or react to the information collected by the detector from the environment and its neighbors. These rules determine into what state the entity should change and also what local knowledge should be released via the effector to the environment. An example of sharable local knowledge is the role pheromones play in an ant colony. It is untargeted, and the communication via the environment is undirected; any ant can pick up the information and react according to its own behavior model.

In order to adapt itself to a problem without being explicitly told what to do in advance, an autonomous entity must modify the rules of its behavior over time. This ability, responding to local changing conditions, is known as the individual's learning capability. Worth noting is that randomness plays a part in the decision-making process of an autonomous entity despite the presence of a rule set. It allows an autonomous entity to explore uncharted territory despite evidence that it should exploit only a certain path. On the other hand, randomness helps the entity resolve conflict in the presence of equal support for suggestions to act in different ways in its own best interests and avoid being stuck by randomly choosing an action in local optima.

The environment acts as the domain in which autonomous entities are free to roam. This is a static view of the environment. The environment of a NIC system can also act as the "noticeboard" where the autonomous entities post and read local information. In this dynamic view, the environment is constantly changing For example, in the N-queen constraint satisfaction problem [7], the environment can tell a particular queen on a chessboard how many constraints are violated in her neighborhood after a move is made. In effect, this violations, or conflicts, report translates a global goal into a local goal for a particular entity. The environment also keeps the central clock that helps synchronize the actions of all autonomous entities, as needed.

Before exploring examples of NIC for characterizing complex behavior or for solving computing problems, we first highlight the central NIC ideas, along with common NIC characteristics, including autonomous, distributed, emergent, adaptive, and self-organized, or ADEAS [5]:

*Autonomous*. In NIC systems, entities are individuals with bounded rationality that act independently. There is no central controller for directing and coordinating individual entities. Formal computing models and techniques are often used to describe how the entities acquire and improve their reactive behavior, based on their local and/or shared utilities, and how the behavior and utilities of the entities become goal-directed.

*Distributed*. Autonomous entities with localized decision-making capabilities are distributed in a heterogeneous computing environment, locally interacting among themselves to exchange their state information or affect the states of others. In distributed problem solving (such as scheduling and optimization), they continuously measure, update, and share information with other entities following certain predefined protocols.

*Emergent*. Distributed autonomous entities collectively exhibit complex (purposeful) behavior not present or predefined in the behavior of the autonomous entities within the system. One interesting issue in studying the emergent behaviors that leads to some desired computing solutions (such as optimal resource allocation) is how to mathematically model and measure the interrelationships among the local goals of the entities and the desired global goal(s) of the NIC system in a particular application.

*Adaptive*. Entities often change their behavior in response to changes in the environment in which they are situated. In doing so, they utilize behavioral adaptation mechanisms to continuously evaluate and fine-tune their behavioral attributes with reference to their goals, as well as to ongoing feedback (such as intermediate rewards). Evolutionary approaches may be used to reproduce high-performing entities and eliminate poor-performing ones.

*Self-organized*. The basic elements of NIC-based systems are autonomous entities and their environment. Local interactions among them are the most powerful force in their evolution toward certain desired states. Self-organization is the essential process of a NIC system's working mechanism. Through local interactions, these systems self-aggregate and amplify the outcome of entity behavior.

# Characterizing Complex Behavior

A complex system can be analyzed and understood in many different ways. The most obvious is to look at it from the outside, observing its behaviors and using models to try to identify and list them. Assumptions about unknown mechanisms must be made to start the process. Given observable behaviors of the desired system, NIC designers verify the model by comparing its behavior with the desired features. This process is repeated several times before a good, though not perfect, prototype can be found. Apart from obtaining a working model of the desired system, an important by-product is the discovery of the mechanisms that were unknown when the design process began.

The human immune system is an example of a highly sensitive, adaptive, self-regulated complex system involving numerous interactions among a vast number of cells of different types. Despite numerous clinical case studies and empirical findings [1], the working mechanism underlying the complex process of, say, HIV invasion and the erosion and eventual crash of the immune system (including how the local interactions in HIV, T-cells, and B-cells affect the process) are still not fully understood (characterized and predicted).

The usefulness of conventional modeling and simulation technologies is limited due to computational scale and costs.

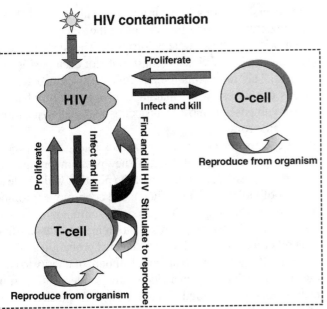

**Figure 2** Modeling HIV, T-cells, and O(ther) cells in a NIC-based system.

Understanding and modeling complex systems (such as the human immune system) is a major challenge for the field of computing for two main reasons: the task of computing is seamlessly carried out in a variety of physical embodiments, and no single multipurpose or dedicated machine is able to accomplish the job. The key to success for simulating self-regulated complex systems lies in the large-scale deployment of computational entities or agents able to autonomously make local decisions and achieve collective goals.

Seeking to understand the dynamics of the immune system during an HIV attack, NIC researchers can use a 2D lattice to build a NIC model. The lattice is circular so the edges wrap around one another. Each site can be inhabited by HIV, as well as by immune cells. HIV and immune cells behave in four main ways:

*Interaction*. T-cells recognize HIV by its signature (protein structure); HIV infects and kills cells;
*Proliferation*. Reactions stimulate lymphoid tissue to produce more T-cells, which are reproduced naturally;
*Death*. Besides being killed by drugs and other deliberate medical intervention, HIV and T-cells die naturally; and
*Diffusion*. HIV diffuses from densely populated sites to neighboring sites (see Figure 2).

Figure 3 outlines the temporal emergence of three-stage dynamics in HIV infection generated from the NIC model [12]:

*Before B*. Primary response;
*B ~ C*. Clinical latency; and
*After D*. Onset of AIDS.

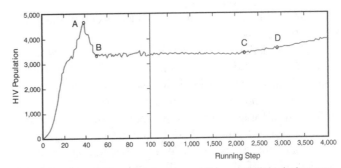

**Figure 3** Simulation results on an HIV population during several phases of AIDS development.

At A, the HIV population reaches a maximum point. Starting from C, the mechanism that decreases the natural ability of an organism to reproduce T-cells is triggered. These NIC-generated results are consistent with empirically observed phenomena [1]. Experiments in [12] have also found that AIDS cannot break out if HIV destroys only T-cells without weakening the T-cell reproduction mechanism. The emergence in "shape space" indicates it is because of HIV's fast mutation that the immune system cannot eradicate HIV as readily as it does other invaders. These discoveries are helping immunology researchers understand the dynamics of HIV-immune interaction.

The NIC approach to systems modeling starts from a microscopic view of the immune system. The elements of the model are the basic units—HIV and immune cells—of the immune system. The model aims to capture the essence of the immune system, though simplification is inevitable. Note that the autonomous entities in the model that belong to the same species types normally have a similar set of behavior rules. The only difference among them is the parameters of the rules, which may be adapted throughout the lifetime of the entities. Probabilistic selection of certain behavior is also common in the entities. It must be emphasized that the environment of the model can also be viewed as a unique entity in the model, with its own behavior rules.

## Self-Organized Web Regularities

Researchers have identified several self-organized regularities related to the Web, ranging from its growth and evolution to usage patterns in Web surfing. Many such regularities are best represented by characteristic distributions following a Zipf law or a power law. Random-walk models [4] have been used to simulate some statistical regularities empirically observed on the Web. However, these models do not relate the emergent regularities to the dynamic interactions between users and the Web, nor do they reflect the interrelationships between user behavior and the contents or structure of the Web. User interest and motivation in navigating the

Web are among the most important factors determining user navigation behavior.

As part of the NIC approach to regularity characterization, [6] proposed a computational model of Web surfing that includes user characteristics (such as interest profiles, motivations, and navigation strategies). Users are viewed as information-foraging entities inhabiting the Web environment or as a collection of Web sites connected by hyperlinks. When an entity finds certain Web sites with content related to its topic(s) of interest, it will be motivated to search sites deeper into the Web. On the other hand, when an entity finds no interesting information after a certain amount of foraging or finds enough content to satisfy its interest, it stops foraging and goes offline, leaving the Web environment.

Experiments in [6] classified users into three groups: recurrent users familiar with the Web structure; rational users new to a particular Web site but who know what they are looking for; and random users with no strong intention to retrieve information but are just "wandering around." The results, which used both synthetic and empirical data from visitors to NASA Web site(s), showed that the foraging agent-entity-oriented model generates power-law distributions in surfing and link-click-frequency, similar to those found in the real world and hence offer a whitebox explanation of self-organized Web regularities.

# Solving Computing Problems

The key factors contributing to the success of these NIC-based models are the distinctive characteristics of their elements. Marvin Minsky of MIT suggested in his 1986 book *Society of Mind* that "To explain the mind, we have to show how minds are built from mindless stuff, from parts that are much smaller and simpler than anything we'd consider smart." So, if we want to formulate a problem-solving strategy based on some observation from nature, how and where should we begin? To formulate a NIC problem-solving system, we must identify and gain a deep understanding of a working system in the natural or physical world from which models can be extracted. As with complex-systems modeling, the abstracted behavior of the working system becomes the property of the elements to be modeled.

Basing their approach on the general principles of survival of the fittest (whereby poor performers are eliminated) and the "law of the jungle" (whereby weak performers are eaten by stronger ones), several NIC systems have been devised [7, 9] to solve some well-known constraint-satisfaction problems. One is the N-queen problem, in which N queens are placed on an N × N chessboard, so no two queens ever appear in the same row, column, or diagonal. Based on the rules of the problem, a NIC model is formulated in the following way: Each queen is modeled as an autonomous entity in the system, and multiple queens are assigned to each row

of the chessboard (a grid environment). This process allow for competition among the queens in the same row, so th queen with the best strategy survives. The system calcu lates the number of violated constraints for each position o the grid. This represents the environmental information a queens can access when making decisions about where t move, with possible movements being restricted to position in the same row.

Three movement strategies are possible: random-mov (involving the random selection of a new position for a queen least-move (involving selection of the position with the lea number of violations, or conflicts); and coop-move (promo ing cooperation among the queens by eliminating certai positions in which one queen's position may create conflict with other queens). All three are selected probabilistically.

This NIC system gives an initial amount of energy to eac queen. Like a character in a video game, a queen "dies" if it energy falls below a predefined threshold. A queen's energ level changes in one of two ways: losing it to the environmen and absorbing it from another queen. When a queen moves t a new position that violates the set constraint with $m$ queens it loses $m$ units of energy. This also causes the queens tha attack this new position to lose one unit of energy. Th intention is to encourage the queens to find a position wit the fewest violations, or conflicts. The law of the jungle i implemented by having two or more queens occupy the sam grid position and fight over it. The queen with the greates amount of energy wins and eats the loser(s) by absorbing al its (their) energy. This model efficiently solves the N-quee problem with only a moderate amount of computation.

> As with complex-systems modeling, the abstracted behavior of the working system becomes the property of the elements to be modeled.

In the commonly used version of a genetic algorithm [3], a member of the family of evolutionary algorithms, the proces of sexual evolution is simplified to selection, recombination and mutation, without the explicit identification of male and female (such as in the gene pool). John Holland of the University of Michigan, in his quest to develop a model to help explain evolution, has developed a genetic algorithm for optimization. The basic unit in this artificial evolution is a candidate solution to the optimization problem, commonly termed a chromosome. A genetic algorithm has a pool of them. Interactions among candidate solutions are achieved through artificial reproduction where operations mimicking natural evolution allow the candidate solutions to produce offspring that carry part of either parent (crossover) with occasional variation (mutation). While reproduction can be viewed as the cooperative side of all the chromosomes, competition among chromosomes for a position in the next generation directly reflects the principle of survival of the fittest.

On the other hand, evolutionary autonomous agents [10] and evolution strategies [11] are closer to asexual reproduction, with the addition of constraints on mutation and the introduction of mutation operator evolution, respectively. Despite this simplification and modification, evolutionary algorithms capture the essence of natural evolution and are proven global multi-objective optimization techniques. Another successful NIC algorithm that has been applied in similar domains is the Ant System [2], which mimics the food-foraging behavior of ants.

## Autonomy-Oriented Computing

As a concrete manifestation of the NIC paradigm, autonomy-oriented computing (AOC) has emerged as a new field of computer science to systematically explore the metaphors and models of autonomy offered in nature (such as physical, biological, and social entities of varying complexity), as well as their role in addressing practical computing needs. It studies emergent autonomy as the core behavior of a computing system, drawing on such principles as multi-entity formulation, local interaction, nonlinear aggregation, adaptation, and self-organization [5, 8].

Three general approaches help researchers develop AOC systems: AOC-by-fabrication, AOC-by-prototyping, and AOC-by-self-discovery. Each has been found to be promising in several application areas [6, 7, 10, 12]. Work on AOC in our research laboratory over the past decade [5, 8] has opened up new ways to understand and develop NIC theories and methodologies. They have provided working examples that demonstrate the power and features of the NIC paradigm toward two main goals: characterizing emergent behavior in natural and artificial systems involving a large number of self-organizing, locally interacting entities; and solving problems in large-scale computation, distributed constraint satisfaction, and decentralized optimization [5].

## Conclusion

The NIC paradigm differs from traditional imperative, logical, constraint, object-oriented, and component-based paradigms, not only in the characteristics of its fundamental concepts and constructs, but in the effectiveness and efficiency of the computing that can be achieved through its ADEAS characteristics. NIC approaches have been found most effective in dealing with computational problems characterized by the following dimensions:

*High complexity.* Problems of high complexity (such as when the system to be characterized involves a large number of autonomous entities or the computational computing problem to be solved involves large-scale, high-dimension, highly nonlinear interactions/relationships, and highly interrelated/constrained variables);

*Locally interacting problems.* They are not centralized or ready or efficient enough for batch processing;

*Changing environment.* The environment in which problems are situated is dynamically updated or changes in real time; and

*Deep patterns.* The goal of modeling and analysis is not to extract some superficial patterns/relationships, data transformation, or association from one form to another, but to discover and understand the deep patterns (such as the underlying mechanisms and processes that produce the data in the first place or help explain their cause and origin).

We will continue to see new NIC theories and methodologies developed and learn to appreciate their wide-ranging effect on computer science, as well as on other disciplines, including sociology, economics, and the natural sciences. Promising applications will help explain gene regulatory networks and drug-resistance mechanisms for anti-cancer drug design, predict the socioeconomic sustainability of self-organizing online markets or communities, and perform real-time autonomous data processing in massive mobile sensor networks for eco-geological observations.

## References

1. Coffin, J. HIV population dynamics in vivo: Implications for genetic variation, pathogenesis, and therapy. *Science 267* (1995), 483–489.
2. Dorigo, M., Maniezzo, V., and Colorni, A. The Ant System: Optimization by a colony of cooperative agents. *IEEE Transactions on Systems, Man, and Cybernetics, Part B, 26*, 1 (1996), 1–13.
3. Holland, J. *Adaptation in Natural and Artificial Systems.* MIT Press, Cambridge, MA, 1992.
4. Huberman, B., Pirolli, P., Pitkow, J., and Lukose, R. Strong regularities in World Wide Web surfing. *Science 280* (Apr. 3, 1997), 96–97.
5. Liu, J., Jin, X., and Tsui, K. *Autonomy-Oriented Computing: From Problem Solving to Complex Systems Modeling.* Kluwer Academic Publishers/Springer, Boston, 2005.
6. Liu, J., Zhang, S., and Yang, J. Characterizing Web usage regularities with information foraging agents. *IEEE Transactions on Knowledge and Data Engineering 16*, 5 (2004), 566–584.
7. Liu, J., Han, J., and Tang, Y. Multi-agent-oriented constraint satisfaction. *Artificial Intelligence 136*, 1 (2002), 101–144.

8.  Liu, J. *Autonomous Agents and Multi-Agent Systems: Explorations in Learning, Self-Organization and Adaptive Computation,* World Scientific Publishing, Singapore, 2001.

9.  Liu, J. and Han, J. A Life: A multi-agent computing paradigm for constraint satisfaction problems. *International Journal of Pattern Recognition and Artificial Intelligence 15,* 3 (2001), 475–491.

10. Liu, J., Tang, Y., and Cao, Y. An evolutionary autonomous agents approach to image feature extraction. *IEEE Transactions on Evolutionary Computation 1,* 2 (1997), 141–158.

11. Schwefel, H.P. *Numerical Optimization of Computer Models.* John Wiley & Sons, Inc., New York, 1981.

12. Zhang, S. and Liu, J. A massively multi-agent system for discovering HIV-immune interaction dynamics. In *Proceedings of the First International Workshop on Massively Multi-Agent Systems* (Kyoto, Japan, Dec. 10–11). Springer, Berlin, 2004.

**JIMING LIU** (jiming@uwindsor.ca) is a professor in and director of the School of Computer Science at the University of Windsor, Windsor, Ontario, Canada. **K. C. TSUI** (tsuikc@comp.hkbu.edu.hk) is an IT manager in the Technical Services and Support Department of Hongkong and Shanghai Banking Corporation, Hong Kong, China.

# Google and the Wisdom of Clouds

**A lofty new strategy aims to put incredible computing power in the hands of many.**

STEPHEN BAKER

One simple question. That's all it took for Christophe Bisciglia to bewilder confident job applicants at Google. Bisciglia, an angular 27-year-old senior software engineer with long wavy hair, wanted to see if these undergrads were ready to think like Googlers. "Tell me," he'd say, "what would you do if you had 1,000 times more data?"

What a strange idea. If they returned to their school projects and were foolish enough to cram formulas with a thousand times more details about shopping or maps or—heaven forbid—with video files, they'd slow their college servers to a crawl.

At that point in the interview, Bisciglia would explain his question. To thrive at Google, he told them, they would have to learn to work—and to dream—on a vastly larger scale. He described Google's globe-spanning network of computers. Yes, they answered search queries instantly. But together they also blitzed through mountains of data, looking for answers or intelligence faster than any machine on earth. Most of this hardware wasn't on the Google campus. It was just out there, somewhere on earth, whirring away in big refrigerated data centers. Folks at Google called it "the cloud." And one challenge of programming at Google was to leverage that cloud—to push it to do things that would overwhelm lesser machines. New hires at Google, Bisciglia says, usually take a few months to get used to this scale. "Then one day, you see someone suggest a wild job that needs a few thousand machines, and you say: Hey, he gets it."

What recruits needed, Bisciglia eventually decided, was advance training. So one autumn day a year ago, when he ran into Google CEO Eric E. Schmidt between meetings, he floated an idea. He would use his 20% time, the allotment Googlers have for independent projects, to launch a course. It would introduce students at his alma mater, the University of Washington, to programming at the scale of a cloud. Call it Google 101. Schmidt liked the plan. Over the following months, Bisciglia's Google 101 would evolve and grow. It would eventually lead to an ambitious partnership with IBM, announced in October, to plug universities around the world into Google-like computing clouds.

## Cloud Computing

### User Friendly

Clouds are giant clusters of computers that house immense sets of data too big for traditional computers to handle—such as the receipts from 100 million shoppers or troves of geological data.

As this concept spreads, it promises to expand Google's footprint in industry far beyond search, media, and advertising, leading the giant into scientific research and perhaps into new businesses. In the process Google could become, in a sense, the world's primary computer.

"I had originally thought [Bisciglia] was going to work on education, which was fine," Schmidt says late one recent afternoon at Google headquarters. "Nine months later, he comes out with this new [cloud] strategy, which was completely unexpected." The idea, as it developed, was to deliver to students, researchers, and entrepreneurs the immense power of Google-style computing, either via Google's machines or others offering the same service.

**It's the computing equivalent of the evolution in electricity, when businesses shut down their generators and bought power instead.**

What is Google's cloud? It's a network made of hundreds of thousands, or by some estimates 1 million, cheap servers, each not much more powerful than the PCs we have in our homes. It stores staggering amounts of data, including numerous copies of the World Wide Web. This makes search faster, helping ferret out answers to billions of queries in a fraction of a second.

Unlike many traditional supercomputers, Google's system never ages. When its individual pieces die, usually after about three years, engineers pluck them out and replace them with new, faster boxes. This means the cloud regenerates as it grows, almost like a living thing.

A move toward clouds signals a fundamental shift in how we handle information. At the most basic level, it's the computing equivalent of the evolution in electricity a century ago when farms and businesses shut down their own generators and bought power instead from efficient industrial utilities. Google executives had long envisioned and prepared for this change. Cloud computing, with Google's machinery at the very center, fit neatly into the company's grand vision, established a decade ago by founders Sergey Brin and Larry Page: "to organize the world's information and make it universally accessible." Bisciglia's idea opened a pathway toward this future. "Maybe he had it in his brain and didn't tell me," Schmidt says. "I didn't realize he was going to try to change the way computer scientists thought about computing. That's a much more ambitious goal."

# One-way Street

For small companies and entrepreneurs, clouds mean opportunity—a leveling of the playing field in the most data-intensive forms of computing. To date, only a select group of cloud-wielding Internet giants has had the resources to scoop up huge masses of information and build businesses upon it. Our words, pictures, clicks, and searches are the raw material for this industry. But it has been largely a one-way street. Humanity emits the data, and a handful of companies—the likes of Google, Yahoo!, or Amazon.com—transform the info into insights, services, and, ultimately, revenue.

This status quo is already starting to change. In the past year, Amazon has opened up its own networks of computers to paying customers, initiating new players, large and small, to cloud computing. Some users simply park their massive databases with Amazon. Others use Amazon's computers to mine data or create Web services. In November, Yahoo opened up a cluster of computers—a small cloud—for researchers at Carnegie Mellon University. And Microsoft has deepened its ties to communities of scientific researchers by providing them access to its own server farms. As these clouds grow, says Frank Gens, senior analyst at market research firm IDC, "A whole new community of Web startups will have access to these machines. It's like they're planting Google seeds." Many such startups will emerge in science and medicine, as data-crunching laboratories searching for new materials and drugs set up shop in the clouds.

For clouds to reach their potential, they should be nearly as easy to program and navigate as the Web. This, say analysts, should open up growing markets for cloud search and software tools—a natural business for Google and its competitors. Schmidt won't say how much of its own capacity Google will offer to outsiders, or under what conditions or at what prices. "Typically, we like to start with free," he says, adding that power users "should probably bear some of the costs." And how big will these clouds grow? "There's no limit," Schmidt says. As

this strategy unfolds, more people are starting to see that Google is poised to become a dominant force in the next stage of computing. "Google aspires to be a large portion of the cloud, or a cloud that you would interact with every day," the CEO says. The business plan? For now, Google remains rooted in its core business, which gushes with advertising revenue. The cloud initiative is barely a blip in terms of investment. It hovers in the distance, large and hazy and still hard to piece together, but bristling with possibilities.

Changing the nature of computing and scientific research wasn't at the top of Bisciglia's agenda the day he collared Schmidt. What he really wanted, he says, was to go back to school. Unlike many of his colleagues at Google, a place teeming with PhDs, Bisciglia was snatched up by the company as soon as he graduated from the University of Washington, or U-Dub, as nearly everyone calls it. He'd never been a grad student. He ached for a break from his daily routines at Google—the 10-hour workdays building search algorithms in his cube in Building 44, the long commutes on Google buses from the apartment he shared with three roomies in San Francisco's Duboce Triangle. He wanted to return to Seattle, if only for one day a week, and work with his professor and mentor, Ed Lazowska. "I had an itch to teach," he says.

He didn't think twice before vaulting over the org chart and batting around his idea directly with the CEO. Bisciglia and Schmidt had known each other for years. Shortly after landing at Google five years ago as a 22-year-old programmer, Bisciglia worked in a cube across from the CEO's office. He'd wander in, he says, drawn in part by the model airplanes that reminded him of his mother's work as a United Airlines hostess. Naturally he talked with the soft-spoken, professorial CEO about computing. It was almost like college. And even after Bisciglia moved to other buildings, the two stayed in touch. ("He's never too hard to track down, and he's incredible about returning e-mails," Bisciglia says.)

On the day they first discussed Google 101, Schmidt offered one nugget of advice: Narrow down the project to something Bisciglia could have up and running in two months. "I actually didn't care what he did," Schmidt recalls. But he wanted the young engineer to get feedback in a hurry. Even if Bisciglia failed, he says, "he's smart, and he'd learn from it."

To launch Google 101, Bisciglia had to replicate the dynamics and a bit of the magic of Google's cloud—but without tapping into the cloud itself or revealing its deepest secrets. These secrets fuel endless speculation among computer scientists. But Google keeps much under cover. This immense computer, after all, runs the company. It automatically handles search, places ads, churns through e-mails. The computer does the work, and thousands of Google engineers, including Bisciglia, merely service the machine. They teach the system new tricks or find new markets for it to invade. And they add on new clusters—four new data centers this year alone, at an average cost of $600 million apiece.

In building this machine, Google, so famous for search, is poised to take on a new role in the computer industry. Not so many years ago scientists and researchers looked to national laboratories for the cutting-edge research on computing. Now, says Daniel Frye, vice-president of open systems development at IBM, "Google is doing the work that 10 years ago would have done on in a national lab."

How was Bisciglia going to give students access to this machine? The easiest option would have been to plug his class directly into the Google computer. But the company wasn't about to let students loose in a machine loaded with proprietary software, brimming with personal data, and running a 10.6 billion business. So Bisciglia shopped for an affordable cluster of 40 computers. He placed the order, then set about figuring out how to pay for the servers. While the vendor was wiring the computers together, Bisciglia alerted a couple of Google managers that a bill was coming. Then he "kind of sent the expense report up the chain, and no one said no." He adds one of his favorite sayings: "It's far easier to beg for forgiveness than to ask for permission." ("If you're interested in someone who strictly follows the rules, Christophe's not your guy," says Lazowska, who refers to the cluster as "a gift from heaven.")

## A Frenetic Learner

On Nov. 10, 2006, the rack of computers appeared at U-Dub's Computer Science building. Bisciglia and a couple of tech administrators had to figure out how to hoist the 1-ton rack up four stories into the server room. They eventually made it, and then prepared for the start of classes, in January.

Bisciglia's mother, Brenda, says her son seemed marked for an unusual path from the start. He didn't speak until age 2, and then started with sentences. One of his first came as they were driving near their home in Gig Harbor, Wash. A bug flew in the open window, and a voice came from the car seat in back: "Mommy, there's something artificial in my mouth."

At school, the boy's endless questions and frenetic learning pace exasperated teachers. His parents, seeing him sad and frustrated, pulled him out and home-schooled him for three years. Bisciglia says he missed the company of kids during that time but developed as an entrepreneur. He had a passion for Icelandic horses and as an adolescent went into business raising them. Once, says his father, Jim, they drove far north into Manitoba and bought horses, without much idea about how to transport the animals back home. "The whole trip was like a scene from one of Chevy Chase's movies," he says. Christophe learned about computers developing Web pages for his horse sales and his father's luxury-cruise business. And after concluding that computers promised a brighter future than animal husbandry, he went off to U-Dub and signed up for as many math, physics, and computer courses as he could.

In late 2006, as he shuttled between the Googleplex and Seattle preparing for Google 101, Bisciglia used his entrepreneurial skills to piece together a sprawling team of volunteers. He worked with college interns to develop the curriculum, and he dragooned a couple of Google colleagues from the nearby Kirkland (Wash.) facility to use some of their 20% time to help him teach it. Following Schmidt's advice, Bisciglia worked to focus Google 101 on something students could learn quickly. "I

was like, what's the one thing I could teach them in two months that would be useful and really important?" he recalls. His answer was "MapReduce."

Bisciglia adores MapReduce, the software at the heart of Google computing. While the company's famous search algorithms provide the intelligence for each search, MapReduce delivers the speed and industrial heft. It divides each task into hundreds, or even thousands, of tasks, and distributes them to legions of computers. In a fraction of a second, as each one comes back with its nugget of information, MapReduce quickly assembles the responses into an answer. Other programs do the same job. But MapReduce is faster and appears able to handle near limitless work. When the subject comes up, Bisciglia rhapsodizes. "I remember graduating, coming to Google, learning about MapReduce, and really just changing the way I thought about computer science and everything," he says. He calls it "a very simple, elegant model." It was developed by another Washington alumnus, Jeffrey Dean. By returning to U-Dub and teaching MapReduce, Bisciglia would be returning this software "and this way of thinking" back to its roots.

There was only one obstacle. MapReduce was anchored securely inside Google's machine—and it was not for outside consumption, even if the subject was Google 101. The company did share some information about it, though, to feed an open-source version of MapReduce called Hadoop. The idea was that, without divulging its crown jewel, Google could push for its standard to become the architecture of cloud computing.

The team that developed Hadoop belonged to a company, Nutch, that got acquired. Oddly, they were now working within the walls of Yahoo, which was counting on the MapReduce offspring to give its own computers a touch of Google magic. Hadoop remained open source, though, which meant the Google team could adapt it and install it for free on the U-Dub cluster.

Students rushed to sign up for Google 101 as soon as it appeared in the winter-semester syllabus. In the beginning, Bisciglia and his Google colleagues tried teaching. But in time they handed over the job to professional educators at U-Dub. "Their delivery is a lot clearer," Bisciglia says. Within weeks the students were learning how to configure their work for Google machines and designing ambitious Web-scale projects, from cataloguing the edits on Wikipedia to crawling the Internet to identify spam. Through the spring of 2007, as word about the course spread to other universities, departments elsewhere started asking for Google 101.

Many were dying for cloud know-how and computing power—especially for scientific research. In practically every field, scientists were grappling with vast piles of new data issuing from a host of sensors, analytic equipment, and ever-finer measuring tools. Patterns in these troves could point to new medicines and therapies, new forms of clean energy. They could help predict earthquakes. But most scientists lacked the machinery to store and sift through these digital El Dorados. "We're drowning in data," said Jeannette Wing, assistant director of the National Science Foundation.

# Cloud Power

Companies and research organizations may eventually hand off most of their high-level computing tasks to a globe-spanning network of servers known as "clouds." These pioneers are in a position to dominate the field:

## Google

The only search company built from the ground up around hardware. Investing more than $2 billion a year in data centers. Far and away the leader in cloud computing.

## Yahoo!

Smaller and poorer than Google, with software not perfectly suited to cloud computing. But as the leading patron of Hadoop, it could end up with a lead over latecomers.

## IBM

King of business computing and traditional supercomputers. Teaming up with Google to get a foothold in clouds. Launching a pilot cloud system for the government of Vietnam.

## Microsoft

Wedded, for now, to its proprietary software, which could be a handicap. But it's big in the fundamentals of cloud science. And it's building massive data centers in Illinois and Siberia.

## Amazon

The first to sell cloud computing as a service. Smaller than competitors, but its expertise in this area could give the retailer a leg up in next-generation Web services from retail to media.

# Big Blue Largesse

The hunger for Google computing put Bisciglia in a predicament. He had been fortunate to push through the order for the first cluster of computers. Could he do that again and again, eventually installing mini-Google clusters in each computer science department? Surely not. To extend Google 101 to universities around the world, the participants needed to plug into a shared resource. Bisciglia needed a bigger cloud.

That's when luck descended on the Googleplex in the person of IBM Chairman Samuel J. Palmisano. This was "Sam's day at Google," says an IBM researcher. The winter day was a bit chilly for beach volleyball in the center of campus, but Palmisano lunched on some of the fabled free cuisine in a cafeteria. Then he and his team sat down with Schmidt and a handful of Googlers, including Bisciglia. They drew on whiteboards and discussed cloud computing. It was no secret that IBM wanted to deploy clouds to provide data and services to business customers. At the same time, under Palmisano, IBM had been a leading promoter of open-source software, including Linux. This was a

key in Big Blue's software battles, especially against Microsoft. If Google and IBM teamed up on a cloud venture, they could construct the future of this type of computing on Google-based standards, including Hadoop.

> **"I had originally thought [Bisciglia] was going to work on education," says Ceo Schmidt. "Google 101" became vastly more ambitious.**

Google, of course, had a running start on such a project: Bisciglia's Google 101. In the course of that one day, Bisciglia's small venture morphed into a major initiative backed at the CEO level by two tech titans. By the time Palmisano departed that afternoon, it was established that Bisciglia and his IBM counterpart, Dennis Quan, would build a prototype of a joint Google-IBM university cloud.

Over the next three months they worked together at Google headquarters. (It was around this time, Bisciglia says, that the cloud project evolved from 20% into his full-time job.) The work involved integrating IBM's business applications and Google servers, and equipping them with a host of open-source programs, including Hadoop. In February they unveiled the prototype for top brass in Mountain View, Calif., and for others on video from IBM headquarters in Armonk, N.Y. Quan wowed them by downloading data from the cloud to his cell phone. (It wasn't relevant to the core project, Bisciglia says, but a nice piece of theater.)

The Google 101 cloud got the green light. The plan was to spread cloud computing first to a handful of U.S. universities within a year and later to deploy it globally. The universities would develop the clouds, creating tools and applications while producing legions of computer scientists to continue building and managing them.

Those developers should be able to find jobs at a host of Web companies, including Google. Schmidt likes to compare the data centers to the prohibitively expensive particle accelerators known as cyclotrons. "There are only a few cyclotrons in physics," he says. "And every one if them is important, because if you're a top-flight physicist you need to be at the lab where that cyclotron is being run. That's where history's going to be made; that's where the inventions are going to come. So my idea is that if you think of these as supercomputers that happen to be assembled from smaller computers, we have the most attractive supercomputers, from a science perspective, for people to come work on."

As the sea of business and scientific data rises, computing power turns into a strategic resource, a form of capital. "In a sense," says Yahoo Research Chief Prabhakar Raghavan, "there are only five computers on earth." He lists Google, Yahoo, Microsoft, IBM, and Amazon. Few others, he says, can turn electricity into computing power with comparable efficiency.

All sorts of business models are sure to evolve. Google and its rivals could team up with customers, perhaps exchanging computing power for access to their data. They could recruit partners into their clouds for pet projects, such as the company's clean energy initiative, announced in November. With the electric bills at jumbo data centers running upwards of $20 million a year, according to industry analysts, it's only natural for Google to commit both brains and server capacity to the search for game-changing energy breakthroughs.

What will research clouds look like? Tony Hey, vice-president for external research at Microsoft, says they'll function as huge virtual laboratories, with a new generation of librarians—some of them human—"curating" troves of data, opening them to researchers with the right credentials. Authorized users, he says, will build new tools, haul in data, and share it with far-flung colleagues. In these new labs, he predicts, "you may win the Nobel prize by analyzing data assembled by someone else." Mark Dean, head of IBM's research operation in Almaden, Calif., says that the mixture of business and science will lead, in a few short years, to networks of clouds that will tax our imagination. "Compared to this," he says, "the Web is tiny. We'll be laughing at how small the Web is." And yet, if this "tiny" Web was big enough to spawn Google and its empire, there's no telling what opportunities could open up in the giant clouds.

It's a mid-November day at the Googleplex. A jetlagged Christophe Bisciglia is just back from China, where he has been talking to universities about Google 101. He's had a busy time, not only setting up the cloud with IBM but also working out deals with six universities—U-Dub, Berkeley, Stanford, MIT, Carnegie Mellon, and the University of Maryland—to launch it. Now he's got a camera crew in a conference room, with wires and lights spilling over a table. This is for a promotional video about cloud education that they'll release, at some point, on YouTube.

Eric Schmidt comes in. At 52, he is nearly twice Bisciglia's age, and his body looks a bit padded next to his protégé's willowy frame. Bisciglia guides him to a chair across from the camera and explains the plan. They'll tape the audio from the interview and then set up Schmidt for some stand-alone face shots. "B-footage," Bisciglia calls it. Schmidt nods and sits down. Then he thinks better of it. He tells the cameramen to film the whole thing and skip stand-alone shots. He and Bisciglia are far too busy to stand around for B footage.

See Senior Writer **STEPHEN BAKER'S** Q&A with Google CEO Eric Schmidt.

# Test-Your-Knowledge Form

We encourage you to photocopy and use this page as a tool to assess how the articles in *Annual Editions* expand on the information in your textbook. By reflecting on the articles you will gain enhanced text information. You can also access this useful form on a product's book support Web site at *http://www.mhcls.com*.


NAME:                                                                          DATE:

_____

TITLE AND NUMBER OF ARTICLE:

_____

BRIEFLY STATE THE MAIN IDEA OF THIS ARTICLE:

_____

LIST THREE IMPORTANT FACTS THAT THE AUTHOR USES TO SUPPORT THE MAIN IDEA:




_____

WHAT INFORMATION OR IDEAS DISCUSSED IN THIS ARTICLE ARE ALSO DISCUSSED IN YOUR TEXTBOOK OR OTHER READINGS THAT YOU HAVE DONE? LIST THE TEXTBOOK CHAPTERS AND PAGE NUMBERS:




_____

LIST ANY EXAMPLES OF BIAS OR FAULTY REASONING THAT YOU FOUND IN THE ARTICLE:




_____

LIST ANY NEW TERMS/CONCEPTS THAT WERE DISCUSSED IN THE ARTICLE, AND WRITE A SHORT DEFINITION: